Almanac & Astro-Sciences

DR. CHALLA SOMASUNDARAM
BE (Civil), MA (Astrology)
Ph.D (Vedanga Jyothisha)

SCIENTIFIC
PUBLISHERS

Published by

SCIENTIFIC PUBLISHERS (INDIA)
5 A, New Pali Road, P.O. Box 91
Jodhpur 342 001 (INDIA)
E-mail: info@scientificpub.com
Website: http://www.scientificpub.com

Distributor

Sri. B. Sobhan Babu, Proprietor,
Telugu Book House,
3-8-362, Kachiguda 'X' Roads,
Hyderabad- 500 027,
Ph -040-65347374,
M -92474 46497,
Email - telugubookhouse@gmail.com

© 2020 Author

Price: ₹ 800/-

ISBN: 978-93-88812-15-3
eISBN: 978-93-88812-55-9

Printed in India

Dedication

This book "Almanac and Astro-Sciences" is dedicated to president awardee, '*Vachaspati*', Jyotisha Vijnana Bhaskara Mahamaho padhyaya, Vastu Kalanidhi; Late Sri. Madhura Krishna Murthy Sastryji by his disciple Shri Challa Somasundaram with Great Reverence, Humable Respects and Pranams to his Lotus Feet.

Chennai **Challa Somasundaram**

Date: 20-10-2019

CONTENTS

PREAMBLE

Professor Sri Kuppa Venkata Krishna Murthy, Ex. Chairman, I-Serve (Institute of Scientific Research on Vedas), resident of Alakapuri, door No. 11-13-279, Road No. 8, Hyderabad had been introduced to me by (Late) Sri Madhura Krishna Murthy Sastry Garu of Rajahmundry in August 2011.

I was learning at that time, the science of casting of Annual Almanac from (Late) Sri Madhura Krishna Murthy Sastry. Every month in 2011 and 2012. I used to go to Rajamundry from Chennai, for a week to learn all the Sutras related to the Science. I also learnt the calculation of Longitudes for 9 planets covering 400 days including the period of Adhikamasa. Sri Madhura Pala Sankar Sarma, Son of (Late) Sri Madhura Krishna Murthy Sastry had helped in understanding the tabular formats prescribed for each planet.

When I met Sri Kuppa Venkata Krishna Murthy in August 2011, he had requested me to write a text book in Telugu captioned, "Panchamga Vijnana Sastramula Parichayamu" as purohits and matriculation-passed students were enquiring about such a text for their benefit of learning the Sciences. Since I was engaged at that time in writing the English Astrology book titled "Jataka Mani Manjusha" I could not accede to his request.

On 5-4-2016 (Late) Sri Madhura Krishna Murthy Sastryji had expired at Rajahmundry. I spoke to Sri Kuppa Venkata Krishna Murthy on 6-6-2016 about the sad demise of Sri Sastryji and conveyed condolence. Sri K.V. Krishna Murthy had again requested me to write the Telugu text mentioned in the preceding para. Immediately in honour of (Late) Sri Madhura Krishna Murthy Sastryji, I had accepted the assignment.

The draft copy of the Telugu text was submitted by me on 25-8-2016 at Hyderabad, to Sri K.V.K. Murthy. He had stated that a Panchamga Kartha be consulted to obtain his opinion on various methods adopted by different almanacs now prevailing in the market. There after, he himself had made his Elder Brother's son Sri Kuppa Anjaneya Sastry to give the necessary writeup and the same being very useful is incorporated as such in the book at Chapter No. 9.

Sri K.V.K. Murthy had also given detailed description of the contents of the book as to the Astro-Sciences that could be dealt with. In the current text not only the fundamental principles of various Sciences listed in the contents were dealt with but also included important additional issues which the students should get acquainted with. The reason being that in future if any student is interested in pursuing further, higher study of any of the subjects, he would be in a better position to know and decide as to which topic he could takeup for study/research.

Many elaborated texts were written by eminent Astrologers on each and every Science mentioned in the book. As the present day trend is such that very few are coming forward to go into these Sciences; an effort is now made to bring to the notice that the sciences that were important in the past, to enable the present generation to come forward in creating interest in any of the subjects and hence they are dealt with at one place. This is the first Text of its kind.

Action is now taken to translate the Telugu Text into English by the author for the benefit of students of all India. Hence the present Text in English titled Almanac & Astro-Sciences is brought-out.

The basis on which these Sciences were written is indicated in the Library of Literature, Annexed at the end of the book.The Text book is written in a common man's language so that it could be easily understood by the presentday students. Scientists, Astrologers and Pundits well versed in all the Sciences could point out any mistakes or suggest any alterations or changes required so that the same will be accepted with humility and corrections are carried out immediately by issue of suitable amendments.

Chennai **Challa Somasundaram**

D/20-10-2019

ASTHANA SIDDANTHI,
SREE KANCHI KAMAKOTI PEETHAMU,
KANCHEEPURAM.
SREE AVADHOOTHA DATTA PEETHAMU,
MYSURU.

PLOT NO-65, NAVODAYA ENCLAVE,
NEAR CNR CRICKET GROUNDS,
KUNTOORU. (NAGOL TO GARELLI ROAD)
HAYATNAGAR MANDAL, PEDDA AMBARPET
NAGAR PANCHAYAT, HYDERABAD-501505, M+914029887088
LOCATION: http://goo.gl/maps/sgGkm9vuJyM2.

SREE RAMA

FOREWORD

सर्वचैतन्यरूपाम्ताम्आद्याम्विद्याञ्च्धीमहिबुद्धिम्यान:प्रचोदयात्

From times immemorial, the inquisitive man has always been fascinated by the celestial objects, the ones visible to the naked eye OR visible using a telescope - the Sun, the Moon, Stars, Constellations, Planets etc and has ever wondered how these luminous bodies affect one's life. This is a common pattern across multiple civilizations and nations. Many an intellectual have also investigated, explored and studied them in terms of their nature, and their effect on human life and existence and have published, publicised and taught their thoughts through various methods. This body of knowledge is called *astrology.* The English word is derived from the early Latin word *astrologia,* which means star divination. In Sanskrit, we call it jyotishya vidya ज्योतिष्यविद्या or jyotirvidya ज्योतिर्विद्याा- meaning the science of the light.

The important relevant questions at this juncture are:

1. With everyone's experience being unique and limited by time and certain other influencing factors, which are also unique, how can these findings be accepted as universal truths with universal application?
2. Even if we accept them to be so, what are we going to gain by this knowledge. Can we prevent or divert the prospect of events' occurrence? Are they not pre-decided?
3. Can we consider human intellect as the final word? The answer to these questions lies in our Indian tradition.

In our Vedic tradition human intellect is not the final word. For us *Parameswara* is the preceptor, whose teachings were heard by the *Maharshis* and they have propagated them further. What did *Maharshis* proliferate? They taught us the knowledge, ways and means for attainment of auspicious cherished desires and prevention of inauspicious events, both worldly and beyond; one of such means is ज्योतिष्यविद्याा. This is not a simple science, it is a divine science and a branch of *Veda* or *Vedanga.* All the aspects of *Veda* apply to this one as well - इष्टाप्राप्त्यनिष्टपरिहारयो: अलौकिकमुपायम्वोवेदयतिसवेद: this is precisely the intent and objective of ज्योतिष्यविद्या for us. It is not mere analysis of natal charts, predictions of personalities, certain astral events like Eclipses, Sunrise, Moonrise etc.

As this science is based on mathematical calculations, there Is an increasing notion that if one learns the calculations, gains knowledge on the Planets, their nature, descriptions etc. combined with an analytical mind, one can easily become an astrologist; can start predicting, providing consultation on muhurtas, publish panchamga etc.

We have mentioned in the beginning Itself that this science is a *Vedanga*. And hence its applications should also be in line with the Smriti. The application of ज्योतिष्यविद्या is beyond predictions and mathematical calculations. These applications should complement observance and performance of the activities and rituals injuncted by the Sruti and Smriti. Panchamga, for example, gives us knowledge of the tithi, vara, nakshatra etc; these will have no relevance if we do not use them in performance of vedic activities or rituals. Beyond this, where else is the utility of Panchamgas? Similarly, the Natal chart analysis and predictions should be directed towards the above-mentioned objective of the Vedas - इष्टाप्राप्ति: and अनिष्टपरिहार: within the boundaries set forth by the Smritis.

Now for these activities to yield good and auspicious, the practitioner must lead a pious life, observing the injunctions of the Smritis and Sruthi such as practice of *Sadachara, Satkarmanushtana, Vairagya, Dayadakshinya etc.* to the extent possible.

In the olden days because of the strong traditional education system basic jyotishya knowledge was fairly common and most people had a good amount of knowledge of the same;it did not need any specific training, education, books or instructions. However, the current day scenario is different. There is a need to provide elaborate training on jyotishya knowledge not only for the common man, but also for practitioners such as purohits, vedic and puranic scholars in the aforementioned lines. Also, there is need to publish, publicise and propagate the correct way of understanding the subject.

In lines with this, I-SERVE, under the direction of Brahmasri Kuppa Krishnamurthy garu (who is my father's brother), has started this exercise of conducting seminars, training camps to impart basic as well as advances Jyotishya Knowledge to the youth, purohits and others interested in learning and understanding the science in the right perspective. I-SERVE also had been conducting sessions and seminars for advanced students and research scholars by bringing the traditional scholars and the new age research scholars, practitioners and professors onto a single platform with the above intent. These efforts have yielded fruitful results as is evident from a wide variety of publications emanating from these sessions and seminars.

In addition to these activities, Sri Krishnamurthy garu has also thought of bringing out a specific publication for imparting fundamental jyothishya knowledge specifically aimed the youth and purohits and for this purpose he had sought the expert help of Sri Challa Somasundaram garu.

Sri Somasundaram garu is an octogenarian well-versed in both vedic traditions and the western education system. A civil engineer by qualification, he had retired from railways after an illustrious career. Simultaneosfy he had trained himself in ज्योतिष्यविद्या under tutelage of able gurus:

1. My guru, a proficient scholar in *Veda,* vedangas, jyotishya and vedartha, nityagnihotri, Sri (late) Edida Suryanarayana Murthy garu BE (Deputy Director, Hydrology and Statistics)
2. Embodiment of ज्योतिष्यविद्या, Sri Chirravuri Subrahmanyam garu, better known as C V B (another guru for me)
3. Mahamahopadhyaya, Receipient of Presidential Award Sri (late) Madhura Krishnamurthy Sastry garu

In addition to the above tutelage, he has gained training from various other scholars and also had obtained Masters and Doctoral degrees in Astrology and vedic Astrology respectively. He further went on to publish English translations to great texts Like *Jatakamani Manjusha, Dwasada Lagna Yogavayoga Nirnaya* and a few others. A great achievement, to Sri Somasundaram garu, his publications are frequently referred by his gurus.

I have reviewed the book only peripherally, not owing to any other reason, than my low status on account of age and knowledge. However, I have found the book to be very useful and practical for the beginners. This has the basic concepts of panchamga, jataka, muhurta, vastu, prasnasastras. In addition to this, other fundamental concepts of the cosmos, ayanamsas, different theories and the related terminology is explained in a brief and yet effective manner. Being an engineer by profession, he had given the entire presentation a very effective look by incorporating diagrams, tables and charts at relevant places.

Sri Somadundaramgaru, has very affectionately asked me to provide my review on this book. I am not acquainted with him except to hear his references from my gurus. Having seen one of my papers on different methods of Panchamga Ganana, he had graciously called me to congratulate and has also included in the current publication. I am thankful to him for his kindness and affection. The only reason that I can attribute to this affection and kindness is Gurvanugraham. I prostrate to the Gurus.

I also bow to this author who is an elderly, well-wishing सतीर्थ owing to common Gurus.

Hyderabad

Date:

20-10-2019

Sri. Kuppa Anjaneya Sastry

Mob. +91-9492888088

PREFACE

1. Daily routine Life of Indians is completely dependent on counting of time on hourly and minute to minute basis. This system of counting is purely dependent on " PANCHAMGAM". This Panchamgam is prepared based on the Siddhanta Bhaga of Ancient Indian Jyothish Sastra. That was how the Ancient Indians had called this as "SASTRA OF THE TIME COUNT".
2. Not only the Ancient Indian system of Vedic Cult but also the activities of arriving at future events in the predictive analysis had all depended on Panchamgam. That was why our Ancient Indians had called both the Ritualistic and Predictive Methods of practices adopted were of Sastras of practical guidance of Nature.
3. This Panchamgam was used and is being used by Purohits, Astrologers, Brahmins conducting Yajnas & Yagas. But the query and doubts regarding points such as:
   (i) How the Panchamgams are made?,
   (ii) What are the various differences between varieties of Panamgams in the Market,
   (iii) The reasons for disputes among these Panchamgams.
   (iv) The causes for various opinions expressed on these matters, etc.

   On all these matters, the Common Man has no idea and knowledge. This was the reason that the Pundits could not answer the query put forward by Younger Generation to their satisfaction. As a result , belief on this Sastra is getting diminished.
4. Taking note of such situation and in order to inculcate confidence among the learned Persons; I, as ex. Chairman of I-SERVE,(Institute of Scientific Research on Vedas), while functioning at Hyderabad up-to 2016, was conducting Classes on Panchamga Gananam to the interested Students, Purohits and Matriculation Passed individuals. There was tremendous response from these students and Teaching Faculty were amazed and astonished. The Teaching Faculty were drafted from Andhra, Telangana, Karnataka, Tamil and Maharashtra areas.

   I started making an effort to get a Book written, which includes the Lectures given by Prominent People from these areas, as this could be prescribed as a Text Book for such Classes in future and also it will be a useful Book to the Public at Large. This ambition of mine could not get fulfilled, as it was found difficult to get the Lectures given by various persons translated into Telugu Language and therefore it could not get materialized.
6. At last fortunately, as a God's sent, the work could be got done through DR. Challa Somasundaram. DR Challa Somasundaram aged + 86 years now, is a knowledgeable person. He Retired as General Manager, of Indian Railway Construction Company. After Retirement, He had not only learnt Panchamga

Ganitham from Late Sri. Madhura Krishna Murthy Sastry Garu of Rajahmundry; but also wrote Dwadasa Lagnamulaku Yogavayoga Nirnayamu in Telugu and Jataka Mani Manjusha in English- these Astrology Books were Printed by obtaining blessings from the highly learned Scholars. He had accepted my request and in order to be useful for Public at large, He had written not only on ' Panchamgam' but also ventilated other Sastras on which the knowledge gained from Panchamgam could be used, which were Annexed to therein. This was the Book printed in 2017, which is more useful for Telugu knowing public of Andhra and Telangana States.

7. Now Dr. Challa Somasundaram has translated the same Telugu Book into English for the benefit of students of other than Telugu speaking States, under the Heading "ALMANAC & ASTRO-SCIENCES". The write-up given by a Panchamga Kartha by name Sri .Kuppa Anjaneya Sastry, of Hyderabad, on the subject ' Introduction on various Panchamgas in the Market' is included as a separate Chapter at Sr. No-9 by Challa Somasundaram, which goes to prove, his deep sympathy for the subject under consideration.

8. I fervently appeal and hope that this book in English ' Almanac & Astro-Sciences' will also be useful to the Students of All Indian States. I hope that there will be more discussions and Seminars on the Subject, and will become popular among Public. I earnestly pray the Almighty that the Author be kept hale and healthy and bestowed with long life.

JAI GURU DATTA.

MYSURU
D/ 20-10-2019.
Mob. +91-9866330060

A Follower of Scholars.
SRI. KUPPA VENKATA KRISHNA MYRTHY.

AP Agrany Publications

MODERN ASTROLOGY

Successor to Dr. B.V. RAMAN'S

THE ASTROLOGICAL MAGAZINE (1936 - 2007)

"Shri Gayatri", 56, ITI Layout, IV East Maia Road, Banashankari III Stage, Bangalore 560 085,

Tel: +91-80-26793479 email: publicationsagrany@yahoo.com

Editor: Gayatri Devi Vasudev **email: gayatridevivasudev@yahoo.co.in**

January 3, 2020

Dr. Challa Somasundaram,

C/O Dr.C.R. Murty, BW-25,

3rd Cross Road, Bonn Avenue,

Adyar, Chennai 600036

Dear Dr.Somasundaram,

Thank you for a copy of your book *Almanac and Astro Sciences* which I have gone through with great interest and would like to share my thoughts on it with you.

Almanac and Astro Sciences is a work of importance to the astrology student covering as it does the entire gamut of principles involved in Panchanga or the Indian almanac making. The Panchanga is not only an integral part of astrology as a subject of study for the student but also a constant reference and guide to most Indians in timing their mundane activities as also for observing fasts and festivals and other religious observances. It is integral to the social and religious life of Indian society.

What amazes me is your enthusiasm and energy in starting the study of the subject of Panchanga-making in your late seventies at a time when most people would like to take total retirement and putting your understanding of the subject in your Telugu book *Panchanga Vignana Sastramulu* which however was confined to the Telugu knowing readership. Thanks to your intiring effort, the present title which is its English version is available to a wider readership. It is an invaluable, and in some ways, a unique addition to extant literature on Jyotisha and in particular, Muhurta or electional astrology.

Starting with the fundamentals such as the definition of terms in astronomy as well as Panchangas, you take one through the principles of Muhurta, Prasna and Vastu in graded steps . The note on Ayanamsa is apt as this is a little understood concept. The chapter on different methods adopted in Panchangas is welcome as it to some extent clarifies on why uniformity is lacking in Panchangas prepared by different maths and others.

The chapter on casting of horoscopes can be of much help to beginners. The 3-part *Appendix* at the end is of much help as it carries the equivalents of English terms in Telugu, of Telugu terms in English and of English terms in Hindi which enable one to understand the Telugu terms that are profusely scattered throughout the text.

Having trained under the scholarly Telugu Siddhanti Sri Madhura Krishnamurty Sastry of Rajahmundry, whom my revered father Dr.B.V.Raman held in great respect, it is no surprise that you have come out with such a detailed text on Panchanga, a subject that has evaded clear and concise treatment and which lacuna is now made good by your work.

I cannot but marvel at your clarity of thought even in your mid-eighties and the stupendous effort that you have put into bringing out this book.

I wish you all the best.

Kind regards,

Gayatri Devi Vasudev

Editor

Message from Dr K S Charak

The cardinal concept at the heart of all Vedic sciences is the intention to uplift the humankind from its basal level to the highest spiritual levels. This according to our scriptures is primarily achieved through the performance of the right Karma, whether physical, mental or spiritual. This universe is subject to the principle of cause and effect. The right Karma is the cause and the subsequent consequence is the effect. In order to attain the desired effect, the performed Karma should be appropriate. One of the most important factors in achieving the right result from an action is the performance of that action at the Tightest time possible. This brings into importance the use of Muhurta or electional astrology which is employed to choose the right moment of time for the performance of a select action. The Panchanga that provides the relevant information about the right moment of time thus attains the vital importance.

It is my considered opinion that the Muhurta is the most important branch of astrology. A horoscope is indicative of the potential inherent in a native. Considered in another way, it is indicative of the limitations that a native is born with. The Muhurta allows the individual to perform an action with the intention of getting the best results from that action, from within his limitations. Muhurta is thus the practical application of astrology in order to attain the best results from a performed Karma, helping in the evolution of the performer of that action. DrChallaSomasundaram has rendered yeoman service to the cause of Vedic astrology by elaborating on the principles of the Panchanga as well as the astronomy relevant to it.

The Panchanga is only one important part of the ***"Almanac and Astro-Sciences".*** The book additionally deals with several other important areas of astrology which would be of relevance to the student and the master alike. While he provides simple examples of casting of a horoscope and arriving at certain Muhurtas, he also takes pains to elaborate on such important branches of Vedic astrology as PrashnaShastra, stellar astrology and VastuShastra. Numerous important astrological principles, rarely found elsewhere in a single book, lie embedded in this compilation. I have full faith that the astrological world would find this work enriching and valuable.

I congratulate DrChallaSomasundaram for his worthy effort in bringing out this valuable work, and wish him all the best in the service of this divine science.

Dr K. S. Charak
MS (Surgery); FRCS UK
Senior Consultant & Chief of General Surgery,
Indian Spinal Injuries Centre,
VasantKunj, New Delhi-110070,
M– +91-9868957363
D/1–2–2020

Naadi Jyothisa Kesari, Jyothir Yogi
Prof. NVRARaja
(Meena2 Jr.)
M.A (Jyothisam), M.A (Philosophy & Religion)
M.Sc. (Psychology) PhD(Jyothisam) PhD (Vedanga Jyothisam)
International Vice-Chancellor,
Yoga Samskrutham University, Florida, USA,
Chairman-JKR Astro Research Foundation
astroraja@gmail.com,
M– +91-9848194591

Jai Meena2

"Almanac and Astro sciences", a book written on the importance of Panchanga and also how Panchanga helps a Purohitha, Daivagna to perform Yagnas, Dhanas, and to fix auspicious Muhurthas for functions like Marriage, Gruhapravesha, Gruharambha etc. Our ancients say that a work started at an auspicious time is half completed and rest will take place automatically without any difficulties. The author Dr. Challa Soma Sundaram is very energetic at the age of 86+ and taken lot of pain in compiling data and messages collected from late Sri. Madhura Krishna Sastry. The author has put his efforts in compiling this work for the benefit of every reader. In olden days every astrologer knew the calculations of PanchagaGanitha and casting of horoscopes. But nowadays many are focusing on PhalithaBhaga leaving almanac calculations. In this work the author has brought out many chapters on almanac and astronomical calculations for everyone to understand specifically he has spent a lot of time in explaining ayanamsa, nirayana and sayana systems.

In the chapter 3 he has explained yoga formed by Rahu - Ketu and also other planets have been dealt very well. In the chapter 4 the author has given introduction to Stellar Astrologythat is, Nakshatra Siddhanthapropounded by Guruji, Sri.N.V.Raghavachary,(Meena 2). I am very happy that he has taken important points from the book written by me on Jeeva and Sareera concept.

Example chart quoted here to arrive Jeeva and Sareera, was explained in stellar effects in astrology Jeeva and Sareera, the same had been reproduced as it is for better understanding for the beginners and masters in astrology. Specifically the gunas table reproduced from the practical stellar astrology written by Guruji Sri.N.V.Raghava Chary is unique and had been given to the world first time by Guruji. That is the reason Guruji Sri.N.V.Raghava Chary (Meena 2) is re-incarnation of Sage Satyacharya who was authority on Nakshatra Siddhantha.

In this chapter Dr. Challa Soma Sundaram referred Kalamsa Gunas written by me and quoted example charts given there, and highlighting how marriage matching is so simple and so lucid. In Astro sciences in the chapter 5, he dealt with Muhurtha Sastra parichayamu - importance of tarabala, Chandra bala, avasthas for the planet and dwadasa bhavas in detail. In chapter 6, Vastu Sastra and its uses, muhurthas for gruhapravesha and rules are dealt wonderfully. Chapter 8 he has given detailed notes on ayanamsa and different concepts. In chapter 10, he has given some practical examples for casting of horoscopes how to fix muhurthas. In this book, author had covered many important points and compiled it very well.

I am proud to write my observations after thoroughly going through the latest work Almanac and Astro sciences being published by Dr. Challa Soma Sundaram. He is a well-known personality in Astro circles and also in spiritual society. After his retirement from railways he has taken up 'astrology' as a full time and read many books, and associated him with many great scholars. During the year 2016, Yoga Samskrutham University, Florida has awarded him a doctorate for his work (Marriage and the 7th bhava). I trust this book will be very popular and useful among astrologers and PanchangaKartas.

May lord Sri Lakshmi Narasimhaswamy and ParamaPoojya Guruji Sri.N.V.Raghavachary's blessings be there with him and his family members for many more contributions towards human society. God's blessings to all.

30.01.2020, Thursday (VasanthaPanchami) **Prof. NVRA Raja**

Secunderabad.

Dr. Prabhakar K Kashyap
Chief General Secretary
Jyotishya Vishwavidyalaya (Regd)
Indian Forum of Yoga Samskrutham University,
Florida, USA
Founder Chairman and President, SCOPE, Bengaluru
M–09986583731

To

Dr Challa Somasundaram
C/o Dr C V R Murthy, BW-25,
3rd Cross Road, Bonn Avenue
Adayar, CHENNAI – 600036
M– 095099 11902

Dear Sir,

Namasthe

Sub: Your Book on 'ALMANAC AND ASTRO SCIENCES'

At the outset, I extend warm greetings on your endeavour to publish a new book on the subject 'Almanac and Astro Sciences' which is translated from your original work in Telugu version.

I have made a cursory glance at the topics highlighted in your book. It appears like a compendium of vital basic data connected to Almanac and Astro Sciences. Your effort to bring different Astro Sciences under one roof for the benefit of aspiring students to have an overall idea of the subject at Introductory level is commendable. You have included therein matters pertaining to Panchanga to start with explaining the different limbs of Panchanga followed by Astromonical terms like Sidereal time and formation of eclipses presented graphically. The chapter on Stellar Astrology summarizing the Jeeva Sarira concept propounded by Dr NVRA Raja gives the basic information on the subject. I have noted with interest the topics on Mhurtha, Vasthu shastra and Prashna shastra covered in your book giving the outline of these subjects. Methods of Panchangams and Casting of horoscopes also find appropriate place in your book.

On the whole, for a beginner interested in learning the limbs of Panchanga and to acquire basic knowledge of Astro Sciences, your book serves as a useful guide.

I heartily wish that the book reaches all the interested people.

With warm regards

DR PRABHAKAR K KASHYAP

FOUNDER PRESEIDENT AND CHAIRMAN – SCOPE (R)

SRI. KV. KRISHNA MURTHY,
EDTOR, BHAKTIMALA,
Sri Ganapathi Sachchidananda Ashramam,
Ooty Road, Datta Nagar, MYSURU-570025
Mob– +91 98663 30060

FORWARD

Vedic daily routine life is mainly dependant on counting the Time element for various activities. This Time factor is relying on Panchamgam. The preparation of Panchagam is based on the principles laid down in the Siddanta Bhaga of Astrological Science. This was the reason that our ancestors called the Astrological Science as the Science of time determination. Not only the Indian performance of daily Ritualistic activities but also their future programmes are dependant on Panchamgam. Therefore our elders had stated that Medical Science and Astrological Sastra are realistic Sciences.

Our learned Pundits, Astrologers and those Karthas who perform Yagnas are utilising Panchamga, but how these are prepared and what are the merits and demerits in these and what are the causes that bring differences of opinion among them and what are the other matters connected with this are not clearly known to many a common man. Even the so called Pundits in this Sastra are not able to clearly answer these questions satisfactorily. As a result, the people started disbelieving this Sastra.

Seeing this trend of uncertainty, it has created interest among of the Educated Class. To bring proper understanding I conducted some Classes, when I was the President of I-SERVE (Institute of Scientific Research on Vedas) at Hyderabad, on the subject of 'Reading and understanding of the contents of Panchamgam'. There was tremendous response from the interested persons, which had surprised me. Classes were organised to teach the Panchamga Sastra by calling Pundits from Andhra, Karnataka, Tamil & Maharashtra areas.

I wanted to prepare a Text covering all the aspects taught by these Pundits, so that the same could become a Reference text for students learning this Science, and also which could be useful to the Public in general; my efforts could not take shape as the Pundits came from different language areas. My intention of bringing a Text in Telugu language had become difficult and as such my ambition could not get fulfilled.

At last, as God sent, fortunately Dr. Challa Somasundaram, could bring out this Book in Telugu, in spite of 86 years of age. Though a Retd. Engineer by profession, after retirement he had undergone training under President Awardee late Sri. Madhura Krishna Murthy Sastryji and became his student and learnt the Science of Panchamga Ganana.

In addition, he had written a Text " Dwadasa Langnamulaku Yogavayoga Nirnayamu" in Telugu and a second Text " Jataka Mani Manjusha" in English with blessings of well noted Astrological Pundits. He had agreed to my request and in order to benefit the public at large, he had not only given a detailed analysis of the five Elements of Panchamga but also added other subjects which are relevant to the knowledge of Panchamga Sastra and brought a book called" Panchamga Vignana Sastramula Parichayamu" inTelugu.

In this text the Article on the subject' Introduction to different methods adopted in Panchamgas' written by Sri. Kuppa Sri. Anjaneya Sastry is included as such at Chapter No-9 of the Text, goes to indicate the magnanimous attitude, of Dr. Challa Somasundaram, which needs to be emphasized.

I am glad and overwhelmed on seeing the fact that Challaji translated his own Telugu book into English, for the benefit of Panchanga admirers of the whole world. This is a noble act and this is done by DR. Challaji at the age of 86 in spite of his non co-operative health conditions. I salute him for this.

I trust that this Book will be utilised by the public at large & hope that the same will be prescribed as Text Book of reference in future Seminars and Discussions that will be held at a future date and brings into wide publicity. I pray the Almighty that the Author be blessed with healthy & long life.

d/ 1-1-2020

Mysuru — Kuppa Venkata Krishna Murthy

Retired Head, Department of Jyothisha Vastu,
Sri Potti Sreeramulu Telugu University,
Hyderabad.
Flat No-101, Swathikuteer,
Yusufguda, Hyderabad-500 045,
Ph:040-2373 4999, Cell: 094400 55415.

TRUTHFUL WORK

Dr. ChallaSomasundaram has written the Book " Almanac and Astro-Sciences" in a simple and common man's language which could be easily understood by the students and those interested in the subject. He has covered the subjects like Ayanamsa, Parasara Astrology, Stellar Astrology, Muhurta, Vastu Sastra, Prasna Sastra, method of casting a horoscope and especially the esteemed advantages of Panchanga Ganana etc. have been enumerated in greater details.

This Book is written as per motivation of Brahmma Sri Madhura Krishna Murthy Sastry garu, Brahmma Sri. Kuppa Vekata Krishna Murthy garu and by adding the Essay written by Brahmma Sri. Kuppa Anjaneya Sastry garu on the subject of' different methods adopted in preparation of Panchamgam' has given a totality to this Book.

By reading this Book one would know as to how the Panchamgam is to be studied and put to useful purpose and the readers will clearly understand the matter concerning different opinions and causes for the same.

Further the important point to be noted is that the Colloquial Stanzas used in Telugu are translated into English and Hindi which will enable the reader to clearly understand the meanings of various technical phrases used in Panchamgams. These Stanzas will be more useful while reading other texts on the subjects of Astrology and Astronomy.

Summing up it is stated that the efforts made by Dr. Challa Somasundaram in bringing out such an excellent Book with blessings of well noted and famous Pundits in Astrology is worth praise worthy. It is hoped that this work will be useful to many who are seeing knowledge on these subjects.

d/ 30-01-2020, Truly Yours

Acharya C.V.B. Subrahmanyam

Pratyaksham Jyothisam Sastram ...

Jyotisha Shastra is a Five branched subject dealing with Siddantha, Samhita, Hora, Prasna, and Sakuna being the five different and unique parts. There is always a scope to include, research and put insight in bringing some more new topics into this vast science. Jyotisham (Astrology) is a Science that deals with Time, its impact on Nature and changes in nature of humans with relevance to the changes in time and nature.

Siddantha part basically is the mathematical calculation part of the Astrology. The various planets, Stars, Satellites, Meteors, in the Solar system , their influence on the individuals on the Earth, distance between Sun and Moon, all these aspects fall under Siddantha part. Compilation of these calculations ,and information about Thithi, Vara, Nakshtra, Yoga and Karana are covered under Panchangam. Panchangam (Almanac) also gives an insight into Karthis, planet positions, their transitions from one sign to another, Weather forecasts, Ascendant calculations, Varjyam, Durmuhurtam timings etc., making it a hand book for astrologers all over. With the changing times and views there is a necessity that we need to adapt to new school of thought in place of old practices of calculations by using new and advanced technological procedures. At the same time there is a call to wipe out the different practices and adapt a single practice for the caicuiations of panchangam.

Samhita branch deals with a lot of other related parts of Astrology. Samhita means a Compilation. This includes Muhurtam, Vastu, Palmistry, Gemology, Waster divination, Dream, Remedial measures etc.,.All these have to be given an individual status these days owing to the importance they gained in present days and the scope to widen the subject.

In regards to the other parts of Prasna, Hora and Sakuna, there is always a continuous effort to understand and widen the knowledge by applying present day living conditions of humans and changes to old practices . Astrology from times immemorial has been playing an important role in human life style by indicating the good and bad times thereby helping the individuals bring the best to themselves and society.

There are many people who worked and many who are working on this vast subject, guiding people, transferring their knowledge to others by teaching etc., Dr. Challa Somasundaram worked on this Panchangam part. Though he was introduced to this subject early, he could work in this area only at an later age owing to his education and professional duties. He started studying this subject more detailedly only in his later age. He even travlled from Chennai to Rajahmundry every week to learn from great scholars like Sri Mathura Krishnamurthy Sastry etc., He also received his Doctorate in Astrology recently.

Sri. Somasundaram has made some additions and changes to his earlier book "Panchanga Vignana Sastramula Parichayam" in Telugu and translated it into English with a view to make it reach more aspirants who study Astrology. In this book he made different heads for Astronomy, Panchang, different calculation methods, making this book a must have for all those who start learning this sufiject. Samhita and Vastu are given prominent importance in this book. A separate head was made for Prasna shastra. In the Hora part, he mentioned the stellar astrology separately. An insight into the way he presented the appendix of technical words used in the book at the last made this book more attractive for study. We can also view Telugu to English, English to Telugu and English to Hindi translations of technical words used.

Dr. Challa Somasundaram not taking his age into consideration, made himself an icon of inspiration to the next generation scholars by bringing out this book. Wishing more and more texts to come out of his pen and wishing him a lot of success in his attempts with the blessings from God Sun as Jyothirmoorthi and from Srimata as Jyothishmathi.

Shubham bhuyath.

HYDERABAD
D/18–2–2020

Dr. Sagi Kamalakara Sharma
Asst. Professor of Telugu,
Osmania University.

Dr. Rallapalli. Venkateswara Rao
Assistant Professor of Astrology(Rtd)
Department of Astrology - Vastu,
Potti Sreeramulu University, Hyderabad, Telangana.
M – +91 9908811188

BLESSINGS

The present book as the title indicates deals with the basic principles "Almanac and Astrological Sciences" prove useful both to the beginner and the advanced students since it starts with the rudimentariness of the science and goes up to the advanced level. This subject being very important required more attention on the part of Astrology as it deals with the daily affairs of the individual. The present author Somasundaram Challa was deeply interested in this branch of science from the beginning and succeeded to a considerable extent after long research to present the material on the subject. His inquisitive knowledge produced commendable work on almanac. He covered all the basic concepts of the Panchanga. As an engineer he tried his level best to present the content in a scientific way. His effort at this age is an inspiration to the youngsters. I wish him great success in his further endeavors in Astrology.

HYDRABAD
D/6–2–2020

Dr. Rallapalli Venkateswara Rao

SRI. POTHUKUCHI SURYANARAYANA MURTHY,
SENIOR ADVOCATE AND FORMER MEMBER
OF A.P. SAHITYA AKADEMY & FORME
CORRESPONDENT OF "THE HINDU",
NATIONAL DAILY, DAN AVAIP ETA,
RAJAMAHENDRAVARAMU.
Ph: 08832475808

BENEDICTION

Dr. Challa Somasundaram was born and brought up in an orthodox Brahmana family. As such he had imbibed all the merits and values of the cultural heritage and ethos of the community and the family.

Trained as a Civil Engineer (On the root of his professional studies) he was employed in the Indian Railways as Engineer for Civil Works and discharged his duties with commendable competence to the satisfaction of his employers and earned encomiums from them for his appreciable fulfilment of the assigned duties.

After retiring from such Engineering services, Dr. Challa Somasundaram evinced interest in Astrology. The interest was not limited only to study but was absolute and abiding which led him to acquire a Masters and Doctorial degrees in his chosen subject from Potti Sreeramulu Telugu University, Hyderabad. Thus Dr. Somasundaram has proved that age is not a bar or restriction to acquisition of new and fresh knowledge in other fields of activity and his success therein has been splendid and exemplary.

At the bidding and encouraging blessings from his Preceptor Brahmma Sri Kuppa Venkata Krishna Murthy (The founder President of I-SERVE, a research Organisation for dissemination of Astrology as a Science, for its propagation and progress) Dr. Somasundaram undertook to write a book (in fact it is a Text Book) for utility of Almanac-writers and students eager to learn the details of Almanac & Astrological Sciences and fulfilled the task with perspicuous out-put thus fulfilling the Preceptor's wish.

The original is in Telugu Language the author's mother tongue. In order to make the contents readable to those who do not know Telugu the author himself translated it into English . I have seen both the versions in their entirety. I am delighted to say that Dr. Somasundaram's English version is a fair rendering of the original in letter and spirit. I congratulate him on this achievement. Dr. Somasundaram is a Sahasra Chandradarsana, a venerable personality, I as a Senior in that line to him by eight years offer my blessings to him for his glorious achievements registered without demonstrative ostentation or creeping desire for the fame.

May the Plemordial Adidampatis (Sacred Couple) Sri Parvathi and Sri. Parameshwara bless him and his family with longevity, health and wealth, thus honoured his Preceptor's desire to the full extent. Om Tatsat.

D/ 21-01-2020 Potukuchi Suryanarayana Murthy

MAHAMAHOOPADHYAYA,
PRESIDENT AWARDEE,
PRACHARYA SALAKA RAGHUNADHA SARMA,
JNANAPURNIMA, 78-10-5/12, C-3,
RESIDENCY APARTMENTS, SHYAMALA NAGAR,
RAJAHMUNDRY, PH:- 0883 2432 906.

GREETINGS

DR. Challa Somasundaram has done extensive research in Jyothis Sastras and had already contributed a few Books which speaks highly of his intellectual capacity and he had done yeoman service to the humanity. In depth study of Jyothish Sastra and Vedanga tantamounts to worshipping Veda Mata itself. The results obtained through such actions speaks of high level of attainment for a research Scholar. Even after crossing 80 years of age his capacity for analytical study is not lacking which is appreciated.

Now Dr. Challa Somasundaram has written another Book called " Almanac & Astro Sciences". I have gone through this Book from over all points of view and felt very much happy for the same. If this Book is studied in greater detail one would know the various

Divisions available in the Jyothish Sastra and how a Panchamgam will be useful in studying those Sastras. This Treatise brings out Astronomical details which is a speciality by itself. I therefore convey my heartfelt greetings to Dr. Challa Somasundaram for bringing out such an excellent Book.

D/ 4-2-2020 Pracharya Salaka Raghunadha Sarma

ALMANAC & ASTRO SCIENCES.

AGAMAACHARYA, RAJA GURU,
Dr.M.R.V. SARMA, M.A., Phd.
AGAMA, MANTRA SASTRA, VASTHU
AGAMA, SMARTHA, PUNDITS.

MANTRA KALANIDHI
H. No-12-17-2, ARYAPURAM
RAJAHMUNDRY-533104, A.P.,
PH-0883-2465 183
M- 97038 67120, 94914 34101

BLESSINGS

DR. Challa Somasundaram garu is well versed in Astrology, Astronomy and the Astrological Sciences. In the recent past He has to his credit in writing & Printing a few Astrological Books. He has now written another Astrological Book titled " Almanac & Astro Sciences"in a simple language and easy to follow by interested Students and in this way He Has done a great service to the readers. He has covered the subjects Astrology, Astronomy & Vasthu by detailed clarifications. He has also written examples for Construction of a Horoscope, fixing Muhurthas etc. In a greater detail.

The 'Forward' by Dr. Kuppa Venkata Krishna Murty Garu and Introduction to 'Panchanga Sastra Parichayamu' given by Sri. Kuppa Anjaneya Sastry garu has enhanced the importance of the Book Value by two fold.

I sincerely convey my whole hearted Blessings to Dr. Somasundaram for a healthy and long life and wish that He will bring out some more such useful Books in future.

Yours Truely,

M.R.V. Sarma

D/ 24-12-2019.

Rajahmundry.

M.R.V. SARMA

ALMANAC & ASTRO SCIENCES.

17-4-6/1, Krishna Nagar,
Jyothisha Vidya Kendramu, Seethampeta,
Rajahmundry-533104, A.P., Ph- 0883-2429272,
Cell: 093979 19902.

COMMENTS

My Dear Sri. Somasundaam Garu,

I am in receipt of your Letter D/ 16-12-2019 asking me to give Blessings on the enclosed Book "Almanac & Astro Sciences" written by you.

I really feel honoured and delightful to go through it's contents. The Book is well written and presented.

It's my sincere opinion that this Book will be of great use not only to Purohits and Metriculation qualified Students but also to General Purohits who believe and follow Panchanga Ganitham. Really you have lived up-to the expectations of your Gurus by writing this Book which will be of immense use all over India.

With Kind Regards. Yours Sincerely,

Rajahmundry,

D/ 24-12-2019. Madhurapala Sankar Murthy Sarma

ALMANAC & ASTRO SCIENCES.

SRI. VRADHA KRISHNA,
WETER SUPLLY & RAILWAYS DIVN.
MADHAPUR, HYDERABAD- 500081.T-S
PH. 040-2326 8888, CELL: 98663 92040.

BLESSINGS

SRI. Challa Somasundaram has written the Book Almanac & Astro Sciences' and wanted me to give Blessings for the same. As I was going through the Book, Sri. Challa Somasundaram has covered many subjects such as Panchanga Ganana Prayojanamu, Science of Astrology etc. In fact Panchanga Ganana is very important and useful for human society. Panchanga Ganana explains the movements of Grahas and their effect on earth.

Human beings use to utilise this informatin to set Muhurthams for fixing up Marriages, calculating Horoscope, performing Poojas, Vrathams, Yagnas, Festivels, Agriculture and for all other purposes. It is needless to say that not only Indian Culture will follow the Panchanga Ganana but also other Westren Countries will follow the auspicious time for all the functions based on movement of Grahas.

Chapters I & II are very important for all Astrology Students and readers to understand the total concept of Astronomy and this technical explanation with detailed diagrams can easily understand the fundamentals of Astrology. Vasthu Sastra, Nakshatra SiddantaJyotisha, Muhurtha Bhagha, Prasna Sastra, Astronomy and Ayanamsa have been dealt. He has not only mentioned fundamentals but also covered the advanced & important issues for the benefit of the Students.

I am associated with Sri Challa Somasundaram for the past two decades and his works. He touched the key subjects in the present Book and I appreciate. His enthusiasm and effort shown in bringing out all the important Astrologial subjects at one place in a Book and this is the probably the first of it's kind.

I wish him all success and I trust that this Book will be received by ever one with enthusiasm and motivate Sri challa Somasndaram to write many more Books.

D/- 24-12-2019

Hyderabad

V. RADYIAKRISHNA

DIRECTOR, N.C.C LTD.

ACKNOWLEDGEMENTS

As per the advice of Sri. Kuppa Venkata Krishna Murthy, former Chairman of I-SERVE, (Institute of Scientific Research on Vedas), Hyderabad; the Book' Panchamga Vijnana Sastramula Parichayamu' was initially written by me in Telugu. In this Telugu version the Article given by Sri. Kuppa Anjaneya Sastry on the subject of' Introduction to the different methods in Panchamgams' was included as it is at Chapter-9.

This Telugu Book is translated by me into English under the heading "Almanac & Astro- Sciences". The Chapter-9 is translated by it's original author. The draft Book was submitted to the following Gurus who are well known on the subject of Astrology, for their blessings,

1. Smt. Gayatri Devi Vasudev, Editor, Modern Astrology Magazine, at 'Sri Gayatri', 56, ITI Layout, IV East Main Road, Banashankari HI Stage, Bangalore-560085, Tel: +91 80 2679 3479.
2. Dr. K.S. Charak, M.S (Surgery), FRCS,UK, Senior Consultant & Chief General Surgery, Indian Spinal Injuries Centre, Vasanth Kunj, New Delhi-110070, M-+9198689 57363.
3. Prof. N.V.R.A. Raja, (Meena-Jr-2), M.A, MSc.,P.hd. (Vedanga Jyotisha), International Vice-Chancellor, Yoga Samskrutham University, Florida, USA, Chairman JKR Astro Research Foundation, Secunderabad- M- +91 9848194591.
4. Dr. K. Prabhakar K. Kashyap, Chief General Secretary, Jyotisha Viswavidyalaya (Regd), Indian Forum of Yoga Samskrutham University, Florida. USA, Founer Chairman & President SCOPE, Bengaluru, M-099865 83731.
5. Sri. K.V.Krishna Murthy, Editor, Bhaktimala, Sri Ganpathi Sachichidananda Ashramam, Ooty Road, Datta Nagar, Mysuru-570025, M-+91 98663 30060.
6. Acharya Dr. C.V.B Subrahmanyam, Retd, Head of Department of Jyothisha Vastu, Sri Pottisreeramulu Telugu University, Hyderabad, Flat-101, Swathi Kuteer, YUsufguda,, Hyderabad.. M- 094400 55415.

7. Dr. Rallapalli Venkateswara Rao, Assistant Professor or Astrology Vastu, Potti Sreeramulu Telugu University, Hyderabad, Telangana, M- +91 99088 11188.

8. Sri. Pothukuchi Suryanarayana Murthy, Senior Advocate, & Former Member of A.P. Sahitya Akademy & Former Correspondent of' The Hindu', National Daily, Danavaipeta, Rajahmundry, Tel:- 0883 247 5808.

9. Mahamahoopadyaya, President Awardee, Pracharya Salaka Ragunadha Sarma, Jnanapurnima, 78-10-5/12, C-3, Residency Apartments, Shyamala Nagar, Rajahmundry. Tel:- 0883 2432 906.

10. Agamacharya, Raja Guru, Mantra Kalanidhi, Agama Mantra Sastra Vastu, Agama Smartha Pundits, Sri. M.R.V. Sarma, Manideepa Peethamu, House No-12-7-2, Aryapuram, Rajhmundry-533104 Tel:-0883 2465 183.

11. Sri. Madhura Pala Sankara Murthy Sarma, 17-4-6/1, Krishna Nagar, Jyothisha Vidya Kendramu, Seethampeta, Rajahmundry-533104,A.P.Tel :- 0883 2429 272.

12. Sri. V.Radhakrishna, Director, Nagarjuna Construction Co. Pvt. Ltd., Water Supply and Railways Division, Madhapur, Hyderabad-500081. T.S. Tel:- 040-2326 8888

13. Jyothisha Praveena, Jyothisha Visharada, Jyothir Vidya Bhushana, Andhra Bhasha Bhushana Daivagna Saman, Sri. Sagi Kamalakara Sarma, Assistant Professor, Head of the Department of Telugu, Osmania University, Hyderabad, M- +91 97042 27744.

I am Thankful for the 'Foreword' given by Sri. Kuppa Anjaneya Sastry of Hyderabad, M-+91 94928 88088 I am highly grateful and thankful for the 'Preface' given by Sri. Kuppa Venkata Krishna Murhy, Mysuru. M-+91 98663 30060.

I am extremely grateful and thankful to all the above Gurus for their kind blessings on my Book' Almanac & Astro-Sciences'.

Challa Somasundaram.

CHAPTER 1

Esteemed Advantages of Almanac

1.1 INTRODUCTION TO ALMANAC

Almanac is also termed as 'Panchamgam' or Tidhipatri' meaning to contain five main divisions. These are Tithi, Vaaram, Nakshatram, Yogam and Karanam. Panchamgam indicate the timings current from and to of these five elements daily. Everyday Varjyamulu, Durmuhurthamulu, Amrita Ghadias, Dina Pramanamu, changes of Planets with Star in which situated including Pada and important festivals are mentioned.

In everyday the routine matters involving issues related to Subha & Asubha Karmas are checked only with the help of Panchamga. Matters relating to travel & journey can be correctly arrived through the Panchamgam.

Indians without the help of Panchamgam no action is taken on their routine activities. For all matters relating to functions and Ceremonies & festival days, Panchamgam is essentially required to be consulted. Tithi periods, timing of Sunrise & Sunset, good and auspicious timings, Nakshatras, different Yogas, Lagnas for all these purposes, Panchamgam is required to be consulted for correct timings of the events.

Correct timings for performance of Vedic Rituals will be made known. The position of Planets in the heavens with their correct Longitudes will be indicated exactly and by knowing these details, good and bad effects are made known through the Panchamgam.

After knowing Tithi, Vaara, Nakshatra, Yoga & Karana auspicious timings can be fixed on correct muhurtha. Such of those days where timings which are not good in Tithi, Vaara decided to be leftout. In all these matters that knowledge is of highest importance. For certain functions specific Tidhi, Vaara and Nakshatra have been laid down for performance.

Hence it is essential to know the timings at which such Tidhi, Vaara, Nakshtra are occurring on those days.

For daily ritual activities such as Bathing, Japam, Homam, & Puja etc. at the beginning of the particular function, details such as Year, Ayanam, Rutuvu, Month, Paksham, Tithi, Vaara and for some functions the Nakshatra are to be mentioned and these can be known only through Panchamgam.

1.2 IMPORTANT INFORMATION AVAILABLE IN PANCHAMGAM

In Telugu Panchamgam from "Chaitra Sudha Padhyami" to "Phalguna Bahula Amavasya" ... daily Tithi upto the timing in hours & minutes is indicated.

For every month in the beginning on first page details such as Year, Name, Month, Saka period, Kalyabdamulu, Huna Sakam, Hijaris etc. are given. For every day Sunrise,

Sunset, English Calander dates, dates of Salivahana Sakam,the names of Planets moving on that day etc. are given. Tithi,Vaara, Nakkshatra, Yoga and Karanam are shown in this order against Sakam dates, Ayanam, Rutuvu and against English dates, Month and Year is written.

The extant to which the tithi & nakshatras are existing on the date will be shown initially in Telugu figures in hours & minutes. Weekday from sunrise to next sunrise on the subsequent date in ghadias, hours & tithi will be identified. Afterwards, yogam and karanam will be shown in ghadias only. Amritaghadias, varjyam in hours, some others in ghadias are indicated. As long as there is no doubt on any issue the matter is shown in the first letter.For example:

'S.R' is meant for Sun Rise and 'R' is understood as for Ravi, Like that etc.

These are abbrievated names. There after mention is made about 'Meshayanam'. Detail of the Planet situated in the Nakshatra with pada is given. Sometimes on a particular date two Tithis are there which is called "Tithi Dwayam". This is followed by festivals and holidays, actions specified by dharma shastras, timings of Moon's aspect on padyami and the Crescent of Moon will be shown. Based on this, the changes expected to take place in the rates of materials in market are indicated. Auspicious timings of 'Vishuwat', timings of subha muhurtha are shown. The extant upto which the Sun had lapsed in a Rasi is shown.

The beginning and end of durmuhurtha is written. In continuation, months of Mohammadan calander, Saura months are mentioned. In every page, at the right hand top corner a table is shown indicating the planetary position at the commencement of the month. That table is to be read either clockwise or anti-clockwise direction. In the middle of the table, the changes which occurred to those Planets are only shown with changed Nakshatras.

After giving details of Almanac for all.the dates, at the bottom, a table of periods of Ascendants is given, indicate both day time and night time, Rasi wise. This is more useful in casting Horoscopes, fixing Subhamuhurthams and Lagnas. In case if any Planet is Retrograde on any day, the same is shown, as (R). If a planet is Retrograde and constant, before moving on direct motion is shown as R.

1.3 ADVANTAGES OF THE INFORMATION MENTIONED IN THE ALMANAC

Kalyabdas are mainly traditional accounts of a hero in an Epic. They are mainly helpful in identifying long durations of periods of time. Currently the issues and instances happening in "Hunasakam" are being accounted. Before the British introduced the "Hunasakam", in our country, the period of time was counted in "Salivahana Sakam". Hizaree belongs to "Mohammadans Sakam".

In Almanac the time counting starts from Sun rise in ghadias. The rituals required to be performed such as Sandhya Vandanam, Agnihotram etc. are also mentioned. Even during Sunset time, Rituals such as "Suryopasana" and "Agnihotram" will also be performed. In the "Sandhya Period", haircutting, mundan etc. of such activities are prohibited. If birth takes place in "Sandhya period of time" santi viz remedial measures are to be performed.

Since the counting of time is being made from the new year of Telugu see, the Calander is being made from Chaitra Suddha Padyami.The order of Seasons is getting backwards, now a days, that means the commencement of "Vasanta Rutuvu" was getting started approximately a month behind.

Based on Tithis, the festival of Sriramanavami is identified. The time specified as"Amrutakalam" is very good for commencement of taking medicines. Varjyam, Durmuhurtham periods are prohibited for performing Subha activities. Devatas and Ancestors are worshipped during the periods of 'Ayanas' and 'Sankramanas'. Almanac is invariably used for house Warming Muhrthas, Casting of Horoscopes and Sumuhurthas for various functions. When two Tithis fall on the same date, the activities relating to "Pitrudevatas" are undertaken.

The Lagna in which Sun is situated at the time of Sunrise is called "Suryodaya Lagna"or "Udaya Lagnam".The Bhukti viz, the extent of Longitude lapsed by Sunrise is mentioned. The remaining period of the same Rasi is called "Bhojyam". From "Bhojyam"the Lagnas are counted up to birth time Lagna, Sumuhurtha Lagna, then Janma Lagna and Sumuhurtha Lagna could be obtained.In some Almanacs the Bhukti and some other Almanacs the Bhojyam are identified. From Lagna pramana, if Bhukti is deducted, then the remaining is Bhojyam. Thereafter, if lagnas are added, we get the desired Lagna.

1.4 INTRODUCTION TO STUDY OF ALMANAC

In Hindu families Almanac is invariably in use. For all activities relating to religious matters, festivals, utsavas, to determine the auspicious timings of commencement, the USE of Almanac is invariably needed.

Almanac gives us mainly five Elements. These are 1. Tidhi, 2. Weekday, 3. Nakshatra, 4.Yogam and 5. Karanam. Since it is giving these five Elements it is named as 'Panchamga' or 'Panchamgam'. It is easy to obtain the required information.

Since Earth is rotating around its own axis, the sun light falls on the spherical surface of Earth, and that period is termed as day light and the surface of Earth on its backside is taken as night. Hence it is how we are getting day and night.

Earth to rotate around its axis once is called a date, Moon to rotate around the Earth once is called a month and Earth to go round the Sun for one complete revolution is called as one year. This is how all countries in the world are following.

The path in which the Planets are moving were identified through imagination by our ancestors as "Jyothish Chakra" and that chakra or circle was divided into 12 equal parts.

This imaginary Circle was termed as "Bhachakra". There are 27 Stars identified in the sky. Each Star is divided into 4 parts (padas) and 9 such divisions are counted as one Rasi. According to the shape of Rasi's their names were prescribed.

Ancestors identified that all Planets in the Heavens are moving around the Sun as shown in sketch 1.4 (a). Their path, distance from Earth is given in the sketch 1.4 (b) shown on page 4.

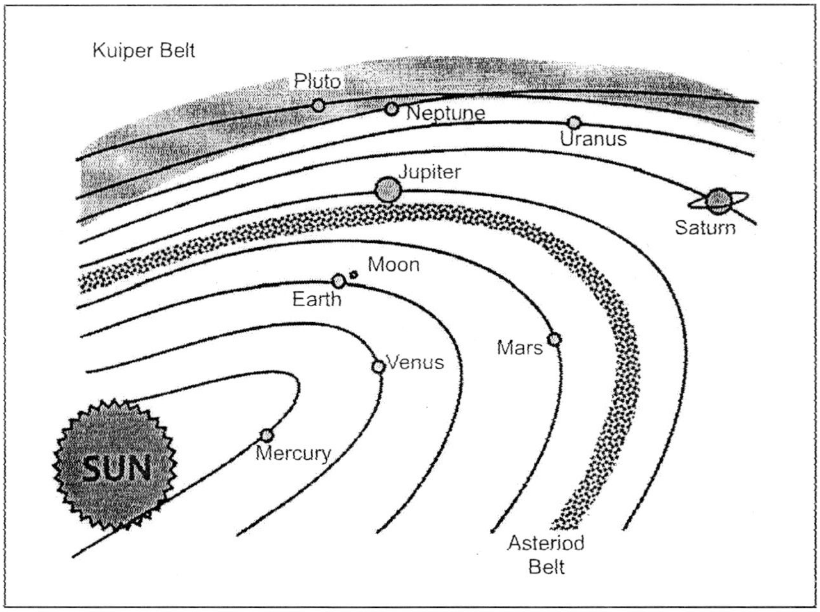

Fig. 1.4 (a)

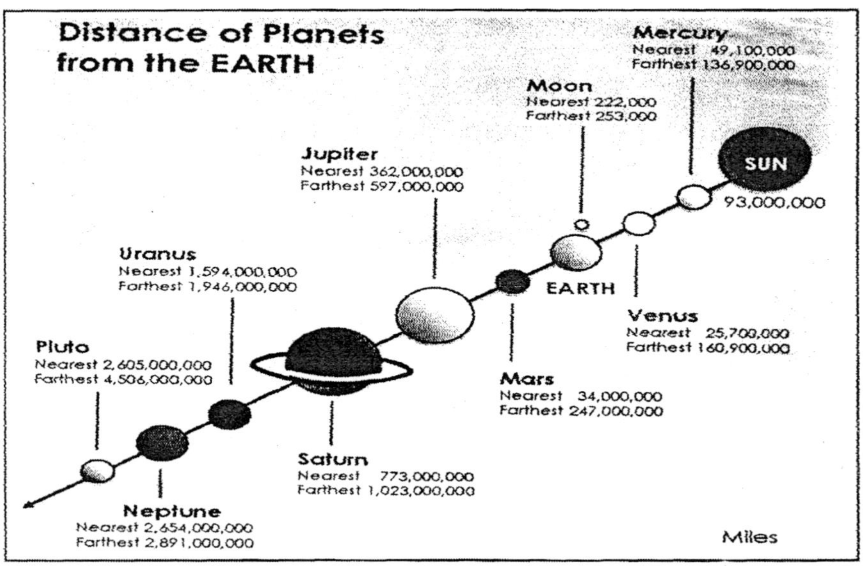

Fig. 1.4 (b)

Since Moon is moving around Earth, we see daily the Moon located in a region of Star. In Almanac the Star in which Moon is situated is counted as the day's Nakshatra for our daily routine activities. On Full Moon day, Moon appears in the region of a Star, then the ancestors called that Month on the name of the Star and therefore the names of the twelve Telugu Calandar Months were arrived as under:-

1. The month in which Full Moon is situated in Chitra Star region was named as "Chaitramasa".
2. The month in which Full Moon is situated in Visakha Star region was named as "Vaisakamasa".
3. The month in which Full Moon is situated in Jyeshta Star region was named as "Jyeshtamasa".
4. The month in which Full Moon is situated in Purvashada Star region was named as "Ashadamasa".
5. The month in which Full Moon is situated in Sravana Star region was named as "Sravanamasa".
6. The month in which Full Moon is situated in Purvabhadra Star reigion was named as "Bhadrapadamasa".
7. The month in which Full Moon is situated in Aswini Star region was named as "Asweejamasa".
8. The month in which Full Moon is situated in Krithika Star region was named as "Karteekamasa".
9. The month in which Full Moon is situated in Mrugasira Star region was named as "Mrugasiramasa".
10. The month in which Full Moon is situated in Pushyami Star region was named as "Pushyamasa".
11. The month in which Full Moon is situated in Makha Star region was named as "Maghamasa".
12. The month in which Full Moon is situated in Uttaraphalguni Star region is named as Phalgunamasa.

1.5 12 RASIS

In table below, the names of 12 Rasis and the Ghadias & Vighadias of time are given. The period of each Rasi is approximately 5 Ghadias or 2 hours as normally understood by everyone,because the Sun is rising every day after 24 hours. These 12 Rasis are changing every day as 12 Lagnas. In Almanac the period of each Lagna on every day for day time and night time are given.

60 Ghadias = 24 hours

2 – 1/2 Ghadias = one hour

S. No.	Name of Rasi	Meaning	Period of time in Ghadias & Vighadias
1.	Aries	Mesha	4-20
2.	Taurus	Oxen	4-36
3.	Gemini	Twins wife & husband	5-26
4.	Cancer	Crab	5-31
5.	Leo	Lion	5-20

S. No.	Name of Rasi	Meaning	Period of time in Ghadias & Vighadias
6.	Virgo	Virgin	5-15
7.	Libra	Balance	5-24
8.	Scorpio	Scorpion	5-33
9.	Sagitterius	Bow & Arrow	5-19
10.	Capricorn	Crocodile	4-43
11.	Aquarius	Pot with water	4-11
12.	Pisces	Twin Fish	4-22
			Total: 60 Ghadias or 24 Hours

The reason for variations in the periods of time of each Rasi is due to movement of Earth around Sun in an Ecliptic form. Hence 12 parts are divided into 360°, the angular duration of each Rasi is 30°, but the distance travelled by Earth in the Ecliptic Arc's is varying and some of them are of longer in distance and some of them are of shorter in distance along the arc as seen in the sketch 1.5 given below.

Almanac & Astro Sciences

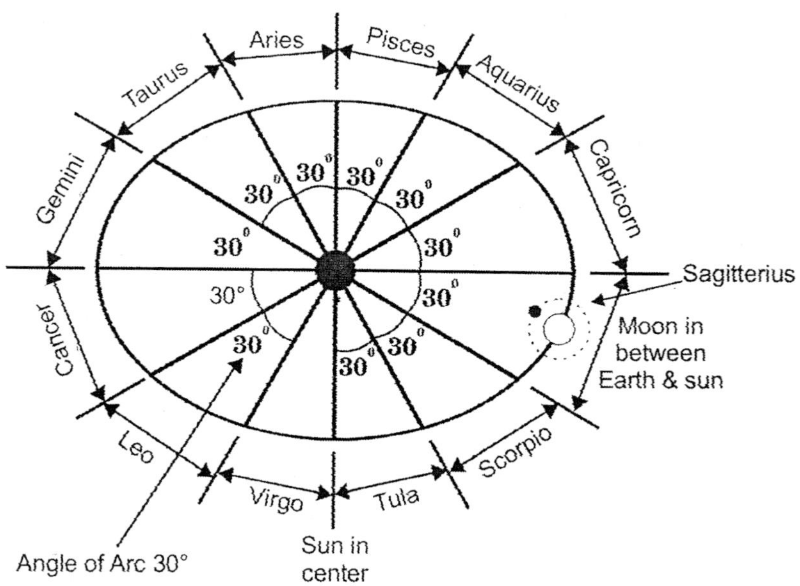

Figure 1.5

Note:

1.6 NAMES OF NINE PLANETS

The following table gives the names of planets with the period of Dasa Pramanam in years.

S.No.	Planet	Dasa Period in Years
1.	Sun	6
2.	Moon	10
3.	Mars	7
4.	Rahu	18
5.	Jupiter	16
6.	Saturn	19
7.	Mercury	17
8.	Ketu	7
9.	Venus	20
		Total : 120 Years

1.7 FORTNIGHTS - PAKSHAS

There are two fortnights everymonth. The first 15 days from Amavasya is called "Sukla Pakshami" and the second set of 15 days from Pournami is called "Krishna Pakshami". Sukla means that increase of Moonlight in the night. The date on which the Moon is full is called "Pournami'. The date on which the Moon is not visible is called "Amavasya". The following sketch at 1.7 shows the Sukla and Krishna Pakshas both.

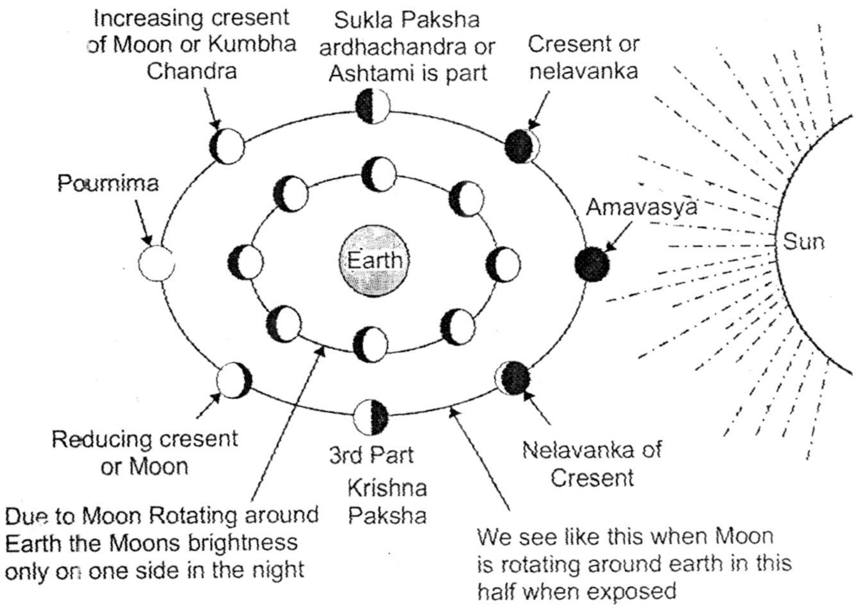

Figure 1.7

1.8 TIDHIS

The name of Tidhis of 15 days Sukla Paksha or Suddha Paksha and Krishna Paksha or Bahula Paksha are given in the following table.

Day S. No.	Name of Day in Sukla / Suddha Paksha	Day S. No.	Name of Day in Krishna / Bahula Paksha
1.	Suddha Padyami	1	Bahula Padyami
2.	Suddha Vidiya	2	Bahula Vidiya
3.	Suddha Tadiya	3	Bahula Tadiya
4.	Suddha Chaviti	4	Bahula Chaviti
5.	Suddha Panchami	5	Bahula Panchami
6.	Suddha Shashti	6	Bahula Shashti
7.	Suddha Saptami	7	Bahula Saptami
8.	Suddha Ashtami	8	Bahula Ashtami
9.	Suddha Navami	9	Bahula Navami
10.	Suddha Dasami	10	Bahula Dasami
11.	Suddha Ekadasi	11	Bahula Ekadasi
12.	Suddha Dwadasi	12	Bahula Dwadasi
13.	Suddha Trayodasi	13	Bahula Trayodasi
14.	Suddha Chaturdasi	14	Bahula Chaturdasi
15.	Suddha Poornima	15	Bahula Amavasya

How Tidhis are formed and how Tidhi increases is given as under.

The Longitude of Moon if deducted from Longitude of Sun and divide that difference by 12, the Tidhi comes out. In every paksha, the distance between Sun and Moon is getting increased and hence the new Tidhi comes.

If both Sun and Moon are on the same Longitude Amavasya comes. If they are 180° apart, then Pournima comes. This can be seen in sketch clearly at para 1.7.

1.9 WEEK DAYS

Since time immemorial, the days of the week are tied to the seven Planets. This fact is well known to every one. The names of week days in Telugu, the names used in Panchamga / Almanac, English names and Hindusthani names are given in the table below.

Names of Week Days in

S. No.	Telugu	Panchamgam	English	Hindi
1.	Aadivaaramu	Bhanuvaaramu	Sunday	Ravivaar
2.	Somavaaramu	Induvaaramu	Monday	Somavaar
3.	Mangalavaaramu	Bhaumavaaramu	Tuesday	Mangalvaar
4.	Budhavaaramu	Saumyavaaramu	Wednesday	Budhavaar
5.	Guruvaaramu	Bruhaspativaaramu	Thursday	Bruhaspativaar
6.	Sukravaaramu	Bhruguvaaramu	Friday	Sukravvar
7.	Sanivaaramu	Mandavaaramu	Saturday	Sanivaar

In India how the earlier civilizations had named the week days is now made known now. In Sanskrit language day and night is called as "Ahooraatra". In this word 'A' the first letter and'tra' the last three alphabets are removed and the remaining six alphabets are called as "Hooraa".This word came into use to give the meaning of 24 hours period, half day part plus half night part are equalled to one full day.

Weekdays (vaaramulu)

Seven days constitute one Vaaramu. These are Ravivaara - Sunday, Somavaara - Monday, Mangalavaara - Tuesday, Budhavaara - Wednesday, Guruvaara - Thursday, Sukravaara - Frinday, Sanivaara - Saturday.

These 7 names of Vaaras are in order of the names of seven Planets. These are Sun, Moon, Mars, Mercury, Jupiter, Venus and Saturn and in Telugu they are called Ravi, Chandra, Kuja, Budha, Guru, Sukra and Sani respectively.

The planets in order of Saturn, Jupiter, Mars, Sun, Venus, Mercury and Moon as seen in heavens from Earth in the decreasing distance are written in the 24 hours of duration commencing from Saturn's day. First hour of Saturday is given to Saturn, 2nd hour of Saturday to Guruvu. In this order if written 3 times 22nd hour comes to Saturn, 23rd hour comes to Guruvu, 24th hour to Kuja and 25th hour to Sun. This is Sunday, the 2nd day's first hour. This is correctly called with the weekday. Like this if continued, the first hour of every day pertains to Planet relevant to the weekday coming. Always the first hour starts with hora of the Planet relevant to the day.

1.10 HOORAADHIPATIS AND WEEK DAY NAMES

Lordship of each one hour from Sunrise to next day's Sunrise is given to the seven planets from Sun, Moon, Mars, Mercury, Jupiter, Venus and Saturn according to their movement of path around Sun. Like this everyday from sunrise, the first hour is given to the lordship of planet that comes in the morning. This is called as that days "Hooraadhipati". This name on Sunday from sunrise.,the first hour is named as "Ravihooraa". Next day from sunrise the first hour is named as "Chandrahooraa". Likewise on all the seven days, the hooraa of that planet relating to the week day comes in the first hour.

Ancestors had believed that the Planets have influence on the human beings. The Rishies from Earth could know how the Planets were moving in the heavens and their path could be established as shown in the sketch at 1.10 (a).

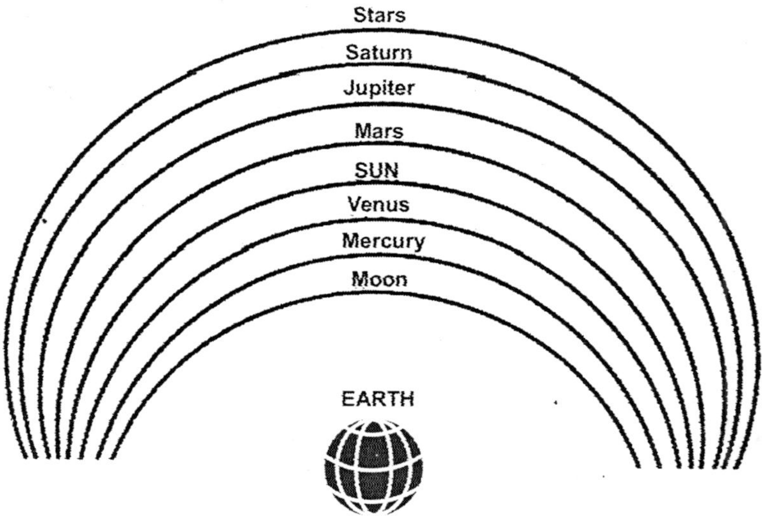

Figure 1.10 (a) Old Method Chakra

Names of seven Weekdays are made equal to the names of seven Planets moving in the sky.This has been shown in table below.

S. No.	Planet Name	Name of the week day
1.	Ravi or Aditya	Ravi or Aadivaaramu
2.	Chandra	Somavaaramu
2(a)	Another name for Moon Somudu	—
3.	Kujudu or Mangaludu	Mangalavaaramu or Bhaumavaaramu
4.	Budha	Budhavaaramu
5.	Gurudu	Guruvaaramu
6.	Sukrudu	Sukravaaramu
7.	Sani	Sanivaaramu

Modern Astronomical Scientists established that all Planets are moving round the Sun in their individual paths.The sketch at 1.10 (b) shows this method.

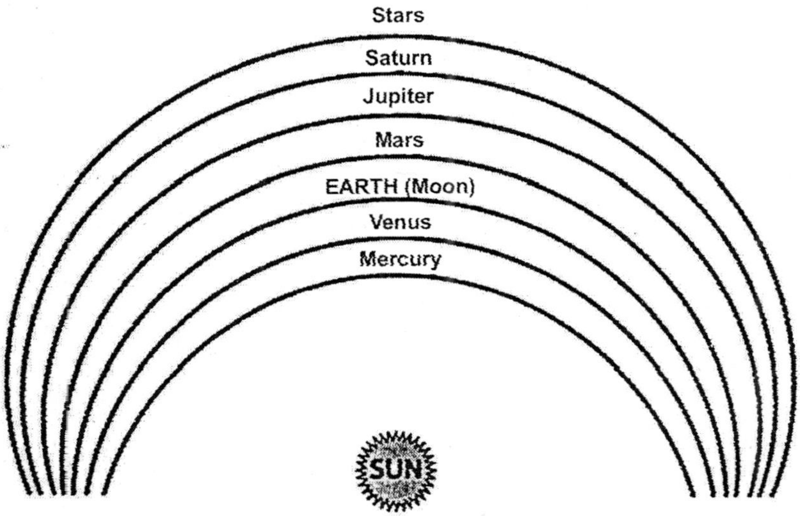

Figure 1.10 (b) New Method Chakra

In ancient Vedanga Jyothisha Sun was considered as 'Paramatma' and Moon as "Jeevatma" and the remaining five Planets represent the five Elements viz ... Earth, Air, Water, Fire and Akash.The sloka in veda says

"Prudhive Vyapastha Teejoo Vaayoo Raakaasaat"

Basing on this Sutra our Ancestors had derived the names of the week days as shown in sketch 1.10(c). This was based on old practice of planets moving around Earth.

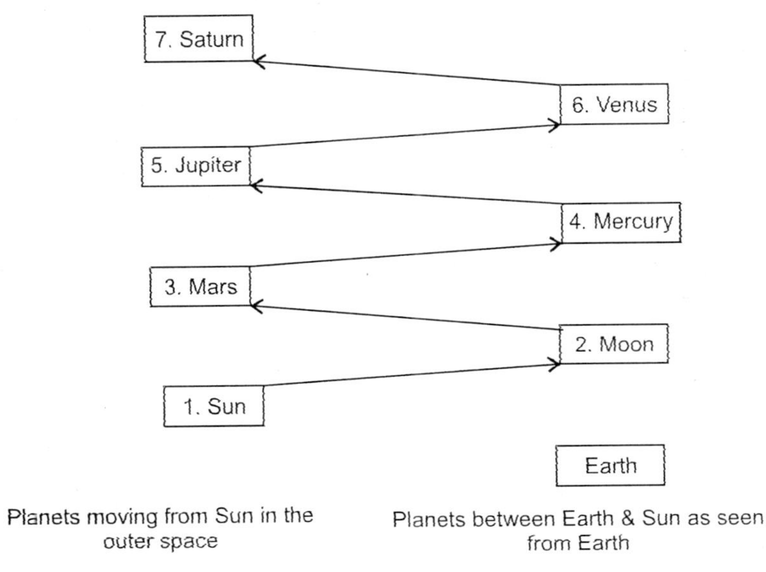

Fig. 1.10 (c)

1.11 THE ORDER OF WEEKDAYS

The counting of week day is an old practice in use. Moghuls came to India in 12th Century and British came in 17th Century and ruled upto 20th Century. None of these dynasties could make any change in the order off Week days followed by Indians. All countries in the world had adopted the Weekdays followed by India and included their names as such in their Almanacs. This shows the superiority of Indian Astronomers in their knowledge of Astronomy connected to Astrological Rules framed at that time.

1.12 STARS AND THEIR PATTERN

All Stars and Planets are in heavens at far off distances.On Amavasya day all stars shine very brightly. Since Earth was found moving around its own axis and moving around the Sun by both Earth and Moon, it was found that the location of Stars was found changing.

Moon moving very fast around Earth in 30 days from one Amavasya to second Amavasya the time taken is 30 days. As a result all Stars are appearing moving under the Moons control and covering all the 12 Rasis.

Since there is relation-ship between Moon and Stars as established by Rishies, the Bhachakra is made as per the following table, linking movement of Moon from one Rasi to another Rasi and inturn Moon's movement also changes in the group by 2-1/4Nakshatra for each Rasi and hence Moon moves all the 27 Stars by the time he completes movement of the 12 Rasis.

This method of counting was prevailing in India from times immemorial.

As per ancient Indian practice, stars are counted from the first point of 'Meshasthana Rasi'. This point is the first point of Bhachakra. A Nakshatra consists of a good number of Stars. The Star which is the brightest in the region of Nakshatra, is named after that Star. The group of Nakshatra in a star is divided into four parts. Hence for 27 Nakshatras, there are 108 parts. If these and divided among 12 Rasis, each Rasi gets 9 Nakshatra Padas parts, Names of 12 Rasis are also linked. The total circumference of all 12 Rasis is 360°. Hence each Rasi gets an angular measurement of 30°. Since there are 9 parts in a Rasi, each part is equal to 3°- 20′. One Star covers 13° - 20′. The limitations of Star divisions are also shown in Nirayana Scale as under.

S. No.	Name of Rasi	Nakshtra Padamulu	Total Padas	Range of Nakshatra	
				From	To
1.	Aries	Aswini-4 parts Bharani-4 parts Krithika-1st part	9	0° – 0′ 13° – 21′ 26° – 41′	13° – 20′ 26° – 40′ 30° – 00′
2.	Taurus	Krithika-2, 3, 4 parts Rohini-4 parts Mrugasira-1, 2 parts	9	30° – 01′ 40° – 01′ 53° – 21′	40° – 00′ 53° – 20′ 60° – 00′

3.	Gemini	Mrugasira-3, 4 parts Aardra-4 parts Punarvasu-1, 2, 3 parts	9	60° – 01′ 66° – 41′ 80° – 01′	66° – 40′ 80° – 00′ 90° – 00′
4.	Cancer	Punarvasu-4th part Pushyami-4 parts Aslesha-4 parts	9	90° – 01′ 93° – 21′ 106° – 41′	93° – 20′ 106° – 40′ 120° – 00′
5.	Leo	Makha-4 parts Pubba-4 parts Uttara-1st part	9	120° – 01′ 133° – 21′ 146° – 41′	133° – 20′ 146° – 40′ 150° – 00′
6.	Virgo	Uttara-2, 3, 4 parts Hasta-4 parts Chitta-1, 2 parts	9	150° – 01′ 160° – 01′ 173° – 21′	160° – 00′ 173° – 20′ 180° – 00′
7.	Libra	Chitta-3, 4 parts Swathi-4 parts Visakha-1, 2, 3 parts	9	180° – 01′ 186° – 41′ 200° – 01′	186° – 40′ 200° – 00′ 210° – 00′
8.	Scorpio	Visakha-4th part Anuradha-4 parts Jyeshta-4 parts	9	210° – 01′ 213° – 21′ 226° – 41′	213° – 20′ 226° – 40′ 240° – 00′
9.	Sagittarius	Moola-4 parts Poovashada-4 parts Uttarashada-1st part	9	240° – 01′ 253° – 21′ 266° – 41′	253° – 20′ 266° – 40′ 270° – 00′
10.	Capricorn	Uttarashada-2, 3, 4 parts Sravanam-4 parts Dhanishta-1, 2 parts	9	270° – 01′ 280° – 01′ 293° – 21′	280° – 00′ 293° – 20′ 300° – 00′
11.	Aquarius	Dhanista-3, 4 parts Satabhisha-4 parts Poovabhadra-1, 2, 3 parts	9	300° – 01′ 306° – 41′ 320° – 01′	306° – 40′ 320° – 00′ 330° – 00′
12.	Pisces	Poorvabhadra-4th part Uttarabhadra-4 parts Revati-4 parts	9	330° – 01′ 333° – 21′ 346° – 41′	333° – 20′ 346° – 40′ 360° – 00′
				Total 108 parts	

The above 27 Stars are called the houses of Moon.For one Nakshatra month there are 27.3217 average days.This is called Moons "Madhyamika Gati". For one revolution of Moon around Earth it is called as one Nakshatra Masa.

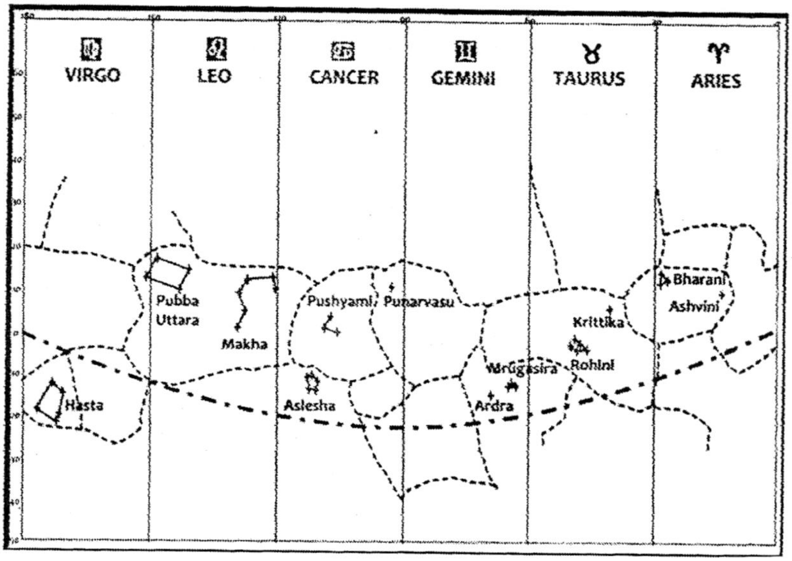

Figure 1.12 (a) Nakshatras and Rasis

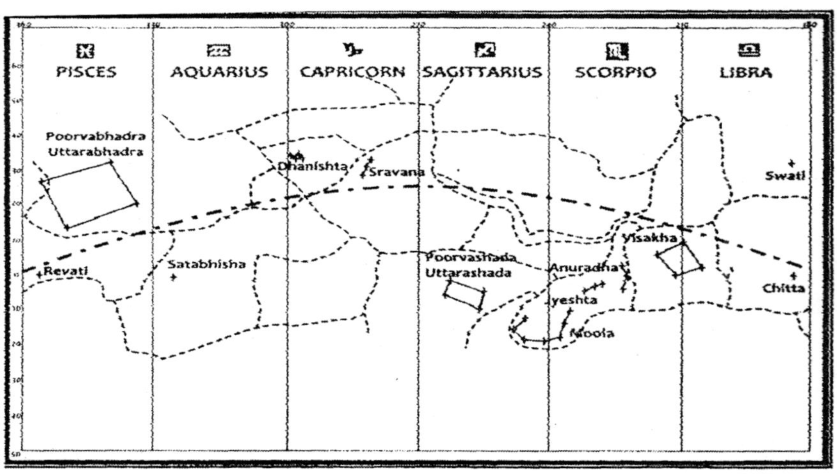

Figure 1.12 (b) Nakshatras and Rasis

The zones of 27 Nakshatras have been shown in sketches 1.12 (a), 1.12 (b) at page-14 The Rasis in heavens and Star groups in the sky are shown in the sketch 1.12(c) at page-15.

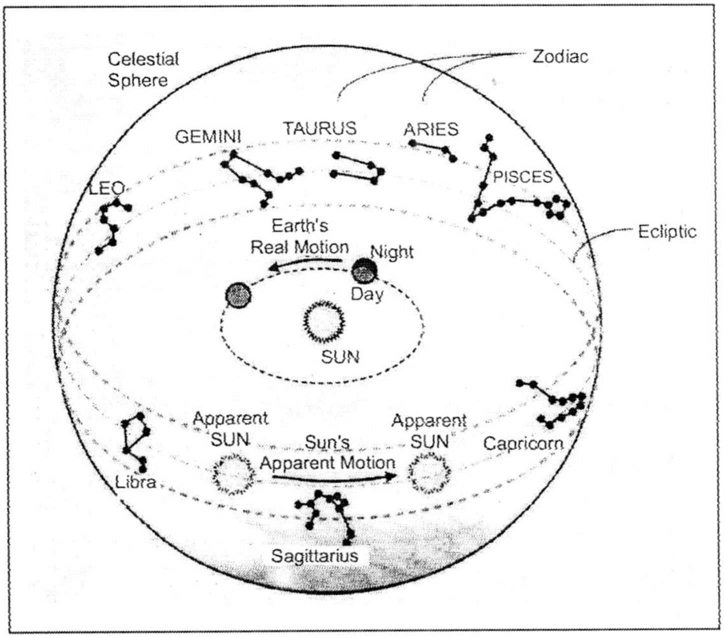

Figure 1.12 (c)The Star groups in the sky are visible thus

1.13 NAKSHTRAS AND THEIR DEVATAS

Table 1.13: *Nakshatras and their dieties*

S. No	Nakshatra	Devata
1.	Aswani	Ganapathy
2.	Bharani	Durgadevi
3.	Krithika	Agni
4.	Rohini	Brahmma
5.	Mrugasira	Chandra
6.	Aardra	Shiva
7.	Punarvasu	Devatas
8.	Pushyami	Bruhaspathi
9.	Aslesha	Adiseshudu
10.	Makha	Pitrudvatas
11.	Pubba	Parvathi
12.	Uttara	Suryudu
13.	Hastha	Shakti
14.	Chitta	Viswakarma

S. No	Nakshatra	Devata
15.	Swathi	Vayuvu
16.	Visakha	Subrahamanya
17.	Anuradha	Lakshmi
18.	Jyestha	Devendra
19.	Moola	Asura
20.	Poorvashada	Varuna
21.	Uttarashada	Eswara
22.	Sravanam	Vishnuvu
23.	Dhanishta	Ashtavasuvus
24.	Satabhisha	Yama
25.	Poorvabhadra	Kubera
26.	Uttarabhadra	Kamadhenuvu
27.	Ravati	sani

1.14 YOGAMULU

These Yogamulu are also 27 in number. If Longitudes of Sun and Moon are added and resultant sum is divided by 13° – 20′. Then it will be known as the name of Yogam. The names of Yogams are as under:-

1.	Vishkambamu	2.	Preeti
3.	Ayushman	4.	Soubhagyamu
5.	Sobhanamu	6.	Atiyoga Gandamu
7.	Suvarnamu	8.	Dhruti
9.	Soolamu	10.	Gandamu – Vruddhi
12.	Dhruvamu	13.	Vyaghaatamu
14.	Harshanamu	15.	Vajramu
16.	Siddhi	17.	Vyatheepathamu
18.	Vareeyaan	19.	Parighamu
20.	Shivamu	21.	Siddhamu
22.	Saadhyamu	23.	Subhamu
24.	Suklamu	25.	Brahmmamu
26.	Indramu	27.	Vaidhruthi

These 27 Yogas in order relate to Aswani to Revathi, 27 Stars.

1.15 KARANAMULU

For every Tidhi there will be two Karanas. In this there are first half and second half, divided into two separate parts and they were named in the following pattern as under, for Sukla Paksha and Krishna Paksha.,

Tidhi	Sukla Paksha		Krishna paksha	
	First half	**Second half**	**First half**	**Second half**
1.	Kimstughnamu	Bava	Balava	Kaulava
2.	Balava	Kaulava	Taitula	Garaji
3.	Taitula	Garaji	Vanaji	Visthi (Bhadra)
4	Vanija	Vishti (Bhadra)	Bava	Balava
5.	Bava	Balava	Kaulava	Taitula
6.	Kaulava	Taitula	Garaji	Vanija
7.	Garaji	Vanija	Vishti (Bhadra)	Bava
8.	Vishti (Bhadra)	Bava	Balava	Kaulava
9.	Balava	Kaulava	Taitula	Garaji
10.	Taitula	Garaji	Vanija	Vishti (Bhadra)
11.	Vanija	Vishti (Bhadra)	Bava	Balava
12.	Bava	Balava	Taitula	Garaji
13.	Kaulava	Taitula	Garaji	Vanija
14.	Garaji	Vanija	Vishti (Bhadra)	Sakuni
15.	Vishti (Bhadra)	Bava	Chatushpata	Nagavam

There are total 11 Karanas. These are 1. Bava 2.Balava 3.Kaulava 4.Taitula 5.Garaji 6.Vanija 7. Vishti (Bhadra) 8. Sakuni 9.Chatushpata 10.Nagavam 11.Kimstughnamu.

In these from Bava to Vishti (Bhadra) all seven, they are called as "Chara Karanamulu".

From Sakuni the remaining four are Sthirakaranamulu.

The Chara Karanas seven will start every month from second half of Sukla Paksha Padyami and will continue upto frist half of Krishna Paksha Chaturdasi. For every Tidhi, two Karanas will be coming.Total 60 divisions will be in 30 days.

From Sakuni Sthirakarana the remaining four will be coming from second half of Bahula Chaturdasi and will continue upto first half of Sukla Padyami Tidhi.

When Tidhi is completed two Karanas get closed fully.

1. Vishti (Bhadra), Sakuni, Chatushpata, Nagavam, Kimsthugnaham all five are inauspicious (Asubha).
2. Bava, Balava, Kaulava, Taitula, Garaji, Vanija 6 Karanams are auspicious (Subha).
3. In Panchamga the second half Karanas are shown.
4. These Karanas are more usefull in Muhurtha Bhaga.

1.16 DIRECTIONS -THEIR LORDSHIPS AND OTHER DETAILS

S. No	Directions	Persons Ruling Directions	Their Wifes	Their Vehicles	Towns in which living	Their Weapons
1.	East	Indra	Sacheedevi	Elephant	Amaravathi	Vajram
2.	South-East	Agnihotrudu	Swahaadevi	Ram	Teejoovathi	Sakthi
3.	South	Yama	Syamaladevi	Buffalo	Samyameni	Dandamu
4.	South-West	Nairuti	Deeghaadevi	Narudu	Krishangana	Kuntamu
5.	West	Varuna	Kalikadevi	Crocodile	Sraddhavati	Pasamu
6.	North-West	Vayuvu	Anjanaadevi	Antelope	Gandhavati	Dhwajamu
7.	North	Kubera	Chitralekha	Horse	Alakapuri	Sword
8.	North-East	Sivudu	Parvatidevi	Bull	Kailasamu	Trisulamu

1.17 RUTUVULU AND THEIR PERIODS

S. No	Months	Rutuvus Seasons as per Hindus	Usefulness & Period prevailing	Kalamulu Seasons as per others
1.	Chaitra Vaisakha	Vasantha Spring	(Feb 19 to Aprl 19) Flowering and Fruits by trees	Hot Seasons
2.	Jyeshta Aashada	Greeshma Summer	(Aprl 20 to June 20) Severe High Temperatures	

S. No	Months	Rutuvus Seasons as per Hindus	Usefulness & Period prevailing	Kalamulu Seasons as per others
3.	Sravana Bhadra	Rainy	(June 21 to Aug. 22) Very heavy Rains fall	Rainy Seasons
4.	Asweeja Kartika	Sarat	(Aug. 23 to Oct. 23) Bright Moonly period	
5	Margasira Pushya	Himavantam	(Oct. 24 to Dec. 21) Snow falls Heavily	Winter Seasons
6.	Magha Phalguna	Sisiramu	(Dec. 22 to Feb. 18) Trees shed their leaves	

1.18 RUTUVULU AND THEIR PERIODS

1. Since Rutuvus are coming regularly in a specific periods of time, importance is gained for Savana Soura year.
2. Commencement of Rutuvu is occuring as per Sun's position. At places where the intensity of hot rays from Sun is not there, and when Sun moving from Southern Hemesphere to Northern Hemisphere crossing the Celestial Equator, the spring season (Vasanta Rutuvu) will come. When Sun is closing the 'Vasant Vishuvat' (Spring - Equinox) happens on the 22nd March.
3. Second Rutuvu hot summer season comes when Sun reaches Northern most point of Northern Hemisphere. This is called 'Summer Solistice'. This comes on June 22.
4. There after the Rutuvu is when Sun crosses "Tula Vishuwat" around September 23 which called as 'Autonomial Equinox'.
5. The Fourth Rutuva is happening when crossing 'Makarayanam' which is called Winter solistice, happening on December 22nd.
6. Spring season from March 22 to June 22 winter gets closed and Sun rays directly fall.The day period is more than nights and trees flower and give fruits.
7. Second season from June 22 to September 23. The Summmer season gets closed. In this period the agricultural rythues will get their Grains from fertile lands.
8. Next season the day time gets reduced and night periods become more. This is from September 23 to December 22. In this period the leaves fall from trees.
9. The last Rutuvu, the fourth is Winter season from December 22 to March 22. The period of day time less and night is longer.

The above seasonal divisions are not favourable to Indian conditions. The above seasons will come to those places / countries which are closer to North pole. The Rutuvus in Places and Countries closer to South Pole will be just opposite. As an example when places close to North pole has Summer season then the places close to South pole will have Winter season.

In India due to movement of Sun close to Equator, only three seasons have mainly formed. These are Summer, Rainy and Winter seasons. These three have been sub divided.

In India the Spring season starts after ending Sisira Rutuvu and for every two months one Rutuvu has formed totalling to six Rutuvulu.

The Rutuvu's are forming as per Sayana Year and not as per Nirayana year.

The seasons start and the ends given above pertain to 21st century. But in the long periods of time due to movement of Vishuwat point, there will be changes in the periods of seasons. But if Soura months are taken into consideration, the changes in the starting and ending of seasons will not have any changes. But this practice is not correct.

In Taittareya Samhita, Soura Months and Rutuvu's are given as under.

S.No.	Rutuvu	Saura Months
1	Vasanta	Madhu, Madhava
2.	Greeshma	Sukra, Suchi
3.	Varsha	Nabhasa, Nabhasya
4.	Sarath	Isa, Oorja
5.	Hemantha	Saha, Sahasya
6.	Sisira	Tapas, Tapasya

1.19 TELUGU MONTHS THEIR NAMES IN ELGLISH, HINDI AND TAMIL LANGUAGES

S.No.	Telugu Months	English Months	Hindi Months	Tamil Months
1	Chaitramu	March	Chait	Chithirai
2.	Vaisakhamu	April	Vaisakh	Vaikasi
3.	Jyeshtam	May	Jyesht	Aati
4.	Aashadamu	June	Aashaad	Aadi
5.	Sravanam	July	Sravan	Aavani
6.	Bhadrapadamu	August	Bhadrapad	Puratasi
7.	Asweejamu	September	Aswin	Ipusi
8.	Kaarteekamu	October	Kartik	Kartikai
9.	Margasiramu	November	Margasir	Margali
10.	Pushyamu	December	Poush	Tai
11.	Maghamu	January	Magh	Moosi
12.	Phalgunamu	February	Phalgun	Panguni

In the Calander year there are 12 months. February has 28 days. Every four years one leap year will becoming when February month has 29 days. 365 days constitute one year. In Leap year there will be 366 days.

1.20 ADHIKA MASAM AND KSHAYA MASAM

The period between two Amavasyas or two Poornimas is called "Chandra Masa". It is nearly 29.530589 days 29 days 12 hours 44 mints. 29 sec. This is called as ...(E)

In Chandramana year, the number of days will be 29 days 12 hours, 44 minutes, 29 seconds × 12 = 354.36706 days (i.e.,) 354 days 6 hrs. 8 mints 98 sec. This is called as ...(G)

But for Madhyamika (Niraya) Saura year, there are 365.256790 days (i.e.,) 365 days, 6hrs, 9 mints, 98 sec. This is called as ...(A) at page 26

Hence the difference between these two will be = 365.530589 days.

	365.256790 days	...(A)
	(–) 354.367060 days	...(G)
Difference	**10.889730 days**	

In India ordinarily as per Sayana Saura counting, the Calendar of Rituvus has formed. But in India the Nakshatra Saura year is being practiced. The Chandrayana year (Siderial year) is accepted as Natural and correctly followed. Because the people at large in India are visually seeing Poornima which is regularly coming after Amavasya., they had accepted that there is un-avoidable natural relationship between Saura year and Chandramana year. This is purely based on natural phenomena and is accepted by every one. There is difference between this Indian method and the Leap year based on Roman Calander.

In India the Soura year and the Chandramana year,both these systems are practiced and followed for performance of activities of religious origin or of matters relating to conducting civil functions.

Chandramana year is less by 10.889730 days when compared to Saura year. When this difference gets accumulated to one Chandramana month, one additional month is added to Chandramana year. This additional month is called as 'Adhikamasa'.

12 Chandramasas constitute as one Chandramana year. In this, there are 354 or 355 days. Chandramana year starts after the first Amavasya. This is Saura Chaitra month (at that time the Sun will be in Pisces Rasi). This Chandramasa is also called as Chaitra masa. But in Tamilnadu this practice is not followed. In Chandra Kalamana the second month starts with Vaisakha. Like this the year comes with 12 Amavasyas.

In Chandramana year, in every Chandramasa, Saura Sankranti or Sankranti is happening. In Tamilnadu the Saura masas names like Meena or Phalguna or Mesha or Chaitra will be coming.

But in some years the Chandramasa will come without full Sauramasa. Then the Surya Sankranti will not come in that year. Such Chandramana month is called 'Adhikamasa'. In this Adhikamasa, Indians will not perform any activities connecting religious matters.

When Adhikamasa comes in a Chandramana year, there will be 383 or 384 days. One Adhikamasa comes for every 33 Chandramana months. Same Adhika Masa also comes once after 19 years. The Adhikamasa will always come in the month of Phalguna/Aswini months. In Chandramana Maghamasa Adhikamasa will never occur.

In case in one Chandramana month, two Sankranthi's come, the Chandramana month is called as "Kshayamasa". But this sort of Kshayamasa comes once in 141 years. But then it comes also at every 19 years. This Kshyamasa comes between Kartika, Margasira and Pushya masas. Because the Sun's paths in these months is more and the Sun is either close to Perigree or Periyah. As a result the Saura month is less than Chandramana month. The month in which Kshyama comes is never called on the name of the month. When one Kshyamasa comes in a Chandramana year, then there will be two Adhikamasas. When two Adhikamasas come, one Adhikamasa will be at the begining of the Chandramana year and the second Adhika will be come at the end of Chandramana year.

In the book of Siddhanta Siromani of Bhaskara –II, Kshayamasa will come for every' 19, 122 and 141 years.

1.21 TELUGU YEARS

The Panchamga (Almanac) starts between March 15 to April 15 every year. Number of years are 60.Every yearwill be coming in the following order.

S. No	Year	Has Come	Will come	S. No	Year	Has/Will Come	Will come
1.	Prabhava	1987	2047	31.	Hevalambi	2017	2077
2.	Vibhava	1988	2048	32.	Vilambi	2018	2078
3.	Sukla	1989	2049	33.	Vikari	2019	2079
4.	Pramoduta	1990	2050	34.	Sarwari	2020	2080
5.	Prajotpathi	1991	2051	35.	Plava	2021	2081
6.	Angirasa	1992	2052	36.	Subhakrut	2022	2082
7.	Sremukha	1993	2053	37.	Sobhakrut	2023	2083
8.	Bhava	1994	2054	38.	Krodhi	2024	2084
9.	Yuva	1995	2055	39.	Viswavasu	2025	2085
10.	Dhata	1996	2056	40.	Parabhava	2026	2086
11.	Eswara	1997	2057	41.	Plavanga	2027	2087
12.	Bahudhanya	1998	2058	42.	Kelaka	2028	2088
13.	Pramadhi	1999	2059	43.	Soumya	2029	2089
14.	Vikrama	2000	2060	44.	Sadharana	2030	2090
15.	Vrusha	2001	2061	45.	Virodhikrut	2031	2091
16.	Chitrabhanu	2002	2062	46.	Paridhavt	2032	2092
17.	Swabhanu	2003	2063	47.	Pramadoha	2033	2093
18.	Tarana	2004	2064	48.	Ananda	2034	2094
19.	Pardhiva	2005	2065	49.	Rakshasa	2035	2095
20.	Vyaya	2006	2066	50.	Nala	2035	2096
21.	Sarvajit	2007	2067	51.	Pingala	2037	2097
22.	Sarvadhary	2008	2068	52.	Kalayukti	2038	2098
23.	Virodhi	2009	2069	53.	Sidhardhi	2039	2099
24.	Vikruti	2010	2070	54.	Roudri	2040	2100
25.	Khara	2011	2071	55.	Durmati	2041	2101
26.	Nandana	2012	2072	56.	Dumdubhi	2042	2102
27.	Vijaya	2013	2073	57.	Rudhirodgari	2043	2103
28.	Jaya	2014	2074	58.	Raktakshi	2044	2104
29.	Manmadha	2015	2075	59.	Krodhana	2045	2105
30.	Durmukhi	2016	2076	60.	Akshya	2046	2106

1.22 CALANDERS AND HINDU PANCHAMGAM

A Calander is very important and essential. A record is kept of Historical happenings and natural instances occurred which will be usefull at a future date.

Keeping a broad view the Panchamga is most usefull. Keeping a record of a particular instances happened with Date, Month and Year specifically, there should be no doubt subsequently in knowing them exactly.

A number of Calenders came into force among people based on their requirements and activities relating to Religious, Social and Civil sectors. In these Calanders-Saura Year, Sayana year, Nirayana year, Chandramana Saura year came into existance based on Amavasyas and Poornimas.

The Calander used by Romans is called as Christian Calander. This was made based on Savana year. Sun travelling from Sarat Vishuvat on the Ecliptical path completes one rotation. This time is called one Sayana year. This period on an average is equal to 365.24219 days. This is equal to 365 days, 5 hrs, for 48 mts, 46 sec. Say this is called as (B). For benefit of population in general for easy use and understanding, it is taken as 365 days only. Juliceaser had added one day extra for every 4 years and it was called as Leap year and total number of days is taken as 366 days.

Since in a year there are 12 months and 365 days, they divided certain months as 30 days and some months as 31 days. In honour's of Juliceaser they named, the month of July on his name. Like that Emporer Augustus's Honour, they named August in his honour and kept 31 days for that month. As a result of this, for the February it is fixed as 28 days and 29 days in Leap year. This is called as Julian Calender which is not scientifically based.

1.23 GREGORIAN CALANDER

From the time Julian Calander was introduced the difference between Saura Calander and Sayana Calander had got reduced considerably. But the Nirayana year was more on an average by 0.00781 days. Hence every one hundred years it becomes 0.781 day.

During 1572 - 1585 AD Pope Gregory, the Authority of Roman Catholic had introduced a New Calander called as Roman Calander. By 16th century this difference got accumulated to 10 days more. A new Calander called Gregorian Calander was introduced with the following changes.

1. The date of October 4, 1982 Thursday was changed as 15 October 1982 as a result there was a reduction of 10 days.
2. As usual similar to Julian Calander February will have 29 days for every four Years.
3. The time of 1600 & 1700 centuries was of Leap year, but if these years are divided by 400, then 1600 AD, 2000 AD would become Leap years in Gregorian Calander. But1700, 1800, 1900 AD years will not be Leap years in this system.

By using Gregorian Calander with the above changes, the difference between Saura year and Sayana year had come down to 0.1216 days.

At the rate of 0.1216 days per every 400 years. It will take 3300 years to get one day. Then by 2000 + 3300 = 5300 AD, one day to be added to the Saura year.

1.24 HINDU'S CALANDER

The Hindu Calander got developed from thousands of years ago, right from the Veda period. During the periods of Veda, Vedanga Jyothisha and Siddanta, the Hindu Calander was revised many a time due to invention of new ideas Astronomically at different times and in various instances which had cropped up during those periods. Mainly there were two practices. First one is Chandra - Sauramana and the second one fully Sauramana. Both these types of Calanders have been explained as under:

(i) **Chandra-Sauramana (or can be called purely Chandramana) Calander:** Ordinarily in Karnataka, Andhra Pradesh, Maharashtra and Gujarat states, Aamanta method i.e, Chandramana is in use. From Padyami after Amavasya right upto the second Amavasya, the entire period is considered as one month.

As per second sub-division the practice is fully Chandramanam which is specified right from Padyami after the end of Poornima, to the end of second Poornima following. This method is in use in Northern India.

In Aamantha method, Chandra Sauramana year starts from Chaitra Sukla Padyami and ends by Phalguna Krishna Amavasya. But in Poornimantha method Chandramana year starts before one fortnight of Aamantha year commencement and starts fifteen days prior to Amavasya. The first Poornimantha month will have its first fortnight in the Phalgunamasa of the previous Aamantha year ended.

The new year of Chandramana method is called one year. 60 years period is called a 'Kalachakra'. This is called also as 'Barhaspatwa Kalachakra'. The twelve year cycle prevailing in Northern India based on Jupiter's movement is one fifth of the 60 years cycle specified in para 1.21 above.

(ii) **Sauramana Calander:** Some groups of Hindus follow fully Sauramana Calander. In Saura (Nirayana) year, Sun's movement on the Ecliptic starts from one Nakshatra for one complete revolution. The Saura year starts when Sun enters Mesharasi (called Mesha Sankramanam).

The Saura year has a period of 12 months Commencement of Saura year starts every year around 14 / 15th of April. One Saura month is counted when Sun travels fully the Mesha Rasi of 30°. The period of time of some Sauramasas are more and some Sauramasas are less. The cause for this is due to Sun's faster movement near Perigree(seeghrochaa) and slower movement near Apooghee (Mandoochaa).

The names of Saura months are Mesha, Vrushabha up to Meena.,similar to the names of Rasis. But while practicing, their names are kept as Chaitra, Vaisakha ... upto Phalguna. The alphabet 'S' is prefixed before Chaitra, Vaisakha etc. The Saura year starts from Saura, Vaisakha month from 14th April and end with Saura Chaitra month.

Though in India the practice of calling Saura months varies at different places, it is advantageous to call the months by Rasi's name based on the position of Sun.

1.25 FESTIVALS FOLLOWED BY HINDUS

The festivals of Hindus were based on either Chandra-Sauramana Calander or Chandramana Calander. For every festival coming in Chandramana the Tidhi and Paksha is unvariably mentioned with the name of the month. The list of important festivals are given with Tidhi, Paksha and Month as under:

S.No.	Festival	Nakshatra / Tidhi / Month
1.	New year	Sukla Pratipat, Amantha Chaitra
2.	Sreerama Navami	Sukla Navami, Chaitra month
3.	Sri Krishna Janmashtami	Krishna Paksha Ashtami, Rohini Nakshatra/Sravana month.
4.	Sri Ganesh Chaturdhi	Sukla Chaturdhi / Bhadrapadamasa
5.	Mahalaya Amavasya	Krishna Paksha Amavasya, Bhadrapadamasa
6.	Dasara	From Sukla Pratipat to Sukla Dasami in Asweeja Masa for 10 days in Bengal, this is called Durgapuja. In Mysore on the name of Chamundeswari Mahishasura Mardini celebrated on Dasami day as festival.
7.	Deepavali	This is a very big festival. Celebrated throughout in entire India. This consists two days. The first day is called 'Naraka chaturdasi' and second day is 'Deepavali' which comes on Krishna Paksha, Chaturdasi and Amavasya in Asweeja Masam
8.	Maha-Shiva Ratri	Saivas perform this festival on Krishna Chaturdasi. In Maghamasam
9.	Holi	Sukla Poornima, Phalguna masam. This is called as festival of colors and mostly celebrated in Northern India

S. No.	Festival	Nakshatra / Tidhi / Month
1.	Saura Vaisakha	This is celebrated as beginning of new year in Assam, Bengal, Orissa, Tamilnadu and Kerala States. On this day Sun enters Mesha Rasi and it is called Chaitra month in Kerala and Tamilnadu.
2.	Makara Sankranti	This is celebrated on 1st day of Sun's Sankranmana into Capricorn Rasi. Falls on Saura Magha month. This festival is called as Pongal in Tamilnadu and Kerala, and as Mahabhihu in Assam.
There are other festival based on the position of Moon and in Nakshatra, which are followed		
1.	Oonam	In Kerala this is celebrated in the day when Moon is situated in Sravana Star during Bhadrapada month. Since the completion of harvest, the paddy had come. The ladies perform dances with songs and celebrated as festival.
2.	Sri Krishna's Brithday	Some Hindus celebrate this festival in Sravanamasa when Moon is in Rohini Nakshatra, but not in Ashtami. It was surprising that on 4-9-2007 both Astami Tidhi and Rohini star had fallen on the same day.

1.26 REVISED HINDU CALANDER

From a long time in India both the Suryamana and the Chandramana Calanders were used. But Chandramana month is naturally the accepted system, as it is visivally proved and established that the period of a month counting is made equal to the time interval between two Amavasya or two Poornimas. The difference to the Sauramana year of 365 days is adjusted for every 33 months by adding one Adhikamasa. By doing this both the Calanders were brought back to a uniform system.

1.27 RECONNING OF THE SYSTEM

1.27.1 Introduction

During Vedic period, time was measured in terms of Ghatikas and Vighatikas. Duration of time from one Sunrise to another was fixed as 60 Ghatikas during Vedic period.

Indian Astronomy based on usage of different types of measurement of time was in force. Measurement of time is divided into two categories, one type defines smallest count and the second type was used to define time in greater periods, right from the beginning of Universe Evolution. In this the method of counting on the basis of 'Yuga' was introduced. It was possible to count the revolutions made by Planets. Where as the Astronomer - Indian Bhaskara-II defined the smallest count as "Truti" which is equal to 1/33.75 seconds.

From the beginning of "Krutayuga" based on the changes occuring in Sunrise, Sunset timings and as New Moon, Full Moon changes in Seasons were noticed. A convenient method of time measurement was used as a day, Fortnight, Month and Year and these divisions were used ever since the human beings lived in this world.

During Vedic period, the Longitude passing through Ujjain (Longitude 75°46'E latitude 23°11'N) was taken for following uniform time and as focal point for all Astrological purposes. The 60 Ghadiyas period is made equivalent to 24 hours thus therefore 1 Ghatika is equal to 24 minutes and one Vighatika is equivalent to 24 seconds.

1.27.2 Indian Standard Time (IST) Introduced in British India

John Goldingham was appointed in 1802 as the first designated Astronomer of Madras Observatory (MO) (Raman 2012). Goldingham made significant contribution while at MO. He ascertained the time of India in relation to Greenwich Mean Time (GMT). He established Longitude of Madras as 80°18'30" East of Greenwich Meridian. Consequently, the MO's clock supplied the Standard Time for whole of India. At 20.00 HRs everyday, Gun was fired to announce that all was well with the Standard Time. The clock at MO was directly connected to the Gun.

To trigger its firing, Indian Standard Time (IST) is the time followed at present throughout India, which is 5-½ hrs ahead of GMT, which is calculated based on the 82°30' E Longitude, from the Clock Tower in Mirzapur (near Allahabad).

During the British period, India followed four different time schemes. In relation to the time at Madras, Bombay presidency operated 49 minutes behind, the Calcutta presidency 21 minutes ahead and Andaman and Nicobar Islands 49 minutes, 51 seconds ahead. In 1802 Goldingham established Madras time as + $5\frac{1}{2}$ Hrs. Madras time was nominated as Indian Mean Time, (IMT) then an Official Standard.

Madras time was later chosen as Railway time, enabling co-ordination of Train Time Tables throughout India, because other areas followed their own constants. For instance, during International Meridian conference held at Washington DC (USA), in 1884 India had two distinct time zones; Bombay time and Calcutta time. On 1st January 1906. Indian Standard Time was established (IST). Nevertheless other time zones continued until India's Independence in 1947 (Raman 2012).

1.28 CIVIL DAY AND SIDERIAL DAY

Since Earth is rotating around its Axis, everyday Sun rises in the East and Sets in the West. From Sunset to next Sunrise, the Sun goes into second half of the Hemisphere during night time. The time measured between two Sunrises is called as a "Civil Day" (In local language it is called as "Soura Dinamu" or "Savana Dinamu".)

After observing the Sunrise and Sunset timings over longer periods of duration, it was found out that the day period and night periods were not uniform and there were differences in the effective time measurements.

Then average period of duration of Day was arrived and it was called as 'Civil Day' or 'Savan Day'. This Savan Day was divided into 60 equal parts and each part was called as one Ghatika, alternatively divided into 24 equal parts and one such division was called as an Hour. This is called as ...(C)

However, taking one Star as basis and the time taken for Earth to rotate one Full Circle to reach the same Star was called "Nakshatra Dinamu" or "Siderial Day". However it should be noted that the time taken for Earth to rotate with reference to Star and to that of Sun, are not equal and there is a difference.

All Planets in the Heavens are moving from East to West. But it was found that Sun with reference to a Star move 1° on the Ecliptic from West to East every Day.

As a result of the above observation, it was established that the time of Savana Day based on a Star is less than the time taken by Earth for one Full Rotation.

As a Corrollary when any Star has come up on the East at a particular time on a specific day, the same Star after 30 days rises 2 hous earlier than the nominated time or after 60 days the Star rises 4 Hrs. earlier than the specified time.

It was established that the time taken by Earth to rotate over a specified Star is less than the time Earth had taken for one Full Rotation around Sun.

It's value being 3 minutes 56 second.

Therefore one Civil Pay = 24 Hrs.

One Siderial Day = 23 Hrs – 56 m – 4s. This is called as ...(D)

1.29 SIDERIAL YEAR AND TROPICAL YEAR

As seen from Earth the time taken for Sun to take one Full revolution is called as Tropical Year. But if you consider different points for count, different timings would come. Hence it was considered only two types of count of Tropical Year. One is 'Siderial Year' and the second is Tropical Year'.

With reference to a fixed Star, the time taken by Earth/Sun for one revolution is called as a 'Siderial' or 'Soura' year (Nirayana).

The Indian Astronomers after careful observations over longer duration of times had established, the average Siderial Year was equal to 365.256364 days or correctly to 365 days 6 Hrs. 9 Minutes 98 Seconds. This is called as ...(A)

As an Equation one Siderial (Nirayana) Year = 365.256364 days

Alternatively, Earth/Sun moving on Ecliptic for one full revolution from Vernal Equinox to the same position, the time taken was called as Tropical Year (Sayana). This period was established as 365 days, 5 Hrs. 48 Minutes, 46 Seconds. Seasons are formed based on Tropical Year. This is called as ...(B)

When we examine Civil Day and Siderial Day, one important point noticed is that the time taken by Earth/Sun for movement with reference to a fixed Star is more than the time taken by Earth/Sun for one Civil Day.

365.25 days average time of Siderial Year is more than the time taken by Earth/Sun for a Tropical Year.

Equations Wise:

'T'is average Civil or Tropical Days = (T + 1) Siderial days

365.25 Civil Days = 366.25 Siderial days

Therefore 1 Siderial Day = T / T + 1 = 365.25 / 366.25

Therefore 1 Siderial Day = 23 Hrs. – 56 M – 4.1 Seconds

It should be noted here that Vedic Astrology time was 1200 BC where as the above derivation was arrived by Astronomer Aryabhatta - 1 in 476 AD.

1.30 SOURA MONTH & CHANDRA MONTH

Ecliptic is 360°. The time taken by Earth/Sun on the Ecliptic is 365.25 days. The timetaken by Sun to move 30° on the Ecliptic is called one Soura month. There are 12 Rasis.

Therefore one average Saura Month= 365.25 / 12 days = 30.43803 days

Moon also similar to Sun moving from West to East.

The movement of Moon is faster than the movement of Sun. The path of Moon is inclined to Ecliptic by 5° – 8′Angular. This being small, it is presummed that Moon is moving on the Ecliptic.

The time taken by Moon with reference to a fixed Star = 27.326615 days. This is called Moon's is Siderial Time (Nirayana). Since Moon moves 360°, the daily angular movement of Moon is = 360° / 27.3216615 = 13° – 10′.

On the Ecliptic the movement of Sun per day is equal to 59′. Therefore the Moon moved forward than Sun in a Day = 13° – 10′ (–) 59′ = 12° – 11′.

From Earth if both Sun and Moon are in the same Longitude, they appear-travelling in the same direction. That day is called New Moon (Amavasya). After 24 Mrs. Moon moves forward from Sun by 12° – 11′.

This Longitude increases daily when it reaches 360°, again both Sun and Moon are moving in the same Longitude, when again New Moon comes (Amavasya). The Astronomers have established the time between two New Moons as 29.530589 Days or 29 Days, 12 Hrs., 44 Minutes, 29 Seconds. This is called as ...(E)

The time between two New Moon's is called as 'Sinodic Month'. This is called as 'Chandra Month' or 'Chandra Masamu' (Lunar Month).

Equation wise:

One Lunar Month = 29.530589 days

The Moon in this 29.530589 days changes his creasent every day. These are called Amavasya, Nelavanka, Arthachandra, Kumbha Chandra, Poornima (on Full Moon Day). Again he starts descending his Cresent right upto Amavasya (New Moon Day) the Figure 1.7 shows the Cresents.

Moon's Siderial Time = 27.3216615 days.

Moon's Siderial month is 27 days, 7 hours, 48 mts., 11 sec. This is called as (F)'.

Ecliptic is divided into 12 parts when Moon moves on the Ecliptic. The time taken is more than Siderial Day. From New Moon, Moon moves everyday 12° - 11[1] faster than Sun. When Moon moves exactly 12°Longitude forward this period is called one 'Tidhi'. In Chandramasa there are 30 Tidhis. Half the period from New Moon to Full Moon is called as "Sukla Paksha" and from Full Moon to New Moon it is called as Krishna Paksha.

The definition of a month is only equal to one Chandramasa. Chandramasa is also called the time between two Poornimas. Please note that Chandramasa is generally considered as the time between two New Moons only (Amavasyas).

In a nut shell, the following are generally the time elements that have formed due to movements of Sun and Moon.

(i)	Siderial (Nirayana) year = 365 days, 6 Hrs, 9 M, 98 sec.	(A) at page 26
(ii)	Sayana Year on the Ecliptic = 365 days, 5 Hrs. – 48 M, 46 Sec.	(B) at page 27
(iii)	Average Civil Day = 24 Hrs. or 60 Ghadias	(C) at page 26
(iv)	Siderial Day (Nirayana) = 23 Hrs. 56 M. 4.1 Sec.	(D) at page 26
(v)	Chandramasa = 29 days, 12 Hrs., 44 M, 29 Sec.	(E) at page 27
(vi)	Moon's Siderial Month = 27 days, 7 Hrs., 43 M, 11 sec.	(F) at page 28
(vii)	Chandramana Year = 354 days 6 hrs. 9 mints. 98 sec.	(G) at page 19

1.31 CHANDRA - SURYA YEAR (OR CHANDRA YEAR)

Chandramasa is the period of time between two New Moons or two Full Moons. Both systems are practiced in India.

1. Chandramasa between two New Moons is called as Amantha or Mukhya Month
2. Chandramasa between two Full Moons is called as Poornimantha or Gauna Masa

The names of Chandramasas will be in the order commencing from the first Amantha Month.

Suryamasa is defined as the period when Sun enters from one Rasi and moves to second Rasi. For example, if in one month Chaitramasa and New Moon comes, the Start of Chandramasa commences from the New Moon which is ahead.

In the second method Chandramasa starts from the Full Moon ahead (Poornimantha). One month is counted after passing New Moon till the second Full Moon.

Sukla Paksha Chandramasa is called as 'Ghadi'

Krishna Paksha Chandramasa is called as 'Vadi'

For all Civil functions, festivals and religious functions, the days are counted as Amantha Chandramana in Karnataka, Andhra and Maharashtra and are followed in these States.The Chaitra month starts on Sukla Prathipath after New Moon.

In Gujarat also Amantha Month is in use. But the year starts from Sukla Paksha Kartika Prathipath after Deepavali. This practice is called as "Karthikadi". Kutch and some Sourashtra areas, Chandrakalamana is followed from Sukla Paksha Ashada Prathipath.

Tripura, Assam, Bengal, Tamilnadu and Kerala states follow the Soura Kala Mana. But for festivals and religious functions Chandra Kala Mana is in use.

Poornimantha Kala Mana is in use in Bihar, Madhya Pradesh, Uttar Pradesh, Rajasthan, Haryana and Kashmir States. But in these states South Kala Mana is used.

One important point to be noted. If Chandramasa is counted from Poornimantha, the year starts from Chaitra 'Vadi' or Krishna Paksha of the previous year. But Chandra Mana Year starts from Amantha of the New Year only.

But Poornimantha year starts only from the middle of Chaitra month after Full Moon from Vadi'.

1.32 NAMES OF CHANDRA MONTHS IN CHANDRAMANA YEAR

Chandramasamulu:

1. Chaitramu	4. Ashada	7. Aswayuja	10. Pushya
2. Vaisakhamu	5. Sravana	8. Karthika	11. Magha
3. Jyeshta	6. Bhadrapada	9. Margasira	12. Phalguna

The duration of Chandramasas on average = 29.530569 days

The difference of duration between Chandramana year, Suryamana Year are dealt in the para No. 1.30

1.33 YUGAS AND METHOD OF COUNTING LONG DURATIONS OF TIME

Right from evolution of this planet and creation as per Indian Astronomers conception, the time was measured by coining a word called 'Yuga'. The word 'Yuga' was used to measure a very long spans of time. In this Yuga period it was possible to indicate revolutions of important planets and for identifying certain specific points for arriving at duration of important aspects noticed in Astronomical observations.

During the period of Vedanga Jyothisha the word 'Yuga' was represented as a period of 5 years. Afterwords the word Yuga was used for measurement of very very long durations of time.

In this method of 'Yuga'. Some lakhs of years of time could easily be specified otherwise any other method would have been combursome and not easily adoptable.

One Maha Yuga = 43,20,000 years

This was divided into 4 parts with time duration of each part as:-

1. Krutayuga	17,28,000 years
2. Tretayuga	12,96,000 years
3. Dwaparayuga	8,64,000 years
4. Kaliyuga	4,32,000 years
Total period of one Maha Yuga	**43,20,000 years**

But Aryabhatta stated that all Yugas were of equal duration of 10,80,000 years.

But Astronomers like Lally, Vateeswara and others assigned the time duration will be in the ratio of 4:3:2:1. It is to be noted that one Maha Yuga is ten times than that of Kaliyuga period.

71 Mahayugas = one Manvantara = 30,67,20,000 years

14 Manvantaras = $14 \times 30672 \times 10^4$ years

Sandhi period as = $14 \times 30672 \times 10000$ years

Between two Manvantaras there is a 'Sandhi' period. Therefore for 14 Manvantaras there would be 15 'Sandhi' periods, as one Sandhi period comes before and after, 1st and last Manvantaras.

One Kalpa = 14 Manvantaras + 15 Sandhi Periods

One 'Sandhi' period is equal to the period of a Krutayuga of 17,28,000 years

Therefore One Kalpa Period = $14 \times 30{,}67{,}20{,}000 + (15 \times 17{,}28{,}000)$

$= 432 \times 10^7$ years

1 Kalpam = 1 Mahayugam $\times 10^3$ years

At present the Swetavahana Kalpam is running. In this 6 Manvantharas have lapsed and 7th Manvantara is running. This is called "Vaivaswatha Manvanthara". In this Manvantara, 27 Mahayugas had lapsed and 28th Mahayuga is running. In this 28th Mahayuga, Kruta, Treta, Dwapara Yugas completed. In Kaliyuga 3102 BC 17th / 18th day, February night 12.00 hrs. the Yuga had started as decided by Indian Astronomers.

At the begining of "Srushti" of this Kalpa (Swethavahana), all Planets including Ketu and Rahu were on one Longitude at the 1st point of Mesha Rasi and there after when Rahu was at 180° from the first point it was assumed that the Tula Rasi started.

Indian Astronomers used Yuga system to identify the revolutions of each Planet at certain specific points of Longitudes.

1.34 SAKAS-ERAS IN FORCE OVER INDIA

From long time ago it was the practice in India for purposes of counting the years the Saka system were in use. The important ones are as under:

1. Sali Vahana Sakam : Used in South India
2. Vikramarka Sakam : Used in both South & Northern India

After India got Independence, the Salivana Sakam is used all over India.

The Salivahana Sakam was started in Sree Vrushabha Nama Samvastara Phalguna Suddha Ashtami of 1924. India was ruled by different Sakahs. Among them the important are Salivahana, British, Hizaries and Phasalies also ruled. Hence if the commencement of Sakas start from Salivana Sakam year, then upto Durmuki nama year (2016-17), the Kaliyuga lapsed will be equal to 5,117 years.

The various Sakas and the years lapsed upto 2016-17 are given as under :

1.	Salivahana Sakam	1930 years
2.	Vikramarka Sakam	2076 years
3.	Budhanirvana Sakam	2560 years

4.	Mahaveera Nirvana Sakam	2543 years
5.	Phasali Sakam	1423 years
6.	Hizari Sakam	1437 years
7.	Adi Sankaracharya Sakam	2061 years
8.	Ramanuja Sakam	999 years
9.	Madwacharya Sakam	909 years
10.	Brahmamgari Sajeeva Samadhi Sakam	313 years
11.	Gandhi Sakam	146 years
12.	Huna Sakam	2016-17
13.	English year	2016 years
14.	Saura year starting	1409-1410
15.	Swatanthraya year staring	from 15-8 – 1947-69 years

1. **Kali Sakam:** This has been taken in Indian Astronomical books. This Yuga started on Friday Mid Night of 17 / 18 February Month 3102 BC and is under count from that day.

   But the Indian Astronomer and Mathematician Arya Bhatta -1 (476 AD) in his text "Aryabhatteeyam" stated that Kaliyuga had commenced about 3600 years before, when he was 23 years old (499 AD). As per this the counting of Kaliyuga was in vogue even much before his period.

   Kaliyuga is more useful as it reveals many items of our Ancient Indian civilization. But the above Sakas given were started much later and were not so useful!. These came into existence to reveal certain instances that occurred during those periods.

   After Mahabharata War the Kaliyuga started. At the same time it was mentioned in our Puranas that Lord Krishna's Niryanam took place. Aryabhatta-I wrote in his text as ending of Dwaraka Yuga or the times related before that Yuga period.

2. **Vikram Sakam:** This Vikram Sakam started from 58 BC. This was the year when king Vikramaditya of Ujjain won the Battle with Sakas and Sythians. But there were no inscriptions of any where written either on stone plaques or in texts. For some time from 5th century AD this Era was called as Malava Sakam. Before that for sometime it was called as "Kruta Sakam". There were roumers that the king Chandragupta = II won battles over Sakas but there was no proof even to accept this argument.

3. **Salivahana Sakam:** This Sakam was started in BC 78. This Saka apperars every year in Soura or Chandramana Panchamgas (Almanacs). There were no proofs to confirm as to when this Saka was started. There was rumour that the king who ruled after Ashoka had started. From the day of his Coronation the King Kanishka had taken the old Saka Era and left 200 years and started this New Sakam. But this had not been confirmed in any of the Indian Historical texts.

4. **Kollam Sakam:** This Sakam was initiated in Kerala State. But there are no evidences to prove as to when this Saka was started. Some people brought similarities with Parasurama Sakam and there were strong belief that this Kollam Sakam started after 1000 years from Parasurama Sakam. It was told that this Kollam Sakam started in 824 AD when Sun entered Mesha Rasi during that year.

5. **Hezeera Sakam:** This Sakam is used by Mohammadans. It was told that this Saka was started in 622 AD on the Moharam festival day and the counting was done from that day onwards.

   As per Calander followed by Mohammadens this Hezeera Sakam started on Thursday the 15th July 622 AD and this was introduced by Calif Umar in 638 - 39 AD. It was told that on the same day the Prophet Mohammad left Mecca.

   Every month when the Moon's first Cescent comes in the evening followed after the end of Amavasya the counting starts. In Islamic year there will be either 354 or 355 days. Every Month has either 29 days or 30 days.

There were many Sakas which were in use such as Saptarshi, Yudhishtara, Buddha Niryana, Mahavir Niryana, Bengali Sun, Lakshmana Sena and Turikilahi (Akbar started this from 1555 AD) and they were not given prominence.

1.35 SMALLEST VALUE OF TIME SCALE MEASUREMENT

In order to perform Ceremonies connected to religious matters, Celebrate Marriages, conduct programmes of Civil nature; for fixing Auspicious time (Subha Muhurtha), the time element has to be reduced to a smallest value possible and has become most essential. In Surya Siddhanta of Indian Astronomy, the smallest value of time proposed was "Prana" for purpose of measurement.

"Prana" is defined as the time taken by a human being to inhale and exhale, while normal breathing. This time period was found equal to the time taken for counting 10 long sylables by Gurujis.

The table runs as under:-

10 Guruvaksara = 1 Prana = 4 seconds
6 Prana = 1 Vinadi
60 Vinadis = 1 Nadi
60 Nadis = 1 day

Sometimes one 'Nadi' is also called as one 'Nadika' or one 'Ghatika'.

In ancient times, as prevailing, the other time scale measurements were also in use and they are given as under:

15 Nimesha = 1 Kastha
30 Kasthas = 1 Kala
30 Kalas = 1 Muhurtha
30 Muhurthas = 1 Day

Here one 'Nimesha' is equal to the time taken for one twinkling of the eye.

Bhaskara-II (1114 AD) in his text "Siddhantha Siromani" had given another type of scale for measurement of time. This was as under:

100 Trutis = 1 Tatparaa
30 Tatparaas = 1 Nimeshaa
18 Nimeshaas = 1 Kasthaa
30 Kasthaas = 1 Kaala

30 Kaalaas = 1 Ghatika

2 Ghatikas = 1 Xenaa

30 Xenaas = 1 Day

Here it should be noted with interest that the smallest time element in our time scale is "Truti", which was defined clearly by the Astronomer and Mathematician the Bhaskara-II.

As per modern time scale, the Equation is

One Truti = 1 / 33.750Second

or In one day we have = 2916×10^6 parts of Truti.

Further Bhaskara - II had clearly stated that one day was divided into 60 Ghatikas and was equal to one Siderial Day (Nakshatra Dinamu).

The time of Siderial Day = 23 Hrs. 56 Min. 4 Sec.and not 24 Hrs.

Hence one Ghatika is slightly less than 24 minutes (Less by 10 seconds of Arc) nearly.

❖❖❖

CHAPTER 2

Introduction of Astronomy

2.0

Many ancient Indian Mythological events are really allegorical descriptions of Astronomical and other physical phenomena. Much of the Indian Mythology is based on hard core Astronomical and Scientific facts and events. Most of the Scholors of Mythology have a background in Languages and Literature and not in Science and therefore possibly could not bringout the inner Scientific meaning. A correct interpretation requires knowledge of Science and Astronomy. Such an interpretation is revealing and makes many obscure notions meaningful.

2.1.1 Astronomy

Vedic Astrology is based on a sound understanding of Astronomy. In Ancient India, Astronomy was a highly developed subject. Knowledge of Astronomy is considered essential for an Astrologer. Ancient Astrologers were well versed with many phenomena, ex: rotation and revolution of Earth, the formation of Seasons, the occurrence of Eclipses, the concepts of Solar and Lunar months, the Equinoxes and the subtle concepts of disposition of Planets and the Stars in the sky. Without the availability of the present day sophisticated Instruments and Telescopes, they were able to decipher fine variations in the descriptions of Heavenly bodies. The fact that they could take into considerations such fine divisions of time, as is possible only through Electronic / Atomic clocks of today is marvelous.

2.1.2

Vedic Astrologers were aware that nothing in the universe was stationary. It was more convenient to imagine them as the central point with the rest of the universe in constant motion around them. Therefore they considered the position and movement of all Heavenly bodies in relation to the Earth itself, which was their residence. Thus the Indian Astronomy is Geo-centric and not Helio-centric, which later considers the Sun as the center.

2.1.3

Indian Astronomers did appreciate the Sun to be the center of Solar system and that the Sun, the Solar system as well as the Stars are all moving. They took the centre of Heavenly bodies in the Galaxy as the Pole Star called the 'Dhruva'. With such profound appreciation of Astronomy, it is preposterous on the part of any one to attribute ignorance of the Earthly movements to the ancient Indian Astronomer.

2.2 THE GEO-CENTRIC ASTRONOMICAL FRAMEWORK

To understand the very basic Astronomical concepts, as pertinent to an understanding of Vedic Astrology, it is important to understand certain facts about the Earth, the movements of the Earth, the apparent movement of Planets around the Earth. Explanations of a few definitions are given below.

2.3.1 Earth as a Sphere

Earth is spherical. It rotates from West to East around its axis. The axis of the Earth is an imaginary line passing through the North and South poles. Another imaginary line is the Equator, which runs across the largest circumference of the Earth, equidistant from Poles and running in the East-West direction.

2.3.2 The Great and small Circles

A great Circle is a circle, whose plane passes through the center of the earth. Equator is the Great Circle. A small circle is a circle, whose plane does not pass through the center of the Earth. Small circles to the North of Equator represent North Latitude and those to the South of Equator as South Latitudes. Imaginary lines drawn on the surface of Earth connecting North and South poles are called Longitudes. These are called also as Terrestrial Maredians.

2.3.3 Imaginary Extention into Space

Celestial Sphere is an imaginary extension of Earth in all directions upto infinity. An extension of the plane of Terrestrial Equator into space is called Celestial Equator. Any great circle that joins Celestial North and South poles is called a Meridian. The Meridian passing through the Greenwich corresponds to Zero Degree Longitude and is termed as Principal Meridian or the Standard Meridian. The Sun crosses the Meridian of a place at mid-day. The intersection of Ecliptic (The Sun's apparent path around the Earth) with the Meridian of a Place is termed as Mid-Heaven, which in other words, corresponds to the Cusp of the Tenth House of a Horoscope. The Meridian of a place thus passes around the Earth, through North pole, Mid Heaven the Zenith (10th house), South Pole, Nadir (4th house) and back to the North Pole.

2.3.4 Declination and Right Ascension

Just as parallels of Latitude and Meridian of Longitudes help to locate a place on the surface of a Terrestrial Sphere, so do their extensions, in the form of Declination and Meridians of Right Ascension help to locate the heavenly bodies on the celestial sphere.

Figure 2.3.4.1 shows how Siderial Time is arrived at. Siderial Time, the Right Ascension and Hour Angle of the star are related. The Siderial Time is equal to the Right Ascension of the Star plus its Hour Angle. When the Star is at upper transit (Hour Angle is zero), the Siderial Time equals to the Right Ascension of the Star.

Declination of a Planet is the angle subtended by it to the Celestial Equator at the Earth. Thus, it corresponds exactly with the Terrestrial Latitude. A planet at Celestial Equator is said to possess zero degree Declination. Right Ascension of a Planet is its angular distance measured Eastwards along the Celestial Equator from Vernal Equinox to the point where a perpendicular drawn through the said Planet falls on the Celestial Equator (Figure 2.3.4.2); Declination is measured North or South from the Equator.

2.3.4.1 Equator and Ecliptic Formation of Seasons

The Earth completes one complete rotation about its own axis in 24 hours. Along with rotation, it completes one complete revolution around the Sun in 365 days 5 hours 48 minutes 46 seconds. This span of time is called Tropical Year. The path of the Earth around the Sun appears to us (from the Earth) as the Sun's path around the Earth and is called the Ecliptic. The Equator runs around the middle of the Earth in the East - West direction and divides the Earth into the Northern and Southern Hemispheres. The Ecliptic or the Sun's path in the apparent East - West direction, does not follow the equator but is placed obliquely to it.Half the Sun's path lies to the North of the Equator and half of it to the South of the Equator.

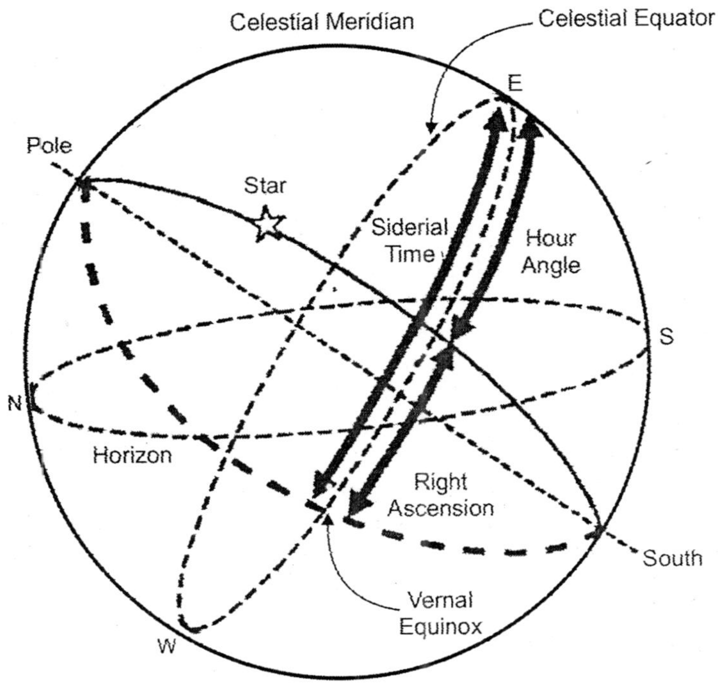

Figure 2.3.4.1 Definition of Siderial Time

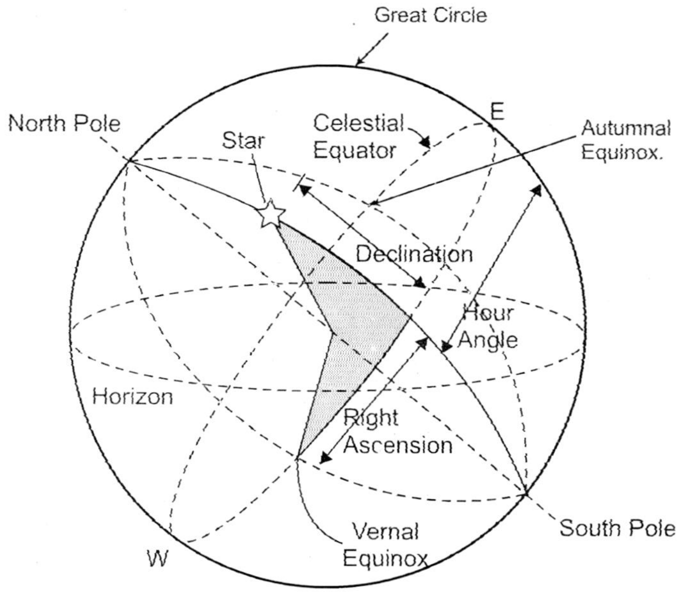

Figure 2.3.4.2 Measurement of the Right Ascension and Declination of a Star

Over 15 centuries ago, Aryabhatta wrote: one half of the Ecliptic, running from the beginning of the Sign of Aires to the end of the Sign of Virgo lies obliquely inclined Northwards (to the Equator). The remaining half of the Ecliptic running from the beginning of the Sign Libra to the end of the Sign of Pisces lies obliquely inclined Southwards (to the Equator). Thus, the Sun happens to cross the Equator twice a year, giving rise to the two Equinoxes, namely the Vernal Equinox (which occurs around 21 March when the Sun is in the Northerly course and the Autumnal Equinox which occurs around 23 September when the Sun is in the Southerly course. After the Vernal Equinox, the Sun pursues the Northerly path and attains a maximum North Declination of 23°28′ around 21 June and is known as Summer Solistice. The Sun is vertically above the Tropic of Cancer at this time. The reverse holds good for the Southern Hemisphere. And, after the Autumnal Equinox, the Sun pursues the Southerly path and attains a maximum South Declination of 23°28′ around 22 December and is known as Winter Solistice. The Sun is vertically above the Tropic of Capricorn at this time. The reverse holds good for the Northern Hemisphere. The obliquity of the Ecliptic to the Equator results in the formation of Seasons. Horizon is a virtual Great Circle, which represents the line where the Earth seemingly meets the Sky.

2.4.0 Astronomy

2.4.1 The Zodiac and the Solar System

Zodiac is a Broad Belt in the Heavens extending to about 8°to 9° on either side of Ecliptic, representing the path of Principal Planets, the Moon and the Sun. Ecliptic is the path of the Sun, a path which exactly passes through the centre of the Zodiac. The Zodiac is a belt of 18° wide and placed obliquely to the Equator. It is divided into 12 equal parts called Rasis and Signs, or 27 equal parts called Nakshatras. The Ecliptic passes through the centre of this belt. Figure 2.4.1 represents these celestial entities.

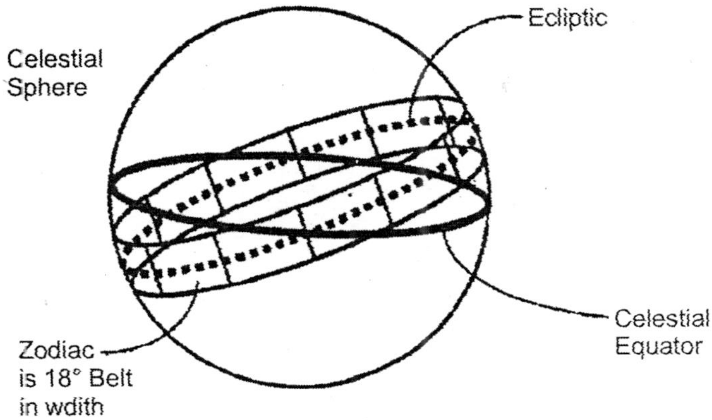

Figure 2.4.1 The Zodiac, Ecliptic, Celestial Equator and Celestial Sphere

The Zodiac is an imaginary circle of 360° and the ancient learned divided the band of seven Celestial Bodies, which influence human affairs and personalities, into 12 equal parts of 30° each. Each equal part of 30° is known as a Sign or a Rasi. The Zodiac is called Bhachakra in Sanskrit, and it revolves on its axis once a day from East to West. There are 12 signs in the Zodiac namely: Aries (Mesha), Taurus (Vrishabha), Gemini (Mithuna), Cancer (Karkataka), Leo (Simha), Virgo (Kanya), Libra (Tula), Scorpio (Vrurchi-kam), Sagittarius (Dhanus), Capricon (Makara), Acquarius (Kumbha) and Pieces (Meena). Each of these signs has a stretch of 30° in the Zodiac. For every two hours, one Sign rises in the Heavens. The Sun's apparent annual motion around the Celestial Sphere results from the Earth's motion around the Sun. As Earth orbits the Sun, different Constellations of the Zodiac appear in the night sky (Figure 2.4.2).

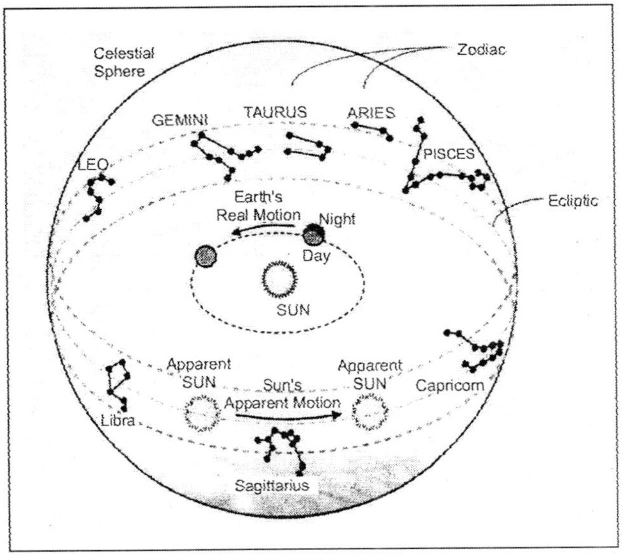

Figure 2.4.2 Celestial sphere, Zodiac, signs with Star groups, Ecliptic, the Sun's apparent motion and Earth's real motion around the Sun

There are nine Planets, which have most powerful influence on the Earth according to Astrology. These are: Sun (Ravi or Surya), Moon (Chandra), Mars (Mangal or Kuja), Mercury (Budha), Jupiter (Guru or Brihaspathi), Venus (Shukra), Saturn (Sani), Rahu and Ketu. The last two are called Shadow Planets (Chhayagrahas), as they do not have physical or Celestial bodies, like the other seven planets. Of the two places, where the Moon crosses the ecliptic (that is the path of the Sun), the North point is known as Rahu and the South point (which is exactly 180° away from Rahu) is Ketu. This is shown in Figure 2.4.3(a) below. Though they are not like the (Terestial Bodies) other Planets, they are sensitive and effective points. It is their powerful influence on the Earth that prompted the ancient people to rank them as Planets in Hindu Astrology. The orbit .of the Earth around the Sun and that of the Moon's orbit intersects the apparent path of the Sun around the Earth. The positions as seen in the night sky of the Rasis (or Signs) with respect to the Nakshatras (or Constellations) are shown in Figure 2.4.3 (b) from 0° to 360° Longitude from the Equator on either side by ± 40° Latitude as seen in the heavens.

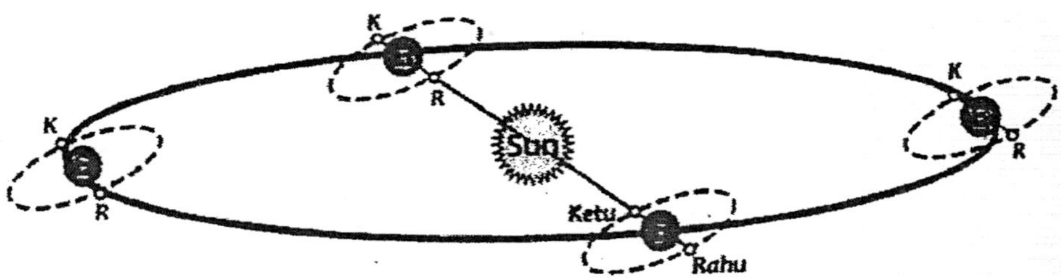

Figure 2.4.3 (a)The Earth's orbit around the Sun

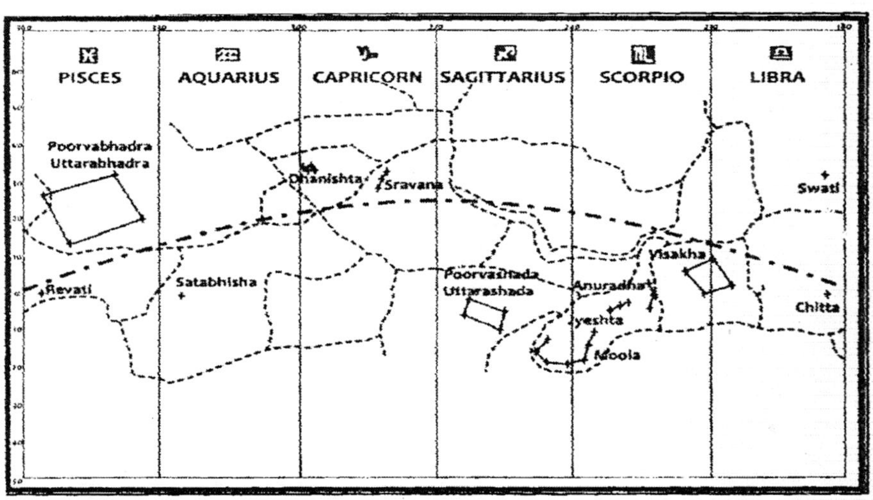

Figure 2.4.3 (b) Position of Rasis or Singns with Nakashatras

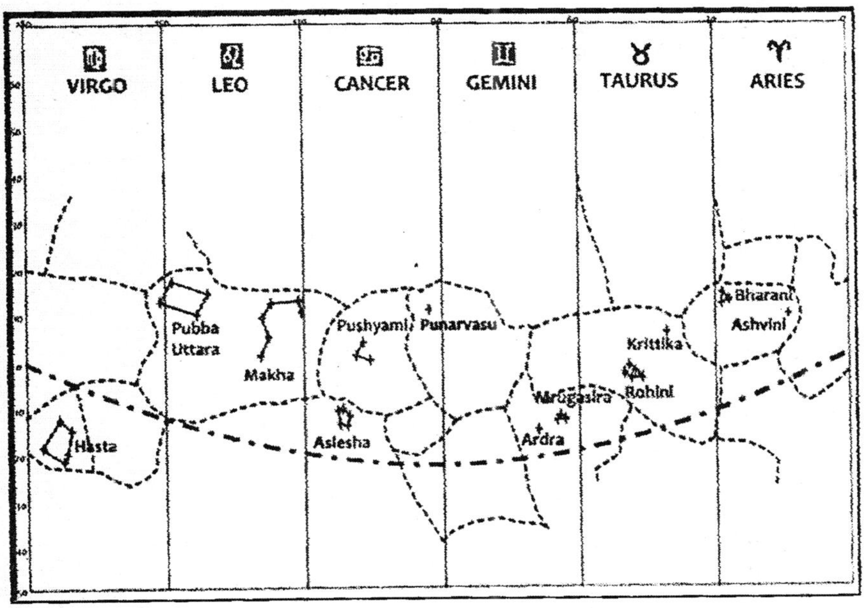

Figure 2.4.3 (b) Continued Positions of Asterisms and Zodiac Signs

The Sun is self-luminous, while Planets and Stars shine by reflected light. Planets revolve around the Sun and Stars do not belong to the Sun's mandala (they are not part of the Solar System). Different shapes of Stars have been described in Satapata Brahmanam and Taitreya Brahmanam. The effect of Stars and their characteristics have been described in certain mantras in Atharvana Veda. Also, it is stressed that a Star is more powerful than Tithi in Atharvana Veda. The study of Stars spread widely during the subsequent times. It is clear from these books / scriptures that study of Stars prevailed in Ancient India.

The Zodiac is marked further by 27 Constellations or Nakshatras.The first Constellation, Ashwini synchronises with the first point of Mesham. Each Nakshatra measures 13°20′ of arc. They are not measurements of time, but just the stretch of Nakshatra. Each Nakshatra consists of four quarters (or padas) of 3°20′ each. These 27 Constellations or Nakshtras comprise of 12 Rasis. Both the Rasis and Nakshatras are reckoned from the same point, namely ZERO degree of the Mesha, the first Rasi (or sign) of Zodiac.

The sketches 2.4.2, 2.4.3(b) Zones, are to be seen as the context demands.

2.5 FORMATION OF SEASONS

The Vishva Bindu or Sampata Bindu is called Vernal Equinox and the point exactly opposite (by 180°) is called Autumnal Equinox. These are the same points, where the Ecliptic intersects the Celestial Equator. Figure 2.5 indicates Celestial Equator inclined to the Ecliptic at 23°30′; the Celestial Equator is inclined by the same amount that the Earth's Equator is inclined to the plane of its orbit around the Sun (Figure 2.5). The Sun crosses the Equator twice a year giving rise to the Equinoxes.

The Vernal Equinox happens on 21 March, when the Sun is on its Northerly course. The Autumnal Equinox happens on 23 September, when the Sun is on its Southerly course. On these two days, the durations of day and night are equal all over the Earth. The Declination of Sun is zero at this time. The Sun attains maximum North Declination of 23°28′ on 21 June, which is called Summer Solistice. On this day in the Northern Hemisphere, the Day is the longest and Night the shortest. And, when the Sun passes to the Southern Hemisphere, maximum South Declination occurs on 22 December, which is called Winter Solistice. On this day in the Southern Hemisphere, the Day is the shortest and Night is the longest. This obliquity of the eclipse to the equator results in formation of Seasons.

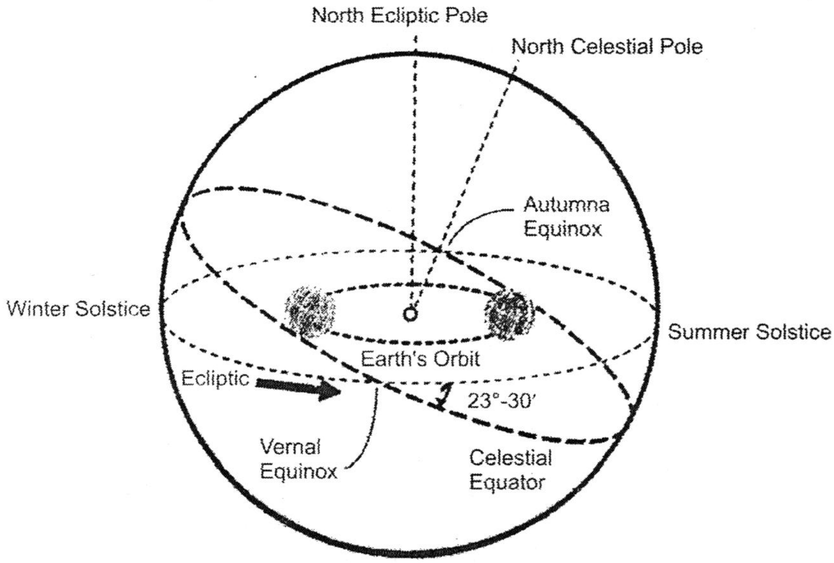

Figure 2.5 The Celestial Equator inclined to the Ecliptic

2.6 PRECESSION OF EQUINOXES

The period that the Sun appears to complete one round of the Ecliptic is called a Tropical Year. At the end of the year, from one Vernal Equinox to the next, the Earth appears to lie some 50.26 seconds of Celestial Longitude to the West of the original position. The Earth to reach this point of time is called Siderial Year. This continuous receding of vernal equinox along the Zodiac is called Precession of Equinoxes.

The Earth is rotating on an axis, which is inclined to the Ecliptic plane of Moon's motion around us. Thus, the Earth resembles a spinning top. The attractions of the Moon and Sun on the Earth's bulging Equator tend to bring it into the same plane with themselves, and thus to straighten up the Earth's axis relative to it's Orbit. Their efforts are restricted by rotation, so that Earth's axis moves slowly around the line joining the Ecliptic poles in the direction opposite to that of rotation, once around 26,000 years at the present rate. This is called Earth's Precession, (Figure 2.6). The pull of the Moon on the bulging Equator is the chief cause of this processional motion.

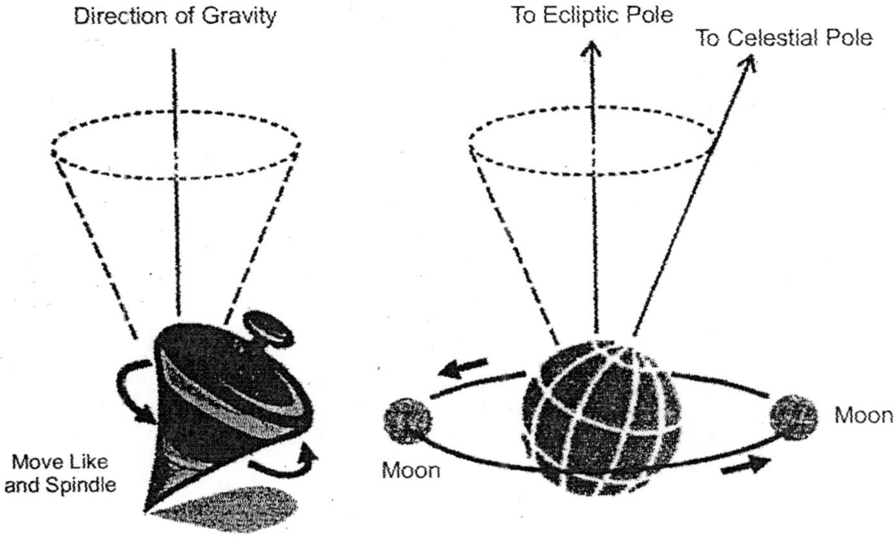

Figure 2.6 Processional motion of the Earth

2.7 CAUSE OF THE PRECESSION

The Earth rotates around its axis, like a spinning top. In doing so, its North Pole (and therefore the Celestial Pole), describes a circle of 47° around the Pole of the Ecliptic. In other words, this means that the plane of the Equator intersects the plane of the Ecliptic at a constantly shifting point. This point, the first point of Aires or the Vernal Equinox, goes on receding westward at a rate of approximately 50.26 seconds. The result of this precession is a slow increase in the Right Ascensions of almost all the fixed Stars in the Zodiac. This precession takes 25,800 (or approximately 26,000) years to complete one circle. As will be seen, an appreciation of this precession is of paramount importance in the understanding of the basic concepts of Vedic Astrology. The wobbling of the Earth's axis, like a spinning top, is in the clockwise direction (Figure 2.8), which causes the precession of the Earth. The axis now points towards Polaris (a). In approximately 13,000 years, it would move to a point with a few degrees from Vega (b).

2.8 NIRAYANA AND SAYANA SYSTEMS AND AYANAMSA

As per Panchamga Reforms Committee appointed by the Government of India, the fixed point of Sampata Bindu was 285 AD. The receding of the Vernal Equinox at the rate of 50.26 seconds per year upto April 2019 comes to 24° – 07' – 18". This difference is called Ayanamsa. Vedic Astrology follows Nirayana System, whereas Western Astrology follows the Sayana System.

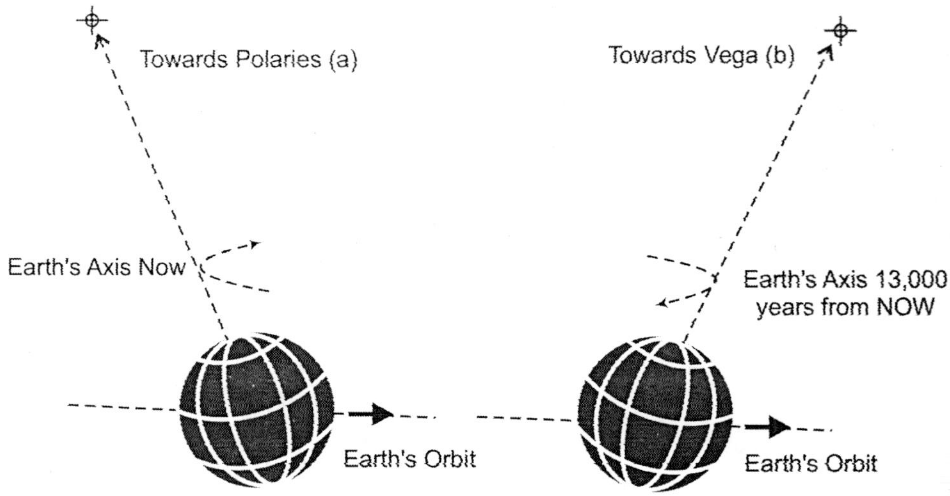

Figure 2.8 Wobbling of the Earth's axis

Nirayana position of Planets, Jyothisha or Hindu Astrology, now increasingly known as Vedic Astrology in the West is gaining greater acceptance world wide for its distinctly superior merits of accuracy in prediction based on the Nirayana Chart. The planetary positions are called Nirayana or Siderial positions; the corresponding Sayana or Tropical positions can be obtained by adding Ayanamsa for the year and month in question.

2.9 LAGNA (ASCENDANT)

The Sign that rise at the Eastern Horizon, at a given moment of time is of primary importance and is called the Ascendant or the Lagna. In a horoscope, this represents the first house.

2.10 SIDERIAL TIME

The Earth completes one full rotation around the Sun in 24 hours, or in what may be called as the Mean Solar Day. Thus, the Mean Solar Day is a function of the Earth's rotation in relation to the Sun. With reference to any particular Star in the Zodiac, the Earth completes one full rotation in 23 hours 56 minutes 4.09 seconds, or in what may be called the Sidereal Day. Thus, the Sidereal Day is the time interval between two successive transits of a fixed Star over the Meridian of a place. The Siderial Day is 3 minutes 56 second (about 4 minutes) shorter than the Mean Solar Day (Figure 2.10).

Since Sidereal Time considers Angular rotation of the Earth in relation to fixed Stars of the Zodiac, the Earth will attain the position with reference to the Zodiac every day at the same Sidereal Time. In other words, for any given location and for the same Sidereal Time, the disposition of Signs of Zodiac (including Rising Sign, the 10th House, the 4th House) will be the same. This is the reason why it is essential to obtain the correct Sidereal Time for the purpose of preparing an Astronomical Chart for any given movement of Mean Solar Time as provided by the watch.

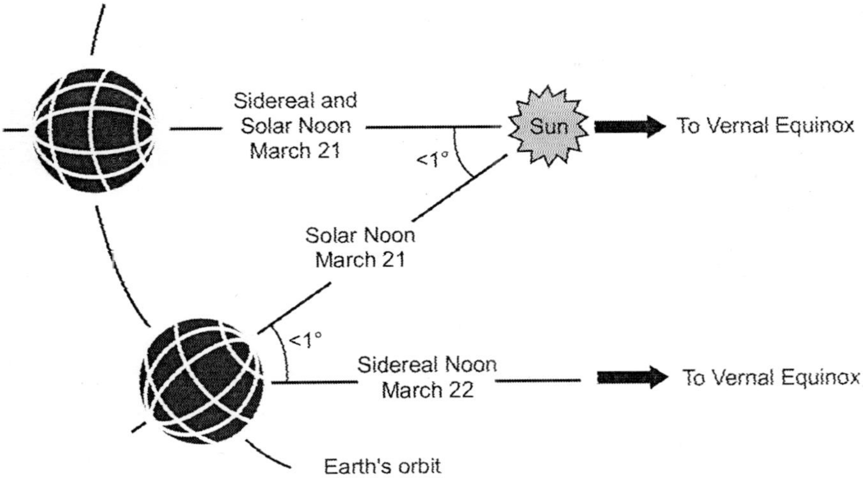

Figure 2.10 Mean Solar Day and Sidereal Day of fixed Star

2.11 MEAN SOLAR DAY AND SIDEREAL DAY

By the time the Earth completes one full rotation with respect to a fixed Star, i.e., in one Sidereal Day, the Sun has moved further along the Zodiac by approximately 1°. For the Earth to reach the same position with reference to the Sun, it has to rotate an extra 1° thereby consuming approximately 4 additional minutes each day. Thus, the Mean Solar Day is longer than the Sidereal Day (Figure 2.10). In Figure 2.11 between positions 1 and 2, the Moon has completed one Sidereal Month. It does not complete the Synodic Month until it reaches position 3; Synodic Month is the time taken from one New Moon to the next New Moon, again covering all the phases and is the Lunar Month of the Calendars.

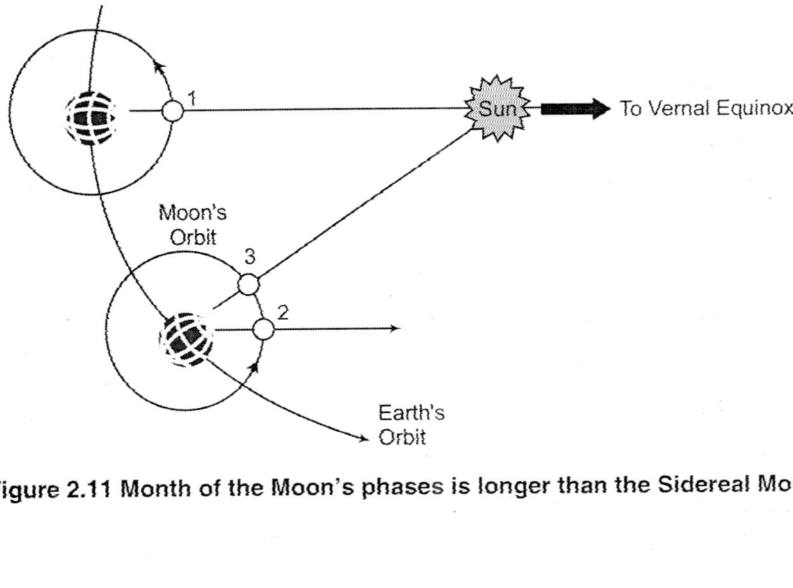

Figure 2.11 Month of the Moon's phases is longer than the Sidereal Month

2.12 ECLIPSE TIMES AND REGRESSION OF NODES

The maximum number of Solar and Lunar Eclipses that can occur in one year is seven. Eclipses do not occur every time we have a New Moon or Full Moon. The Moon's orbit is titled at 5.2° to the plane of the Earth›s orbit. In most months, the Moon is either above or below the Sun-Earth line at New and Full Moon phase, and hence Eclipse may not occur (Figure 2.12).

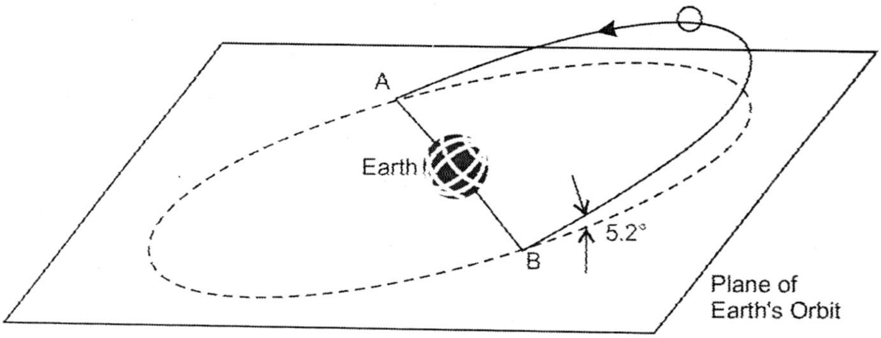

Figure 2.12 Moon's orbit titled 5.2° to plane of the Earth›s orbit

2.13 RETROGRESSION AND DIRECT MOTION OF PLANETS

The Planets move along the Zodiac from West to East around the Sun. However, when seen from the Earth, sometimes their motion appears to be occurring in a reverse direction against the background of the Stars. This apparent motion in the reverse direction is called Retrogression of Planets and has special significance in Predictive Astrology. Rahu and Ketu, which are not true Planets, always move in Retrograde Motion (Figure 2.13).

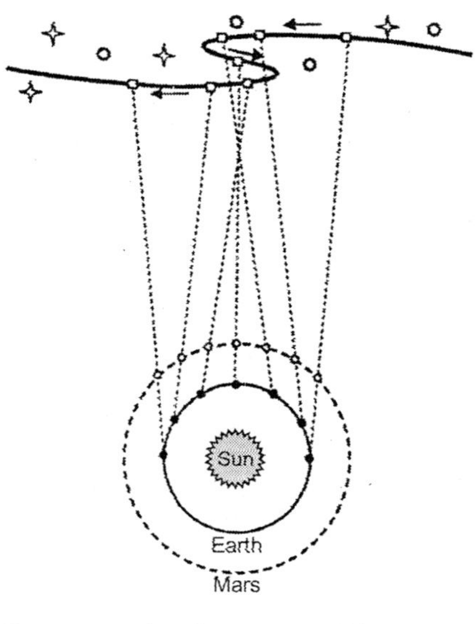

Figure 2.13 Apparent Retrogression in an outer Planet as viewed from the Earth

2.14 ECLIPSE OF MOON

Eclipse of Moon will form when Earth comes between Sun and Moon. This can be seen in Fig. 2.14(a).

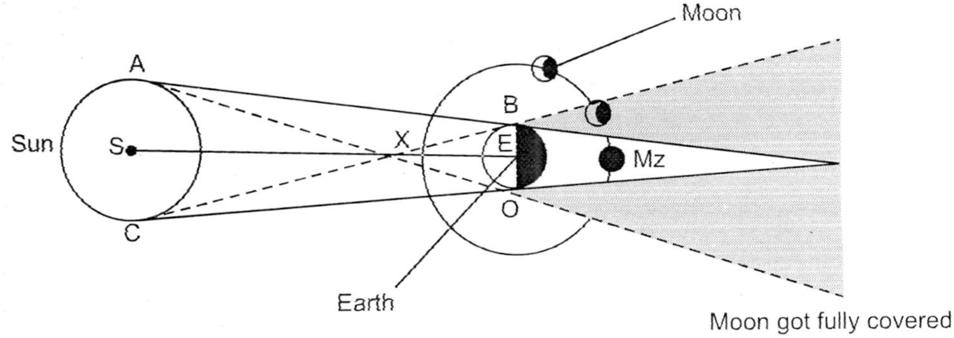

Figure 2.14(a)

In the middle of the Moon's Eclipse, Earth and Moon will appear as shown in Fig. 2.14(b)

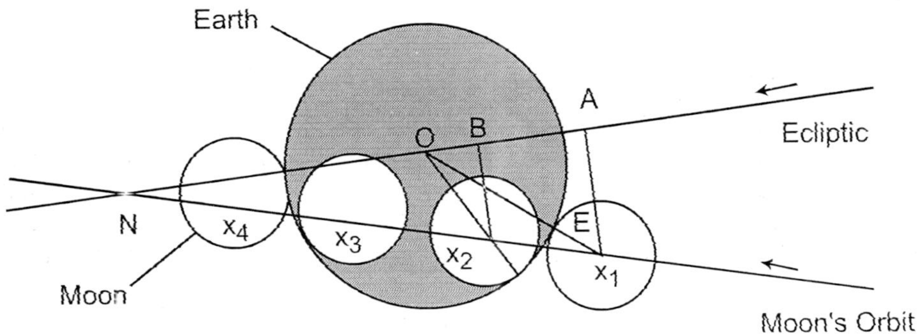

Figure 2.14(b)

2.15 ECLIPSE OF SUN

When Moon comes between Sun and Earth.Sun's eclipse is formed as shown in Fig. 2.15(a)

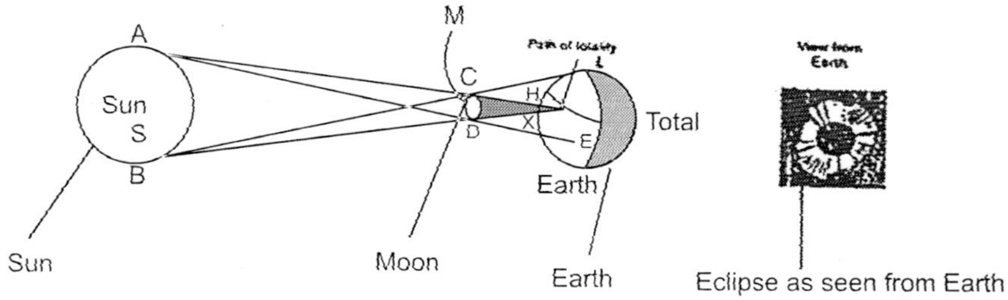

Figure 2.15(a)

When Sun is halfway in Eclipse Fig. 2.15(b) shows the position.

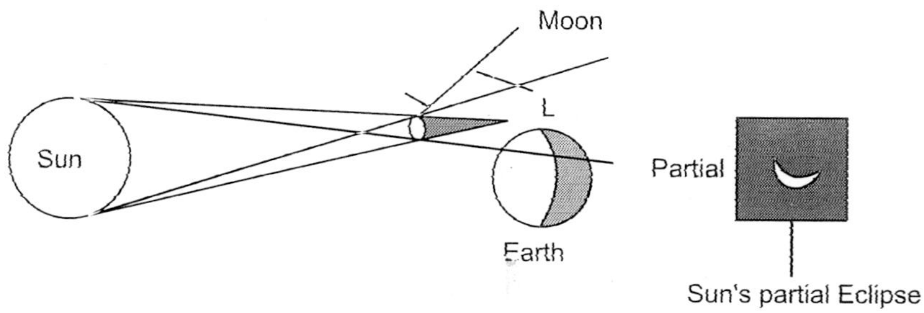

Figure 2.15(b)

Sometimes Sun appears like a Ring which is shown in Fig. 2.15(c)

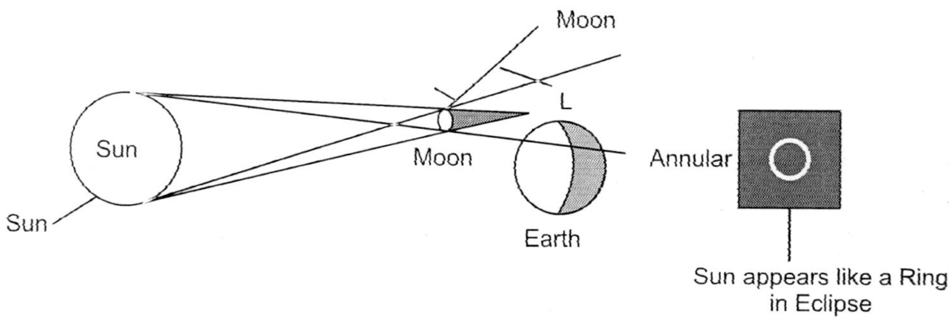

Figure 2.15(c)

❖❖❖

CHAPTER 3

Astrology Acquaintence

3.1 WHAT IS MEANT BY JYOTHISH SASTRA

Jyothish Sastra's meaning, its sub-divisions and inter-relation between these subdivisions are dealt in this chapter. In our daily life the term 'Jyothish Sastra' is mentioned frequently. It is observed that use of Jyothish Sastra has become inevitable in important activities & occasions. For example Commencement of House Construction, House Warming Activity, Marriage, Birth of a Child, Religious functions such as Vratas & Pujas etc. In all such activities an Astrologer is invariably consulted.

In view of the importance attached the information needed to be known from Astrological points; to find the related information concerning the various sub-divisions and when such information is necessary to be utilized will be known. Therefore it is absolutely essential and necessary to introduce the information related to Astrology Sastra.

3.2 DEFINITIONS OF JYOTHISHA

Jyothi means Light. Immediately it strikes the meanings leading to Sun and Stars. From times immemorial, it was recognized that the Heavenly bodies such as Sun, Moon, Planets and Stars are considered as bright spheres emitting light from the sky. One can imagine that it was creating happiness in Humans by seeing light being emitted from these objects.

The main reasons for evolution of Jyotish Sastra was attributed to anxiety about the spheres emitting Light and Research there on, the effect of these Rays emitted on Human Beings. Changes occurring in a standard pattern on climates and seasonal variations and the relationship of these changes and their effect in totally on Human beings. The Man from Ancient Times of Creation had complete knowledge about Directions, Countries and Time Measurement and these were learnt by them after careful observations of the movements of Sun, Moon and Stars over longer durations.

3.3 STARS-DESCRIPTIONS GIVEN IN VEDAS

In the beginning during ancient periods Jyothish Sastra was defined and understood as information related to Stars as seen in the sky and identifying their shapes etc.

In 'Yajurveda' the "Nakshtra Darsa" was used, giving the meaning as Astrologer.

In 'Chandoogyoopanishat' the word "Nakshtra Vidya" was used to mean 'Jyothisha'. Vedas specified performance of Yagnas. The time at which 'Yagna' is performed is decided by Jyothisha. That was the reason how Jyothisha become one of the 'Vedangas'. The Siddhanta Bhaga which gives the Longitudes of Planets has been captioned as 'Jyothisha'.

Daily Routine of Human Beings is linked to Sunrise, Sunset, Moonrise and its changes in Crescent and lights emitted by Stars in the sky.

Jyothish Sastra describes the effects on Human Beings due shape and character of Stars. Sun, Moon and Planets being spheres emitting light and also their influences on the nature and changes noticed seasonally.

It was established and recognized gradually that Sun and Moon and Planets had influenced the actions of Human Beings. Then they started framing rules for the Jyothish Sastra.

In the sound of the word 'Ahooratra". 'A' and Tra' Vowel and Consonant were omitted leaving the 'Hoora' Sound, as opined by sage Varahamihira. This part of Astrology is called the Predictive portion. The main aim is to predict for every human, based on Planetary position of birth time, the coming future events of Good and Bad.

3.4 DEFINITION OF YUGA

In the beginning the word 'Yuga' or 'Yugam' was used to give the meaning of 'a pair'.In daily routine activities, for a day of 24 Hrs. there is day portion and night part. In a month, there is Sukla Paksha followed by Krishna Paksha. In an year there is Uttarayanam and Dakshinayanam. All these were in pairs.

The time of five years period was called as "Panchavarshaatmika Yuga". In order to coincide Chandramana year with Souramana year, one additional "Adhikamasa" was introduced for every 33 months time.

The time taken by Sun from one specified Star to go round and back to the same Star is equal to 365.25 days. Similarly the period of Chandramana year is approximately 354 days.The difference between these two periods is 11.25 days. For every 33 months, 28.12 days will get accumulated additionally. Hence for 5 years 2 Nos. of additional months are coming. These are a pair of 'Adhikamasas' and keeping this broad meaning, the period of five years is called as "Panchavarshaatmikayuga". Gradually the word Yuga is used as a time clock.

In Human Body, this word 'Yuga' related to various parts of Human Body and it had taken highest importance. In the later periods, the longer durational periods of time such as those called by the names of Kruta Yuga, Tretayuga, Dwaparayuga and Kaliyuga were coined to convey that meaning.

During the starting periods of Jyothisha, a complete knowledge was available about the Stars. As a result of constant observation, the 'Vishuvat Point' or "Sampatha Bunduvu" was moving in 4th pada of 'Bharani' Star. Hence the counting of time was commenced from 'Krittika' Star.

The information related to Jyothish Sastra were mentioned in Samhita part of Vedas and also revealed by way of lectures in 'Brahmanas'. The divisions of time in 'The Kala Chakra' were defined as Kalpa, Yugam, Year, Month, Fortnight, Day and Night.

Sun situated in Heavens is "Eternal Luminous" or 'Paramjyothi' Sun incites Drive and Affection in all Human Beings. Sun is the cause for creation and formation of seasons. From one Vernal Equinox to next Vernal Equinox it is recognized as one year.

The year was divided into 12 parts as Madhu, Madhava etc. as mentioned at page. (Chapter 1, para 1.18, page 19). In seasons Spring, Summer and Rainy the Sun moves

Northward from Vernal Equinox (when duration of times are equal in day and in the night). This time is auspicious for Paramatma - The Lord. In seasons Sarat, Hemanta and Sisira the Sun moves in Southern Direction. The period is auspicious for "Pitrudevatas".

Moon moves along 'Bhachakra'. Stars are 27 Nos. In one full rotation along Bhachakra, one full Chandramasa gets completed. When Sun and Moon are in the same plane, with Earth, then Eclipse is formed.

Due to influence of Planets and Stars, the Human Beings experience, auspicious and in-auspicious results in their lives. The Karma performed in auspicious time gives good results.

Hence the matters related to Astronomy and Astrology had been mentioned in Vedas which are beneficial for use by Human Beings.

The word "Vishuvat" was mentioned in "Taithariya" and "Itareya Brahmmanas". In these Mantras similarity was drawn between 'Vishuvat' and 'Human Beings' when humans have their body parts such as Eyes, Ears, Nose, Hands and Legs in 'Yugma' pattern from the head, so the period of one year is divided into 6 months to the right front and 6 months to the left behind. Similarly a Bird, compared to an year, Vishuvat is its Head and 6 months each are its left / right wings.

As per Mantra **"Chandrama Manaso Jataha Chakshoo Suryoo Ajaayatata".**

When examined, Moon is Karaka for Mind and Sun is Karaka for Vision. Like this the foundation was laid in Mantras for Astrology / Jyothisha in Veda periods.

3.5 VEDANGA JYOTHISHAM

Rishees had observed from ancient times that the effect and influences of Planets and Stars on Human Beings was considerably high. It was found that they were able to predict their future. They decided that the counting of periods such as times of Auspicious and in auspicious would be beneficial for progress in the lives of Human Beings. The Rishees by their Divyadrishti could see the movements of planetary positions in advance and made it clear in various parts of Vedas, not only matters connected with Literature, but also to decide the auspicious timings. For learning and study of Vedas, the knowledge of Astrology had become inevitable and had become a part of the Vedangas.

The information for all matters connected with Hundu Mythology and Dharma are given in the 18 Sastras mentioned below.

1. **Four Vedas:** Rigveda, Yajurveda, Samaveda and Adharvanaveda.
2. **Six Vedangas:** These are Siksha, Vyakarana, Chandas, Niruktha, Jyothisha and Kalpa.
3. **Four Subsidiary Vedangaas (Upaangaas):** Mimamsa, Nyaya, Puranas and Dharmasastra.
4. **Later four more were added these were:**Ayurveda, Arthasastra, Dhanurveda and Ghandharvaveda.

Siksha, Vyakarana, Chandas and Nirukta, all these four though part of Vedangas, they literally deal with pronunciation of words in the language. But all these have relationship with Human's Social and Cultural Activities.

Eventhough Astrology was also connected with daily activities of Human Beings it had become a Sastra, as it deals with Planet's time and direction in the Astronomical Science. In ancient times the Astrology had gained highest importance and now in modern times it had grown as a Big Banian Treee and it is now helping the mankind in all its Scientific, Social and Mythological activities. Therefore the Jyothisha was considered as Eye of Vedapusha. Birth chart will convey the information regarding leading a happy life as influenced by the World and its Nature. Hence the following sayings are well noted and made public.

"Tamasomaa Jyothirgamaya Mrutyormaa Amrutangamaya"

In "Taittariya" mention was made about 'Panchavarshaas' meaning the period of five years. These were named as Samvatsara, Parivatsara, Idaavatsara, Anuvatsara and Idvatsara.

They had been compared to Devatas-Fire, Aditya, Air,Mrutyu and Vasthu. They had been named as Agni, Aditya, Moon, Prajapathi and Rudras. The five categories of positions, leading to formation of Uttarayana and Dakshinayana, were defined as the five years of Yuga.

Names of Stars, dieties of each Star had also been mentioned. In Predictive Astrology, the division of time, Ferocious Stars, Calm Stars, Auspicious Stars and introduction was made for formation of daily karanas in each fortnight and Yogas for each Star.

It was established that the counting of daily Stars, movement of Vishuvat point and study of movement of Ayanas. South / North was in vogue even before B.C. 1400 of Vikram Sakam.

The first independent text on Indian Astrology was only the "Rukjyothisham". During the period of Varahamihira BC 427, the Vishuvat movement to Northerly direction had commenced when Sun and Moon were in 2nd part of "Uttarashada" Star and when they are in 4th pada of "Punarvasu" Star, the Dakshinayana starts.Now a days Uttarayana starts when Sun and Moon enters 'Poorvashada' Star on the Ecliptic. In the beginning when Sun entered "Ardra" Star, it was considered that Dakshinayana period was commenced. During later periods, this commencement of 'Ayana' time was gradually getting shifted. The movement of "Sampata Bindu" was estimated as 50 seconds per year approximately

3.6 PART PLAYED BY PLANETS IN "KARMA SIDDHANTA"

It was known through Jyothisha that by performing remedial measures in the present life, one would win over. "The through forward Karma" of the previous life. By understanding the "Karma Siddhanta", one would clearly know the relationship between Jyothisha and Karma Siddhanta. Through this process, the individual would become progressive and prosperous. The information concerning this topic is mentioned as under.

The efforts made by Human Being to know the details of his future life had culminated in the form and development of 'Jyothisha Sastra". Since the Human Beings, from ancient times had experienced the advantages of following Jyothis Sastra, this science became live even till today. It is a well known fact that Karma Siddhanta was widely in use in this world. That there is strong belief among people one has to undergo the results of past karma. The reasons unknown to you will be revealed by Jyothisha. During present day times, the activities now undertaken in the present life and the timings at which such actions would fructify could be known by study of Astrology. For every karma performed, there are two advantages, of which one could be clearly seen and felt and the second one would not be seen. Therefore by earring out the effort as per Karma Siddhanta all the actions would be made advantageously to get the desired results. Jyothish Sastra would indicate methods by which one would avoid getting the undesired results. Jyothish Sastra has become a supportive science to Karma Siddhanta as it would clearly indicate the methods which would give the desired results and those undesired results.

Ancient Indian Sciences belonged to only one category of knowledge. The ultimate aim of all Sastras is to attain Mosksha by Human individual. If there is any controversy in the Siddhanta Rules, it would not over rule the ultimate aim of Indianness.

The Karma is of three varieties

1. Prarabdha
2. Sanchitam
3. Agaami

1. **Prarabdha:** Results now faced as a result of Karma performed in the previous life. It is not so easy to win over this.
2. **Sanchitam:** The Karma performed in earlier life which is transfored to the present life.
3. **Agami:** Results of Karma performed which will fructify in future periods.

The Karma which is now performed will be advantageous to overcome the result of the past Karms. In order to avoid facing the bad results of Past Karma and improve the Good results, the present karma will help in mitigating earlier bad Karma results. Both Karmas are interrelated in support of each other and are not adversely affecting each other.

Birth of a human being has a special importance when compared to crores of living species in the creation of the entire universe.

Therefore, to make the present life successful, the bad results of past karma could be overcome by using the remedial principles mentioned in Astrology. To avoid the bad effects, the Japa, Oushadha, Manis, Mantra, Homas, Donations etc. of different methods and practices are invogue. To mitigate the bad effects of planets, the smallest rays emanating from the Jewels and Diamonds will act as remedial medicine and gives relief. All remedial measures such as Color therapy, Gem therapy, Yoga therapy and Sun rays therapy are intended to win over bad results by carrying out proper karma in the present life, as per saying.

"Karmanaa Karmaanaam Havaha",which is a reality in the present day world.

3.7 PREDICTIVE PART OF JYOTHISHA

Now an introduction is given for Jyothish Sastra.

In Jyothish Sastra, there are certain traditional percepts (Sampradayas). It is necessary to know them and follow them is of utmost importance. Over a period of time, these traditional percepts were lost sight off. But these traditions are even now Live and followed in a few families only. As a result of this, even certain Astrologers who are fully conversent with the Sastra were giving predictions which are not fruitfying in actual practice. This had happenied because of shortage of suitable Astrology texts. Hence this Sastra could not get developed even upto the first decade of 20th century.

But late Sri Vadrevu Suryanarayana Murthy was born on 8-10-1904 at Vizayanagaram. He had made untrining efforts to study Astrology indepth. He went to Madras and studied "Talapatra Grandhas". He studied Astrology at Varanasi under Guruvus. In 1925 he had writen a text in Telugu titled "Jataka Narayaneeyamu Part I".Later in 1945 as per demand of Jyothisha Pundits, he had written another Text called "Yogavali Khandamu" as Part-II.

He had covered in Part-I, all 12 Bhavas, Stree Jatakam, special chapters dealing rules for Yogas. In Part-II he had written rules for all 9 planets - planetwise for 12 Lagnas including combinations of planets in different positions. In 1957 the citizens commence of Rajahmundry gave a rousing reception and gave an award to him titled as "Jyothisha Vidya Bhushana". He expired on 5-5-1978 at Rajahmundry.

For purposes of giving prediction based on their positons in the Horoscope, Sri V. Suryanarayana Murthy had categorised the positions of planets as under from Lagna.

	From Lagna
1. Kendra Positions	1, 4, 7, 10 Houses
2. Kona positions	5, 9 Houses
3. Inauspicious Positions	3, 6, 8, 12 Houses
4. Nir-veerya Position (Strengthless)	2, 11 Houses

3.8 STARS - RASIS - LORDHIP OF PLANETS

The following table gives these details

S. No	Stars	Padas	Rasis	Lordship of Rasis
1.	Aswini Bharani Krithika	4 4 1	Aries	Mars
2.	Krithika Rohini Mrugasira	3 4 2	Taurus	Venus
3.	Mrugasira Aardra Punarvasu	2 4 3	Gemini	Mercury
4.	Punarvasu Pushyami Aslesha	1 4 4	Cancer	Moon
5.	Makha Pubba Uttara	4 4 1	Leo	Sun
6.	Uttara Hastha Chitta	2 4 2	Virgo	Mercury

7.	Chitta Swathi Visakha	2 4 3	Tula	Venus
8.	Visakha Anuradha Jyestha	1 4 4	Scorpio	Mars
9.	Moola Poovashada Uttarashada	4 4 1	Saggitarius	Jupiter
10.	Uttarashada Sravanam Dhanishta	3 4 2	Capricon	Satrun
11.	Dhanishta Satabhisha Poorvabhadra	2 4 3	Aquarius	Saturn
12.	Poorvabhadra Uttarabhadra Revati	1 4 4	Pisces	Jupiter

3.9

The Rasi's have been assigned qualities concerning Human Body and Mind. Kalidasa had introduced two new planets as Gulika and Maadi. Planets have been assigned the characters of friendship, enimity and neutral between themselves. Planets were given Shapes, Attitudes, Castes, Qualities, Genders, Metals and Arts. For all these matters readers are requested to refer to "Jataka Mani Manjusha" or other Astrological texts.

3.10 DASA PERIODS OF PLANETS-VIMSHOTTARI METHOD

S.No.	Stars	Adhipayya Planets	Dasa Periods
1.	Krittika, Uttara, Uttarashada	Sun	6
2.	Rohini, Hasta, Sravanam	Moon	10
3.	Mrugasira, Chitta, Dhanista	Mars	7
4.	Aardra, Swathi, Satabhisham	Rahu	18
5.	Punarvasu, Visakha, Poorvabhadra	Jupiter	16
6.	Pushyami, Anuradha, Uttarabhada	Saturn	19
7.	Aslesha, Jyesta, Revati	Mercury	17
8.	Makha, Moola, Aswini	Ketu	7
9.	Pubba, Poorvashada, Bharani	Venus	20
		Total	120 Years

3.11 METHOD OF CASTING THE BIRTH CHARTS

Navamsa, Bhava and Rasi charts, based on Birth Date, Time and Place, Dasa Sesham etc. can be seen in the Example - 1 given at chapter – 10.

3.12 PLANETS - CAUSATIVE FACTORS / INDICATORS

The following table gives the main causative factors for each planet.

Sun	Pita	Venus	Wife/husband
Moon	Mother	Sani	Longevity
Mars	Brothers & Sisters	Rahu	Relations from Mother's side
Mercury	Business	Ketu	Relations from Father's side
Jupiter	Children		

3.13 BHAVAS - PRINCIPAL PLANETS

Lagna	Sun	7th Bhava	Venus
2nd Bhava	Jupiter	8th Bhava	Saturn
3rd Bhava	Mars	9th Bhava	Sun, Jupiter
4th Bhava	Moon, Mercury	10th Bhava	Sun, Mercury, Jupiter, Saturn
5th Bhava	Jupiter	11th Bhava	Jupiter
6th Bhava	Mars & Saturn	12th Bhava	Saturn

3.14 CAUSATIVE FACTORS FOR BHAVAS AND STATES OF PLANETS

For the above information, limits of combustion for Planets, Adhidevatas etc. all can be obtained from Jataka Mani Manjusha Text.

3.15 PLANETS AND THEIR ASPECTS

1. All planets aspect 7th house and planets positioned there in.
2. In addition the following plants have special aspects which are very important
   (a) Mars aspects 4, 8 houses and planets positioned there in.
   (b) Jupiter aspects 5, 9 houses and planets positioned there in.
   (c) Saturn aspects 3, 10 houses and planets positioned there in.

3.16 AUSPICIOUS AND INAUSPICIOUS PLANETS

Auspiciousness

1. Jupiter-Poornasubha
2. Venus-¾ Subha

3. Mercury-½ Subha
4. Moon-A Subha from Sukla Dasami to Bahula Saptamti – Equal to Jupiter
5. Moon-Suklapaksha-¾ Subha from Saptami to Sukla Dassmi – Equal to Venus
   (a) ½ Subha from Sukla Panchami to Saptami – Equal to Mercury
   (b) ¾ Papi-Mars from Sukla Vidiya to Panchami – Equal to Mars
6. Moon-Krishna Paksha
   (a) ½ Subha as Mercury from Krishna Chaturdasi to Sukla Vidiya
   (b) ½ Papi as Ravi (Sun) from Krishna Saptami to Chaturdasi

Strength of Planets

1. Krishna Saptami to Dwadasi-Weak Planet
2. Krishna, Dwadasi, to Chaturdasi-Old Person, (Vrudhudu) Kshneenu.
3. Krishna-Chaturdtsi to Sukla Vidiya-In Combustion Nil Strength
4. Sukla Vidiya to Panchami-In Balyavastha
5. Sukla Panchami to Saptami-A weak planet
6. Sukla Saptami to Krishna Shashti-A full Subha

3.17 FOR THE FOLLOWING SUB-CHAPTERS READERS ARE REQUESTED TO SEE THE TEXT "JAYAKA MANI MANJUSHA"

1. Decide the strength of Lords of 2 & 3, 1 & 2, 2 & 12
2 Strength of Lords of Kendra, Kona, Labha and Vyaya positions.
3. Strength of 8th Lordship.
4. The speciality in the Dosha Lordship of Kendras.
5. Decide the Dosha in Lordship of Kendras for Jupitor & Venus.
6. Maraka Planets
7. 8th Lordship of Mercury and Moon.
8. Strength of Lordship of Kendra or Kona for Mars.
9. Strength of Rahu and Ketu planets
10. Yogas for Rahu and Ketu.
11. Other relationships of Kendra-Kona Lords & Yoga decession.
12. Planets having lordship of inauspicious houses
13. Predictive results of Dasa and Antardasa Lords.

3.18 FOR SOME OF THE ABOVE SUB-SECTIONS, THE MATTER HAS BEEN DEALT HERE WITH AS UNDER.

Planets: Auspicious and Inauspicious

There are 9 planets and they are classified as under

Naturally Good Planets	Naturally Bad Planets
1. Jupiter	1. Saturn
2. Venus	2. Mars
3. Mercury	3. Sun
4. Full Moon	4. Rahu
	5. Ketu
	6. Moon Not full

3.19 DOSHA IN THE LORDSHIP OF KENDRAS

1. Lordship of Kendra is Asubha for Naturally Good Planets.
2. Lordship of Kona is Asubha for Naturally Bad Planets.
3. Barring Sun and Moon for the remaining 5 planets, there will be lordship of two houses.
4. As per traditional concept, for Naturally Bad Plantes getting Kendradhipatya and later becoming Lord of Kona is Dosha.
5. The three Naturally, bad plantes are Saturn, Mars and Sun. Excepting Sun, for Saturn and Mars there will be two Lordships.

   In this if first is Konadhipatya and 2nd is Kendradhipatya, then the Planet becomes strong and gives Rajayoga.

   But if the 2nd lordship is of Kona, the Papa quality gets doubled and the Planet gives bad results.
6. If Naturally Good Planets get Kendradhipatya Dosha.
   (a) If they are in Papasthana, they will give Yoga.
   (b) If Subhagraphas get Papadhipatya and remain in Kendras the Yoga given is less than that of (a) above.
7. In respect of Naturally Bad Planets
   (a) If they get Konadhipatya and remain in Papasthana they will give Yoga.
   (b) If they get Papadhipatya and remain in Kona the Yoga gets reduced when compared to (a) above
8. Papadhipatya effect is equal for both Naturally Good / Bad Planets.

3.20 MARAKA PLANETS

(a) Maraka Positions

Since 3rd and 8th houses are Ayusthana, Lagna invariably comes into the same category. Therefore the 12th houses of 1st, 3rd and 8th namely 12th, 2nd, 7th houses are becoming Marakasthanas.

(b) In these Maraka Sthanas there is higher upgradtion

The Higher to Lower order is as under:-

(i) Lords of Houses (1, 8, 3)

(ii) Lords of Naturally Good Planets having Kendradhipatya (1, 4, 7, 10)

(iii) Lords of Naturally Bad Planets having Konadhipatya (5, 9)

(iv) Lord of 2, 7 and 12 Houses

(v) Lords of Houses (6, 11)

(vi) Rahu - If in Maraka Sthanas

(vii) Ketu - If in Maraka Sthanas

(c) Maraka Planets taking into account the Lordship and its Position

Prabala Marakas in decending order is as under:-

1. Planets having Maraka character as per lordship and also has Maraka Character by virtue of its position.
2. Planets having Marka Character as per Lordship and not having Maraka Character as per position.
3. Planets do not have Maraka Character as per Lordship but has Maraka Character as per position.
4. Natually Good Planets having Kendradhipatya Dosha and remain in Kendras and Maraka Sthanas
5. Naturally Bad Planets Saturn, Mers & Sun having Konadhipatya Dosha and remain in Konas or in Maraka positions (12, 2, 7).

In all these 5 categories, the strength of Planets for Marakam gets reduced from top to bottom.

3.21 THE STRENGTH OF PLANETS OF RAHU AND KETU

It's a commen saying that Rahu and Ketu will give their own Yoga irrespective whether they are Aspected or Conjoined with others, or positioned in any House. This opinion is not accepted by every one. For Rahu and Ketu, it was decided that they have houses of Exaltation, Own house and friendly house. As per the opinion of some others, the Yoga for Rahu and Ketu is to be decided based on their position and association with others, similar to the main 7 planets.

Ketu when positioned in 3rd and 12th houses is giving Rajayoga, irrespective of their Lords. Further it is stated that the Yoga / Avayoga given by other Planets, the Ketu has power to create obstruction for such Yogas.

From Karakamsa Lagna, if Ketu is positioned in 9th House. The Native will be obstructed to go after other women. Rahu, Ravi combination will independently bestow more Sons to the Native similar to Jupiter.

Rahu, Ketu when conjoined with other Planets will not behave independently, but will take good / bad of those Planets in so far as the Lordship is concerned and if Rahu / Ketu is stronger and accordingly give either Yoga or Avayoga as the case may be.

If there are more than 2 / 3 Planets in a Rasi, these planets become stronger due to their combination and give either Yoga / Avayoga.

But Rahu / Ketu when they join with other Planets, the other Planets cannot take the power from Rahu and Ketu, where as Rahu / Ketu are taking strength from other Planets conjoined with them.

Rahu / Ketu when conjoined with Naturally Bad Planets having Kendradhipatya Dosa and remain in kendras, they give very good Rajayoga. In case these Rasi's are Sthira Rasis or Papa Rasis, the Yoga will get increased considerably. In such situations, the combination of Saturn with Ketu is very good for Yoga.

For Rahu / Ketu, the Moon's association is very good. Between the two, Moon joining Rahu is very good.

If the Moon is the Lord of Konas and remain in Konas / Kendra and join with Rahu gives very good Yoga.If this position is either Aries or Leo, Yoga is much higher.

If Sun gets Kendradhipatya and joins Rahu in Kendra / Kona gives Rajayoga. Similarly it should be decided for other Papagrahs.

For Rahu / Ketu positioned in Kendra should have either associations or aspect of Planets having Kendradhipatya, then they give Yoga. But association with Lords of Papasthana is also causing Yoga.

While deciding Yogas for Rahu / Ketu, the following points should be kept in mind and results arrived at.

1. Ordinarily Rahu / Ketu situated in Kendras are good planets.
2. The association of Kendra Lords is also good.
3. It is incorrect to say that Rahu / Ketu will not give Yoga if
   (a) Rahu / Ketu in Kendras are associated with Kona Lords

   and

   (b) Rahu / Ketu in Kona are associated with Kendra Lords.
4. Since Kendra and Kona Rasis are good Rasis, it is correct to say that Rahu / Ketu positioned there are good Planets. But in practice it is not happening always.
5. In the following cases planets get only Kendra and Kona Lordships but not Lordship of Papasthanas.
   (a) If Gemini, Virgo, Sagittarious and Pisces have become Lagna then Jupiter and Mercury will only have Kendradhipatya.
   (b) If Capricorn becomes Lagna the Venus gets Konadhipatya and Kendradhipatya.
   (c) If Cancer and Leo becomes Lagna, for Mars they get only Kendra and Kona Lordships
   (d) In the case of Sun and Moon they get Lordship of either Kendra or Kona only and they will never get Lordship of Papasthana for Aries & Scrpio Lagnas
6. In respect of 5 Lagnas viz Aries, Taurus, Libra, Scorpio and Aquarious, the planets will get Papasthanadhipatya, in addition to, the Lordship of either Kendra / Kona.
7. Everyone is aware that though Rahu / Ketu being declared as Shadow Planets, they do not give Yogas in the same manner due to their natural character or Lordship and position wise. Hence while deciding Yoga / Avayoga, Rahu and Ketu are to be examined separately.

Hence Gaimini Maha Rushi had stated as "Vepareetham Ketoo". Meaning, not similar to Rahu, Ketu gives opposite Yogas, when in Konas, barring other Naturally Bad Planets and hence Ketu is to be considered as a Naturally Good Planet and Yogas are decided.

3.22 YOGAS OF PLANETS OF RAHU AND KETU

1. If Rahu / Ketu are positioned, either of them alone, in 5th house from Lagna and (a) Associated with Lords of either 2nd or 7th houses or (b) Aspected by the Lords of 2nd of 7th houses; then Rahu / Ketu in their Dasa / Anthardasa periods, cause Marakam.
2. If Rahu / Ketu are positioned either in 2nd or 7th house from Lagna and if they are aspected by the Lords of Kona of 5th or 9th Houses;
   (i) then in their Dasa / Antardasa periods, the Longevity gets increased.
   (ii) but if any Papagraha is associated with them, then that Papagraha would cause Marakam.
3. If Rahu / Ketu are positioned in Dual Sign Rasis - such as Gemini, Virgo, Sagittarious and Pisces. (a)and associated with Lords of Kendra or Kona or (b) and Rahu / Ketu has Lordship of Kendra / Kona then (i) In their Dasas / Antardasas, they give wealth, kingdom and happiness or (ii) If associated with Rasi Adhipathis or aspected by them, then Rahu / Ketu will give very little yoga. But will cause, hardship to Maternal relatives and Marakam to the Mother.
4. If Rahu / Ketu are positioned in Chara / Sthira Rasis and (a) Conjoined with Lords of Kendra / Kona
   (i) Then who ever of Rahu / Ketu is positioned in Subha Rasi, that planet would give great wealth.
   (ii) Then who ever of Rahu / Ketu are positioned in Papakshetra, will spoil the Yoga, but the native will only be kept happy otherwise.
   (b) Conjoined with Naturally Good Planet having Lordship of Papaskhetra.
   Then Rahu / Ketu will become Maha Marka Planets.
   Naturally Good Planets are Jupiter, Venus, Mercury and Full Moon.
5. If Rahu / Ketu are in 6th, 8th, 12th Houses and (i) Aspect these 6, 8, 12 positons or (ii) Aspected by the Lords of 6th or 8th or 12th Houses or (iii) (a) Conjoined with the Lords of 6th, 8th or 12th houses or (b) Aspect the Lords of 6th, 8th or 12th houses; then Rahu / Ketu will become Marakas (iv) If they are (Rahu / Ketu) associated with Lords of Kendra and Kona, (Subhadhipathis) and Yoga giving planets combine with them these Rahu / Ketu will make the Native suffer from disceases, wounds caused by swords or drowning in water leading to death. (v) If they do not cause Yoga then they loose their capacity to cause Marakam. But in their periods, they will cause great hardship and create the life fully painful.
6. (i) If Rahu / Ketu are positioned in 5 - 9, 1-4-7-10 then they will give very high great Raja Yoga. But they should have association of Naturally Good Planets also.
   (ii) If Rahu / Ketu are in 2nd, 7th houses or aspected by the lords of 2nd and 7th houses. Theywill cause loss of wealth and Marakam also.

7.

S.No.	Description of Character	Rahu	Ketu
1.	Exaltation	Taurus	Scorpio
2.	Own House	Aqurious	Scorpio
3.	Moola Trikona	Gemini	Virgo
4.	Satru Khetra	Leo	Cancer
5.	Friendship of planets	Libra	Capricorn
6.	Neutral houses	Aries	Sagittarious and Pisces

Rahu / Ketu when in exaltation house they become highly strengthened.

8. Rahu / Ketu when positioned in any Bhava and have conjunction with other Bhavadhipatis; then they will take the strength of those Bhavadhipathis and become strong and give either good or bad results according to the Bhavadhipathis character of Yoga or Avayoga of Karaka Planet. Rahu / Ketu takes the strength of the Bhava Lord in which they are positioned. Rahu / Ketu have no independant force. They only have the strength of the House in which they are positioned.

3.23 LORDS OF KENDRA AND KONA -YOGA NIRNAYAMU BASED ON THE ASSOCIATION OF OTHER PLANETS

1. (a) When Naturally Bad Planets like Saturn, Mars and Sun get Kendradhipatya and Naturally Good Planets like Jupiter, Venus, Mercury and Full Moon become Lords of Konas then their association gives Atyanta Raja Yoga

   (b) For such Kendra and Kona Lords when associate with Lords of 2, 3, 6, 8, 11, 12 houses the combination will not give good result.

   (c) When Naturally Good Planets become Kendra Lords and join with Naturally Bad Planets with Konadhipatya then their combination will not give Yoga, but gives Avayoga. Then such planets when joined with lords of Papadhipathis, viz. Lords of houses 2, 3, 6, 8, 11 and 12 they become good and such combinations give Yoga also.

2. (i) For Mesha Lagna Sun is the Lord of 5th House and (ii) For Midhuna, Dhanur Lagnas - Sun, Mars, Saturn, Jupiter and Mercury have Lordships of 3, 9; 6, 11, 5, 12; 8, 9, 2, 3; 7, 10, 1, 4; 1, 4, 7, 10 respectively.

   The above Planets will give Yoga only when situated in Papasthanas or with the Lords of Papasthanas. They will not give Yoga without the association of Papas.

3. Kalidasa stated : when association of

   (i) Bhagya Rajyadhipathis and

   (ii) Kendra, Konadhipathis only when happened, they give yoga.

   (a) One of the Konadhipathis who should be slow moving should be ahead and the second one should be fast moving should be behind.

   (b) However they should not be far apart by more than 12°.

   (c) If Moon is positioned between them, it causes Yoga.

4. Kalidasa wrote outstanding Raja Yogas.

   Lords of 6, 8, 12th houses, if combindly or separately situated any where in 6, 8, 12th houses, causes, outstanding Rajayoga.It should be noted that these three planets should be either together in any one of 6, 8, 12 houses or positioned independently distributed among the same three houses.

   This is an outstanding Rajayoga.

5. Jaimini stated:

   (a) Lords of Lagna and 5th House gets more prominence

   (b) An Avayogadasa coming between two Rajayogadasas will also give Yoga.

   (c) A strong Naturally Good Planet Karakadasa falling between two Avayogadasa's will not give yoga.

6. (i) When Planets get Lordship of Houses 3, 6, 8, 12; they become good and give yoga when associated with Yoga Karaka Planet.

   (ii) As Sun, Mars, Saturn are Naturally Bad Planets they give Yoga only when associated with Yoga Karaka Planet.

   (iii) Here the Papi's are those who have attained Papadhipatya.

7. It is not difficult to establish in case of Sun and Moon as they only have one Lordship.

   But for other Planets, they get two Lordships, hence along with Lordship of Parasthanas; they will either get the Lordship of Kendra or Kona.

   Planets become papis only when they get Lordships of both Papasthanas.

3.24 YOGAS OF PLANETS HAVING PAPADHIPATYA

The following table give Lords of Papasthanas, for all 12 Rasis.

	Lordship of Houses			Lordship of Houses	
1. Aries	Mercury	3, 6	8. Scorpio	Mercury	8, 11
2. Taurus	Moon	3	9. Sagitterious	Venus	6, 11
Taurus	Jupiter	8, 11	Sagitterious	Moon	8
3. Gemini	Sun	3	10. Capricorn	Sun	8
Gemini	Mars	6, 11	Capricorn	Jupiter	3, 12
4. Cancer	Mercury	3, 12	11. Aquarious	Moon	6
5. Leo	Moon	12	12. Pisces	Venus	3, 8
6. Virgo	Sun	12		Saturn	11, 12
Virgo	Mars	3, 8		Sun	6
7. Libra	Jupiter	3, 6			

2. For Mesha Lagna, Mars gets Lagnadhipatyam in addition to 8th Lordhsip, hence Mars is not a Papi.Therefore Mars is not listed above.

3. Similarly for other Lagnas - The Lords of Kendra, Kona and Dwiteeya positions have not been taken.

4. (i) The Paragraphs listed in the table above are giving Yogas only when they join with Lords of Kendras.

(ii) The Kendradhipatis join with Konadhipatis they give limitless Rajayoga (Aparimita Rajayoga). In this Kendra Lords should be Naturally Bad Planets and Kona Lords should be Naturally Good Planets.

(iii) Similarly such Kendra and Kona Lords, if they join in Kendra or Kona either positioned together or situated independently they will give Atyanta Raja Yoga.

(iv) If the above combinations take place in Aqurius, Leo, Scorpio and Taurus Lagnas, they become stronger due to "Uttarotra" and give Yoga.

(v) If these Houses are their own or they exchange their own Hosues, it is Atyanta Subham.

(vi) For these Planets the association of Naturally Good Planets having Konadhipatya in Kendra or Kona is very good.

5. The association of Planets with Lordship of Kendra of Naturally Good Planets and Lordship of Kona of Naturally Bad Planets in Kendra and Kona causes very bad Yoga. This Yoga gets increased due to Lordship of higher Houses (Uttarothara much).

6. When Naturally Good Planets are Lords of Kendras and Naturally Bad Planets are Lords of Konas, then they become good planets if they are positioned in 3, 6, 8 and 12 Houses.

   In case of Venus for Capricorn and Scorpio, Lagna. Venus and Mars for Cancer and Leo lagnas - it is utmost auspicious when these planets are situated in Papathanas.

7. In so far as Naturally Good Planets are concerned namely of Jupiter and Mercury for Gemini and Saggitarious Lagnas and of Mercury and Jupiter for Virgo and Pisces Lagnas;

   (i) It is auspicious if Sun, Mars and Saturn with Kona Lordship are in Papasthanas.

   (ii) The Yoga is good even if these Planets conjoin or remain independantly in these Papa Houses.

8. In case of Aquarius, Leo, Scorpio and Taurus Lagnas, the combination of Kendra and Kona Lords in Papasthana (3, 6, 8, 12) will cause Avayoga.

   For these Lagnas even if they are not joined and remain alone, they still give Avayoga.

9. It is better and the Yoga is more when not joined in Kendras and remain independant in respect of the Planets who have Lordship of Konas of Naturally Good Planets and Kendras of Naturally Bad Planets.

10. When Naturally Good Planets get Kendra Lordship and Naturally Bad Planets get Kona Lordship the Yoga is more for these planets if they are not joined in Papasthanas, than when con-joined there.

11. When Naturally Good Planets become Lords of Kendra and conjoin with Lords of Papasthanas and remain in Kendra and Kona, the Kendradhipatyadosha gets nullified and become Yogakaraka Planets

12. Similarly when Naturally Bad Planets become Lords of Kona and conjoin with Lords of Papasthanas and remain in Kendra / Kona, the Konadhiptyadosha gets nullified and become Yogakaraka Planets.

It is very good Yoga if they are not conjoined and remain independently in papasthanas.

13. For Mesha Lagna 9th Lord is Jupiter; 10th Lord is Saturn.But Saturn gets 11th Lordhip. Hence the combination of Saturn with Jupiter is not Good for Yoga.

14. For Gemini Lagna 9th Lord is Saturn and 10th Lord is Jupiter.But Saturn has Lordhip of 8th house. Hence it is not good if these two join and there is no Yoga.

    But the above conclusions in respect of items 13 and 14 are not tallying with actual experience gained in practice. The following examples are given.

    (a) For Gemini Lagna, Jupiter Lord of 10th with Saturn Lord of 8th give Yoga when situated in Kendra and Kona.

    (b) For Taurus Lagna, Saturn Lord of 9th and 10th Houses with Jupiter Lord of 8th when posited in Kendra gives Yoga.

    Hence from the above, it is concluded that Naturally Good Planets with Kendradhipatya with Naturally Bad Planets having Konadhipatya will not give Yoga unless they join Papi planets having 8th Lordship.

15. For Gemini Lagna Saturn gets Lordship of 8th and 9th houses. Similarly for Aries Lagna Saturn get Lordship of 10 and 11th as per tradition Saturn in such cases will not give Yoga.

    The reason is that the planet having Lordship of 9 and 10th becomes Adhipatyapapi. Such planets

    (i) If positioned in 8 and 11th Houses even if owned by them and also in other Papasthanas are not giving Yoga.

    (ii) If that Planet having Kona Lordship and even if remained in Kona, it will cause Avayoga.

    (iii) Saturn in 10th house being his own house, the Yoga given is much less than when positioned in other Kendras.

16. For Planets Yoga is to be decided taking into account its Natural Quality, Lordship and its position and should not be decided on any single account of the three factors for any Lagna.

17. Decision of finding out strength of Lords of 2 and 12, Lords of 2 and 3 and Lords 1 and 2 are given as moder.

    1. 2nd Lord will give mixed result. Some yoga of 3rd Lord plus some Yoga of 1st Lord.
    2. Lord's of 11 and 12, they have no force and are not independent.
    3. If 11th and 12th Lords gets 2 Lordships, they will give Yoga good or bad according to their Lordships.
    4. There is another tradition that only Lagna is to be taken for Kendradhipatya. Lagna has also Konadhipatyadosha. But this need not be taken necessarily.
    5. For Leo and Aqurius Lagnas the Jupiter and Mercury will become lords of 2nd and 11th Houses. They both give yoga only related to mixed Yoga of 2nd Lordship.

(a) If Jupiter and Mercury gets associated with Lords of Kendra and Kona and positioned any where in Kendra and Kona they not only give Yoga but also make the Planet joined give Yoga.

(b) If they do not join with any other Planets and remain in 2nd they will give mixed results.

(c) When they are associated with Naturally Good planets having Kendradhipatya dosha in 2nd House, their dosha gets reduced to some extant.

(d) Similarly the case with Naturally Bad Planets is to be seen.

(e) Good effect get reduced when associated with Naturally Bad Planets with Kendradhipatya Subham.

(f) When Naturally Good Planets with Papadhipatya join with Naturally Bad Planets with Papadhipayta their Papatwa gets much increased.

18. Strength of Planet having Lordship of 8th House

(a) Since 8th House being Vyayasthana to 9th House no Yoga is given. But if 8th Lord is also the Lagna Lord, he gives good result.

(b) In practice it is found that dosha is more in respect of Naturally Bad Planets than when compared to Naturally Good Planets.

(c) For Leo Lagna in respect of Jupiter the Lord of 5th and 8th, in general for Naturally Good Planets, the Dosha is for Kendradhipatya and not for Papadhipatyam and the same is good.

19. Deciding the strength of Mars when he is the Lord of Kendra or Kona. Mars when becomes 10th Lord, will not give Yoga only when he has Lordship of 5th House. He gives Yoga as written in 'Poorva Parasari' grandha.

But this is opposite to the actual results seen from practice. This rule applies only for Cancer Lagna. Then Mars is the 5th and 10th Lord, he gives Yoga in 10th House. Mars will not give Yoga in 5th House.

20. Results of Dasa, and Antardasa Planets

1. Any planet when his own Dasa and Antardasa is running, he gives Yoga, Avayoga of the previous Dasa only, he will not be independent in giving Yoga, Avayoga of his own. This rule applied only to 7 Nos. of planets but not to shadow planets of Rahu, Ketu.

2. In case of utmost powerful Planet when its own Yogadasa starts, it is causing Yoga even in its sub-period.

3. (a) If in a previous Dasa, Yoga had commenced and if later Dasa is also a Yogadasa, then ordinarily it gives good yoga in its own Swabhukti in the later Dasa.

(b) If in a previous Dasa Yoga had commenced and if the later dasa is an Avayoga Dasa, then after the period of Swabhukti, the planet causes Avayoga only throuhout its period.

4. The Vimshottari Dasa system as laid down by Parasara Rishi is followed throughtout India right from Himalayas to Kanyakumari by all States. As a sensible standard, established by its usage in experience and also appraised as utmost easyest method.

5. (a) In any Horoscope, if it is decided that a particular yoga will be in operation during a Yogakaraka Planets period, then that Yoga starts in the Antardasa of a planet in association with Yoga Karaka Planet's Dasa i.e. to mean that the yoga related to the Bhava only will be given during that Antardasa period of the Yogakaraka Planet.

   (b) Sometimes the Yoga commences in the Antardasa period and gradually the Yoga gets increased. Sometimes, the Yoga related to the Bhava is only given depending upon the Bhava Karakatwam of the sub-planet.and also due to its overall strength of the Bhava supported by him, This is the speciality.

6. Sometimes in the sub periods of Antardasa Planets, depending upon their position, they give Yoga which is not related to the character of the Main Dasa Lord. Such Yoga will be known depending upon the location of that Antardasa Planet.

7. There are two systems in deciding Dasa-Antardasas results. These are

   (a) Yoga is given in their Bhukti in accordance with Main Lord.

   (b) Results given will be those of opposite character of the Dasanath.

8. The planets associated with Dasanath will give results in their sub-period in accordance with the Yoga of Main Lord. That is if Dasanath is a good planet it gives Yoga and if Dasanath is a Papi it gives Avayoga only in respect of Yoga.

   As regards Bhava result depending upon his Bhava Lordship and his Karakatwam, the Yoga given by him has direct relation to these two aspects either good or bad yoga as the case may be.

9. The Yoga of Dasanath is decided only after deciding overall Yoga on the Peethika. The Antardasa Lords can never give yoga which Dasanath cannot give.

   The Planets who are not in association with Dasanath will give less yoga depending upon their own Yoga based on their Nature, Lordship and position.

10. Sometimes the Dasanatha will give very good Rajayoga in the begining and afterwords in his own Dasa he will give opposite results or even prevent the Yoga. Then even,if sub-sequent Dasas are good when compared, the Yoga gets spoiled. These are extreme results.

    Sometimes at a week point in a period, an Avayoga is caused which has no relationship to the Dasanath. This is done to handover to suit to the coming Dasa. This is found to be correct in actual practice.

11. (i) Yoga gets started in the Dasa of Naturally Bad Planet who had no Lordship of Kona and also in the sub-period of the Planet of Naturally Good Planets who has no Lordship of Kendra.

    (ii) That means Dasanatha when he is a Naturally Bad Planet, he should not have Konadhipatya and in that Dasa and Antardasa of Naturally Good Planets who are not Lords of Kendras will cause good yoga or good yoga commences.

    (iii) Similarly in Dasa's of Naturally Bad Planets with Kendradhipatya and in Antara of Naturally Good Planets with Konadhipatya, the Yoga starts or in Dasas of Naturally Good Planets with Konadhipatya and in Antardasasa of Naturally Bad Planets who have Kedradhipatya the Good Yoga starts or gives good yoga.

12. (a) Sometimes at the begining of Dasa (i.e) the yoga commences in his own Swabhukthi. Again in his own Maindasa in the Antara of Papi, viz of a Maraka; then if Dasanatha has Maraka character, the Dasa / Antardasa Lords become Marakas and cause Marakam.

(b) Ordinarily if Dasanatha has no Maraka Lakshanas, even during Antaras of Prabala Marakas, there is no danger of Marakan.

(c) Similarly in so far as Yoga's concerned; if main Lord is not a Yoga Karaka Dasa, the sub-lord even if he is good can never give the Yoga which Dasanath cannot give.

(d) Similarly in the sub-periods of Papa Planets in Main Yoga Dasa, they cannot cause Avayogamm but only create difficulties.

(e) If any Planet is effective in causing Prabala Rajayoga and if they have Maraka character, then after deciding Longevity falling in Alpa, Madhyama or Poornima periods and when that period comes the planet causes Marakam. Then in his Dasa, Prabala Raja Yoga starts and gradually after some period of lapse, in the Papi's Antara Period who have Maraka Character, the Marakam is caused.

(f) The word Prabala Raja Yoga was used because those who had given Rajayoga earlier in their periods, but when their Antara period comes, suddenly it gives very good un-expected yoga and there after causes Marakam.

(g) Sometimes the yoga starts in the Main Dasa and his own Swabhukthi with Maraka Lakshanam and after deciding longtvity of Alpa / Madhya and Poorna; no Marakam is caused as the Longevity is estimated as Poorna, in the Alpaayuvu period.

13. (a) In deciding the Yoga-Bhuktis, some people:

Take Shadvarga Characters, ascending and descending from exalted signs, balance of Cusps and AshtakaVarga are taken. Based on these factors yoga is , decided.

(b) By taking the above chracters only yoga connected with Bhava could be decided; but will not be useful in deciding weather the Dasa or Antàrdasa is aYoga period or not.

(c) In deciding Yoga of Dasa or Anthardasa Lords on the Peethika the strength of planets decided taking into account - the natural qualities of the planet, their Lordship and the position, association and aspects.

14. The planets associating the Dasanath gives equal yoga to the dasanath in their sub-periods.

(a) Those planets which are not associated with Dasanath; will give ordinary yoga in their sub-periods. But planets who are Yogakaraka Planets by themselves will give Yoga in their sub periods though they are not associated with Dasanath.This is correct from the points of view of experience in many cases.

(b) An important aspect is to be accepted in this case:

While deciding the Yoga of Dasanath and Antardasanath, the strength of each planet is to be first decided. Then based on relationship between Dasanath and Antardasanath; it should be decided the extant Rajayoga given in every sub periods of main periods. This opinion is of utmost importance. Because when a Planet comes in one Dasa, it gives Yoga and in a different way in another Dasa, the same planet gives Yoga completely of opposite nature to that of first Dasa referred.

15. (a) Rahu / Ketu when not in association and positioned in Subha Rasis, then they will give Rajayoga in their sub-periods.

(b) Rahu / Ketu are Subhas when they are in Kendras / Kona. These Kendra / Kona should be owned by Papis, rather Papi rasis. If these Rasis are fixed Rasis, it is all the more advantageous.

(c) In Chara Rasi Aires; in Sthira Rasis - Taraus; and if they are Kendra / Kona and then if Rahu and Ketu are positioned in those Rasis; they give Atyanta Subham.

(d) Rahu / Ketu are also giving Yoga in Papa Rasis.

16. (a) When Dasanath becomes Papi and give Avayoga, then the planets associated with Dasanath in their own sub-periods give Papa result only. If they are Subhas, the results will be mixed.

(b) The good planets who are not associated with Dasanath will also give mixed results based on experience.

(c) Those good planets who are not associated with the Dasanath will also give Papaphala.

(d) The Subhagraha not in association with Dasanath will also gvie Papaphala and this tallies with actual experience.

17. The Sukra Sub period in Saturn Main period; and Saturn Sub period in Venus Main Dasa the results will be good if they are good Planets and results will be adverse if they are not good planets.

Sometime this opinion is not correct. As per actual experience they are giving yoga in both the cases referred to.

Some times due to extraneous special factors, Yoga is given but the quantum given is much less.

There is a special effect in respect of Saturn. If he is in Kendra and Venus is in another Kendra, excepting Lagnam;then good Raja Yoga is given

Similarly Saturn - Rahu Dasas are also to be considered.

Advise to Students: There are many other Astrology Books, they are requested to take any book and proceed further to accomplish and attain proficiency.

CHAPTER 4

Introduction to Stellar Astrology

4.0

Introduction to Stellar Astrology Rules for Prediction. Planets, Jeeva and Sareera & Kalaamsa-Guna, sub-division (New Method).

4.1 JEEVA & SAREERA SUBDIVISION

Not only an introduction to Astrology is given to students but also a new method under the caption Stellar Astrology is brought in the predictive technology, to learn at Phala nirupana to enable students to fore cast future events very easily.

The Stellar Astrology was initially invented by Sri Maharshi Satyacharya. There after Parama Poojya Sri. N.V. Raghavachari (Called as Naadi-2). Based on Stellar Astrology, he had laid down the methods by which this subject was taught to arrive at correct predictions. Along with Sri Raghavachari, Sri R. Gopal Krishna Rao Garu (called as Naadi-1) had both combindaly studied this Stellar Astrology and founded most important rules.

Sri. N.V.R.A. Raja, Son of Late Sri N.V. Raghava Chari was also his student, had thoroughly studied the Stellar Astrology. There after Sri Raja took training under Gurus like Shri Prof. Gorasa Veera Bhadra Rao & Shri P.V.K. Punneswsara Rao and Mastered the subject of Stellar Astrology. Sri Raja had written the following two Books.

1. Advantages of Stars in Stellar Astrology and to make predictions based on Jeeva & Sareera.
2. Characters are attributed to Stars in Stellar Astrology. New factors such as Kalaamsa & Guna of planets is required and by using these two, the Phala Nirupana is made.

For writing the above two Books, Sree Potti Sreeramulu Telugu University had awarded the Ph.Degree to Sri N.V.R.A. Raja (He is called as Junior Meena-2).

Dr. N.V.R.A. Raja was my Guruvu. Students should necessarily read the above two Books.

4.2 IMPORTANT NECESSITY OF STARS

Literally the meaning of Star is that which never gets extinguished. In Bhachakra situated in theavens has both Rasis are attributed to it and Stars studded to it. As per Karma Siddhaanta of Hindus, the results of past karma is indicated by Stars and when ever it has to show up its result, it will act in the Dasa & Antardasas currently running, relavent to a particular individual.

Initially the Stars absorb the power from the sky and there after it will be passed to mankind at appropriate time & manually.

In the life cycle of Human beings the importance of Stars is very much stressed & known. When ever any auspicious function is performed such as Marriage, House Warming Ceremony etc. the usefullness of Star is well known.

The necessity of Stars will be known at the following timings.

1. The first point in Vimshoari Dasa System is the Star.
2. It is also decided whether the Horoscopes are matching for Marriage, based on Birth Stars of the intended Boy & Girl.
3. In order to know the "Nama Nakshtra" at the time of naming Ceremony after the birth of a child, Star's necessity is of much importance.
4. For fixing Subha Muhurtha for any auspicious function the Star is invariably to be known.
5. One should know the Nakshtra for either Yoga commencement or 'Naming' of the child.

4.3 BHAVAS & BHAVA KARAKAS-RESULTS OF STARS

In Stellar Astrology there are important subjects and topics which are very usefull such as:

1. Stellar lord
2. Stars, Strength in Digbala directions strength.
3. Planets of Jeeva & Sereea and their qualities.
4. These new sub-divisions were made and fully described and were given signs. Importance is given in Stellar Astrology to Rasis, Stars, Planets, Karakatwas & Characters.
5. In order to obtain good results, the Stellar Lord of the Bhavathipati, the Stellar Lord of Bhava Karaka (Nakshatra) are necessary that both these planets should be in Subha Rasis in Rasi Chakra.
6. When Planets are in action or Debilitation, the extent of directional strength of their Stellar Lords is to be known to know the Planets strength. Sometimes the planet would not give the expected good results. The reason being that the Star Lord is posited in 6/8/12 Houses. In the Stellar Siddhanta, Superior strength Planets and lesser strength Planets are shown below in that order.
   1. Rahu & Ketu are strongest of all Planets.
   2. Sun
   3. Moon
   4. Venus
   5. Jupiter
   6. Staturn
   7. Mars
   8. Mercury-having lowest strength of all planets

When 3 to 4 Planets are in the same House the Planets in Moola Trikona Rasi will be the strongest than the planets in own, exaltation rasis.

(a) Naturally Good Planets are stronger in odd rasis.

(b) Naturally Bad Planets are stronger in even Sings.

Some time one or two Planets control the Jataka Chakkra. It should not be told that the native will have good future and reach high positions in life. Because, it should be examined whether the Planets attained Subbaadhipatya or Papaadhipatya. If any plant is having yoga Karaka strength, then it gives good results.

4.4 STELLAR LORD STHITHI SIDHANTA

In Stellar Astrology the Stellar Lord of the Planet will give either good or bad results, but it is not the result based on the position of Planets.

If a Planet becomes the Dasanath, the results given by him will not be uniform. The results will be varying according to the Nakshatra Part in which the Stellar Lord is situated.

In Stellar Astrology predictive results are given based on the position of Stellar Lord. Hence this is also called as Stellar Lord Sthithi Siddhanta. According to this Siddhanta for Planets & Bhavas, the procedure of arriving Jeeva & Sareera planets has been established.

In this Human world the life (Jeeva) and Body, (Sareera) are always together. In Astrology the Prana is called as Jeeva the human figure with life is called as Sareeram. In any Horoscope Jeeva & Sareera Planets are of advantageous nature for each Bhava & Karaka, then good results are achieved. Both are inter-dependent on each other.

In Stellar Astrology Moon gets the lordship for Sareera and Sun gets the Lordship of Jeeva. Mars and other Planets become lords of Pancha Bhavas. (the sloka-prudhivyapasthejovayurakasat is well known)

Rahu, Ketu & Gulka are enemies to Sun. These planets will cause difficulties to Jeeva & Sareera Planets.

4.5 METHOD OF FINDING OUT THE JEEVA & SAREERA PLANETS FOR BHAVAS AND THE PLANETS

Method of calculating Jeeva & Sareera Planets for Bhavas & Planets.

Example: Rasi Chart

		Ketu	Lagna
Mars			Venus
			Sun Jupiter
	Rahu Sani Moon		Mercury

1. **Ascendant Lagna:** In Hastha Star (Lord Mercury)
2. **Sun:** In Poorva Phalguni star (Lord-Venus)
3. **Moon:** In Anuradha Star (Lord-Saturn)
4. **Mars:** In Poorvabhadra Star (Lord-Jupiter)
5. **Mercury:** In Hastha Star (Lord-Moon)

6. **Jupiter:** In Poorvaphalguni Star (Lord-Venus)
7. **Venus:** In Pushyami Star (Lord-Saturn)
8. **Saturn:** In Anuradha Star (Lord-Saturn)
9. **Rahu:** In Anuradha Star (Lord-Saturn)
10. **Ketu:** In Krittika Star (Lord-Sun)

The method of finding out for 12 Bhavas and Planets the Jeeva or Sareera Characters is given in greater detail as under.

Bhavas

Bhava S. No	Jeeva	Sareera	Deciding Jeeva & Sareera planets
1.	Saturn	Mars	Lagna Lord Mercury is in Hastha Star. Moon is Stellar Lord. He should become Jeeva. But Moon is in debilitation with Sani. Sani is in his own star Anuradha, Sani becomes stronger, hence, Sani is Jeeva. Jeeva planent Sani is in has own star Anuratha, posited in Scorpio Rasi and in his own star. Hence lord of Vruchika-Mars became Sareera.
2.	Saturn	Mars	2nd Lord is Moon. He is in Saturn Star. Sani is Jeeva. Sani is in Scorpio Rasi hence Sareera is Mars.
3.	Venus	Saturn	3rd Lord is Sun. He is in Poorvaphalguni Star. Lord is Venus. Jeeva planets is Venus. Venus is in Pushyami star. It's lord is Saturn. Hence Saturn is Sareera Planet.
4.	Saturn	Mars	4th Lord is Mercury in Hastha Star. Lord is Moon. Hence, similar to Lagna-Jeeva is Saturn; Sareera is Mars.
5.	Saturn	Mars	5th Bhava Lord is Venus. He is in Pushyami Star. Hence Saturn is Jeeva. As per item-4 Sareera is Mars.
6.	Sun	Venus	6th Bhava Lord is Mars in Poorvabhahra Star. Lord Jupiter is with Sun, who is in own house, very strong. Hence Sun becomes Jeeva. Sun in Poorvaphalguni Star. Its lord is Venus. Hence Venus is Sareera.
7.	Venus	Saturn	7th Bhava Lord Jupiter. He is in Venus's own star. Then Venus is Jeeva. Venus is in Pushyami Star. Lord is Saturn. Then Saturn is Sareera.
8.	Saturn	Mars	8th Bhava Lord is Saturn, in his own Star Anuradha. Here Saturn is Jeeva. Saturn in Vruchika, its Lord is Mars. Hence Mars is Sareea.
9.	Saturn	Mars	9th Bahva Lord is Saturn. As mentioned in above Saturn is jeeva and Mars is Sareera.
10.	Venus	Saturn	10th Bhava Lord is Jupiter. Similar to 7th Bhava, Venus is Jeeva and Saturn is Sareera.
11.	Sun	Venus	11th Bhava Lord is Mars. He is in Poorvaphalguni. Sun is the Lord here Sun is Jeeva. Sun is in Venus Star, hence Sareera is Venus.
12.	Satrun	Mars	12th Bhava Lord is Venus. Similar to 5th Bhava, hence Jeeva is Saturn and Sareera is Mars.

Planets

Sun	Venus	Saturn	Sun is in Venus Star. Jeeva is Venus. Venus is in Saturns Star, Sareera is Saturn.
Moon	Saturn	Mars	Moon is in Saturns Star. Jeeva is Saturn. Saturn is in his own Star, in Mars house. Hence Mars is Sareera.
Mars	Sun	Venus	Mars is in Jupiters Star but Jupiter is with Sun. Sun is this own house & strong. Hence Sun is Jeeva. Sun is in Venus Star. Hence Venus is Sareera.
Mercury	Saturn	Mars	Mercury is in Moon's Star but Moon is in debilitation combined with Saturn. Satrun is in this own Anuradha Star. Hence Jeeva is Saturn. Saturn is in Mars house. Hence Sareera is Mars.
Jupiter	Venus	Saturn	Jupiter in Venus Star. Hence Venus is Jeeva. Venus is in Saturn Star. Sareera is Saturn.
Venus	Saturn	Mars	Venus is in Saturn Star. Jeeva is Saturn. Saturn is in his own Star in Mars house Sareera is Mars.
Saturn	Saturn	Mars	Saturn in his own Star. Jeeva is Saturn. Saturn is in his own Star in Mars house. Sareera is Mars.

4.6 IMPORTANT FORMULAE

In Stellar Astrology, as per Stellar Lord of the Planets Star, the Jeeva & Sareera Planets of the Bhavas are arrived at, as described in para 4.5.

Rule 1: For one Bhava, find out the Star in which the Bhavadhipathi is situated and the Star Lord becomes Jeeva Planet. The Star Lord of Jeeva Planet is the Sareera.

Rule 2: If Jeeva Planet joins with another strong Planet, then the Jeeva Planet will become Sareera Planet. The planet which is stronger will take the full force from Jeeva Planet. This will happen to Sareera Planet also.

Rule 3: If Bhava Lord is in his own Star, Bhava Lord himself becomes Jeeva Planet. If Jeeva Planet is posited in a particular Bhava then, the Bahva Lord becomes Sareera.

Rule 4: Some times the Bhava Lord is not only in his own Star but also posited in his own house. Then Jeeva planet becomes Sareera planet.

4.7 STARS AND THEIR ADVERSE STARS

S. No	Star	Adverse star	S. No	Star	Adverse star
1.	Aswini	Cihtta (14) Moola (19)	14.	Chitta	Aswini (1) Moola (19)
2.	Bharani	Jyeshta (18)	15.	Swathi	Mrugashira (5)
3.	Krittika	Anuradha (17)	16.	Visakha	Rohini (4)
4.	Rohni	Visakha (16)	17.	Anuradha	Krittika (3)
5.	Mrugasira	Swathi (15)	18.	Jyeshtha	Bharani (2)
6.	Ardra	Dhanishta (23)	19.	Moola	Aswini (1)

S. No	Star	Adverse star	S. No	Star	Adverse star
7.	Punarvasu	Sravanam (22)	20.	Poorvashada	Alesha (9)
8.	Pushyami	Utarasahada (21)	21.	Uttarashada	Pushyami (8)
9.	Aslesha	Poorvashada (20)	22.	Sravanam	Punarvasu (7)
10.	Makha	Revathi (27)	23.	Dhanishta	Ardra (6)
11.	Pubba or Poorvaphalgumi	Uttara bhadra (26)	25.	Poorva bhadra	Uttraphalguni (12)
12.	Uttaraphalguni	Poorvabhadra (25)	26.	Uttarabahadra	Poorvaphalguni (11)
13.	Hastha	Satabhisham (24)	27.	Revathi	Makha (10)

4.8 STARS, STAR LORDS, THEIR CHARACTERS

S. No.	Names of Stars	Star Lords	Character of Planet
1.	Aswini/Makha/Moola	Ketu	Tamasika
2.	Bharani/ Pubba/Poorvashada	Venus	Rajasika
3.	Krittika/ Uttara/Uttara shada	Sun	Rajasika
4.	Rohini/ Hastha/Sravanam	Moon	Rajasika
5.	Mrugasira/Chitta/Dhanishta	Mars	Tamasika
6.	Aradra/Swati/Satabihsham	Rahu	Tamasika
7.	Punarvasu/Visaka/Poorvabhadra	Jupiter	Satwika
8.	Pushyami/Anuradha/Uttara-bhadra	Saturn	Tamasika
9.	Aslesha/Jyeshtha/Revati	Mercury	Satwika

4.9 GUIDELINES TO GET GOOD AND FAVORABLE RESULTS

In order to get good & favorable results, the following factors and points are to be considered for examination.

1. Jeeva & Sareera should not be adverse between them selves.
2. The character attained by Jeeva & Sareera Planets should be incosonance with their natural qualities.
3. Jeeva & Sareera Planets should be positioned in good Bhavas.
4. Jeeva & Sareera should not join with Enemies, should not be aspected by Enemies and should not be posited in enemy houses.

The Jeeva & Sareera Theory laid down above, was in accordance with Stars and their Star Lords and the rules laid down.

4.10 TWO IMPORTANT FORMULAE IS GIVEN AS UNDER

Rule 1: Dasanatha will give results of Star Lord and of those Planets associated with it.

Rule 2: If Dastantha is in the Star of Bhuktinath or Bhukthinath is in the Star of Dasanath and based on association of other planet.

The forecast of incidents would positively happen could be inferred in Bhukthianath's period only. The time of Happening the future events could be known through the Jeeva & Sareera Sidhanta.

1. To get good results the Jeeva & Sareera Planets should not be enemies between them selves.
2. The Jeeva & Sareera Planets should not be in 6th or 8th houses.
3. It should be fully examined as to the following issues.
   (a) Owning houses
   (b) Position of Jeeva & Sareera in the Horoscope
   (c) And Planets position in the Star and there after the predictive results announced.
4. It should be found out as to which are the planets aspecting Dasanath
5. Star Lord's position in the Horoscope and it's associations etc. should all be examined.
6. It should be found out as to which Bhava, the Jeeva & sareera Planets are related.
7. When Dasanath is in association with other 2 or 3 Planets, the strength of Dasanath and the other Planets are to be kept in mind and then only the predictive decision is taken.
8. It should be examined whether the Dasanath & Star Lord are Friends or Ememies before deciding the predictive results.

4.11 DASANATH & BHUKTINATH

The following guide lines will be usefull to take final decision taking into account the relationship between Dasanath & Bhauktinath's Jeeva & Sareera Planets and also in revealing the time of occurrence of the event.

1. For any Bhava and Karaka, Planet's Jeeva & Sareera Planets have relationship with Dasa/Bhukti/Antra, Lords; the incidents will occur during their periods.
2. When Jeeva & Sareera Planets of a Bhava or Karaka Planets come into their own houses in Gochara and join with Dasa/Bhukti Antara Lords then they will assist the Bhava & Karaka Planets to give good results.
3. When Jeeva & Sareera Planets have aspects between them selves in Gochara and have relationship by way of association with Dasa/Bhuki Anthara Lords then, either that Bhava or Karaka Plant will give good results.

4.12 SHARP GOCHARA

In Stellar Astrology predictions are not to be given based on the position of Planets. Always the prediction should be given based on Stellar Lord of a Planet. This is called sharp Gochara.

4.13 PERIOD OF TIME IN DAYS/MONTHS/YEARS WHEN PLANETS ARE MOVING IN DIRECT/RETROGRADE, MOTIONS IN ONE, DAY OR RASI OR 12 RASIS.

When in direct motion

Planets	Average movement per day	Time to cover one Rasi	Time taken to move 12 Rasis
Sun	0°-59′	1 month	1 year
Moon	10°-10′	2¼ days	1 month
Mars	0°-31′	1½ month	18 months
Mercury	4°-5′	27 days	1 years
Jupiter	0°-5′	1 year	12 years
Venus	1°-36′	28 days	1 year
Saturn	0°-2′	2½ years	29 years
Rahu	0°-3′	1½ years	18-2/3 years
Ketu	0°-3′	1½ years	18-2/3 years

Apart from Sun & Moon, the remaining five Planets, when for away from Sun some times they appear as fixed and for some times in retrograde motions. The following table gives the periods of Stable & Retrograde motion for the 5 Planets.

In Stable and Retrograde Motion

Planets	Distance away from Sun	Planets appear Stable in days	Planet appear in Retrograde in days
Mars	228°-132°	3	80
Mercury	14°20-17°20′	1	29
Jupiter	245°-115°	5	120
Venus	29°-26°	2	42
Saturn	251°-109°	5	140

4.14 PLANETS & THEIR STARS ASPECTS IN STELLAR ASTROLOGY

In Vedic Astrology there are aspects to Rasis & Planets. In a similar manner in Stellar Astrology the details of aspects of a Stellar Lord on another Stellar Planet are given in the following table.

The positions which a Star Lord aspects and also in other Stars in which the planets are posited there in are given below–

1. If Sun is in a Star & that Star aspects positions	On 7, 8, 11, 16, 21, 24 Stars from that star and also the Stars in which the Planet posited there in.
2. If Moon is in a Star and that Star aspects positions	On 4, 8, 10, 15, 16 positions from that star and also the stars in which the Planet posited there in.
3. If Mars is in a Star and that Star aspect positions	On 3, 7, 8, 15 positions from that Star and also the Stars in which the Planet posited there in.
4. If Mercury, Jupiter, Venus and Saturn are in a Star and that Star aspect positions	On 3, 5 positions from that Star as also the Stars in which the Planet positioned there in.
5. If Saturn is in a Star, that Star has spical aspect	On 15, 16 positions and alsc the Stars in which Planets are posited there in.
6. If Jupiter is in a Star that Star has special aspects	On 10, 19 positions and also the Stars in which the Planets posited there in.

4.15 STELLAR ASTROLOGY-CLARIFICATION ABOUT BINNAPADA

Star-Krittkia (3), Mrugasira (5), Punarvasu (7), Uttarphalguni (12), Chitta (14), Visakha (16), Uttarashada (21), Dhaninshta (23), Poorvabhadra (25) these 9 stars have their Padas distributed in two adjacent Rasis. In these circumstances that Star Lord gives the results of the two relevant Rasis.

4.16 STELLAR ASTROLOGY-CLARIFICATION ABOUT RAHU AND KETU

Rahu and Ketu both Planets are shadow Planets. These two are formed at the junction of Moon's orbit with that of Earth's orbit. Their movement is always anticlockwise. Their angular distance is always 180°. In an year they move by 19°-20′.

	Rahu	Ketu
1. Exaltation Sign	Taurus	Scorpio
2. Debilitation Sign	Scorpio	Taurus

When Rahu/Ketu are in combination with other Planets and if they happen to become Karaka Planets, then Rahu/Ketu will give the results during their Dasa/Bhukti periods.

4.17 SETLLAR ASTROLOGY-DIRECTIONAL STRENGTH OF PLANETS

In order to know the strength of Planets the following rules have been laid down.

In Vedanga Jyothisha Sastra, the Directions & the Rasis in which the Plaents gain strength is given as under.

1. In Lagna Kendra-Jupiter and Mars are strong.
2. In 4th Bhava-Moon & Venus are strong.
3. In 7th Bhava-Saturn & Rahu are strong.
4. In 10th Bhava-Sun, Mars & Ketu are strong.

But in Stellar Astrology the Planet need not be positioned in strong Rasi. If any Planet is not having Directional strength and if any other planet having Directional strength is in association then, that first Planet tantamounts to have directional strength.

When Horoscope chart is being examined, the Star in watch the Planet is posited should be known. From this the Rasi in which the Star Lord is posited should be known. Accordingly the results are to be decided.

4.18 WHEN PLANETS ARE IN GROUPS-THEN THE STRENGTH OF EACH PLANET IN THE GROUP

In Stellar Astrology for Stars on the basis of Lords the Jeeva & Sareea Planets are decided for all Bhavas. For this method, the following 4 Rules as laind down in para 4.6 are again given here.

Rule 1: The Star in which the Bhava is positioned then, that Star Lord will be Jeeva. The Star in which Jeeva Planet is situated and its Lord will be the Sareera.

Rule 2: If Jeeva Planets joins another stronger Planet, then that strong planet will be Jeeva. That means that the stronger Planet will take the strength from Jeeva Planet and this can happen to Sareera Planet also.

Rule 3: If Bhava Lord is in his own Star then Bhava lord will be Jeeva. The Rasi Lord of the House in which Jeeva is posited will be the Sareera.

Rule 4: Sometimes not only the Bhavadhipathi is in his own star but will also be in his own house. In this ease Jeeva Plants is also the Sareera Planet.

4.19 RULES FOR GETTING GOOD AND FAVORABLE RESULTS

1. Jeeva-Sareea Planets should not have Stars which are adverse to each other.
2. The characters which Jeeva & Sareera got should be in consonance with their own characters.
3. Jeeva-Sareea Planets should be in Subha Rasis.
4. Jeeva-Sareea Planets should not be associated with Enemies or positioned in Enemy's houses or have aspects from Enemy Planets.
5. Whether Jeeva-Sareera Planets are in friendly Houses, or in Exaltation or in their own Houses and whether they got good planet's aspect are to be examined.

Persons having tamasika character

Their food items contain more of bitterness, highly pungent, sourness, with spicy powders, dipped in oil, Roasted and fried.

These persons are lazy, dull headed and will not bother for any thing. They worship lowly, ferocious, wild Devatas, Ghosts & Demons.

The food, eaten by them is not all healthy type. It is stale & harm full. These persons will eat the left over food items.

Every Planet will have all three characters viz. Rajasika, Tamasika and Satwika. When one character gets prevailed the other two will remain doorment and stay away in the back ground. While assessing the character of the Planet, it should be seen as to in which Star the Planet is positioned. Then one need not necessarily, see, either the Star Lord or the aspects of Planets or conjunction with other Planets or its position.

Ordinarily Satwika Plent will be in its Satwika character, Rajasika Planet will be in its Rajasika character and Tamasika Planet will be in its Tamasika character, then in all these cases the Planets will inverιably give good results.

Rajasika Planet: Can get Satwika character. Then the results will be via media. It should not get Tamasika. For this Plant the results are experienced in the beginning of the Natives career.

Tamasika Planet: These Planets should never get Rajasika character. The results are experienced in the last spell of the Native's life.

Satwika Planet: If they get Rajasika character, the results will be via media. Good results are not given if they get Tamasika character. The results are felt in the middle of Natives life.

4.20 USE FULLNESS OF CHARACTERS IN PREDICTIVE SUB-DIVISION

Stars, Star Lord-Their natural character/qualities are shown in para 4.8 table. Three characters got evolved from Nature. These are 1. Satwika, 2 Rajasika 3. Tamasika.

Persons having Satwika Character

Their faces emit brilliance, worship Devatas, no harm is caused to any one, they do good to every one. They wish that all should be safe. The food that is eaten by them gives intelligence, wisdom, health, longevity, strength and happiness.

Persons having Rajasika character

Their Devatas are more. They crave for sensual enjoyment. They have love & affection. They worship Yaksha (Demi-God) & Rakshasas (Demons)

4.21 RESULTS OF CERTAIN IMPORTANT EXPERIENCES

After detailed examination of many Horoscopes, various points such as happenings of incidents in future, timings at which the results will be fructified, the changes likely to occur in the results of Bhavas are listed below:

1. If Jeeva-Sareea Planets are Yoga Karaka Planets and they have relationship with either of each Bhava or Karaka Planet	Then that person will attain highest status in his life.
2. If for all the Jeeva & Sareera are the same than the Natives Horoscope will be fully under the control of both these Planets.	Then if these Jeeva & Sareera Planets have association with Dasa/Bhukti Lords then they will give good results of the Planets.
3. If Jeeva & Sareera Planets have association with the Yoga Karaka Planets or aspected by Yoga Karaka Planet or positioned in Yoga Karakas Planet's own house.	Then the good results of that Bhava gets imporved. The Native will achieve good and appropriate results.

4. While matching two Horoscopes the Jeeva & Sareera Planets of Gent's 7th Bhava, have relationship with Female's 6th Bhava Planets of Jeeva and Sareera OR The Gent's 6th Bhava's Jeeva & Sareera Planets have relationhip with Female's 7th Bhava Planets of Jeeva & Sareera	Then they experience difficulties in leading their family life.
5. If Jeeva & Sareera Planets of Husband's 7th Bhava has relationship with wife's Jeeva & Sareera Planets of 5th Bhava or even if they have no relationship.	Then both their Horoscopes get matched very well and they lead a happy married life.
6. (a) If Jeeva & Sareea Planets of Husbands 5th Bhava or Karaka Jupiter have (a) relationship with Dasa/Bhukti/ Antara Lords OR (b) Relationship with 6th or 8th Bhava or 5th or 6th Bhava and 5th or 8th Bhava	Then the Native will positively get Yoga of a Child Birth. The Native begets a Male Child OR The Navtive will not be happy with that child.
7. If Sun and Jeeva & Sareera Planets of 10th Bhava are strong and have relationship with 11th Bhava	The native will attain high Status in the professional carrier
8. If Mercury, Saturn, Jupiter have relationship with 10th and 11th Bhava's	Then the Native becomes a famous Astrologer. OR Becomes a big Spiritual & Phylosophical Leader with an Asounding self confidence person. He help's others.
9. (a) If Jeeva & Sareea Planets of Bhagyadhipathi, Maraka Lord, 6th Lord, 8th Lord and 12th Lord have relationship with Antara lords. (b) If Jeeva & Sareera Planets have relationship with 6th and 12th Bhavas and in addition have relationship with Dasa/Bhukti/Antaka Lords.	The Native will face lot of difficulties and suffer from torture. Sometimes faces dangereous conditions to the life itself. The native will get narrowly escapes from serious danger to life and remain alive.
10. Somes times even if Jeeeva & Sareera Planets have relationship with 6/18/12 Bhavas and the Jeeva & Sareera Planets are Yoga Karaka Planets and they are in their own character and had Directional Strength.	Then the native will experience good results only.
11. If Jeeva & Sareera of Bhava or Karaka have relationship with 6/8/12 bad houses, or aspects or posited there only; and have relationship with Dasa/ Bhaukti/Antara Lords and Jeeva-Sareera Planets of 6/8/12 Bhavas.	The Native will suffer badly during the periods of Bhava Karakas.

12. Even if sometimes Jeeva-Sareera Planets are in debilitation and they are in their own character or have relationship with Karaka Planet.	Those debilitated Planets give good results only.
13. Jupiter/Mercury have relationship with Jeeva-Sareera Plaents of 9, 10, 11 Bhavas	The Native will become a highly learned & famous Astrologer OR A big Philosophical person.
14. For all Bhavas and Karaka Grahas if their Jeeva-Sareera Planets have connection to Rahu & Ketu.	Then that Native Person will lead a difficult life and will go down deeply into bad state of affairs.
15. For any Bhava/Karaka, the Jeeva-Sareera Planets are Enemy to Dasa/Bhukti, Auttkra Lords.	In case if Jeeva-Sareera Planets are in Sookshma Nakshatra Parivarthana; then no harm will happen either to the Bhava or to the Karakatwa.

4.22 IMPORTANT POINTS IN STELLAR ASTROLOGY

1. By reading Stellar Astrology, one would come to know certain hidden Secret opinions. It is all the more necessary to have full faith and carry out study of research.
2. To what extant the results could be enjoyed depends upon various factors which determine the Strength of Planets viz, whether the Planets (a) in Exaltation or (b) in Own House, or (c) in Moola Trikona position or (d) aspected by good Planets or (e) Has aspects between themselves.
3. Sometimes the planet gives adverse results, the reasons being that the Planet has no strength due to factors like (a) the Planet being in Debilitation or (b) the Planets have moved from Exaltation to Debilitation or (b) the Planet in Enemys house or (c) the Planet is sandwhiched between two bad Planets or (d) the Planet is in combustion.
4. It should also be examined based on Parasara Astrology both, the Birth Chart & the Gochara Chart as per specified rules there in viz.

   (a) The combination of Planets

   (b) The Planets are posited exactly in opposite direction

   (c) The Planets have certain aspects.

   All these factors have to be taken into consideration.
5. When the Planetary positions & combination in Birth Chart and Gochara Chart are in similar fashion, the chances of getting good results will be in the duration of the period when they are together in the same position
6. Depending upon the characters of Jeeva-Sareera Planets, the time of the expected results of the incidents, that could happen, could be examined very minutely.
7. If strength of Jeeva-Sareera Planets of Sun, 10, 11 Bhavas are strong, then the Native will attain high positions in the professional field & Career.

4.23 FRIENDLINESS/ENIMITY OF BHAVAS AND IN AUSPICIOUS STARS WHEN THESE MATERS ARE EXAMINED, THE IMPORTANT POINTS ON WHICH STRESS IS TO BE LAID ORDINARILY

1. There are many Karakatwas for each Bhava, and they will be applicable for every person in their life at some time or other. Hence the relationship between Bhava & the Karaka Planets should be carefully examined.
2. If Bhavadhipahi & Bhava Karaka Planets are possessing good strength (a) in Exaltation (b) Moola Trikona position (c) in Own House; they give good results.
3. If Bhava Lord is between two good Planets or Planets having Subha Nakshatras then that Bhava gets highly improved. This is called Subha Karathiri Yoga.
4. If Bhava Lord is in 6, 8, 12 position that Bhava will not be able to give any good results.
5. If Bhava Lord is in Vipat, Pretyak and Veedha Stars, the results of that Bhava gets reduced drastically.
6. If Bhava Lord is between two Asubha Planets then those bhavakarakatwas will become feeble.
7. If Bhava Lord is in Combustion or in Debilitation that Bhava will fully gets spoiled.
8. If Bhava Lord is positioned in Kendra & Kona, then the Karakatwa of that Bhava will get improved to very good status.
9. If Bhava Lord is well within 6 Houses from its own House, then the Karakatwas of that Bhava gets improved.
10. If any Planet is close to its Exaltation Sign, Got many Subha Vargas or in Virgothama and in conjunction with Subha Planets, then that Bhava gets improved
11. If for any Planet the points obtained are 6, 7 or 8 in Ashtakavaga, then those Bhava Karaktwas get improved.
12. If any Planet is not in the manner described in the item 10 above the Bhava gets harmed. Meaning that if the Planet joins two Asubha Planets or gets aspected by them.
13. If Bhava is between two good planets (Subha) or both in the same state of Bhava, then the Bhava gets improved. If not or has an asubha planets posited in that bhava or a bhava is between two ashubha planets or aspected by that or located between two Papa grahas, then that Bhava gets spoiled.

4.24 OTHER MATTERS

1. **Rasis:** Karakatwas, Professions, Rays, Difference between past, present & future characters, Genders-Heights blind, cripple, lame. Ojha, Yugama, Dhatu, Moola, Division, Moola Trikonas.
2. **Planets:** Karakatwas Friendships and Enemies-Bhavas. Strength of Planets who are Lords of 2 Bhavas. Exaltation Debilitation, Metals, Subhas, Asubhas, Sons, Bhava – factors and the results given by Star Lords divisions based on profession, Paksha

balam, places of worship, Cerels, Characters, aspects, sepcieal aspect, Dancers, Devatas, vehicals, directions, Nava Ratna's.

3. Their Lords, Devatas, color, qualities, ruling direction, body parts, places of dwelling characters, clock wise or anticlockwise, friends Enemies. Their Gender, Yogas, Characters of those born in Stars Chart, Taras.

For the the subjects under the three categories momentioned above detailed explanations are given by Dr. N.V.R.A. Raja in the text of Jeeva-Sareera and these may be perused.

4.25 DIVISION OF KALAAMSA GUNA

It is very important to know the strength of Bhavas and Plants as per Meena 2 method. This method is based on rules laid down in Dhrura Naadi, Budha Naadi and Sugar Peru Naadi and detailed description and explanation is given as under for the subjects dealt below such as:-

1. Kalaamsa (Sub-Lord Theory) & its Characters
2. Jeeva-Sareera Planets
3. Directional Strength of Bhava/Karaka

If Kalaamsa Lord is his own Character, the results are given immediately. If Kalaamsa Lord is in Satwika Character, the results will be soft and are acceptable Sometimes if he has the character of Tamasika/Tamasika/Tamsika; Bhava results will be alright but the Native becomes greedy and even if the has exerted he remains in a state of stress mentally all the time.

Here what is meant by Kalaamsa is explained. In the Birth Chart obtained from Computer the Lagna and 9 Planets its Rasi position with Degrees Minutes are known. In the same table, Rasi Lord Nakshatra Lord, Sub-Lord and sub-lord are given. In that the Sub-Lord is called as Kalaamsa.

One Rasi is of 30° Angular time. One Star covers in 13°-20′. In this the sub-lord Angle is obtained by multiplying the Dasa period and Divided by 120. This is sub-lord's measurement.

4.26 SUB DIVISIONS OF KALAAMSA OR SUB-LORD

In the year 1950, both Meena-1 and Meena-2 had thought of further sub-divisions of Sub-Lord of each Star. They found out that such Sub-divisions of AMSA is giving good results. In Parasara text for any individual Horoscope, the Lagna and 9 planets are given with their Longitudes. Then they decided the Planet results based on its Longitude.

But in Stellar Astrology certain modification is made. In this method, they had introduced the Sub-Lord. The duration of a star is 13°-20′ and the Division of sub-lord was found out to be as per the period of Dasa. The total period of all the Planets is 120 years. In this every Planet has its own period. The measurement of sub-lord is based on its Dasa lord. In this manner the duration of sub-lord for each Dasa was decided.

A table is given in pages 86 to 92. In this right from Aries Rasi to Meena Rasi for all the Rasi-Lords, Star Lords Sub-Lords or Kalaamsas the extent of duration has been shown. The Table gives clearly how the Kalaamsa Sub-Division is made.

Kalaamsa or Sub-Table

Rasi	Sign	From (Deg/min/sec)	To (Deg/min/sec)	Duration	Sign Lord	Star Lord	Kalaamsa Sub Lord
Mesha	Arise	00°00′00″	00°46′40″	00°46′40″	Mars	Ketu	Ketu
Mesha	Arise	00°46′40″	03°00′00″	02°13′20″	Mars	Ketu	Venus
Mesha	Arise	03°00′00″	03°40′00″	00°40′00″	Mars	Ketu	Sun
Mesha	Arise	03°40′00″	04°46′40″	01°06′40″	Mars	Ketu	Moon
Mesha	Arise	04°46′40″	05°33′20″	00°46′40″	Mars	Ketu	Mars
Mesha	Arise	05°33′20″	07°33′20″	02°00′00″	Mars	Ketu	rahu
Mesha	Arise	07°33′20″	09°20′00″	01°46′40″	Mars	Ketu	Jupiter
Mesha	Arise	09°20′00″	11°26′40″	02°06′40″	Mars	Ketu	Saturn
Mesha	Arise	11°26′40″	13°20′00″	01°53′20″	Mars	Ketu	Mercury
Mesha	Arise	13°20′00″	15°33′20″	02°13′20″	Mars	Venus	Venus
Mesha	Arise	15°33′20″	16°13′20″	00°40′00″	Mars	Venus	Sun
Mesha	Arise	16°13′20″	17°20′00″	01°06′40″	Mars	Venus	Moon
Mesha	Arise	17°20′00″	18°06′40″	00°46′40″	Mars	Venus	Mars
Mesha	Arise	18°06′40″	20°06′40″	02°00′00″	Mars	Venus	Rahu
Mesha	Arise	20°06′40″	21°53′20″	01°46′40″	Mars	Venus	Jupiter
Mesha	Arise	21°53′20″	24°00′00″	02°06′40″	Mars	Venus	Saturn
Mesha	Arise	24°00′00″	25°53′20″	01°53′20″	Mars	Venus	Mercury
Mesha	Arise	25°53′20″	26°40′00″	00°46′40″	Mars	Venus	Ketu
Mesha	Arise	26°40′00″	27°20′00″	00°40′00″	Mars	Sun	Sun
Mesha	Arise	27°20′00″	28°26′40″	01°06′40″	Mars	Sun	Moon
Mesha	Arise	28°26′40″	29°13′20″	00°46′40″	Mars	Sun	Mars
Mesha	Arise	29°13′20″	30°00′00″	02°00′00″	Mars	Sun	Rahu
Rishabha	Taurus	00°00′00″	01°13′20″	02°00′00″	Venus	Sun	Rahu
Rishabha	Taurus	01°13′20″	03°00′00″	01°46′40″	Venus	Sun	Jupiter
Rishabha	Taurus	03°00′00″	05°06′40″	02°06′40″	Venus	Sun	Saturn
Rishabha	Taurus	05°06′40″	07°00′00″	01°53′20″	Venus	Sun	Mercury
Rishabha	Taurus	07°00′00″	07°46′40″	00°46′40″	Venus	Sun	Ketu
Rishabha	Taurus	07°46′40″	10°00′00″	02°13′20″	Venus	Sun	Venus
Rishabha	Taurus	10°00′00″	11°06′40″	01°06′40″	Venus	Moon	Moon
Rishabha	Taurus	11°06′40″	11°53′20″	00°46′40″	Vensu	Moon	Mars
Rishabha	Taurus	11°53′20″	13°53′20″	02°00′00″	Venus	Moon	Tahu
Rishabha	Taurus	13°53′20″	15°40′00″	01°46′40″	Venus	Moon	Jupiter
Rishabha	Taurus	15°40′00″	17°46′40″	02°06′40″	Venus	Moon	Saturn
Rishabha	Taurus	17°46′40″	19°40′00″	01°53′20″	Venus	Moon	Mercury
Rishabha	Taurus	19°40′00″	20°24′40″	00°46′40″	Venus	Moon	Ketu
Rishabha	Taurus	20°26′40″	22°40′00″	02°13′20″	Venus	Moon	Venus
Rishabha	Taurus	22°40′00″	23°20′00″	00°40′00″	Venus	Moon	Sun

Rasi	Sign	From (Deg/min/sec)	To (Deg/min/sec)	Duration	Sign Lord	Star Lord	Kalaamsa Sub Lord
Rishabha	Taurus	23°20'00"	24°06'40"	00°46'40"	Venus	Mars	Mars
Rishabha	Taurus	24°06'40"	26°06'40"	02°00'00"	Venus	Mars	Rahu
Rishabha	Taurus	26°06'40"	27°53'20"	01°46'40"	Vensu	Mars	Jupiter
Rishabha	Taurus	27°53'20"	30°00'00"	02°06'40"	Venus	Mars	Saturn
Mithuna	Gemini	00°00'00"	01°53'20"	01°53'20"	Mercury	Mars	Mercury
Mithuna	Gemini	01°53'20"	02°40'00"	00°46'40"	Mercury	Mars	Ketu
Mithuna	Gemini	02°40'00"	04°53'20"	02°13'20"	Mercury	Mars	Venus
Mithuna	Gemini	04°53'20"	05°33'20"	00°40'00"	Mercury	Mars	Sun
Mithuna	Gemini	05°33'20"	06°40'00"	01°06'40"	Mercury	Mars	Moon
Mithuna	Gemini	06°40'00"	08°40'00"	02°00'00"	Mercury	Rahu	Rahu
Mithuna	Gemini	08°40'00"	10°26'40"	01°46'40"	Mercury	Rahu	Jupiter
Mithuna	Gemini	10°26'40"	12°33'20"	02°06'40"	Mercury	Rahu	Saturn
Mithuna	Gemini	12°33'20"	14°26'40"	01°53'20"	Mercury	Rahu	Mercury
Mithuna	Gemini	14°26'40"	15°13'20"	00°46'40"	Mercury	Rahu	Ketu
Mithuna	Gemini	15°13'20"	17°26'40"	02°13'20"	Mercury	Rahu	Venus
Mithuna	Gemini	17°26'40"	18°06'40"	00°40'00"	Mercury	Rahu	Sun
Mithuna	Gemini	18°06'40"	19°13'20"	01°06'40"	Mercury	Rahu	Moon
Mithuna	Gemini	19°13'20"	20°00'00"	00°46'40"	Mercury	Rahu	Mars
Mithuna	Gemini	20°00'00"	21°46'40"	01°46'40"	Mercury	Jupiter	Jupiter
Mithuna	Gemini	21°46'40"	23°53'20"	02°06'40"	Mercury	Jupiter	Saturn
Mithuna	Gemini	23°53'20"	25°46'40"	01°53'20"	Mercury	Jupiter	Mercury
Mithuna	Gemini	25°46'40"	26°33'20"	00°46'40"	Mercury	Jupiter	Ketu
Mithuna	Gemini	26°33'20"	28°46'40"	02°13'20"	Mercury	Jupiter	Venus
Mithuna	Gemini	28°46'40"	29°26'40"	00°40'00"	Mercury	Jupiter	Sun
Mithuna	Gemini	29°26'40"	30°00'00"	01°06'40"	Mercury	Jupiter	Moon
Karkataka	Cancer	00°00'00"	00°33'20"	01°06'40"	Moon	Jupiter	Moon
Karkataka	Cancer	00°33'20"	01°20'00"	00°46'40"	Moon	Jupiter	Mars
Karkataka	Cancer	01°20'00"	03°20'00"	02°00'00"	Moon	Jupiter	Rahu
Karkataka	Cancer	03°20'00"	05°26'40"	02°06'40"	Moon	Saturn	Saturn
Karkataka	Cancer	05°26'40"	07°20'00"	01°53'20"	Moon	Saturn	Mercury
Karkataka	Cancer	07°20'00"	08°06'40"	00°46'40"	Moon	Saturn	Ketu
Karkataka	Cancer	08°06'40"	10°20'00"	02°13'20"	Moon	Saturn	Venus
Karkataka	Cancer	10°20'00"	11°00'00"	00°40'00"	Moon	Saturn	Sun
Karkataka	Cancer	11°00'00"	12°06'40"	01°05'40"	Moon	Saturn	Moon
Karkataka	Cancer	12°06'40"	12°53'20"	00°46'40"	Moon	Saturn	Mass
Karkataka	Cancer	12°53'20"	14°53'20"	02°00'00"	Moon	Saturn	Rahu
Karkataka	Cancer	14°53'20"	16°40'00"	01°46'40"	Moon	Saturn	Jupiter
Karkataka	Cancer	16°40'00"	18°33'20"	01°53'20"	Moon	Mercury	Mercury

Rasi	Sign	From (Deg/min/sec)	To (Deg/min/sec)	Duration	Sign Lord	Star Lord	Kalaamsa Sub Lord
Karkataka	Cancer	18°33′20″	19°20′00″	00°46′40″	Moon	Mercury	Ketu
Karkataka	Cancer	19°20′00″	21°33′20″	02°13′20″	Moon	Mercury	Venus
Karkataka	Cancer	21°33′20″	22°13′20″	00°40′00″	Moon	Mercury	Sun
Karkataka	Cancer	22°13′20″	23°20′00″	01°06′40″	Moon	Mercury	Moon
Karkataka	Cancer	23°20′00″	24°06′40″	00°46′40″	Moon	Mercury	Mars
Karkataka	Cancer	24°06′40″	26°06′40″	02°00′00″	Moon	Mercury	Rahu
Karkataka	Cancer	26°06′40″	27°53′20″	01°46′40″	Moon	Mercury	Jupiter
Karkataka	Cancer	27°53′20″	30°00′00″	01°06′40″	Moon	Mercury	Saturn
Simha	Leo	00°00′00″	00°46′40″	00°46°40″	Sun	Ketu	Ketu
Simha	Leo	00°46′40″	03°00′00″	02°13′20″	Sun	Ketu	Venus
Simha	Leo	03°00′00″	03°40′00″	00°40′00″	Sun	Ketu	Sun
Simha	Leo	03°40′00″	04°46′40″	01°06′40″	Sun	Ketu	Moon
Simha	Leo	04°46′40″	05°33′20″	00°46′40″	Sun	Ketu	mars
Simha	Leo	05°33′20″	07°33′20″	02°00′00″	Sun	Ketu	Rahu
Simha	Leo	07°33′20″	09°20′00″	01°46′40″	Sun	Ketu	Jupiter
Simha	Leo	09°20′00″	11°26′40″	02°06′40″	Sun	Ketu	Saturn
Simha	Leo	11°26′40″	13°20′00″	01°53′20″	Sun	Ketu	Mercury
Simha	Leo	13°20′00″	15°33′20″	02°13′20″	Sun	Venus	Venus
Simha	Leo	15°33′20″	16°13′20″	00°40′00″	Sun	Venus	Sun
Simha	Leo	16°13′20″	17°20′00″	01°06′40″	Sun	Venus	Moon
Simha	Leo	17°20′00″	18°06′40″	00°46′40″	Sun	Venus	Mars
Simha	Leo	18°06°40″	20°06′40″	02°00′00″	Sun	Venus	Rahu
Simha	Leo	20°06′40″	21°53′20″	01°46′40″	Sun	Venus	Jupiter
Simha	Leo	21°53′20″	24°00′00″	02°06′40″	Sun	Venus	Saturn
Simha	Leo	24°00′00″	25°53′20″	01°53′20″	Sun	Venus	Mercury
Simha	Leo	25°53′20″	26°40′00″	00°46′40″	Sun	Venus	Ketu
Simha	Leo	26°40′00″	27°20′00″	00°40′00″	Sun	Sun	Sun
Simha	Leo	27°20′00″	28°26′40″	01°06′40″	Sun	Sun	Moon
Simha	Leo	28°26′40″	29°13′20″	00°46′40″	Sun	Sun	Mars
Simha	Leo	29°13′20″	30°00′00″	02°00′00″	Sun	Sun	Rahu
Kanya	Virgo	00°00′00″	01°13′20″	02°00′00″	Mercury	Sun	Rahu
Kanya	Virgo	01°13′20″	03°00′00″	01°46′40″	Mercury	Sun	Jupiter
Kanya	Virgo	03°00′00″	05°06′40″	02°06′40″	Mercury	Sun	Saturn
Kanya	Virgo	05°06′40″	07°00′00″	01°53′20″	Mercury	Sun	Mercury
Kanya	Virgo	07°00′00″	07°46′40″	00°46′40″	Mercury	Sun	Ketu
Kanya	Virgo	07°46′40″	10°00′00″	02°13′20″	Mercury	Sun	Venus
Kanya	Virgo	10°00′00″	11°06′40″	01°06′40″	Mercury	Moon	Moon
Kanya	Virgo	11°06′40″	11°53′20″	00°46′40″	Mercury	Moon	Mars

Rasi	Sign	From (Deg/min/sec)	To (Deg/min/sec)	Duration	Sign Lord	Star Lord	Kalaamsa Sub Lord
Kanya	Virgo	11°53′20″	13°53′20″	02°00′00″	Mercury	Moon	Rahu
Kanya	Virgo	13°53′20″	15°40′00″	01°46′40″	Mercury	Moon	Jupiter
Kanya	Virgo	15°40′00″	17°46′40″	02°06′40″	Mercury	Moon	Saturn
Kanya	Virgo	17°46′40″	19°40′00″	01°53′20″	Mercury	Moon	Mercury
Kanya	Virgo	19°40′00″	20°26′40″	00°46′40″	Mercury	Moon	Ketu
Kanya	Virgo	20°26′40″	22°40′00″	02°13′20″	Mercury	Moon	Venus
Kanya	Virgo	22°40′00″	23°20′00″	00°40′00″	Mercury	Moon	Sun
Kanya	Virgo	23°20′00″	24°06′40″	00°46′40″	Mercury	Mars	Mars
Kanya	Virgo	24°06′40″	26°06′40″	02°00′00″	Mercury	Mars	Rahu
Kanya	Virgo	26°06′40″	27°53′20″	01°46′40″	Mercury	Mars	Jupiter
Kanya	Virgo	27°53′20″	30°00′00″	02°06′40″	Mercury	Mars	Saturn
Thula	Libra	00°00′00″	01°53′20″	01°53′20″	Venus	Mars	Mercury
Thula	Libra	01°53′20″	02°40′00″	00°46′40″	Venus	Mars	Ketu
Thula	Libra	02°40′00″	04°53′20″	02°13′20″	Venus	Mars	Venus
Thula	Libra	04°53′20″	05°33′20″	00°40′00″	Venus	Mars	Sun
Thula	Libra	05°33′20″	06°40′00″	01°06′40″	Venus	Mars	Moon
Thula	Libra	06°40′00″	08°40′00″	02°00′00	Venus	Rahu	Rahu
Thula	Libra	08°40′00″	10°26′40″	01°46′40″	Venus	Rahu	Jupiter
Thula	Libra	10°26′40″	12°33′20″	02°60′40″	Venus	Rahu	Saturn
Thula	Libra	12°33′20″	14°26′40″	01°53′20″	Venus	Rahu	Mercury
Thula	Libra	14°26′40″	15°13′20″	00°46′40″	Venus	Rahu	Ketu
Thula	Libra	15°13′20″	17°26′40″	02°13′20″	Venus	Rahu	Venus
Thula	Libra	17°26′40″	18°06′40″	00°40′00″	Venus	Rahu	Sun
Thula	Libra	18°06′40″	19°13′20″	01°06′40″	Venus	Rahu	Moon
Thula	Libra	19°13′20″	20°00′00″	00°46′40″	Venus	Rahu	Mars
Thula	Libra	20°00′00″	21°46′40″	01°46′40″	Venus	Jupiter	Jupiter
Thula	Libra	21°46′40″	23°53′20″	02°06′40″	Venus	Jupiter	Saturn
Thula	Libra	23°53′20″	25°46′40″	01°53′20″	Venus	Jupiter	Mercury
Thula	Libra	25°46′40″	26°33′20″	00°46′40″	Venus	Jupiter	ketu
Thula	Libra	26°30′20″	28°46′40″	02°13′20″	Venus	Jupiter	Venus
Thula	Libra	28°46′40″	29°26′40″	00°40′00″	Venus	Jupiter	Sun
Thula	Libra	29°26′40″	30°00′00″	01°06′40″	Venus	Jupiter	Moon
Vrichika	Scorpio	00°00′00″	00°33′20″	04°06′40″	Mars	Jupiter	Moon
Vrichika	Scorpio	00°33′20″	01°20′00″	00°46′40″	Mars	Jupiter	Mars
Vrichika	Scorpio	01°20′00″	03°20′00″	02°00′00″	Mars	Jupiter	rahu
Vrichika	Scorpio	03°20′00″	05°26′40″	02°06′40″	Mars	Saturn	Saturn
Vrichika	Scorpio	05°26′40″	07°20′00″	01°53′20″	Mars	Saturn	Mercury
Vrichika	Scorpio	07°20′00″	08°06′40″	00°46′40″	Mars	Saturn	Ketu

Rasi	Sign	From (Deg/min/sec)	To (Deg/min/sec)	Duration	Sign Lord	Star Lord	Kalaamsa Sub Lord
Vrichika	Scorpio	08°06′40″	10°20′00″	02°13′20″	Mars	Saturn	Venus
Vrichika	Scorpio	10°20′00″	11°00′00″	00°40′00″	Mars	Saturn	Sun
Vrichika	Scorpio	11°00′00″	12°06′40″	01°06′40″	Mars	Saturn	Moon
Vrichika	Scorpio	12°06′40″	12°53′20°	00°46′40″	Mars	Saturn	Mars
Vrichika	Scorpio	12°53′20″	14°53′20″	02°00′00″	Mars	Saturn	rahu
Vrichika	Scorpio	14°53′20″	16°40′00″	01°46′40″	Mars	Saturn	Jupiter
Vrichika	Scorpio	16°40′00″	18°33′20″	01°53′20″	Mars	Mercury	Mercury
Vrichika	Scorpio	18°33′20″	19°20′00″	00°46′40″	Mars	Mercury	ketu
Vrichika	Scorpio	19°20′00″	21°33′20″	02°13′20″	Mars	Mercury	Venus
Vrichika	Scorpio	21°33′20″	22°13′20″	00°40′00″	Mars	Mercury	Sun
Vrichika	Scorpio	22°13′20″	23°20′00″	01°06′40″	Mars	Mercury	Moon
Vrichika	Scorpio	23°20′00″	24°06′40″	00°46′40″	Mars	Mercury	Mars
Vrichika	Scorpio	24°06′40″	26°06′40″	02°00′00″	Mars	Mercury	Rahu
Vrichika	Scorpio	26°06′40″	27°53′20″	01°46′40″	Mars	Mercury	Jupiter
Vrichika	Scorpio	27°53′20″	30°00′00″	02°06′40″	Mars	Mercury	Saturn
Dhanus	Sagittarisu	00°00′00″	00°46′40″	00°46′40″	Jupiter	Ketu	Ketu
Dhanus	Sagittarisu	00°46′40″	03°00′00″	02°13′20″	Jupiter	Ketu	Venus
Dhanus	Sagittarisu	03°00′00″	03°40′00″	00°40′00″	Jupiter	Ketu	Sun
Dhanus	Sagittarisu	03°40′00″	04°46′40″	01°06′40″	Jupiter	Ketu	Moon
Dhanus	Sagittarisu	04°46′40″	05°33′20″	00°46′40″	Jupiter	Ketu	Mars
Dhanus	Sagittarisu	05°33′20″	07°33′20″	02°00′00″	Jupiter	Ketu	Rahu
Dhanus	Sagittarisu	07°33′20″	09°20′00″	01°46′40″	Jupiter	Ketu	Jupiter
Dhanus	Sagittarisu	09°20′00″	11°26′40″	02°06′40″	Jupiter	Ketu	Saturn
Dhanus	Sagittarisu	11°26′40″	13°20′00″	01°53′20″	Jupiter	Ketu	Mercury
Dhanus	Sagittarisu	13°20′00″	15°33′20″	02°13′20″	Jupiter	Venus	Venus
Dhanus	Sagittarisu	15°33′20″	16°13′20″	00°40′00″	Jupiter	Venus	Sun
Dhanus	Sagittarisu	16°13′20″	17°20′00″	01°06′40″	Jupiter	Venus	Moon
Dhanus	Sagittarisu	17°20′00″	18°06′40″	00°46′40″	Jupiter	Venus	Mars
Dhanus	Sagittarisu	18°06′40″	20°06′40″	02°00′00″	Jupiter	Venus	Rahu
Dhanus	Sagittarisu	20°06′40″	21°53′20″	01°46′40″	Jupiter	Venus	Jupiter
Dhanus	Sagittarisu	21°53′20″	24°00′00″	02°06′40″	Jupiter	Venus	Saturn
Dhanus	Sagittarisu	24°00′00″	25°53′20″	01°53′20″	Jupiter	Venus	Mercury
Dhanus	Sagittarisu	25°53′20″	26°40′00″	00°46′40″	Jupiter	Venus	Ketu
Dhanus	Sagittarisu	26°40′00″	27°20′00″	00°40′00″	Jupiter	Sun	Sun
Dhanus	Sagittarisu	27°20′00″	28°26′40″	01°06′40″	Jupiter	Sun	Moon
Dhanus	Sagittarisu	28°46′40″	29°13′20″	00°46′40″	Jupiter	Sun	Mars
Dhanus	Sagittarisu	29°13′20″	30°00′00″	02°00′00″	Jupiter	Sun	Rahu
Makara	Capricorn	00°00′00″	01°13′20″	02°00′00″	Saturn	Sun	Rahu

Rasi	Sign	From (Deg/min/sec)	To (Deg/min/sec)	Duration	Sign Lord	Star Lord	Kalaamsa Sub Lord
Makara	Capricorn	01°13′20″	03°00′00″	01°46′40″	Saturn	Sun	Jupiter
Makara	Capricorn	03°00′00″	05°06′40″	02°06′40″	Saturn	Sun	Saturn
Makara	Capricorn	05°06′40″	07°00′00″	01°53′20″	Saturn	Sun	Mercury
Makara	Capricorn	07°00′00″	07°46′40″	00°46′40″	Saturn	Sun	Ketu
Makara	Capricorn	07°46′40″	10°00′00″	02°13′20″	Saturn	Sun	Venus
Makara	Capricorn	10°00′00″	11°06′40″	01°06′40″	Saturn	Moon	Moon
Makara	Capricorn	11°06′40″	11°53′20″	00°46′40″	Saturn	Moon	Mars
Makara	Capricorn	11°53′20″	13°53′20″	02°00′00″	Saturn	Moon	Rahu
Makara	Capricorn	13°53′20″	15°40′00″	01°46′40″	Saturn	Moon	Jupiter
Makara	Capricorn	15°40′00″	17°46′40″	02°06′40″	Saturn	Moon	Saturn
Makara	Capricorn	17°46′40″	19°40′00″	01°53′20″	Saturn	Moon	Mercury
Makara	Capricorn	19°40′00″	20°26′40″	00°46′40″	Saturn	Moon	ketu
Makara	Capricorn	20°26′40″	22°40′00″	02°13′20″	Saturn	Moon	Venus
Makara	Capricorn	22°40′00″	23°20′00″	00°40′00″	Saturn	Moon	Sun
Makara	Capricorn	23°20′00″	24°06′40″	00°46′40″	Saturn	Mars	mars
Makara	Capricorn	24°06′40″	26°06′40″	02°00′00″	Saturn	Mars	Rahu
Makara	Capricorn	26°06′40″	27°53′20″	01°46′40″	Saturn	Mars	Jupiter
Makara	Capricorn	27°53′20″	30°00′00″	02°06′40″	Saturn	Mars	Saturn
Kumbha	Aquarius	00°00′00″	01°53′20″	01°53′20″	Saturn	Mars	Mercury
Kumbha	Aquarius	01°53′20″	02°40′00″	00°46′40″	Saturn	Mars	Ketu
Kumbha	Aquarius	02°40′00″	04°53′20″	02°13′20″	Saturn	Mars	Venus
Kumbha	Aquarius	04°53′20″	05°33′20″	00°40′00″	Saturn	Mars	Sun
Kumbha	Aquarius	05°33′20″	06°40′20″	01°06′40″	Saturn	Mars	Moon
Kumbha	Aquarius	06°40′20″	08°40′00″	02°00′00″	Saturn	Rahu	Rahu
Kumbha	Aquarius	08°40′00″	10°26′40″	01°46′40″	Saturn	Rahu	Jupiter
Kumbha	Aquarius	10°26′40″	12°33′20″	02°06′40″	Saturn	Rahu	Satun
Kumbha	Aquarius	12°33′20″	14°26′40″	01°53′20″	Saturn	Rahu	Mercury
Kumbha	Aquarius	14°26′40″	15°13′20″	00°46′40″	Saturn	Rahu	ketu
Kumbha	Aquarius	15°13′20″	17°26′40″	02°13′20″	Saturn	Rahu	Venus
Kumbha	Aquarius	17°26′40″	18°06′40″	00°40′00″	Saturn	Rahu	Sun
Kumbha	Aquarius	18°06′40″	19°13′20″	01°06′40″	Saturn	Rahu	Moon
Kumbha	Aquarius	19°13′20″	20°00′00″	00°46′40″	Saturn	Rahu	Mars
Kumbha	Aquarius	20°00′00″	21°46′40″	01°46′40″	Saturn	Jupiter	Jupiter
Kumbha	Aquarius	21°46′40″	23°53′20″	02°06′40″	Saturn	Jupiter	Saturn
Kumbha	Aquarius	23°53′20″	25°46′40″	01°53′20″	Saturn	Jupiter	Mercury
Kumbha	Aquarius	25°46′40″	26°33′20″	00°46′40″	Saturn	Jupiter	Ketu
Kumbha	Aquarius	26°33′20″	28°46′40″	02°13′20″	Saturn	Jupiter	Venus
Kumbha	Aquarius	28°46′40″	29°26′40″	00°40′00″	Saturn	Jupiter	Sun

Rasi	Sign	From (Deg/min/sec)	To (Deg/min/sec)	Duration	Sign Lord	Star Lord	Kalaamsa Sub Lord
Kumbha	Aquarius	29°26'40"	30°00'00"	01°06'40"	Saturn	Jupiter	Moon
Meena	Pisces	00°00'00"	00°33'20"	01°06'40"	Jupiter	Jupiter	Moon
Meena	Pisces	00°33'20"	01°22'00"	00°46'40"	Jupiter	Jupiter	Mars
Meena	Pisces	01°20'00"	03°20'00"	02°00'00"	Jupiter	Jupiter	Rahu
Meena	Pisces	03°20'00"	05°26'40"	02°06'40"	Jupiter	Jupiter	Saturn
Meena	Pisces	05°26'40"	07°20'00"	01°53'20"	Jupiter	Saturn	Mercury
Meena	Pisces	07°20'00"	08°06'40"	00°46'40"	Jupiter	Saturn	Ketu
Meena	Pisces	08°06'40"	10°20'00"	02°13'20"	Jupiter	Saturn	Venus
Meena	Pisces	10°20'00"	11°00'00"	00°40'00"	Jupiter	Saturn	Sun
Meena	Pisces	11°00'00"	12°06'40"	01°06'40"	Jupiter	Saturn	Moon
Meena	Pisces	12°06'40"	12°53'20"	00°46'40"	Jupiter	Saturn	Mars
Meena	Pisces	12°53'20"	14°53'20"	02°00'00"	Jupiter	Saturn	Rahu
Meena	Pisces	14°53'20"	16°40'00"	01°46'40"	Jupiter	Saturn	Jupiter
Meena	Pisces	16°40'00"	18°33'20"	01°53'20"	Jupiter	Mercury	Mercury
Meena	Pisces	18°33'20"	19°20'00"	00°46'40"	Jupiter	Mercury	Ketu
Meena	Pisces	19°20'00"	21°33'20"	02°13'20"	Jupiter	Mercury	Venus
Meena	Pisces	21°33'20"	22°13'20"	00°40'00"	Jupiter	Mercury	Sun
Meena	Pisces	22°13'20"	23°20'00"	01°06'40"	Jupiter	Mercury	Moon
Meena	Pisces	23°20'00"	24°06'40"	00°46'40"	Jupiter	Mercury	Mars
Meena	Pisces	24°06'40"	26°06'40"	02°00'00"	Jupiter	Mercury	Rahu
Meena	Pisces	26°06'40"	275320	014640	Jupiter	Mercury	Jupiter
Meena	Pisces	27°53'20"	30°00'00"	02°06'40"	Jupiter	Mercury	Saturn

4.27 DETAILS OF KALAAMSA SUB-DIVISION

The meaning of Kalaamsa is defined as under:-

One Nakshatra Pada occupies an angle of 3°-20′. Total angle of four Padas is equal to 13°-20′. This is the extant of one Nakshatra, there are 27 stars × 4 Padas = 108 padas. These 108 Padas make 360° one full Elipse.

In Predictive Astrology, even in a Pada different angular positions, give various results. All 27 stars were made into 9 groups each group consist of 3 stars at 120° apart. Hence one star duration of 13°-20′ is divided by 120. Then that figure is multiplied by the number of years of Vimshomari Dasa of the Planets total duration.

Then that value of the angle is called that Planet's Kalaamsa Division. For 27 stars lined upto 9 Vimshomari Dasas will give a total of 243. For Rahu & Moon 6 more Kalaamsa are added, then the ground total of 249 Kalaamsa Divisions will come.

Rahu's parts Kalaamsas (from Sun's Star)

Between Aries & Taurus – 1

Between Leo & Kanya – 1

Between Dahnus & Makaram – 1

Moon's part Kalaamsaa (From Jupiter star)

Between Midhunam & Karkatakam – 1

Between Tula & Vruchikam – 1

Between Kumbham & Meenam – 1

The extent of these parts of Rahu &Moon's Kalaamsa have been shown in the Table 4.27 at proper palces.

4.28 UTTAMA DREKKANA RESULTS OR STARS

In Stellar Astrology if the Planet's Star Lords strength has any relation to Ascendant or 10th Bhava, then such a Native will be helped to reach highest status in the life.

Every 10° angular measurement is called one Drekkana. If for every Rasi three Drekkanas are made. Then for all 12 Rasis 36 Drekkanas will come. Since three are 9 Star Padas, for each Drekkana we get 3 Nakshatra Padas. Out of 3 Drekkanas in a Rasi, only one Drekkana is called Uttama Drekkana. These are detailed as under.

1. **In Chara Rasis:** The first one is Uttama Drekkana
2. **In Sthira Rasis:** The second one is Uttama Drekkana
3. **In Dwiswabhava Rasis:** The third one is Uttama Drekkana

In the above Drekkanas, the Pada is called Virgottama Pada Drekkana, and the remaining two Padas are called Parivarthana Pada Drekkanas.

The following table gives the Virgottama Pada & Parivarthana Padas for all the 12 Rasis

Table: Vargothama & Parivarthana Padas

S. No.	Rasi/Sign	Vargothama pada	Parivarthana Padas
1.	Mesha/Aries	Aswini 1	Aswini 2nd & 3rd
2.	Rishaba/Taurus	Rohini 2	Rohini 1st and 3rd
3.	Mithuna/Gemini	Punarvasu 3	Punarvasu 1st and 2nd
4.	Karkataka/Cancer	Punarvasu 4	Pushyami 1st and 2nd
5.	Simba/Leo	Pubba 1	Magha 4th and Pubba 2nd
6.	Kanya/Virgo	Chitha 2	Hastha 4th Chitha 1
7.	Thula/Libra	Chitha 3	Chitha 4th and Swati 1
8.	Vrichika/Scorpio	Anuradha 4	Anuradha 3rd and Jesta 1
9.	Dhanus/Sagittarisu	Uthiradam 1	Pooradam 3rd and Pooradam 4th
10.	Makara/Capricorn	Uthiradam 2	Uthiradam 3rd and Uthiradam 4th
11.	Kumbha/Aquarius	Sadabisha 3	Sadabisha 2nd and Sadabisha 4th
12.	Meena/Pisces	Revati 4	Revati 2an and Revati 3rd

4.29 KALAAMSA GUNA-PREDICTIVE RULES WERE LAID BASED ON THESE FACTORS

Rule 1: If Kalaamsa Lord gets good character (Para 4.8) then its Jeeva & Sareera Plaents are posited in Konas (1, 5, 9 Houses) then Kalaamsa Lord give wonderfull results during his Dasa Bhukthi/Anthara periods.

When Jeeva & Sareera has relation during Gochara, then it could be confirmed that the right time has come for beneficial results to get fructified and the Native enjoys the results during that time.

Rule 2: If Kalaamsa Lord gets Directional Strength (para 4.17) and is in conjunction with a Yoga Karaka Planet; then during the period of Dasa/Bhukti/Antara of Kalaamsa Lord, Native gets good results.

Rule 3: If Kalaamsa Lord did not get good Character and Jeeva & Sareera Planets are reported to be posited in 6/8/12 Houses, then during Dasa/Bhukthi/Anthara periods the native will have to be very carefull in all his matters.

Rule 4: If a Bhava or Karaka Planet is to give good results then strength of the Planets Jeeva & Sareera of Kalaamsa Lord should be carefully examined based on its position in Birth Chart & also in Gochara Chart. At this time it should be foundout by carefull examination whether the Birth Chart is in order or not.

4.30 THREE VARIETIES OF CHARACTERS FOR PLANETS & STARS

1. In order to know the results for a Bhava or Karaka Planets the theory of Jeeva & Sareera and Kalaamsa & Guna has to be made applicable to Kalaamsa Planet.
2. If for a Bhava the Planet Jeeva & Sareera are in good positions, the Bhava gives good results provided the Character obtained for Kalaamsa Planet and the Character obtained for Bhava Lord should be in consonance with each other.
3. If the Kalaamsa Planet for a Bhava got Satwika Character and that Planet first got Rajasika or Tamasika character the results of that Bhava will be soft.
4. If Kalaamsa Planet got mixed Character the results will be mixed. Character will be in 3 varietys first the Character of Planet in Rasi, second the Character of the Planet Star Lord and third will be the Character of the (Sub Lord) Kalaamsa.

   That is the reason why the Kalaamsa Guna is depicted in the short from by showing the alphabet of the three Characters in order as under

   Satwika – 'S' Alphabet

   Rajasika – 'R' Alphabet

   Tamasika – 'T' Alphabet

For every Planet – Star wise Pada wise – the three are shown in the Table below.

Table: Planets Stars 3 Varietys of Characters

Planet	Padas/Stars	Aswini	Bharant	Kertika	Rohini	Murgasira	Ardra	Punarvasu	Pushtama	Aslesha	Makha	Pubba	Uttara-phalguni	Hastha
Sun	1	TRT	RSR	RRS	RRT	TSR	TRS	SRT	TSR	SRS	TRT	RSR	RRS	RRT
	2	RSR	RTS	RRT	RSR	TTS	TRT	SSR	TTS	SRT	TSR	RTS	RRT	RSS
	3	TSS	RTR	RRT	RSS	TTR	TRT	SSS	TTR	SRT	TSS	RTR	RRT	RSR
	4	TSR	RRT	RRS	RSR	TRT	TRS	SSR	TRT	SRS	TSR	RRT	RRS	RST
Moon	1	RTR	RTR	RRS	RRT	TTR	TRS	SRT	TTR	SRS	TRT	RTR	RRS	RRR
	2	TRR	RTS	RRT	RRR	TTS	TRT	SRR	TTS	SRT	TRR	RTS	RRT	RRS
	3	TSS	RTR	RRT	RSS	TTR	TRT	SSS	TTR	SRT	TSS	RTR	RRT	RSS
	4	TSR	RRT	RRS	RSR	TTT	TRS	SSR	TTT	SRS	TSR	RTT	RRS	RST
Mars	1	TST	RSR	RRS	RST	TSR	TRS	SST	TSR	SRS	TST	RSR	RRS	RRT
	2	TTR	RSS	RRT	RTR	TSS	TRT	STR	TSS	SRT	TTR	RSS	RRT	RTT
	3	TTS	RSR	RST	RTS	TSR	TST	STS	TSR	SST	TTS	RSR	RST	RTR
	4	TTR	RST	RSS	RTR	TST	TSS	STR	TST	SSS	TTR	RST	RSS	RTS
Mercury	1	TST	RRR	RTS	RST	TRR	TTS	SST	TRR	STS	TST	RRR	TRS	RST
	2	TSR	RRS	RTT	RST	TRS	TTT	SSR	TRS	STT	TSR	RRS	RTT	RSS
	3	TSS	RTR	RTT	RSS	TTR	TTT	SSS	TTR	STT	TSS	RTR	RTT	RST
	4	TRR	RTT	RTS	RRR	TTT	TTS	SRR	TTT	STS	TRR	RTT	RTS	RRR
Jupiter	1	TRT	RSR	RSS	RRT	TSR	TSS	SRT	TSR	SSS	TRT	RSR	RSS	RR
	2	TRR	RSS	RTT	RRR	TSS	TTT	SRR	TSS	STT	TRR	RSS	RTT	RRT
	3	TRS	RSR	RST	RRS	TSR	TST	SRS	TSR	SST	TRS	RSR	RST	RRS
	4	TRR	RST	RSS	RRR	TST	TSS	SRR	TST	SSS	TRR	RST	RSS	RRS
Venus	1	TST	RTR	RRS	RST	TTR	TRS	SST	TTR	SRS	TST	RTR	RRS	RSS
	2	TSR	RTS	RRT	RSR	TTS	TRT	SSR	TTS	SRT	TSR	RTS	RRT	RST
	3	TSR	RSR	RRT	RTS	TSR	TRT	STS	TSR	SRT	TTS	RSR	RRT	RTS
	4	TTR	RRT	RRS	RTR	TRT	TRS	STR	TRT	SRS	TTR	RRT	RRS	RRS
Saturn	1	TTT	RRR	RRS	RRT	TRR	TSS	STT	TRR	SSS	TTT	RRR	RSS	RTT
	2	TRR	RRS	RST	RRR	TRS	TST	SRR	TRS	SST	TRR	RRS	RST	RRT
	3	TRS	RRS	RST	RRS	TRR	TST	SRS	TRR	SST	TRS	RRR	RST	RRR
	4	TRR	RST	RTS	RRR	TST	TTS	SRR	TST	STS	TRR	RST	RST	RRS
Rahu	1	TTT	RRR	RSS	RTT	TRR	TSS	STT	TRR	SSS	TTT	RRR	RSS	RTT
	2	TTR	RRS	RST	RTR	TRS	TST	STR	TRS	SST	TTR	RRS	RST	RTT
	3	TRS	RRR	RST	RRS	TRR	TST	SRS	TRR	SST	TRS	RRR	RST	RRS
	4	TRR	RRT	RTS	RRR	TRT	TTS	SRS	TRT	STS	TRR	RRT	RTS	RRR
Ketu	1	TST	RRR	RSS	RST	TRR	TSS	SST	TRR	SSS	TST	RRR	RSS	RSS
	2	TTR	RRS	RST	RTR	TRS	TST	STR	TRS	SST	TTR	RRS	TST	RTR
	3	TRS	RRR	RST	RRS	TRR	TST	SRS	TRR	SST	TRS	RRR	RST	RRT
	4	TRR	RRT	RSS	RSS	TRT	TSS	SRR	TRT	SSS	TRR	RRT	RSS	RRR

R-Rajasika S-Satwika T-Tamasika

Planet	Padas/Stars	Chtita	Swatha	Visakha	Anyrasha	Jyeshta	Moona	Poorvashada	Uttarashada	Sravanam	Dhanha	Satabaisha	Poorvarhasba	Uttrabhadra	Remti
Sun	1	TSR	TRS	SRT	TSR	SRS	TRT	RSR	RRS	RRT	TSR	TRS	SRT	TSR	SRS
	2	TTS	TRT	SSR	TTS	SRT	TSR	RTS	RRT	RSR	TTS	TRT	SSR	TTS	SRT
	3	TTR	TRT	SSS	TTR	SRT	TSS	RTR	RRT	RSS	TTR	TRT	SSS	TTR	SRT
	4	TRT	TRS	SSR	TRT	SRS	TSR	RRT	RRS	RSR	RTR	TRS	SSR	TRT	SRS
Moon	1	TTR	TRS	SRT	TTR	SRS	TRT	RTR	RRS	RRT	TTR	TRS	SRT	TTR	SRS
	2	TTS	TRT	SRR	TTS	SRT	TRR	RTS	RRT	RRR	TTS	TRT	SRR	TTS	SRT
	3	TTR	TRT	SSS	TTR	SRT	TSS	RTR	RRT	RSS	TTR	TRT	SSS	TTR	SRT
	4	TTT	TRS	SSR	TTT	SRS	TSR	RTT	RRS	RSR	TTT	TRS	SSR	TTT	SRS
Mars	1	TSR	TRS	SST	TSR	SRS	RSR	RRS	RRS	RST	TSR	TRS	SST	TSR	SRS
	2	TSS	TRT	STR	TSS	SRT	RSS	RSS	RRT	RTR	TSS	TRT	STR	TSS	SRT
	3	TSR	TST	STS	TSR	SST	RSR	RSR	RST	RTS	TSR	TST	STS	TSR	SST
	4	TST	TSS	STR	TST	SSS	RST	RST	RSS	RTR	TST	TSS	STR	TST	SSS
Mercury	1	TRR	TTS	SST	TRR	STS	TST	RRR	RTS	RST	TRR	TTS	SST	TRR	STS
	2	TRS	TTT	SSR	TRS	STT	TSR	RRS	RTT	RSR	TRS	TTT	SSR	TRS	STT
	3	TTR	TTT	SSS	TTR	STT	TSS	RTR	RTT	RSS	TTR	TTT	SSS	TTR	STT
	4	TTT	TTS	SRR	TTT	STS	TRR	RTT	RTS	RRR	TTT	TTS	SRR	TTT	STS
Jupiter	1	TSR	TSS	SRT	TSR	SSS	TRT	RSR	RSS	RRT	TSR	TSS	SRT	TSR	SSS
	2	TSS	TTT	SRR	TSS	STT	TRR	RSS	RTT	RRR	TSS	TTT	SRR	TSS	STT
	3	TSR	TST	SRS	TSR	SST	TRS	RSR	RST	RRS	TSR	TST	SRS	TSR	SST
	4	TST	TSS	SRR	TST	SSS	TRR	RST	RSS	RRR	TST	TSS	SRR	TST	SSS
Venus	1	TTR	TRS	SST	TTR	SRS	TST	RTR	RRS	RST	TTR	TRS	SST	TTR	SRS
	2	TTS	TRT	SSR	TTS	SRT	TSR	RTS	RRT	RSR	TTS	TRT	SSR	TTS	SRT
	3	TSR	TRT	STS	TSR	SRT	TTS	RSR	RRT	RTS	TSR	TRT	STS	TSR	SRT
	4	TRT	TRS	STR	TRT	SRS	TTR	RRT	RRS	RTR	TRT	TRS	STR	TRT	SRS
Saturn	1	TRR	TSS	STT	TRR	SSS	TTT	RRR	RSS	RTT	TRR	TSS	STT	TRR	SSS
	2	TRS	TST	SRR	TRS	SST	TRR	RRS	RST	RRR	TRS	TST	SRR	TRS	SST
	3	TRR	TST	SRS	TRR	SST	TRS	RRR	RST	RRS	TRR	TST	SRS	TRR	SST
	4	TST	TTS	SRR	TST	STS	TRR	RST	RTS	RRR	TST	TTS	SRR	TST	STS
Rahu	1	TRR	TSS	STT	TRR	SSS	TTT	RRR	RSS	RTT	TRR	TSS	STT	TRR	SSS
	2	TRS	TST	STR	TRS	SST	TTR	RRS	RST	RTR	TRS	TST	STR	TRS	SST
	3	TRR	TST	SRS	TRR	SST	TRS	RRR	RST	RRS	TRR	TST	SRS	TRR	SST
	4	TRT	TTS	SRR	TRT	STS	TRR	RRT	RTS	RRR	TRT	TTS	SRR	TRT	STS
Ketu	1	TRR	TSS	SST	TRR	SSS	TST	RRR	RSS	RST	TRR	TSS	SST	TRR	SSS
	2	TRS	TST	STR	TRS	SST	TTR	RRS	RST	RTR	TRS	TST	STR	TRS	SST
	3	TRR	TST	SRS	TRR	SST	TRS	RRR	RST	RRS	TRR	TST	SRS	TRR	SST
	4	TRT	TSS	SRR	TRT	SSS	TRR	RRT	RSS	RRR	TRT	TSS	SRR	TRT	SSS

5. The importance of result of Pada of Star has been emphasized. Since a Planet has Lord Ship of Padas of two Rasis, then the Planet gives results of both the Rasis.
6. In the Stellar Astrology which was obtained as a result of continuous Application and Research, sometimes the Birth Chart is under the control one or two Planets. The opportunities for the controlling factors could be either Star Lords or Bhava Lords.
7. Which ever Planet or Bhava is controlling Birth Chart the results are decided by that planet or Bhava.

(a) At this moment it is stated that sometimes results obtained are good and acceptable because of Planet which is fully, Tamisika in Character got fully Rajasika Character for the Bhava & Kalaamsa Planet.

(b) It was examined as to how the above got happened. It was found out that all Planet Bhavas are under the control of a Planet was in Rajasika Character that was the reason as to why the entire Horoscope is under the control of one Rajasika Planet.

(c) When one Bhava is under examination the Kalaamsa & its Character can be found out then it can be decided whether the Bahva or Kalaamsa Planet could give good or bad results.

(d) If in case it is otherwise, that is the Character obtained by Kalaamsa Planet for Bhava and Karaka Planet are different from each other; then that Native experience bad results during the periods of Bhava & karakatwa Planets.

(e) If the Character & Directional Strength Rules are applied to Kalaamsa Planet, then the future periods as to when the results given by Bhava Karaka could happen be decided.

4.31 SUB DIVISION OF KALAAMSA LORD BASED ON NAKSHATRAS

In the Stellar Astrology Theory, importance is given to Planets Virgottama Position. If a planet is in Virgottama or in his Own House, it attains good strength but all Virgottamas are not good. These have to be sub-divided into Stawika, Rajasika and Tamasika Character. Virgottma alone cannot give the result for the Planet. They should be in proper strength to give good results.

For Dasa of each Planet, it has 3 Stars under it's control. The duration of Kalaamsa was arrived at based on the theory of sub-divisions of Stars. The following tables give the duration of Kalaamsa in Minutes and Seconds, for each Sub Lord for all 9 Planet Dasas.

This is the duration of each sub-division of a constellation in proportion to the Dasa periods of the sub-lord.

Virgothama Constellations: Aswini, Makha, Moola-Ketu Dasa

Bhukthi (sub period)	**Kalas** (Minutes)	**Vikalas** (Second)
Ketu	46	40
Venus	133	20
Sun	40	00
Moon	66	40
Mars	46	40
Rahu	120	00
Jupiter	106	40
Saturn	126	40
Mercury	113	20
Total Kalas	800	00

Constellations: Bharani, Pubba, Poorvahsadha-Sukra dasa

Bhukthi (sub period)	**Kalas** (Minutes)	**Vikalas** (Second)
Venus	133	20
Sun	40	00
Moon	66	40
Mars	46	40
Rahu	120	00
Jupiter	106	40
Saturn	126	40
Mercury	113	20
Kethu	46	40
Total Kalas	800	

Constellations: Krithika, Uthiram, Uthiradam-Sun Dasa

Bhukthi (sub period)	**Kalas** (Minutes)	**Vikalas** (Second)
Constellations: Bharani, Pubba, Poorvahsadha Sukra dasa		
Sun	40	00
Moon	60	40
Mars	46	40
Rahu	120	00
Jupiter	106	40
Saturn	126	40
Mercury	113	20
Kethu	46	40
Venus	133	20
Total Kalas	800	

Constellations: Rohini, Hastha, Sravana-Moon Dasa

Bhukthi (sub period)	**Kalas** (Minutes)	**Vikalas** (Second)
Mon	66	40
Mars	46	40
Rahu	120	00
Jupiter	106	40
Saturn	126	40
Mercury	113	20
Kethu	46	40
Venus	133	20
Sun	40	00
Total Kalas	800	

Constellations: Mirgasira, Chitta, Dhanishta-Mars Dasa

Bhukthi (sub period)	**Kalas** (Minutes)	**Vikalas** (Second)
Mars	46	40
Rahu	120	00
Jupiter	106	40
Saturn	126	40
Mercury	113	20
Kethu	46	40
Venus	133	20
Sun	40	00
Moon	66	40
Total Kalas	800	

Constellations: Aridra, Swathi, Satabhisha-Rahu Dasa

Bhukthi (sub period)	**Kalas** (Minutes)	**Vikalas** (Second)
Rahu	120	00
Jupiter	106	40
Saturn	126	40
Mercury	113	20
Kethu	46	40
Venus	133	20
Sun	40	00
Moon	66	40
Mars	46	40
Total Kalas	800	

Constellations: Punarvasu, Visaka, Poorvabhadra-Jupiter Dasa

Bhukthi (sub period)	**Kalas** (Minutes)	**Vikalas** (Second)
Jupiter	106	40
Saturn	126	40
Mercury	113	20
Kethu	46	40
Venus	133	20
Sun	40	00
Moon	66	40
Mars	66	40
Rahu	120	00
Total Kalas	800	

Constellations: Pushyami, Anuradha, Uthrabhadra-Saturn Dasa

Bhukthi (sub period)	**Kalas** (Minutes)	**Vikalas** (Second)
Saturn	126	40
Mercury	113	20
Kethu	46	40
Venus	133	20
Sun	40	00
Moon	66	40
Mars	46	40
Rahu	120	00
Jupiteer	106	
Total Kalas	800	

Constellations: Ashlesha, Jyestha, Revathi-Mercury Dasa

Bhukthi (sub period)	**Kalas** (Minutes)	**Vikalas** (Second)
Mercury	113	20
Kethu	46	40
Venus	133	20
Sun	40	00
Moon	66	40
Mars	46	40
Rahu	120	00
Jupiter	106	40
Saturn	126	40
Total Kalas	800	

4.32 IMPORTANT CAUSATIVE FACTORS FOR ALL THE 12 BHAVAS-THE RELAVENT BHAVAS FOR EXAMINATION

The following Table gives the Bhavas to be examined for different and causative factors Bhava wise and this examinanation will reveal the likely time of fructification of results in future of the Kalaamsa Lord for every such occasion.

Important causative factors	**Bhavas to be examined**
1. For Lagna Bahva	
(a) To attain high status in life	1, 10, 3, 11
(b) For Deergha Ayuvu	1-3-5-8-10
(c) For Alpa-Ayuvu	2-7
(d) Sudden Accident Happening	Relationship for Bhadhaka Sthana to Bhava 1-6-8-12

Important causative factors	Bhavas to be examined
2. Second Bhava	
(a) Second Marriage	2, 7 Rasis to Dwiswa bhava Rasi & the relationship with Mercury
(b) To become Healthy	2-6-10-1
(c) Loss in Business	5-8-12
(d) Profit in Business	2-6-11
(e) Good Predictive Speech	Have relationship of Jupiter & Mercury to Rasis 7-2-10-6
3. Third Bhava	
(a) To obtain agency to carry out Business activities	3-10-6-11
(b) Travel for short duration	3-12-1
(c) To enter into Rightful Contracts and Agreements	3-1-11-7
(d) For Negotiation	3-11
(e) To meet Important Personalities	1-3-9-11-7
4. Bhava	
(a) For Higher Studies & to attain Higher Standards.	4-9-11
(b) For construction of a House	4-11-12 Relationship with Mars
(c) Purchase of House already built	4-6-9-12-1
(d) To purchase Land	4-11-12 Kalaamsa planet to be Mars
(e) Only get upto Primary Education	4-11
(f) Acquire Ancestral Property	4-9-11-6-1
(g) Remain at one Place & do the job	4-10
(h) Always unhealthy	1-4-6
5. Bhava	
(a) Betting & Lottery	5-10-11-8-6-2
(b) To Learn Mantras	3-5-11-4
(c) Love affairs	7-5-11-1
(d) Not successful in Love affairs	5-9-10-12-1
(e) Child Birth	2-5-11
(f) To become a famous Astrologer	2-5-10-11-27 Kalaamsa Lord should have relation with Jupiter, Mercury
(g) To Earn unlimited money	2-6-5-11-3 Kalaamsa Lord to be Jupiter, relationship should not have with 8/12 Bhavas
(h) No Child Birth	4-12-10-6
(i) Good knowledge & capacity to examine	5-11-39-10-1
(j) Not having proper thinking capacity, mentally deranged, Insane & Non-Sensical	5-8-6-1-12 Relationship with Ketu

Important causative factors	Bhavas to be examined
6. Bhava	
(a) Debts	6-8-12
(b) Success	6-11
(c) Divorce	6-12
(d) Health & Diseases	1-6
(e) Attain Higher jobs in profession	2-6-10-11
(f) Loss of wealth	2-6-11
7. Bhava	
(a) Love Marriage	2-5-7-11
(b) Remain Unmarried	6-10-12
(c) To become a Partner	7-11
(d) More than one Marriage	2-7 Jupiter & Mercury relation in Dwiswabhava Rasi
(e) Marriage	2-7-3-11
(f) Separated after Marriage	2-7-6-12
(g) Marry a Widow	Kalaamsa Lord of 2nd Bhava will be Rahu or Saturn
8. Bhava	
(a) Acquire another House through a will of	8-6-11-3-10
(b) Acquire property from Wife side	8-2-11-6-7
(c) Alpha Ayuvu	2-7 In addition Bhadhaka Planet
(d) Deegha Ayuvu	8-5-10-3-1
(e) Suicide	8-1-12-7-6 Bhadhaka sthanamu should be 8th Kalaamsa Lord Ketu
(f) Earn money through Gratuity Insurance or deceased Persons Property	8-2-6-11-5 8th Kalaamsa Lord is Jupiter
(g) To marry a Widower	8-2-7-11 Kalaamsa Lord should be Saturn/Rahu
9. Bhava	
(a) Spiritual life and devine worship	1-9-5-11-12 Kalaamsa Lord-Saturn has relation with Jupiter
(b) Highly Learned	2-9-10-11
(c) To become an important Scientist	9-2-10-11-3 Kalaamsa Lord has relation to Saturn & Mercury
(d) Research & Invent new findings	9-12-6-11 Kalaamsa Lord should be Saturn
(e) Politician Acceptable to all & Acquire Chief Minister Post	9-10-11-2-6 Kalaamsa Lord to be Mars or Sun they remain in 10th Bhava or deposited in the star of Lord 10. Kalaamsa Star Lord has relation with Saturn.
(f) Go to foreign Countries	9-3-12 Rahu/Ketu/Sani to become Kalaamsa Lord. If Kalaamsa Lord is Rahu/Ketu the Native remains permanently.

Important causative factors	Bhavas to be examined
10. Bhava	
(a) Change in Job	29-10-11
(b) Change of place in Profession	3-10-12
(c) To go higher up in Politics	9-10-11 Kalaamsa Lord will be Jupiter/Mercury
(d) Become a Minister	29-10-11-6 The Kalaamsa lord should be Mars or Sun & Jupiter
(e) Start commeneing the Job	2-10-11 No relation of 10th Kalaamsa Lord to those Bhavas
(f) Profit & Losses	2-6-10-11 10th Kalaamsa Lord should have relation to these Bhavas
(g) To get loss in the current Job	5-8-12
(h) Good Intelligent Astrologer but not famous.	2-8-9-10 Mercury and Jupiter
11. Bhava	
(a) To pass in the class studying	4-9-11
(b) To become famous in acting	5-11 Kalaamsa Lord to be Mercury or Venus
(c) The best among Oral musicians	2-3-10-5-11 Kalaamsa Lord should be Mars or Sun
(d) Give Health	2-6-11
(e) Advantage in Profession	2-6-10-11
(f) Construct many Houses	4-11-12
(g) Purchase a House already constructed	6-9-4-11
(h) Happy Married life	2-7-5-11 Venus in Good Houses
(i) Safe & happy Child Birth	5-3-11
(j) Winning in Competition	6-11
(k) Successful in Love Affairs	5-11
12. Bhava	
(a) Spiritual development	12-1-10 Kalaamsa Lord to be Saturn
(b) To become Acetic	4-1-12 Kalaamsa Lord to be Saturn/ Ketu
(c) Happening of sudden Accident	6-8-12 Mars in Lagna
(d) Suicide or attempting to comit Suicide	1-6-8-12 Rahu/Ketu relation. If combined with Rahu the attempt will be highly serious in nature.
(e) Getting Loss in profession	5-8-12
(f) To go to Foreign Countries	1-3-9-12 Connection with Venus-pleasure trip. Mercury education, and Rahu or Saturn medical treatment
(g) Live in Foreign Countries	1-3-10-9-12

4.33 EXAMPLES-1

Number 1: To find out Jeeva & Sareera Planets See Para 4.5

Number 2: Marriage in early life, See Para 4.35 below.

4.34 EXAMPLE-2

7th Bhava Early Marriage, date of birth = 1-7-1967

Time = 01-14 Hrs.

Place of Birth-Dharma Puri, Tamilnadu, India

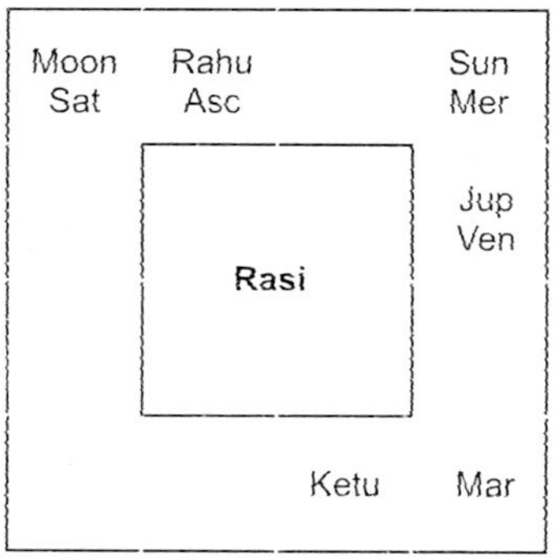

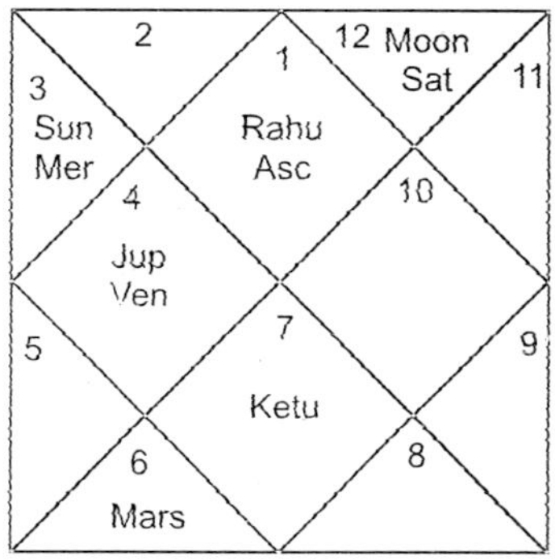

Name/Ret	Sign	Degrees	Star	Qtr.	Lord	KL/SL
Ascendant	Aries	3°5′	Aswini	1	Ketu	Sun
Sun	Gemini	14°55′	Aridra	3	Rahu	Ketu
Moon	Pisces	26°16′	Revati	3	Mercury	Jupiter
Mars	Virgo	28°33′	Chita	2	Mars	Saturn
Mercury	Gemini	27°49′	Punarvasu	3	Jupiter	Venus
Jupiter	Cancer	13°44′	Pushya	4	Saturn	Rahu
Venus	Cancer	29°55′	Ashlesha	4	Mercury	Saturn
Saturn	Pisces	18°33′	Revati	1	Mercury	Ketu
Rahu	Aries	11°26′	Aswini	4	Ketu	Mercury
Ketu	Libra	11°26′	Swati	2	Rahu	Saturn

For marriage 7th Bhava.

Husband & Wife to lead a happy Married life, Calm Temperament. Enjoy Sexual happiness, Partnership in going to foreign Countries. Combination of Semen of both Men & Women for Fertlity, well noted & famous, are the normal causative factors

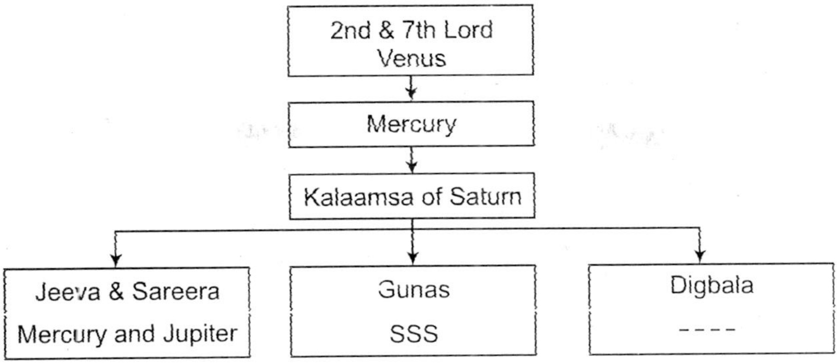

On examination of the above Table Rasi Lord for 2 & 7 Bhavas is Venus. Venus is in Aslesha Pada-4. Saturn is in Kalaamsa. Kalaamsa Lord of 2 & 7 is Saturn. Saturn is in Revati Star in I[st] Part. This is Virgomama Padam. Hence, Jupiter is Sareera Planet 2/7 Kalaamsa Jeeva Planet is Mercury is with 10th lord Sun. Mercury in this own House.

Sareera Planet Jupiter is posited with 2nd and 7th Lord with Venus in 4th house Cancer the Exalted house for Jupiter 2nd and 7th Kalaamsa Lord SAT got SSS Character.

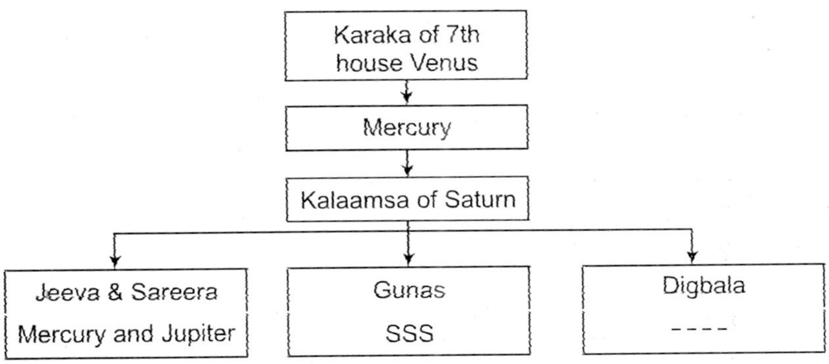

Karaka for wife is Venus is also Lord of 7th Bhava. Hence the argument given above will equally apply to Venus here. The character of 7th Bhava obtained is SSS Guna. On the day of Marriage Kalaamsa Lord Saturn gave the desired result of 7th Bhava.

Important to be noted is that Dasa Lord Venus is transiting on Kalaamsa Lord Saturn's Sareera plant.

Bhukthi Lord Sun transiting on Netal 7th Jeeva Planet Mercury is posited in Midhuna Rasi.

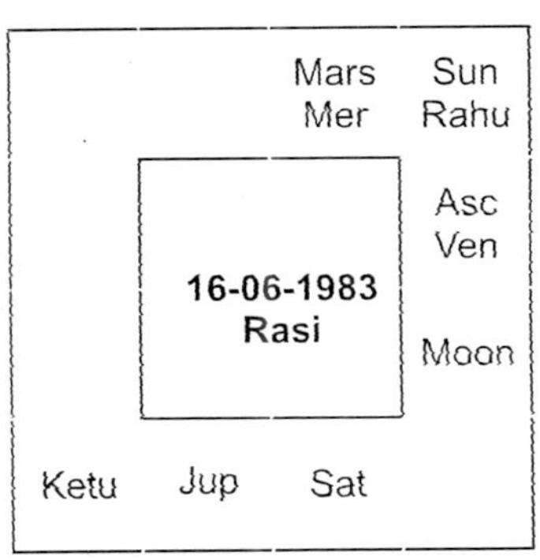

On the day of Marriage Dasa/Bhukthi/Antara Lords had connection to 2 & 7 Bhavas & Karaka Venus, Kalaamsa Lord of Jeeva Sareera Planets Mercury & Jupiter have complete relationship.

Since the Character obtained for Kalaamsa Lord Saturn is SSS Character at the age of Sixteen only a happy Married life combination had occurred. Though Ketu, is in 7th Bhava Saturn in 2nd Bhava had led to have Married the girl at the age of 16th year. The reason being Venus is the lord of 2 & 7 Houses. This planet got SSS Character which is the main cause for early Married life.

❖❖❖

CHAPTER 5

Muhoortha Sastra Parichayamu

5.1 INTRODUCTION TO MUHOORTHA SASTRA

In Jyothisha Sastra there are separate Divisions like Dharma Sastra, Vasthu Sastra & Muhoortha sastra which were described by Maharshis as very important. These Divisions in our Country, are always required for every individual in his daily routine life of activities. The matters related to us, are, describded in the following paragraphs. This Chapter is written in 1968 (Lived from 1904-1978) based on the text titled Muhoortha Sindhuvu written by a Famous & Well noted Jyothisha Pundit who was native of Rajahmundry by name Jyothisha Vidya Bhuhana Sri. Vadrevu Suryamarayama Murthy Garu.

5.2 THE AIM OF MUHOORTHA BHAGHA

Every Human being performs Karma. But the results of that Karma cannot be predicted just because the activity is performed. Main reason being that it is not sufficient for the human being to make an attempt. For these activities the period of time at which it was taken up & performed should be strong enough to give the desired result. It is therefore said that both Time & Karma should come together, by elders and nothing would without the combination of both these factors.

The Job we do is solid and is known to us. But the time factor is unknown, its very small and is like God pervading all over. The Sanskrit Sloka Reads as under

Sloka: Sarwagatwaa Tathsatsyata
Strasthaat Sarwatmaa
Twanmaheswar:!!

The above was stated by Maharsihs. There fore the time is all over pervading and is related to all activities of Karma; then when the fructification time gets approached it is becoming the main cause for getting either a good or a bad result. To decide that particular moment of time is the main aim of the Muhoortha Bhaga.

Hence based on movement of Planetary position, Maharsish's had decided the time for all Subha functions including laying down the Commands to be observed. Rishis intension was that based on the Commands, if the Function's are held by Human beings then they would attain good results.

Hence Muhoortha Bhaga was considered with utmost importance.

One more important aspect to be noticed. When fixing Muhoortha, it should first been seen that there are no Doshas for Muhoortha. Then the strengths of Lagna & Planets are to be decided. It is incorrect to say time dosha gets nullified if the planet is strong. Small

Doshas will be there very many. Some Doshas will come into effect suddenly. For such Doshas the strength of Planet will only be considered as remedy.

Cne more important aspect to be observed. Depending on the type of work, the suitable Lagna for that work & Planets strength has to be evolved separately. It should be noted that the commands laid down for one Muhoortha will not be usefull for another Muhoortha.

Sri. Vadrevu Suryamaraya Murthy a famous Astrologer of Rajahmundry had written a text with 10 Chapteras under the title Muhoortha Sindhuvu. The main Heads are Signs for Muhoortha, Dosha, Menstruation, Child Birth, Upanayana, Marriage & other matters, then Marriage, Travel Rules, Dreams & Ceremonies. This Chapter deals with Signs and are described as under:

Since the remedial measures are to be conducted for Santhi Nakshatras these are important to be known, they have also been dealt in this chapter. In the sub-division concerning Travel not only important points to be examined are mentioned but also the necessary Rules to be followed for travel Muhoortha have been laid down.

In olden days, lot of importance was given for Travel. Now a Days Travel has become a routine matter due to matters concerning Social, Religious, Business, Professional & other necessary functions. Therefore based on past experience the Travel Chapter is written on new matters which were not specified in the Sastra written in the past.

5.3 SIGNS DIVISION

This is the main factor on which all good & asubha functions are held and for 'time' there is no beginning nor there is an end. The entire Universe is functioning based on time factor only.

We have had experience that one work which was performed at a predetermined time was giving good results and the work if done at the end of the specified time, was not only not giving the desired result but giving an un-successful result.

In the circumstances it is difficult to know as to the time at which a particular work is to be taken up to get the desired result. Therefore our Rishies were kind enough, who had Super Natural future Drishiti Aspects, had specified the timings at which both the types of work that could be under taken and also those works which should not be take up. Our main job is only to fully understand the Rules laid down and make them applicable in a better way.

The Yagnas & Yagas as laid down in Vedas, Nuptional Marriages as Specified in the Scriptures, Maharshis had laid down specified periods of timing for performance. This 'Time' only is called Muhoortha Timing. What are these Muhoorthas and their necessity are detailed here in. The Signs Chapter lays down various informations in order to understand properly and take correct decisions. In this Text for Marriages & other good functions detailed directions have been given for taking necessary correct decision on Muhoortha Timing. Sufficient Rules been given to take proper & concise decisions.

The following Topics were dealt with in chapter-1

1. No of years – 60
2. Ayanas – 2

The readers may refer to Chapter – 1.

The Times at which 'Samkramana starting' are called and considered as Punyakala or 'Auspicious Timing'. These Timings are considered Lovable by Pitrudevatas and hence they are called Sankramama timing.

Sloka Ayance Vimshathihi
Poorvemakaree
Vimshathihi Paree!"

As per the above sloka, 20 Ghadias before Sun entering Karakataka Rasi is called Dashanatyana Punyakala and when Sun enters Makara Rasi & passes 20 Ghadias from that time onwards Uttarayana Punyakala is forming. When Sun enters Karkataka Rasi Dakshinayana Punyakala and when Sun enters Makara Rasi Uttarayana Punyakalas are commenced. From the beginning of Uttarayana to beginning of Dashinayana Kala, this period is considered as Auspicious for all functions and punya functions as intended by Rishis.

3. Rutuvus – 6
4. Months – 12
5. Manas – 5

These Manas are given as under.

1. Chandra mana
2. Soura Mana
3. Savana Mana
4. Barhaspatya Mana
5. Nakshatra mana

Chandramana is followed in Andhra Pradesh. Soura Mana is practiced in Kerala & Tamil Nadu and Barhasptyamana is followed by all countries North of Vindhya Range Mountains.

Chandra Mana forms based on the crescent of Moon. The Tidhi & Pakshas are formed based on the Moons Cresent. Amavaasya means that both Sun and Moon on the same Longitude. At that time Moon is in Combustion and will have no strength and he will have no Cresent at time. There after for every one day Moon increases in it's Cresent and by the time he comes to Poornima, He has attained 15 Cresents (Tidhs). This period is called as Sukla Paksha. Then from Bahula Padyami daily one cresent gets reduced till, the time of Amavaasya. This Period is callled Krishna Paksha. Tidhis are formed based on Cresents of Moon.

The Chandramana was considered as best of all Manas and it was certified as such by our Ancient Rishis. The reason being prescribed as religious actions for

(a) For performing Karma is of utost importance
(b) It was laid down in Vedas
(c) Tidihs are important for Veda Karmas
(d) Tidhis are formed based on Moon's cresents as per Chandramana.

The Chandramana was considered as of Primary importance and as the best.

This Chandramana is followed by all States for Marriages, Vedic Functions and for all Auspicious Functions. But in respect of other matters viz. beginning of New years counting the period of years etc. they were using their related Manas.

Soura Mana had formed based on Sun's Ingress into Mesha Sign. This means that when Sun enters Airies Sign, it is called Mesha and similarly when Sun enters into other Signs it is called Vrushabha Month etc. The names of the Month are given based on the Sign. That is why in just as in Chandra Mana the new year started from Chaitra-Suddha Padyani, in Souramana the year commencement is from the day Sun entering Mesha Sign. The Rishes had emphaszied that in the Jyothisha Sastra the Rules of sub-divisions Ganita, Siddhana and Perdicition were based on Soura Mana.

The Barhaspatya Mana is forming based on Jupiters movement. When Jupiter entering from one Rasi to another Rasi, Barhaspatya Mana New year is forming. Based on this, the decision of Pushkaran is made for each River in India.

When Jupiter enters Aries and to all 12 Rasis, the Pushkara formation is occurring for all the 12 live rivers in India.

Two Pakshas viz, Sukla Paksha and Krihna Paksha i.e. 15 Tidhes for every Paksha will be coming. The 15 Tidhis are:-

1. Padyami	6 Shashti	11 Ekadasi
2. Vidiya	7 Saptami	12. Dwadasi
3. Tadiya	8 Ashtami	13 Trayodasi
4. Chaviti	9 Nanami	14 Chaturdas
5. Panchani	10 Dasami	15 Poornima or Amansya

The Tidhis are categorized into five divisions

1. Nanda
2. Bhadra
3. Jaya
4. Riktha
5. Poorna

Week days:	Seven
Stars:	27
Rasis:	12

Rasi Lords		Planet lordship
Rasis S. No	Owning Signs	
5	For Leo	Sun
4	For Ctaner	Moon
1, 8	For Aries & Scorpio	Mars
3, 6	For Gemini &Virgo	Mercury
9, 12	For Sagittarius & Pisces	Jupiter
10, 11	Capricorn & Aquarius	Saturn

Owing Sign for Planets-Their Own Signs.

For Rahu & Ketu, they being Shadow Planets there are no owning signs for them. Planets are 9 in numbers.

5.4 EXALTATION, DEBILITATION, MOOLA TRIKONA SIGNS FOR PLANETS

S.No.	Planet	Exhaltation		Debilitation		Swakshetra	
		Exaltation	Maximum Ealtation	Debilitation	Maximum Debilitation	Swakshetra	Moolatrikona
1	Sun	Aries	1°-10°	Libra	1°-10°	Leo	1°-21°
2	Moon	Taurus	1°-3°	Scorpio	1°-3°	Taurus	3.1°-30°
3	Mars	Capricorn	1°-28°	Cancer	1°-28°	Aries	1°-12°
4	Mercury	Virgo	1°-15°	Pisces	1°-15°	Virgo	16.1°-20°
5	Jupiter	Cancer	1°-5°	Capricorn	1°-5°	Sagitarius	1°-10°
6	Venus	Pisces	1°-27°	Virgo	1°-27°	Libra	1°-15°
7	Saturn	Libra	1°-20°	Aries	1°-20°	Aquarius	1°-20°
8	Rahu	Gemini	13°20′ -16°40′	Sagitarius	13°20′ -16°40′	Aquarisu/ Virgo	6°40′ -10°00′
9	Ketu	Sagitarius	0°0′ -3°20′	Gemini	0°0′ -3°20′	Scorpio/ Pisces	0°0′ -3°20′

Even though for Rahu & Ketu are not having Lordship of any signs, in Vruddha Parasara concpt, the following have been laid down.

	Rahu	Ketu
1. Exaltation	Cancer & Leo	Capricorn & Aquarius

In respect of Ownership of Rasis for Rahu & Ketu Varahamihra & Kalidasa had laid down their own rules.

In Muhoortha Bhaga, many Rishes were of the impression that Rahu & Ketu are not to be considered. They are of the opinion that in the Muhoortha Lagna for Marriages and other Auspicious Functions even if Rahu & Ketu are situated functions are performed without any objection.

5.5 MITRA, SHATRU, SAMA, VISHAMA RASIS FOR PLANETS

S.No.	Planet	Mitra	Shatru	Sama	Vishama
1	Sun	Cancer Pisces	Taurus Libra Aquarius	Gemini Virgo	Vruchika Dhanus Makaram
2	Moon	Gemini Virgo Leo	—	Rest all 9 Rasis	—
3	Mars	Cancer Leo Pisces Sagitarius	Taurus Gemini Virgo Aquarius Capricorn	—	—
4	Mercury	Taurus Leo Libra	Cancer	Rest all 8 Rasis	Cancer

5	Jupiter	Aries Cancer Leo Scorpio	Taurus Gemini	Aquarius	—
6	Venus	Gemini Aquarius Capricorn	Pisces Cancer Leo	—	—
7	Saturn	Taurus Gemini Virgo Libra	Aries Cancer Leo Scorpio	Sagitarius Pisces	—
8	Rahu	Aries	—	—	—
9	Ketu	Libra	—	—	—

5.6 FRIENDSHIP OF PLANETS

S.No.	Planets	Mitra	Sama	Shatru
1	Sun	Moon Mars Jupiter	Mercury	Saturn Venus
2	Moon	Sun Mercury	Rest 4 planets	None
3	Mars	Jupiter Moon Sun	Saturn Venus	Mercury
4	Mercury	Sun Venus	Rest 3 Planets	Moon
5	Jupiter	Rest 3 planets	Saturn	Mercury Venus
6	Venus	Mercury Saturn	Mars Jupiter	Sun Moon
7	Saturn	Venus Mercury	Jupiter	Sun Moon Mars

5.7 GENDER SIGN TO PLANETS

Male planets	Sun, Mars, Jupiter
Female planets	Moon, Venus
Impotant or Neuter	Mercury, Saturn
Female or Neuter	Some were of opinion in case of Rahu & Ketu

5.8 ASPECTS OF PLANETS

(a) From the House situated all planets Aspect	7th house with full Aspect
(b) Jupiter has Special Aspect in addition to full Aspect from the House situated	5th & 9th Houses Special Aspect
(c) Mars from the House situated in addition to full Aspect	4th & 8th House has Special Aspect
(d) Saturn from the House situated in addition to full Aspect	3rd & 10th Houses has Special Aspect

5.9 SHADOWY ASPECT ON ADJACENT HOUSES BY PLANETS (AACHCHADANA ASPECT)

Shadowy aspect is similar to Direct/Specific Aspect. Planets have Shadowy aspect from their situated houses on 2nd & 12th Rasis, asper Rule given below.

(a) **Full Moon, Jupiter, Saturn & Ketu:** On both 2nd & 12th houses.

(b) **Jupiter if in combination with a Naturally Bad Planet the Doshas increase:** Then aspect only the 12th House No aspect on the 2nd House

5.10 PARTIAL ASPECTS ON PLANETS

(Pada Drushti)

(a) All Planets except Saturn from their House on	3rd & 10th House & other Planets situated there in	Have ¼ Aspect
(b) All Planets except Jupiter from their House on	5th & 9th Houses & other Planets situated there in	Have ½ Aspect
(c) All Planets except, Mars, from their House on	4th & 8th houses & Planets situated their in	Have ¾ Aspect
(d) All Planets from their House on	7th house & all Planets situated there in other	Have full Aspect

(i) Planets having Special Aspects are strong. Special aspect planets are viz. Saturn, Jupiter, Mars

(ii) Sun, Mercury Moon, Venus: Strong in full Aspect on 7th only

(iii) Sun, Moon, Mercury, Venus: Give complete higher good results in full Aspect rather than these Plants viz. Saturn, Jupiter & Mars having Special Aspect.

5.11 EFFECTIVE TIME PERIOD OF PLANETS RESULTS

This issue will be use-full in "Prasna Jyothisha Sastra"

Find out the Planet of Navansa related to Prasna Lagna, then during the time period of that Planet the results either good or otherwise will start happening. These time periods-Planet wise are given below.

Sun – 6 Months　　Jupiter – 1 Month

Moon – 2 Ghadias　　Venus – 15 Day

Mars – 1 Day　　Saturn – 1 Year

Mercury – 2 Days

5.12 TASTE SIGN (KATUKADI SIGN) FOR SUN & OTHER PLANETS

Sun= Pungent　　Jupiter = Sweetness

Moon= Salty　　Venus = Sourness

Mars = Bitter　　Saturn = Souro Bitter

Mercury = Mixture of all six tastes

Lagna Navamsa Lord will decide the Taste Sign related to that Planet and the Native likes that taste.

5.13 STAR LORDS

The subject was dealt fully in chapter 3.

5.14 KSHIPRAADA SIGNS (FAST OR OTHER WISE) OF STARS

1. Kshidraa (Speedy) Stars	Aswini, Hasta, pushyami, Quick result
2. Horrible Stars	Moola, Ardra, Jyeshta, Aaslesha, fearfull results
3. Soft stars	Chitta, Revati, Mrugasira, Anuradha, Soft results
4. Fixed Stars	Bharani, Makha, Pubba Poorvashada, Poorvabhadra fixed results.
5. Terrible Stars	Rohni, Uttara, Uttarashada, Uttarabhadra Terrible results.
6. Ordinary Stars	Krittika, Visaka, ordinary results.
7. Chara Stars	Swathi, Punarvasu, Sravanam, Dhanishtha, Satabhisham Shaky, Unsteady, Fickle inconsistent results.

5.15 BLIND OR OTHERWISE SIGNS FOR STARS

1. 4 stars from the Star in which Sun is posited	Blind Stars
2. Stars 5 to 10 from Sun's Star	Two eyed Stars
3. Stars 11 to 19 from Sun's Star	One eyed Stars
4. Stars 20 to 25 from Sun's Star	Two eyed Stars
5. Stars 26 to 27 from Sun's Star	Blind Stars

5.16 STARS LIVE OR NON-LIVE DIFFERENCES

(a) Star in which Sun is there in 26th Star from which Sun has left to 3 Star in which Sun is about to enter	These four have no life Stars (Nirgeeva)
(b) Thereafter from 3 to 9 Stars	Half life (Ardha Jeeva) Stars
(c) Thereafter 10th Star	Dead Star
(d) From 11 to 18 Stars	Full live Stars
(e) 19th Star	Dead Star
(f) from 20 to 26 Stars	¼ live Stars

5.17 TYAJYA (AVOIDED) GHADIAS COMMENCEMENT FOR STARS

1.	Aswini	50	**10.**	Makha	30	**19.**	Moola	2 & 56
2.	Bharani	24	**11.**	Pubba	20	**20.**	Poorvabhadra	24
3.	krithika	30	**12.**	Uttara	18	**21.**	Uttarabhadra	20
4.	Rohini	40	**13.**	Hastha	21	**22.**	Sravanam	10
5.	Mrugasira	14	**14.**	Chitta	20	**23.**	Dhanishta	10
6.	Ardra	21	**15.**	Swathi	4	**24.**	Satabhisham	8
7.	Punarvasu	31	**16.**	Visakha	14	**25.**	Poorvabhadra	1
8.	Pushyami	20	**17.**	Anuradha	10	**26.**	Uttarabhadra	24
9.	Aslesha	32	**18.**	Jyeshta	14	**27.**	Revathi	30

These stars are to be avoided at the specified Ghadias

5.18 NAKSHATRA BASED ON FIRST ALPHABET OF THE NAME

1. CHOO, CHEE, CHOO, LA	Aswini
2. LEE, LOO, LEA, LOOYO	Bharani
3. AA, EE, VOO, EEA	Krittika
4. OOA, VAA, VEE, VOOO	Rohini
5. VEEA, VOOE, KAA, KEE	Murgasira
6. KOO, KHAM, GNA, CHCHA	Ardra
7. KEE, KOOA, HAA, HEE	Punarvasu
8. HOOO, HEEA, HOOA, DHAA	Pushyami
9. DEE, DOOO, DEEA, DOOA	Aslesha
10. MAA, MEE, MOOO, MEEA	Makha
11. MOO, TAA, TEE, TOO	Pubba
12. TEEA, TOOA, PAA, PEE	Uttara
13. POO, SHAM, NAAA, DHAA	Hastha
14. PEEA, POOA, RAA, REE	Chitta
15. ROOU, REEA, ROOA, TAA	Swathi
16. TEE, TOOU, TEEA, TOOA	Visakha
17. NAA, NEEA, NOOO, NEEA	Anuradhaa
18. NOOA, YAAA, YEEE, YOOU	Jyeshta
19. YEEA, YOOU, BAA, BEE	Moola
20. BOOO, DHAA, BHAA, DHAA	Poorvashada
21. BEEA, BOOU, JAA, JEEA	Uttrashada
22. KHAA, KHEE, GHAA, KHEA	Sravanam
23. JOOU, JEEA, JOOO, KHAA	Dhanista
24. GAA, GEE, GOO, GEEA	Satabhisham

25. GOOA, SAA, SEE, SOOO — Poorvabhadra
26. SEEA, SOOA, DAA, DEE — Uttarabhadra
27. DEEA, DOOU, CHAA, CHEE — Revathi

For every Star has four Alphabets are given to represent the 4 Padas of the Stars

5.19 HERLOTS (SOOLALU) FOR TRAVEL (THESE ARE PAINFUL)

S. No.	Direction	Varamu day	Tidhi	Nakshatra	Lagna
1.	East	Saturday & Monday	1-9 First 8 Ghadias	Jyeshta Dhanishta	Tula Aquarius
2.	South East	Saturday & Thursday	3 & 11	—	Capricorn
3.	South	Thursday	5 & 13 First 22 Ghadias	Sravanam Aswini	Meena Vruchikam
4.	South West	Monday & Friday	4 & 12	—	Karkatakam
5.	West	Sunday & Friday	6 & 14 First 15 Ghadias	Rohini Pushyami	Dhanus Simham
6.	North West	Sunday & Tuesday	7 & 15	—	Mesham
7.	North	Tuesday & Wednessday	2 & 10 First 12 Ghadias	Pubba Hastha	Vrushabham Kanya
8.	North East	Wednessday	3 & 30	—	Midhunam

While travelling the above should be avoided and Travel under taken:

5.20 YOGAS – 27 given at Para 1.14

5.21 KARANAS - 11 given at Para 1.15

These have been dealt in Chapter-Para 1- Sub paras 1.14 & 1.15 at page 16.

5.22 VARARUCHI-STATEMENTS

The following Vararuchi statements will indicate the time in Ghadias left already related to Lagna of the Star as found out in the Night at the head.

Sanskrit Sloka

Sravanaa Meshe Rataa, Dhanishtaa Veushabce Nabha, Satabhisha Grvaru Shabu Raamaha, Prooshtapsadhu Nee Varaha, Ahrbudhinni Midhunee Bhanuhu, Revati Karki Yagnaha, Aswani Karka Moonmaarupa, Bharani Karkra Sasataka, Krittika Simsteetaaya, Rohinee Simhee Guruhu, Mrugasiraa Kanyaa Neeya, Ardra Kanya Yutee, Punaruasu Tulaa Nilaa, Pusityastu Tula Raaamha, Aslesha Too Boogea, Makhaa Vrucihkeekaea, Phalgune Vruchikalataa, Uttara Dhanurnama, Hasthha Dhnuschalaan, Chitta Panuschairaha, Swati Makareekaama, Visakha Makhareepanam, Anuradhaa Kumbhee Naabhihi, Jyehtee Kulabhee Kadhaa, Moolla Kumbhegachcha, Poorvashda Meeneekalm, Uttarashada Meenee Gaadhaa.

As for the above sloka the period of time elapsed in the Star is given under.

Period of Time Elapsed in the Star & Lagna

S. No.	Star passed at head in night	Lagnam	Bhukti-Kaalam time elapsed GHA & Vi-GHA
1.	Sravanam	Mesham	1-48
2.	Dhanishta	-do-	3-19
3.	Satabhisham	Vrushabham	4-25
4.	Poorvabhadra	Midhunam	0-43
5.	Uttarabhadra	-do-	2-28
6.	Revathi	Karkatakam	0-38
7.	Aswini	-do-	1-52
8.	Bharani	-do-	4-3
9.	Krittika	Simham	1-20
10.	Rohini	-do-	3-23
11.	Mrugasira	-do-	5-14
12.	Ardra	Kanya	1-2
13.	Punarvasu	Tula	0-49
14.	Pushyami	-do-	2-48
15.	Aslesha	-do-	2-58
16.	Makha	Vruchchikam	1-12
17	Poovarhalguni	-do-	4-12
18.	Uttara	-do-	5-12
19.	Hastha	Dhanus	2-5
20.	Chitta	-do-	4-15
21.	Swathi	Makaram	1-12
22.	Visakha	-do-	3-50
23.	Anooradha	Kumbham	0-54
24.	Jyeshta	-do-	2-2
25.	Moola	-do-	4-1
26.	Poorvashada	Meenam	2-19
27.	Uttarashada	-do-	3-20

5.23 DURATION OF TWELVE RASIS

S. No.	Rashi	Duration GHAVI-GHAH	S. No.	Rasi	Duration GHAVI-GHAH
1.	Mesham	4-20	7.	Tula	5-24
2.	Vrushabham	4-56	8.	Vruchikam	5-13
3.	Midhunam	5-26	9.	Dhanus	5-19
4.	Karkatakam	5-31	10.	Makaram	4-43
5.	Simham	5-20	11.	Kumbham	4-11
6.	Kanya	5-15	12.	Meenam	4-2

5.24 TAJYA GHADIAS FOR LANGAS

S. No.	Type of Rasis	Detail of Rasis	Tyajya Ghadias
1.	Chara Rasis	Mesha, Karkataka, Tula, Makaram	First ½ GHA To be left out
2.	Sthra Rasis	Vrushabha, Simha, Vruchkam, Kumbham	Middle ½ GHA, To be left out
3.	Dwi-Swa-Bhava Rasis	Midhunam, Kanya, Dhanus, Meena	Last ½ GHA To be left out

Just as Varjya and Dwamuurtha are avoided for Moohurthas, similarly it is most important to ensure that Lagna Tajya Ghadias are also implemented (Avoided) while fixing Marriage or other Moohurthas.

5.25 CHARA-STHRA & DWISWABHAVA RASIS

These have been described in Para 5.24 above.

5.26 RASIS ANDHA KADI (BLIND EYE SIGNS)

(a) Blind Rasis (Andhakamulu): 1. Aries, 2. Taurus, 3. Gemini, 4. Cancer, 5. Leo, 6. Virgo

Note:

1. 1, 2,5 Rasis are fully Blind at Mid Night
2. 3, 4, 6 Rasis are fully Blind at Afternoon Time.

Hence in the afternoon period they give Inauspicious results

(b) Cheviti Rasis (Badhiramulu): 7. Tula, 8 Scorpio, 9. Saggitterius, 10. Capricorn.

1. 7, 8 Rasis are fully Chtviti Rasis during midnoon & afternoon.
2. 9, 10 Rasis are fully Cheviti Rasis during Night time.

(c) Kunti Rasis or Lame Rasis (Pungu Rasis)

11. Aquarius, 12 Pisces: These Rasis are Kunti-Rasis during the time of Sun rise and Sun set.

It should be noted that these two Rasis will give bad results during their prescribed periods and at other timings good results will be given.

5.27 SAMA AND VISHAMA RASIS

(a) Sama Rasis	2 Taurus	8 Scorpio
	4 Cancor	10 Capricorn
	6 Virgo	12 Pisces
(b) Vishama Rasis (Basi rasi)	1 Aries	7 Libra
	3 Gemini	9 Sagittarius
	5 Leo	11 Aquarius

5.28 RASIS - RISING

From Head, from Back, from Bottom

(a) **Head Raising Rasis (Sirshtodaya):** Gemini, Leo, Virgo, Libra, Scorpio, Aquarius.

(b) **Back Raising Rasis (Prushtodaya):** Aries, Taurus, Saggiterious, Cancer, Capricorn.

(c) **Tirya Gudaya Rasis:** Pisces

5.29 RASIS STRENGTH AS PER TIMINGS

(a) **Night Jala Rasis:** Aries, Taurus, Gemini, Cancer, Capricorn.

(b) **Days Jala Rasis:** Leo, Virgo, Libra, Scorpio, Aquarius Pisces.

Some Astrologers take Pisces Rasi is always strong at all times.

5.30 FOUR CATEGORIES OF JALA RASIS

(a) **Poorna Jala Rasis:** Cancer, Capricorn, Pisces.

(b) **Ardha Jala Rasis:** Taurus, Aquarius.

(c) **Pada Jala Rasis:** Gemini, Libra, Scorpio.

(d) **Nirjala Rasis:** Aries, Leo, Virgo Saggiterious

5.31 EXALTATION, MAXIMUM EXALTATION, DEBILITATION AND MAXIMUM DEBILITATION FOR PLANETS IN DIFFERENT RASIS

S. No.	Planet	Exaltation	Max Exaltation	Debilitation	Max Debilitation	Friendship part	Enemy part	Equal part	Moola Trikona
1.	Sun	Aries 1° to 9°	Aries 10°	Libra 1° to 9°	Libra 10°	Aries 11° to 30°	Libra 11° to 30°	—	—
2.	Moon	Taurus 1° to 2°	Taurus 3°	Scorpio 1° to 2°	Scorpio 3°	—	Scorpio 4° to 30	—	Scorpio 4° to 30°
3.	Mars	Capricorn 1° to 27°	Capricorn 28°	Cancer 1° to 27°	Cancer 28°	Capricorn 29° to 30°	Cancer 29° to 30°	—	—
4.	Mercury	Virgo 1° to 14°	Virgo 15°	Pieces 1° to 14°	Pieces 15°	—	Pieces 16° to 20°	Virgo 21° to 30°	Virgo 21° to 30°

S. No.	Planet	Exaltation	Max Exaltation	Debilitation	Max Debilitation	Friendship part	Enemy part	Equal part	Moola Trikona
5.	Jupiter	Cancer 1° to 4°	Cancer 5°	Capricorn 1° to 4°	Capricorn 5°	Capricorn 6° to 30°	Aqurius 6° to 30°	—	—
6.	Venus	Pieces 1° to 26°	Pieces 27°	Virgo 1° to 26°	Virgo 27°	Pieces 28° to 30°	Virgo 28° to 30°	—	—
7.	Saturn	Libra 1° to 9°	Libra 10°	Aries 1° to 9°	Aires 10°	Libra 21° to 30°	Aries 21° to 30°	—	—

5.32 DIRECTIONAL STRENGTH OF RASIS

(a) On East	1. Aries,	5. Leo,	9. Saggiterious
(b) On South	2. Taurus,	6. Virgo,	10. Capricon
(c) On West	3. Gemini,	7. Libra,	11. Aquarius
(d) On North	4. Cancer,	8 Scorpio,	12. Pisces

The usefulness of this strength is described in the division of (i) Chandra Kantakam (Sammukha Chandara Lakshanam) and (ii) Yatra, Prayana (Travel) Nirnaya.

5.33 SHADVARGU

The following Sub-Divisions (Charit) are called Shadvargu.

1. Rasi,
2. Hora,
3. Drekkana,
4. Navamsa,
5. Dwadasamsa,
6. Trimsamsa.

1. **Rasi:** This has been described in chapter no. 1.
2. **Hora:** The Lagna Rasi is to be divided into two equal parts, to see in which part the Muhoortha Ghadia has fallen.

   If Muhoortha Lagna falls in fist half of Odd Rasi, that part is called Surya Hora. If in the second part, it is called Chandra Hora.

   If Muhoortha Lagna falls in first half of Even Rasi, that part is called Chandra Hora. If it is in the second part it is called Surya Hora.
3. **Drekkana and Lords of Drekkana:** Muhoortha Lagna pramanam is divided into 3 equal parts and each one is called as a Drekkana.
   1. If Lagna falls in the first part, Lagna Lord is the Drekkanadhi part.
   2. If Lagna falls in the second part, then 5th House Lord is the Drekkanadihpathi.
   3. If Lagna talls in the third part, then 9th House Lord is the Drekkanadhipathi.

Lagna is Chara/Sthira/Dwiswabhava	Drekkana Lords
(a) If it is Chara Rasi	Lords of Lagna, Panchama & Navama
(b) If it is Sthira Rasi	Lords of Navama, Lagna & Panchama
(c) It it is Sthira Dwiswabhava Rasi	Lords of Panchama, Navama and Lagna

4. **Navamsa:** The Muhoortha Lagna is divided into 9 parts, then find out in which part the Lagna Ghadia is falling.
   (a) If the Muhoortha Lagna falls in (1) Mesha (5) Simha (9) Saggiterious then the count will be from Mesha Navamsa.
   (b) If Muhoortha Lagna falls in Cancer (4) Scropio (8), Piece (12) then the count will start from Cancer Navamsa.
   (c) If Muhoortha Lagna falls in Libra (7) Aqurious (11) Gemini (13) then the count will start from Libra Navamsa.
   (d) If Muhoortha Lagna falls in Capricorn (10), Taurus (2) Virgo (5) then the count will start from Capricorn Navamsa.
5. **Dwadasmsa:** If the Muhoortha Lagna is divided into 12 equal parts, then each part is called Dwadasamsa.

   For this, the Rasi Lords will be similar to what is given for Navamsa.
6. **Trimsamsa:** The Muhoortha Lagna is divided into 30 equal Rasis.

   The Divisions & Planets for both Odd & Even Lagnas are given as under.

	If Lagna is Odd Sign	**If Lagna is Even Sign**
(a) First 5 parts belongs to	Mars	Venus
(b) 6-10 parts belong to	Saturn	6-12 parts Mercury
(c) 11-18 parts belongs	Jupiter	13-20 parts Jupiter
(d) 19-25 parts belongs to	Mercury	21-25 parts Saturn
(e) 26-30 parts belongs to	Venus	26-30 parts Mars

5.34 VIRGOTHAMAMSA & PUSHKARAMSA

(a) Virgothmamsa	
1. Chara Rasis	
Aries, Cancer, Libra, Capricorn	First Navamsa will be Virgothamamsa
2. Sthira Rasis	
Taurus, Leo, Scorpio, Aquarius	5th Navamsa will be Virgothmamsa
3. Dwiswabhava Rasis	
Gemini, Virgo, Saggiterious, Pisces	9th Navamsa is the Virgothmamsa
(b) Pushkaramasa	
Every Rasi is divided into 30 parts thus. The following parts are Pushkaramsas.	Pushkaramsa Division
1. For Aries (1), Simha (5), Sagghertous (9), Rasis	21st part
2. For Taurus (2) Virgo (6), Capricorn (10) Rasis	14th part
3. For Gemini (3), Libra (7), Aquarius (11) Rasis	24th part
4. For Cancer (6), Scorpio (8), Pisces (12), Rasis	7th part

The table given on page 122 gives for each Rasi, its period of time and Virgohamamsa & Pushkaramsa, showing the divisional part and extent of duration from & to.

			Period of Divisions in Ghadia/Vigihadias					
			Virogthamama			Pushkaramsa		
S. N.	Rasi	Division of rasi	Part number	From Gah-Vigha	To Gha-Vigh	Part number	From Gha-Vigh	To Gha-Vigh
1	Aries	4-20	1	0-00	0-29	21	2-53	3.02
2	Taurus	4-56	5	2-12	2-45	14	2-08	2-18
3	Gemini	5-26	9	4-50	5-26	24	4-10	4-21
4	Cancer	5-31	1	0-00	0-37	7	1-06	1-17
5	Leo	5-20	5	2-22	2-58	21	3-33	3-58
6	Virgo	5-15	9	4-40	5-15	14	2-17	2-27
7	Libra	5-24	1	0-00	0-36	24	4-08	4-19
8	Scorpio	5-33	5	2-28	3-05	7	1-07	1-18
9	Saggterious	5-19	9	4-44	5-19	21	3-33	3-43
10	Capricorn	4-43	1	0-00	0-31	14	2-03	2-12
11	Aquarius	4-11	5	1-52	2-19	24	3-12	3-21
12	Pisces	4-02	9	3-35	4-02	7	0-48	0-56

For every Muhoortha Vargottamansa is considered as most important but if Lagna Kala Sandhi and Lagna Tajya Ghadis come for Virgottamamsa then that Muhoortha is to be rejected.

Example: For Mesha first Navansa is Virgotama. In this the Lagna Tajya Ghadia also comes. Hence for Aries Lagna Virgottamamsa is not taken & is rejected.

Similarly for Pisces the last Navamsa is Virgottamamsa. This time is Lagna Sandhi. Here for Pisces, Virgortamtmasa is not accepted.

Langna Sandhi Kala has been specially dealt in this chapter separately.

If it is not possible to fix Virgottamamsa for Muhoortha time, then it should be fixed for Pushkaramsa. This aspect is not known to many Pundits and for muhoorthas only fix Pushkaramsa and leaving Virgottamamsa fully. This practice is against the Rishis Sampradayas.

5.35 SANDHIKALAM (JUNCTION TIME)

1. In the 60 years cycle Akshaya year is the Sandhi year. Similarly for that year in the end from Phalguna Bahula Padyami to Amavasya and each other Month, Bahula Trayodasi to Suddha Vidiya, are called Sandhi Kalas.
2. The middle period between Amvasya to Pratipath, Dasame to Ekadasi and Poornima to Pratipadh is two ghadias of 48 minutes.
3. Between two Stars & Yogas is 4 Ghadias 1 hour 36 minutes.
4. Between two Karanas is 2 Ghadias = 48 minutes.
5. For Lagna the Sandhi kala is one Ghadha = 24 minutes. That means ½ Ghadia for the previous Lagna and ½ Ghadia for the Forward Lagna, equal to total one Ghadia of 24 minutes

6. (a) Before Sun rise $1\frac{1}{2}$ Ghadias as Night to Day Sandhi Kala, after Sun set $1\frac{1}{2}$ Ghadias as Day to Night Sandhi Kala.

   (b) When the duration of night is made into equal parts and the first $1\frac{1}{2}$ Ghdias after the first half is called Nisedha Kala Sandhi. But in the Bharadwaja Samhita the following Sloka reads.

Sloka: Udayatpratsa kanee sandhya Ghatikadwaya muhyatee! Sayamshandya dwighatika!

This concept is only acceptable.

Sloka: Vindhyasyottaram Digbaagee Shashtyamtam Vatasram Tyajeet!
Tasya Dakshma Deeseethu
Trimasa Varjayee Tadaa!!

Sloka: Yaa Daa Phalguna Meenau! Dwaowva Yaga satviritingatau
Tadha Pakstoo Varashantee hee yoo Manayatra kurachit!!

Sloka: Dasa Chaadreetu varshaantee Souracheeddutu hee vasaram!
Tadhaa dwi raatrim jaivaantee Varjayeechehu Subhakarmasu!!

In view of the above it is stated that Akshaya year in the 60 years need not be rejected fully. If 6 months are left upto in Aswayuja Month it is acceptable. Similarly Chandramana persons if they leave 5 days before the year end and 5 days after commencement of the year, it is adequate.

In Ghadantara Rasis viz.

Mesha-Meena

Karkataka-Simha

Vruchika-Dhanus

Half Ghadia in Rasyantham and half Ghadia at the beginning of Rasi if left, is adequate.

But in other Rasis one fourth Ghadia is to be left at the end of a Rasi and beginning of the next Rasi which is considered as adequate.

For Birth also it is to be considered as above in the preceding para.

Two Ghadias of the previous Star and two Ghadias of the Star they follow total 4 Ghadias are called Sandhi Kala, this is only in respect of Gandantara Star as opined by Rishis.

Upto seven days after Eclipse no Muhoortha should be fixed. Some persons one day & before after, the Eclipse; some others upto 2 Days before & after Eeclipse, no Muhoorthas are fixed

Some others from the 4th Lagna before Sun rise and upto 4th Lagna after Sunrise and in Rasis of Sunrise & Sunset except for travel Muhoortha, are left out for all Subha Functions as it was considered as Sandhi Kala.

5.36 GANDANTARA RASIS

Meena-Mesha
Karkataka-Simha
Vruchika-Dhanus

For these the Sandhi Kala is one Ghadia.

This period in Births & Muhoorthas, it is considered as death.

Last half ghadia of Meena and half ghadia at the beginning of Aries is called Gandantarakala. Similarly it is to be considered for other Rasis.

5.37 GANDANTARA STARS

Revati-Aswini
Aslesha-Makha
Jyestha-Moola

These are Gandantara Stars. For this, total 4 Ghadias Gandantakalam.

Example: The end 2 Ghadias of Aslesha, Jyestha & Revati Stars and two Ghadias at the beginning of Stars Aswini, Makha & Moola are called Gandantara Stars. These timings are to be left out for all Subha Functions.

5.38 PAKSAHA CHAHDRAMULU–VARJYA KALAS

In Sukla Pakshasa Dwadasi, Shashti, Chaviti, Chaturdasi Ashtami, Navami Tidhis are called Paksha Chchidras. Hence no Subha functions are considered in these Tidhis.

5.39 VARJYA KALAS IN PAKSHA CHCHIDRAS

	Beginning Ghadias
In Chaturthi	8
In Shashti	6
In Ashtami	14
In Navami	14
In Dwadasi	10
In Chaturdasi	25

The above beginning ghadias are inauspicious and no Subha Functions are fixed and the remaining times are considered.

Sudha Padyami, Amavasya both these days are avoided for all Subha Functions.

5.40 ANADHYAYA TIDIHS

(i) Padyami, Ashami, Chaturdasi, Poornima Amavasya-Tidhis	(a) For 5 Ghadias from Sun Rise in Krishna Tidhs (b) For 3 Ghadias from Sun Rise in Sukla Tidhis
(ii) Padyami, Ashtami-Tidhis	(c) Utpo 5 Ghadias or more than 5 ghadias in the Morning both Krishna & Sukla Pakshas in Ashtama & Chaturdasi Tidhis
(iii) Saptami, Trayodasi-Tidhis	No harm
(iv) Chaitra Suddha Vidiya	-do-
(v) Vaisaka Suddha Tadiya	-do-
(vi) Aashada Suddha Navami, Dasami Ekadasi	-do-
(vii) Bhadrapada Suddha Tadiya, Ekadasi	For all items from (i) to (xvi) both Morning & Evening Sandhi Kalas, Clouds resounding with sparks time are to be avoided for daily Rituals & Routine Study. Even performing thread ceremony function is to be avoided.
(viii) Aasweja Suddha Ekadasi	-do-
(ix) Kartika Suddha Padyami, Ashtami Ekadasi	-do-
(x) Pushya Suddha Vidiya Ekadasi	-do-
(xi) Magha Suddha Saptami, Dwadasi	-do-
(xii) Aashada Bahula Vidiya	-do-
(xiii) Bhadrapada Bahuha Trayodasi	For all the items (i) to (xvi) Morning and Evening Sandhi Kala, and resounding of Coulds time with sparks emitting-daily routine study is to be avoided. Even performing thread ceremony is also to be avoided.
(xiv) Before Bhadrapada Bahula Trayodasi when Bharani Star comes into a Tidhi that Tidhi	-do-
(xv) Kartika Bahula Vidiya	-do-
(xvi) Phalguna Bahula Vidiya	-do-

5.41 DWADASA BHAVA DETAILS

(i) The following are to be counted from Lagna for all 12 Bhavas.

1. Tanu Bhava
2. Dhanu Bhava
3. Bhatru Bhava
4. Matru and Vidya Bhava
5. Putra Bhava
6. Satru Bhava
7. Kalatra Bhava
8. Ayur Bhava
9. Pitru Bhava
10. Karma and Business Bhava
11. Labha and Elder Brother Bhava
12. Vyaya Bhava

(ii) Planets joining Sun are under Combustion that means they become weak.

(iii) If Planets join Moon it is called Samagama, Planets strength gets increased.

(iv) Moon gives more strength when joined with Naturally Bad Planets than when joining Naturally Good Planets.

(v) Moon should not join with any Planet in any Muhoortha Lagan. This is only for Muhoortha and not for Astrological purposes.

(vi) If Sun & other Planets join Mars, there is fight between them. The Planets which has more Longitude in the Rasi will win over. Those Planets getting less Longitude will get defeated.

5.42 CHADHAKA, VEEDHAKA, BANDHAKA, PRATIBANDHAKA PLANETS

For any Bhava or for any Mhoortha lagna:

	Planet called as
(i) Planet in 2nd house from Lagna	Chaadhaka
(ii) Planet in 3rd house from Lagna	Veedhaka
(iii) Planet in 4th house from Lagna	Bandhaka
(iv) Planet in 8th house from Lagna	Pratibandhaka

(v) In all the above situations the presence of Naturally Good Planets is considered most auspicious.

(vi) For all Muhoorthas 8th House being Pratibandhaka House is not considered even if it has Subha Grahas.

(vii) In respect of muhoortha the 3rd house is not considered as Veedhaka Sthana. If naturally Bad Planet is positioned in 3rd house, it is considered as most auspicious from Rishis points of view.

5.43 PLANETS BAALATWADYAVASIHAS

(i) Moon, Jupiter, Venus Naturally Good Planets	These 3 planets being Naturally Good Planets are considered as good for Subha Muhoorthas.
(ii) Moon from Suddha-Vidiya to Panchami	Bala Graha having less strength
(iii) Moon from Suddha-Shasashte to Dasami	Having half strength
(iv) Moon from Suddha Ekadasi to Bahula Panchami	Full strength
(v) Bahula Ashtami to Bahula Ekadasi	As Old person (Vruddhudu)
(vi) Bahula Dwadasi to Bahula Chaturadasi	Ksheenudu very old person
(vii) Amavasya to Suddha Padyami	In Combustion without any strength

Here Moon is to be considered as Naturally Good planet from Suddha Panchami to Bahula Ekadasi. That is why the Sloka

"Baaloo Vruddhaa Khagasthoopi
Pasyannapi Napasyati!"

Kalidasa in respect of Moon had stipulated similar to Naturally Good Planets, cartain Avasthas like Balya, Vruddhatwa and attributed Lameness to the Moon, when he in not is full.

(viii) (a) After rising Jupiter: as a Baludu upto 15 days

(b) Before setting of Jupiter: for 15 days before setting as an old man (Vruddhdu)

(ix) Venus while raising from East: Upto 3,days, he is considered as a Boy.

(x) Venus while raising from West: Upto 10 days, he is considered as a Boy.

(xi) Venus when raising from East: 15 Days before raising he is considered as an old Man.

(xii) Venus when setting in West: For 10 days before setting, he is considered as old Man. Some people take only 5 day as old person.

(xiii) In respect of Jupiter & Venus the Baalatwa & Vruddhatwa; was attributed for a penod of 5 days and if considered likewise is accepted.

Sloka: Edoomoodhoo bhaveeducacha swoochcha mitraamsa gooyataha!
Saraasimitra Gataschchana Mudhya dooshoono vidyatee!!

Sloka: Moodhdhastoopt Bhrugorbalavaan!
Kalidasa meaning of this is

(xiv) If any one of Jupiter/Venus are in Combustion and the second is Shining or in both Combustion or while in Own House or in a Friends house or in Exaltation or all in own Namamsa; there is no effect of Moudhyami as for Maharshi Mandavya. Kalidasa has stated that there is no moudhya Dosha for Venus.

(xv) Moudhya Dosha should in variably be followed in Muhurtha Bhaga.

But Rishis had laid down certain variations for each Country. In respect of five places the Rishies had laid down the period for which the Moudhyadosha continues.

(xvi) In the text Vashishta, it is laid down the extent of period in days of both Balatwa & Vruduhawa as under.

A. (a) Vindhyamara Desa – 16 days
(b) Avani desa - 7 days
(c) Banga desa - 6 days
(d) Houna desa – 5 days
(e) Other desa – 3 days

This Dosha is to be observed.

B. For Jupiter & Venus in States below South of Vindhyranges, the period to be considered is 3 days for Baalatwa & Vruddhatwa.

(xvii) Bhargava had opined that there is no Moudhya dosha for Venus provided Jupiter is strong in Muhoortha Lagna and Naturally Bad Planets are situated in houses 3, 6, 11.

But many Rishes had opined that Moudhya Dosha is of very little in magnitude and that too for Venus, it is too very little. It is therefore to be considered accordingly.

(xviii) Sloka: 'Budhana, Papatva Paapaha!'

The Mercury when not joined with Naturally Bad Planet is to be considered as Naturally Good Planets like Jupier, Moon & Venus.

(xix) Mercury when joined with a Papagraha is to be considered as a Bad Planet. This is followed both in respect of Muhoortha & Astrology Bhavas.

5.44 TIDIHS & THEIR LORDS

S. No.	Tidhi	Diety lordship	S. No.	Tidhi	Diety Lordship
1	Padyami	Agni	9	Navavami	Ashtavasuvulu
2.	Vidiya	Brahmma	10.	Dasami	Diggajas
3.	Tadiya	Parvati	11.	Edadashi	Yama
4.	Chaviti	Vigneswara	12.	Dwadashi	Vishnovu
5.	Panchami	Adisheshudu	13.	Tryodashi	Manmadhu
6.	Shashti	Kumaraswami	14.	Chaturdasi	Kalipurushudu
7.	Saptami	Sun	15.	Poornami	Moon
8.	Astami	Siva	16.	Amavasya	Pitrudevatas

5.45 WEEKDAYS AND LORDSHIP

1. Sunday-Sun
2. Monday-Moon
3. Tuesday. Mars
4. Wednesday-Mercury
5. Guru or Thurday or Lakasami-day Jupiter
6. Friday-Venus
7. Saturn or Mandavaaram-Saturn

The Hora Lord for Ist hour being Sun is the Lord Hora and the Day is called as Sunday.

Similarly for all the week days the order of Hora Lords is given as under for eaeh one hour.

DINA HORADHIPATI TABLE

Day Time Hours	Sun	Mon	Tue	Wed	Thur	Fri	Sat
6-7	Sun	Mon	Tue	Wed	Thu	Fri	Sat
7-8	Fri	Sat	Sun	Mon	Tue	Wed	Thu
8-9	Wed	Thu	Fri	Sat	Sun	Mon	Tue
9-10	Mon	Tue	Wed	Thu	Fri	Sat	Sun
10-11	Sat	Sun	Mon	Tue	Wed	Thu	Fri
11-12	Thu	Fri	Sat	Sun	Mon	Tue	Wed
12-1	Tue	Wed	Thu	Fir	Sat	Sun	Mon
1-2	Sun	Mon	Tue	Wed	Thu	Fri	Sat
2-3	Fri	Sat	Sun	Mon	Tue	Wed	Thu
3-4	Wed	Thu	Fri	Sat	Sun	Mon	Tue
4-5	Mon	Tue	Wed	Thu	Fri	Sat	Sun
5-6	Sat	Sun	Mon	Tue	Wed	Thu	Fri

Day Time Hours	Sun	Mon	Tue	Wed	Thur	Fri	Sat
6-7	Thu	Fri	Sat	Sun	Mon	Tue	Wed
7-8	Tue	Wed	Thu	Fri	Sat	Sun	Mon
8-9	Sun	Mon	Tue	Wed	Thu	Fri	Sat
9-10	Fri	Sat	Sun	Mon	Tue	Wed	Thu
10-11	Wed	Thu	Fri	Sat	Sun	Mon	Tue
11-12	Mon	Tue	Wed	Thu	Fri	Sat	Sun
12-1	Sat	Sun	Mon	Tue	Wed	Thu	Fri
1-2	Thu	Fri	Sat	Sun	Mon	Tue	Wed
2-3	Tue	Wed	Thu	Fri	Sat	Sun	Mon
3-4	Sun	Mon	Tue	Wed	Thu	Fri	Sat
4-5	Fri	Sat	Sun	Mon	Tue	Wed	Thu
5-6	Wed	Thu	Fri	Sat	Sun	Mon	Tue

5.47 SOONYAMASAS-DECISION

(i) When Sun in Meena Rasi-Chaitramasam

(ii) When Sun in Midhuna Rasi-Aashadhamasam

(iii) When Sun in Virgo Rasi-Bhadrapadamasam

(iv) When Sun in Sagittarius Rasi-Pushyamasam

5.48 SOONYAMASAS

There were difference of opinions as expressed by Maharshis in respect of deciding Soonya Masas. Certain exceptions were given in performing Subha Function & Marriages even in Soonya Masas, when there are peculiar circumastances these situations are

(a) When persons of either Boy or Girl are in critical conditions due to accidents.

(b) When either the Boy or Girl may have to leave India and go Abroad.

In these unavoidable circumastances this Dosha of Soonyamasa is ignored. Muhoorthas can be fixed taking into consideration the strength of the Planets.

These exceptions are also agreed to, due to changes in the Country. Maharshis had in their mind this aspect of different practices in various Countries based on Geographical conditions and then only wrote the Rules in this manner.

There are differences in the practices followed due to seasonal climatic conditions which is an acceptable reason. Now it is difficult to know the reason for changes in the Countries. The Divisions of States in older times during Rishis existence and the present day division of States on political considerations has lead to the conclusion that these would not be identical or comparable and it can never be correct all the time.

Hence as acepted by all Rishis in general to leave Soonya Masas, for Marriages & Subha Function. It is recommended as far as possible to leave Soonya Masas and carryon the Function at other periods. In exctptional circommastances & in the conditions stipulated the Marriages and of Subha Functions can be taken up even during Soonya Masas.

5.49 THE METHOD OF FINDING OUT TARABALAM

Count from Janma Nakshatra to the Nakshatra prevailing on that date and divide by 9, and if the balance is:

1. It is Janma Tara.
2. Sampt Tara.
3. Vipat Tara
4. Kshema Tara
5. Pratyak Tara
6. Saadhana Tara
7. Naidhana Tara
8. Mitra Tara
9. Parmamitra Tara

If Janma Nakshatra is not known, then Nama Nakshatra to be taken & followed.

These taras are not seen while examining Astrology.

Balance No.	Tara	Result	Balance No.	Tara	Result
1.	Janma Tara	Difficulties for individual body	6.	Saadhana Tara	Work accomplished
2.	Sampat Tara	Gain wealth	7.	Naidhana Tara	Leads to death
3.	Vipat Tara	Suffer from Poverty	8.	Mitra Tara	Friendship develops
4.	Kshema Tara	Every thing is safe	9.	Paramamitra Tara	Friendship becomes Permanent & gets stronger
5.	Pratyak Tara	Work Anticipated gets spoiled			

There are three groups of 9 Stars each. The group is called as Navakam. The following Stars getting the Taras shown should be totally avoided at all times in all cases.

	Star in Navakam	Tara to be left
1.	In first Navakam	Janma Tara
2.	In the second n Navakam	Vipat Tara
3.	In the third Navakam	Pratyak Tara

The Naidhara Tara which comes in 3rd Navakam is considered as Dosha & is to be left out in all Navakams.

For the same Tara obtained in other two Navakams, the Dosha can be reduced by conducting certain remedies like Danam given to others. For these objectionable Taras the first Ghadia is to be fully avoided. These are shown as under.

Tara	Objectionable Ghadias in the begining	Materials to be given as Danam (Donate)
1. In 2nd & 3rd Navakam Janma Tara	7	Leafee vegetable
2. In 1st & 3rd Navakam Vipat Tara	3	Jaggary
3. In 1st & 2nd Navakam Pratyak Tara	8	Salt

If these Danas are given the Dosah gets nullified.

Some people opion that leaving the first Nindhya Ghadia, the remaining Ghadias are acceptable.

5.51 LORD SHIPS OF TARAS

S. No	Tara	Lordship	S. No	Tara	Lordship
1.	Janma Tara	Sun	6.	Saadhana Tara	Moon
2.	Sampat Tara	Mercury	7.	Naidhana Tara	Saturn
3.	Vipat Tara	Rahu	8.	Mitra Tara	Venus
4.	Kshema Tara	Jupiter	9.	Paprma Mitra Tara	Mars
5.	Pratyak Tara	Ketu			

Some people opione that Mars being the lord of Parama Mitra Tara, it is considered as not that good. Some others viewed that Paramamitra Tara is also good, as Kuja has another name as Mangaludu.

5.52 CHANDRABALAM

Based on Janma Nakshatra the Moon's rasi is known and on the day's Nakshatra, the Moons Rasi is also known. From Janma Rasi to the day's Rasi, if the count becomes 1, 3, 6, 7, 10, 11 it is considered that Moon is stronger in both the fortnights.

If the count is 4, 8, 12, Moon is strong only in Krishna Paksha.

5.53 PANCHAKA RAHITHAMU

The meaning is that due to combination of Tithi, Vaara, Nakshatra & Lagna, certain bad & good results are expected and Aspects are to be examined in the case of every Subha Muhoortha.

The main reason being that all the factors should become good on a day, then there is strength in the Muhoortha.Maharshis had opined that for all Subha Functions the time is of utmost importance to get the desired good results viz., with proper, strength power and auspiciousness. The pick of such Muhoorthas can be done by a speciallist.

After deciding the proper combination of these factors, then for the appointed time, if Lagna has strength, then Muhoortha will be considered as the best and all the actions taken will give very good results. This is the ingenuity of the Astrologers. Here Subha Tithi, Nakshatra, Lagna, means that those Tithis, Vaaras, Nakshatras & Lagnas which are specified for Subha Muhortha are to be taken.

Sloka: Tidhivaaroo dubhi ryuktham
Tat kaaloo dayamisritam!
Navabhinthu haareedbhagam
Seesham panchakmeeretam!!

This means, the serial numbers of Tithi, Vaara, Nakshatra & Lagna are added then the total sum is devided by 9, the balance number is called as Panchakamu. If the balance figure is 1, 2, 3, 4, 5, 6, 7, 8, the figure 1, 2, 4, 6, 8 are to be left out, as they are considered inauspicious and they mean as under.

If Balance is	Result indicative of
1	Death
2	Fire
4	Raja Panchaka
6	Chora (theft) Panchaka
8	Roga (disease) Panchaka

The other figures 3, 5, 7 as balance they have been considered as auspicious.

In the bad Panchakas the figure 1, 2, 8 are most inauspicious.

The figure 4 Raja Panchaka is considered as not that bad for Travel, to serve the Kings (now a days there are no kings) or Politicitions, it is considered acceptable. Similarly for Travelling, House construction ceremony, Upanayanam, Stone laying Ceremony, and Griha Pravesa Functions for these the Agni Panchakam and for Upanayantam, Marriage & Subha Functions Mrutyu Panchakam should invariably left out.

During Night time-Chora & Agni Panchakam and During Day time-Raja Panchakam are considered inauspicious.

Further:

On Sunday-Roga Panchakam

On Monday – Raja -Do-

On Tuesday-Agni -Do-

On Wednessday & Friday-Chora -Do-

On Saturday-Mrutyu -Do-

These are said to be very bad. In this, except Raja and Chora all other Panchakams are to be left out.

Raja & Chora Panchakams are to be left out for Gruha Pravesa & Travel Times. For others we need not insist to satisfy.

(i) Raja Panchkam is said to be bad and it should be avoided while meeting Kings or Politicians or doing their works. This is based on shear experience.

(ii) For Travelling, Chora Panchakam is said to be bad. This is correctly specified.

(iii) Even while House Warming Functions, Chora Panchakarm should be avoided. Along with this Agni Pancharakm Chora Panchakams are to be left out. At Gruha Praesa time Raja Panchakam is also recommended to be left out. This opion is not correct. But Agni Chora, Roga & Mrutyu Panchakms are to be left out.

(iv) For Marriages & Upanayana Functions Agni, Chora and Mrutyu Panchakas are to be left out.

(v) Mrutyu Panchakam should be left out for all Muhoorthas.

Time Day week days	Timings of Durmuhurtha Gh-V.Gha	Timings of 2nd Dumuhoortha Gh.-V.Gha	Timings of Rahu-kala Gh-V.Gha
Sunday	26-0	—	26-0
Monday	16-0	22-0	3-30
Tuesday	6-0	11-50 Night	22-15
Wednessday	14-0	—	15-0
Thursday	10-0	22-0	16-30
Friday	6-0	16-0	11-15
Saturday	4-0	—	7-15

Durmuhoortha timings which are based on day timings will be changing. The above Gh. & V.Gh are given on the assumption that the duration of day time is equal to 30 Ghadias and the Sun Rise & Sun Set are 6 am & 6 pm respectively.

Except on Sunday, Wendessday & Saturday the Durmuhoortha will come twice in a day.

(i) The period of Durmuhoortha is normally .... 2 Ghadias (48 minutes)

(ii) The period of Rahu Kalam is .... 4 ghadias (1 hr-36 minutes)

5.54 JAPA COUNT & DANAS (DONATIONS) FOR NINE PLANETS

S. No.	Planet	Japa count	Materials to be given as Danan
1	Sun	6,000	Wheet
2	Moon	10,000	Rice
3	Mars	7,000	Harardal
4	Mercury	17,000	Moong dal
5	Jupiter	16,000	Chana dal
6	Venus	20,000	Jwar
7	Saturn	19,000	Til
8	Rahu	18,000	Urad dal
9	Ketu	7,000	Horse grain

The weight of materials will be 1¼ Kgs. for each item

5.55 OTHER CHAPTERS

These are

1. Dosha: There are 21 Maha Doshas. There is a Sub-Chapter as Remedial Measures.
2. Rajaswala. (First Menses for Girls)
3. Jananam, Upanayana, Vivaha other than Marriage, Travel, Dreams and Asubha Karma.

In so far as the above Chapters, the readers are advised to consult 'Muhoortha sindhuvu' or other. Standard Texts.

5.56 EXAMPLES

Four examples are given in chapter 10.

1. Casting of a Horoscope.
2. Marriage Muhoortha.
3. New House Warming Muhoortha.
4. Upanayana Muhoortha.

5.58 TIDHI, VAARA, NAKSHATRA,LAGNA SUDDHI FOR HOUSE CONSTRUCTION & OTHER SUBHA MUHOORTHAS DETAILS OR RULES LAID DOWN IN THE FOLLOWING TABLE FOR COMPLIANCE

S. No.	Subha function	Tithi	Weedays	Nakshatras	Lagnas	Important matters
1	House construction	2, 3, 5, 7 11, 13, 15	Mon-Wed Thurs-Fri,	Aswa-Roo-Mruga-Puna-Uttara Trayam-ha-ch-swa-anu-sra-dhani-sata-revati	Vrusha-Midhuna-Kanya-Dhanu-Kumbha-Meena (Simha-Vrichika)	Ashtama Suddihi kartairi-meena kanya, midhuna-dhanur-Masas-are-objectionable
2	House warming	2, 3, 4, 7, 10 11, 13, 15	Mon-Wed Thurs-Fri	Roo-mru-Umtha-ratrayam-chi-anu-ravati (pushya)	Vrushabha-Midhu-Sim-Kan-Vruch-Dhanu-Kum-Meena	Ashtama suddhi, Kalasa Chakra suddhi, Vrushbaha Chakra suddhi
3	Nishekamu	2, 3, 5, 10	Mon-Wed Thurs-Fri-Sat	Aswa-roo-mru-push-puna-uttara trayam-has-Cha-swa-anu-moo-sra-dha, sat- re	Subha yoga drushatamulu	Sandhya-prava pradosha-vrata-sarddha days objectionable
4	Grabha danamu	2, 3, 5, 7, 11, 13	Sun-Mon-Wed-Thru Fri	Roo-mru-pun-pusa-uttara trayam hatha-swa-anu-sra-dani-sata-ardra-poorva-trayam	Subha yoga drushtamulu	Sandhya parva pradosha vrata-srar-dosha-days objectionable lagna shuddhi.
5	Pumsavanam or Seemantham	2, 3, 5, 7 10, 11, 13, 15	Sun-Mon-Wed-Thur Fri	Mru-puna-push has-anu-sra-dha-satav-asw-roo-cht-swa-ttaratrayam	Aries, Taurus Gemini, Libra, dhanus, kumbha, Meena	For punsavanam 3rd month and for seemantham 4, 6, 8 months.
6	Jatakarma, Namakaraam	2, 3, 5, 7 10, 11, 13	Sun-Mon Wed-Thur Sat	Asw-roo-mru-pun-push-has-chh-swa-anu-uttara trayam-sra-dha-sat,re	Subha Lagnas	Ashatma suddi
7	Dolaro-haranam	2, 3, 5, 7, 10 11, 13, 15	Sun-Mon Wed-Thru Fri	Asw-roo-mru-pun-push-uttaratrayam has-cha-swa-anu-re-(sra)	Subha Lagnas	Ashatma suddhi

S. No.	Subha function	Tithi	Weedays	Nakshatras	Lagnas	Important matters
8	Nishkra manam	2, 3, 5, 7 10, 11, 13	Mon-Wed Thur-Fri	Asw-roo-mrpum-push-uttaratranam, has-chh-swa-anu-sra-dha-rev	Mesha-taurus karaktaka Libra Dhanus-meena	4th Month good 3rd Month also good
9	Annaprasana	2, 3, 5, 7 10, 13, 15	Sun-Mon Wed-Thru Fri	Aswa-roo-Mru-Puna-push-uttapatrayam-has-chi-swa-anu-sra-dha-sata-rev	Subha lagna	Dasama suddhi fore-noon-for men even months for women-odd month
10	Karana-veedha	2, 3, 5, 7 10, 11, 13	Sun-Mon Wed-Thru Fri	Aswa-roo-mru-puna-push-uttaratrayam-has-chh-sra-dha-anu-ree (ardra)	Taurus Gemini, caner, kanya, tula, dhanus meena (mesha makara)	9, 7, 8 months & ashtama suddhi
11	Kesha-khadana	2, 3, 5, 7 10, 13, 15	Mon-Wed Thru-Fri	Aswa-roo-mru-puna-push-has-chh-sra-dha-sata-ree (Jyesth)	Subha lagnas	Uttaraayana poorvarnam vishama varshamulu to be left out ashtama suddhi
12	Ashara bhyasam	2, 3, 5, 7 10, 11, 12	Mon-Wed Thur-Fri	Aswa-puna-has-chh-swa-anu-sra-rev (ardra-mru-dah-sata)	Midhuna kanya dahanus meena	Ashtama suddhi, uttarayanam 5th year is good
13	Vidyaa rambhamu	2, 3, 5 10, 11, 12	Wed-Thur Fri	Asa-mru-ardra-puna-push-asle-poorvatrayam-has-chi-swa-moila-sra (ardra-sata-anu)	Mesha midhuna karamtaka kanya, tula, dhanus makaram meenam	Day time
14	Upanayanam	2, 3, 5 10 11, 6, 12	Mon-Wed Thur-Fri	Asw-roo-mru-puna-push-uttaratrayam has-chh-swa-anu-sra-dha-sata-rev	Subha Lagna	Ashtama suddhi, Meena, chaitram subham
15	Marriage	2, 3, 5, 7 10, 11, 12, 13, 15	Mon-Wed Thur-Fri	Roo-mru-makh-uttaratrayam-has-swa-anu-moo-rev (Asw-sra-chi-dha)	Subha Lagnas	Jamitra suddhi. Meena chatram objectionable
16	Nava-vadhu pravasam	2, 3, 5, 7 10, 11, 13	Mon-Wed Thur-Fri	Aswa-roo-mru-pun-push-uttaratrayam, has-chi-swa-anu-moo-sra-dha-sata rev	Subha Lagnas	Dwadasa suddi Vishama-Varsha months
17	Nava-vas-traabharana dhramam	2, 3, 5, 7, 10 11, 13, 15	Wed-Thru Fri	Asw-has-chi-swa-anu-dha-(Poorvardham roo-puna-push-uttaratrayam)	Vrbshabha midhna karkataka kanya tula dhanus meena	Truteeya suddhi

S. No.	Subha function	Tithi	Weedays	Nakshatras	Lagnas	Important matters
18	Vapi-Koopadikam	2, 3, 5, 7, 10 11, 13, 15	Mon-Wed Thur-Fri	Asw-roo-mru-push-uttaratrayam, has-anu-moo-sra-dha-sata-rev (Jye)	Karkataka, makara, kumbha meena	South East, south, south west, north west-directions and centre of house not permitted
19	Beejaa vaapam	2, 3, 5, 7, 10 11, 13, 15	Mon-Wed Thur-Fri	Roo-push-uttaratrayam has-swa-anu-mo-sra-sata-re (asw-mru-puna-dha)	Vrushabha, karkatama, simha, makara (tula-midhuna-kumbha)	Ashtama suddhi, in 3, 6, subhas should not be there
20	Vrusha latadi stapanam	2, 3, 5, 7, 10 11, 13, 15	Mon-Wed Thur-Fri	Asw-roo-mru-push-uttaratrayam, chi-visa-anoo-moo-sra-sata-rev	Subha lagnas	There should be good planet's aspect to 4th house
21	Devata pratishta	2, 3, 5, 7, 8 10, 11, 12, 13	Sun-Mon Wed-Thru Fri	Aswa-roo-mru-puna-push-uttaratraya, has-cih-swa-ano-sra-dha-sata-rev (Deva nakshatra)	Taurus scropio leo, meena, kanya, dhanus, Khumbha, Meena	Soumya devatas uttarayamam. for Ugra Devatas dakshanayam
22	Yatra	2, 3, 5, 7 10, 11, 13	Wed-Thur Fri	Asw-mru-pun-push-has-anu-dha-sata-rev-roo-uttaratrayam-Moo (sra)	Mesha vrusha-bha, karkataka, tula, dhanus, makara, meena	Panchama suddhi subha sakunam
23	Halakarma	2, 3, 5, 7, 10 11, 13, 15	Sun-Mon Wed-Thur Fri	Asw-roo-mru-puna-push-uttaratrayam, has, chi, swa, visa, moo-sra-dha-sata rev	Taurus Gemini, virgo, scorpio, dhanus, pisces	Kartari is not permitted.

It is to be counted as Paksha wise only.

1. For Subha Muhoorthas-Maha Doshas should be left out.
2. The particular day's Nakshatra is the basis for count (separately for Sukla & Krishna Pakshas) for all Subha Functions listed above.
3. The number obtained for their serial for Nakshatra, Varra, Lagna & Tidhi are to be added and the sum obtaied is divided by 9, then if the balance number is 1-Mrutyu, 2-Agni, 4-Raja, 6-Chora, 8-Roga will cause these Asubha Phalas.
4. The balance to get 1 & 2 is most objectionable & Highly Dosha.
5. The balance 3, 5, 7, 9 if obtained it is auspicious.

To count from previous Tithi is not as per Rules. It is to be counted as Paksha wise only. The number obtained after Division is not to be added. Tithi is not to be counted from the beginning of the Month it is not as per Rules. It as to be counted pakshawise only.

CHAPTER 6

Introduction to Vaasthu Sastra

6.1 KNOWLEDGE OF VAASTU SASTRA

The important texts in Vaasthu Sastra are- 1. Manasaara, 2. Viswakarma Mata, 3. Maya Mata, 4. Aparajitha Pruchcha, 5. Samarangana Sutra Dhaara, 6. Raja Vallabha and 7. Mandeeya etc.

6.2 KSHETRA KNOWLEDGE

Kshetra means the Land. For any construction the first & foremost requirement is the Land. The main objective of this chapter is to choose a proper Land which is most suitable from the Rules laid down as per Vasthu Sastra points of view.

It is possible only for a person who had accepted Gruhastashrama, to attain the four Purshardhas viz, Dharma, Artha, Kama & Moksha. In Gruhasthashrama the House is the most important item of attainment. The House should be such that it is Livable from the points of view of having good breeze, get bright lighting inside the House, so that it helps the owner in maintaining good health, feel always enthusiatic and delightful and also assist in improveing the mental calmness alround. This is most important. The Vasthu Sastra lays down Rules & Regulations for Construction, to enable enjoyment of all the comforts & conveniences.

Vaasthu Sastra depends upon the following considerations:-

1. The effect of surroundings.
2. The physical character of land meant for Construction
3. Co-ordination of Rules specified for healthy living.
4. Ensure the Architectural Beauty of the building constructed.
5. Defining the necessities of life.
6. The advatnaege obtained as a result of examination of land characteristics and the forces within.
7. The influence of Atmospheric chanages occurring on this Planet.
8. Accounting for changes noticed in various places and the time differences involved.
9. The influnces of changes occurring in the Human Life due to movement of Planets and their effects.

For Construction, the first & foremost to be examined is the Land for which the Land taken for construction of a House. The four sides are to be fixed. Fencing or boundary walls constructed. The Land taken for purpose of Construction is popularly known as Kshetra.

For all Vaasthu Karmas the land is of great importance and is called as an important vastuvu. Those Constructions which are built on Vasthuvu are called Vaasthuvulu. The Vaasthu Sastra Text had laid down certain Rules for construction of vaasthuvu. Before deciding to take the Land for Construction, the following points are to be examined.

1. Importance of Nama Nakshatra.
2. Directions & Vargus.
3. Vargu–Lordship of Vargu.
4. Examination of Land.
5. Examination of Village.
6. Physical Characters of the soil inside the Land.

6.3 THE IMPORTANCE OF NAMA NAKSHATRA

The Indian Astrology had elaborately described the relationship between Stars, Planets & Rasis. In Vaasthu Sastra, Utmost importance is given for Nama Nakshatra, than the Janma Nakshatra. In the House construction based on Nama Nakshata the following sub-division have to be worked out.

1. Varga Arvanam
2. Kshetra Arvanam
3. Gruha Arvamam
4. Grama Arvamam

From the fifty one Alphebets starting from 'A' to 'Ksha', the Vaasthu Sastra had laid down Eight Vargus such as.

'A-KA-CHA-TA-THA-PA-YA-SA'. These eight 'Vagu's starting from East have Lordship for the eight Directions. Taking these eigiht Vargus into considereation the Vaasthu Sastra decides Gruhaarvanam and the position of Main Door etc. The Nama Nakshatra is considered in Vassthu Sastra than the Janma Nakshatra and is the basis that was established on Sampradaya, & Rules laid down as such from long standing periods of practice.

This practice is in vogue even in other Countries, to enable them to findout Auspicious and Inauspicious results based on the system of Nama Nakshatra.

We had considered the '51' alphabet in the Telugu Language as equivament to Pancha Bhutas (Five Premordial Elements) Character and distributed to them as under.

Sky-Akaasham	Water-Jala, Aru, Aroo	Earth-Prudhvi Uo Uoo, Aoo	Air-A, AA, Yee	Fire-IE, IEE
Raa, Va	Yo, Ja Doa	Ga, Ja, Da, Dha	Ka, Cha Ta	Na, Kha
Ma, Sa, Maa	Ddha, Bha Va, Na	Ba, Bbha La	Ta Pha Ya	Cha, Ra

6.4 NAMA NAKSHATRA TABLE WITH RASIS

S. No.	Nakshatra	First alphabet of the name				Rasi
1	Aswani	Chu	Chee	Choo	Laa	
	Bharani	Lee	Loou	Lyee	Looo	Aries
	Krittika	AA	—	—	—	
2	Krittika	—	Yee	Uoo	EEA	
	Rohini	Yoo	Vaa	Vee	Yuoo	Taurus
	Mrigasira	Vee	Voo			
3	Mrigasira			Kaa	Kee	
	Arudra	Kuoo	Kham	Ja	Chhaa	Gemini
	Punarvasu	Kee	Kooo	Haa	—	
4	Punarvasu	—	—	—	Heee	Cancer
	Pushyamui	Huoo	Heee	Hooo	Ddaa	
	Aslesha Elements					
5	Makha	Maa	Me	Mooo	Mmee	
	Pubba	Mmoo	Tta	Ttee	Ttoo	Leo
	Uttara	Ttea	—	—	—	
6	Uttara	Ttoo	Paa	Ppee		
	Hastha	Ppoo	Sham	Ninaa	Dhaa	Virgo
	Chitta	Pee	Ppou	—	—	
7	Chitta			Raa	Rree	
	Swati	Rooo	Reee	Rooe	Thaa	Libra
	Visakha	Ttee	Thoo	Thee		
8	Vishkah	—	—	—	Ttoo	
	Anuraadha	Nau	Nee	Noo	Nnee	Scorpio
	Jyestha	Nooo	Yaaa	Yee	Youu	
9	Moola	Yaa	Yooo	Baa	Bee	
	Porvashda	Bboo	Dhaa	Chchaa	Ddhaa	Sagitterious
	Uttarashada	Bbee	—	—	—	
10	Uttarashada	—	Jjou	Jjaa	Jjee	
	Sravanam	Jjoo	Jeee	Jooo	Khaa	Capricorn
	Dhanishta	Gaa	Gee	—	—	
11	Dhanishta	Ggoo	Ggee	—	—	
	Satabhisham	Gggo	Ssaa	Ssee	Ssuu	Aquarius
	Poorvabhadra	Ssee	ssoo	Dhaa	—	
12	Poorvabhadra				Dhee	
	Uttarabhatra	Ddoossam	Jjhoo	Ddhaa		Pisces
	Revati	Jjee	Doo	Chha	Chee	

When an individual is unwell, thinking of Country & Village at the time of House Warming, when employing a Servant, when you go in for a War, in Business Matters, when sending an Ambassador, while giving money-for all these activities importance is to be given for Nama Nakshatra.

But when you go on Travel & Conduct Marriage the Janma Nakshatra is important.

6.5 DIRECTIONS-VARGUS

In our daily routine life knowledge about direction is absolutely necessary. To know the areas & regions and for travel, the knowledge of directions is very useful.

When we face Sun rise the direction will be known. The Devatas in charge for each direction is also indicated in the following manner.

1. East: Direction of Sun rise, Indra
2. West: Sun setting direction, Varuna
3. South: Right side direction facing Sun, Yama
4. North: Left side direction facing Sun, Kubeera
5. South East: Middle of East & South, Agni, Agneya
6. South West: Middle of West & South, Parvati, Niruti
7. North West: Middle of West & North, Vayuvu
8. North East: Middle of East & North, Eeswarudu

The last four Directions are called sub-directions (Vi= Dkkulu) total eight directions. The 51 Alaphabets have been distributed into these 8 Directions and they are called Vargus in eight.

Similarly Animals & Brids have been divided from East to North-West in the name of their gender Yonees for all the eight Vargus. These details are given below.

Vargu	Lordship	Bird	Direction
'AA'	Indra	Garuda	East
'KA'	Agni	Cat or Marjalam	Southest East (Aagneya)
'CHA'	Yama	Lion	South
'TTA'	Nirti	Sunakam (Dog)	South West (Nairuti)
'TA'	Varuna	Sarpent (Snake)	West
'NA'	Vayuvu	Mooshikam (Elaka)	North-wast (Vayavya)
'YA'	Kubera	Elephent	North
'SSA'	Eeswarudu	Sasakam (kundelu)	North-east (Eesanya)

The above are shown with the Table given in a separate page 141.

If a Person's Name belongs to a particular Vargu, then it become its 'Own-Vargu'.

The 5th Vargu, leaving the 'Own Vargu'; becomes the 'Enemy-Vargu'

6.6 KSHETRAAR VARGU

'Aarvanam' means the suitable one Ksihetraarvanam means, election of the direction which gives good results. Based on the suitable kshetra for construction of a House according to the Vargu arrived depending upon the Owner's Name.

Every Direction is divided into 9 eqal parts, leaving 2 divisions on either side for sub-directions, the middle five divisions belongs to that Direction.

The 5th Vargu, from Own Vargu, (ii) the 6th one becomes Enemy Vargu Leaving Satru Vargu the construction can be done in any Direction.

The results of Vargus will be as under.

Swa vargu	Financial Gain
2nd Vargu	Gain is small
3rd Vargu	Subha Pradam
4th Vargu	Disceases
5th Vargu	Enemy
6th One	Fight
7th One	Soubhagyam
8th One	Death

See in which rasi the kshetram falls for construction as counted based on nama nakshatra rasi and from that rasi the results will be as under:-

If the Graha Rasis is	1, 5, 9 Rasis good results
If the Graha Rasis is	3, 7, 11 Rasis not that good result
If the Graha Rasis is	4, 8, 12 Rasis very bad results
If the Graha Rasis is	2, 6, 10 Rasis bad results

It is better to decide after examining Kshetraarvanam & Vargaarvanam. For this the following table will help.

	Eesanyam	**East**	**Agneya**	
	'SSA'-VARGU-EESANU-DU SASAKAM SSA, SHA, SA, HAA	'AA' = VARGU, GARUDA INDRA AA, AAH, YE, YEE, UO, UOO, ARU, AROO, YEE, IE, YOO, YOE	'KA'-VARGU, MARJALAM' AGNI, KA, KHA, GA, GHA, GNA	
North	'YA'-VARGU-ELE-PLANET, KUBERA, YA, RA, LA, VA	BRAHMMA POSITION	'CHA'-VARGU, LION, YAMA, CHA, CHHA, JA, JJHA, IGNE	SOUTH
	'PA'-VARGU-MOO-SHIKAM, VAYUVU, PA, PHA, BA, BBAMA	'TA'-VIRGU-SARPA, VARUNA, TA, TTHA, DA, DHA, NA	'TTA'-VARGU, DOG, NIRUTI TA, THHA, DA, DDHA, NNA	
	Vayavya	**West**	**Nairuti**	

6.7 GRAMAARVANAM

When a person migrates from one Village to another Village, it should examined before hand whether the Village is worth living or not and then only moved as opined by our Ancesstors. The Vasthu Sastra Pundits had stipulated these conditions based on the practice prevailing in those days.

In 'Kalamrutham' Text, it is stated.

Staring from 'AA' Alphabet count upto the Planets first Alphabet, then that figure is obtained as '9', then from 'AA' count upto the owner Names first Alphabet and if that figures is 4, then both these figures placed kept side by side to get 49. This is divided by 8 and the balance is one.

In the same manner the same figures reversed to make 94 and if this is divided by 8, the balance will be 6. This will become Debt.

If Badarayan's concept is followed, count from Own Nama Rasi to the Village where a new construction is made or already living in a house there. Then if the Rasi count is 2-5-10-11 any one of them comes, it is Auspicious. If 4-8-12 Rasi then the tenanets will spend their life there only and if 1-3-6-7 Rasi comes, then Own Finances will be spent. In the Ratnavali, Text.

NAKSHATRA SAREERA

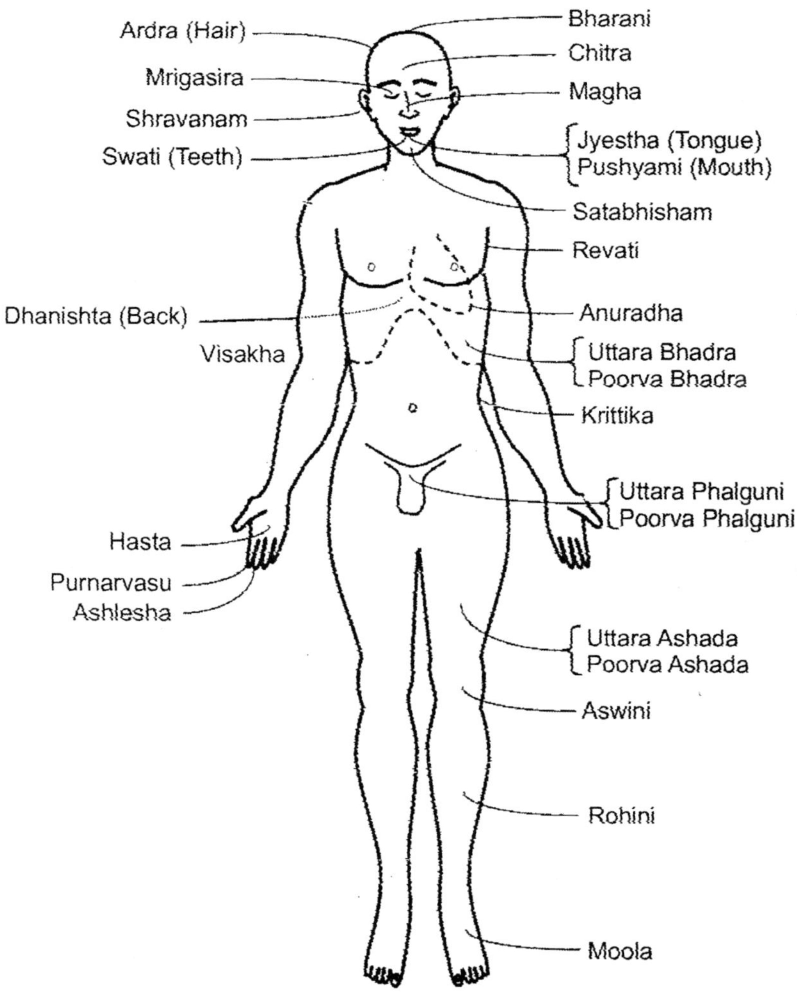

Fig. *The nakshatra Shareera of Lord Vishnu [Charak, 2010]*

Draw a figure of Human & then counting from Grama Nama Nakshatra.

Fix 5 Stars in the Head

Fix 3 Stars in the Face

Fix 5 Stars in the Chest

Fix 6 Stars in the Feet

Fix 1 Stars back Near anus

Fix 4 Stars at an Biblical Chord

Fix 1 Stars at Private part

Fix 1 Stars Right Hand

Fix 1 Stars Left Hand.

Then find out as to where the Star pertaining to House construction comes or Nama Nakshatra comes. Then if the Star comes is in the

Head-Financial gain

Face-Loss of Finance/Wealth

Ambilical-Wealth

Private Parts-Fear & Trouble some

Chest-gain of Wealth

Feet-Poverty to Women

Back-Danger to Life

Right hand-Unhappy or Sorrowfulness

Left hand-Do---Do---

6.8 EXAMINATION OF LAND

Before selection of Land site for construction, one should examine the surroundings & their influence and the four sides of that site should be such that it gives:-

1. Happines
2. Causes Enthusiasm
3. Should be in conformity with Rules laid down for good health, and from Social secutiry poits of view, the following places are not fit for construction site.
    1. The Land which is in the out-skirts of a Village.
    2. The Land which is closer to Burial grounds.
    3. The Land on which the shadows of the Temple falls.
    4. The Land adjacent to Temples with Grama Devatas and Shakthi Peethamulu.
    5. The Land which is opposite to the site where congregations takes place for conducting Night Functions throught the entire night time.
    6. The Land at the junction of four roads.
    7. The Land closer to shady trees of Ravi & Madde where Villagers congregate now and then.
    8. The Land which is behind the Temple of Lord Vishnu.

6.9 DIGMOODHAM

Taking help of Compass, the Land taken should be examined and correct Directions fixed. If it is done like that the Absolute Directions are known.

Before examination by Compass the site selected should be seen for level differences by stacking Water over the plot. Then adjustments carried out correctly to get the Land to the correct level. If site selected is not in comfirmty with Absolute Directions and if it coincides with sub-direction (Vi-dikkulu) then the Land site is said to have Dosha from the Direction and is called 'Digmoodhami'.

Direction of Moodhatwam	Result
1. In East-West Direction	Causes loss of Wife
2. In North Direction	Causes no Children
3. In South Direction	Causes Disceases leading to death

6.9.1 Direction and Rasis

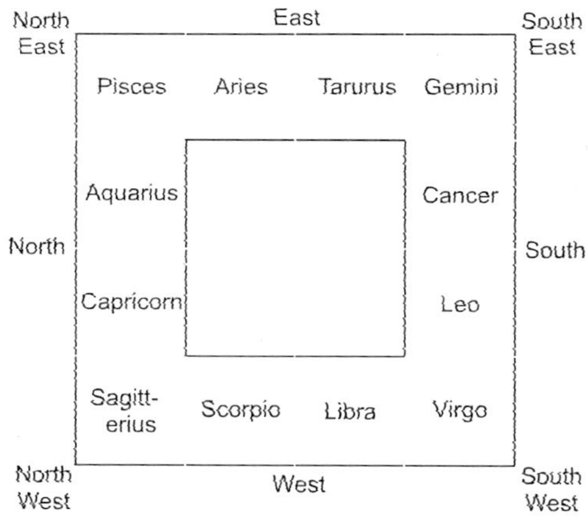

6.10 SITES HIGH & LOW

If Sites are having level difference then the results Direction wise, are given in the following Table:-

The sites which are High in the Direction or Sub-direction & their results	Sites which are Low & their results Direction wise
1. East-Loss of Son	1. East-Imporves future
2. S.E-Gain wealth	2. North-Get wealth
3. South-Good health	3. West-Loss of wealth
4. S.W-Happyness from women	4. South-Death
5. West-Loss of wealth	
6. North-Get Discease	
7. N.E-Uncurable Discaeses	

The results of Directions & Subdirections for the sites can also be seen in other Text- such as. Aparajitha Pruchcha ' Jyothir Nibandham' & 'Vastu'.

The soil of the site proposed for selection should be tested with the following.

1. Color
2. Taste
3. Feeling by touch
4. Smell
5. Outlook
6. Sound
7. Shape

From all these angles tests are to be conducted and suitable site selected.

Tests such as:

1. Filling up soil after excavation back in the same pit and if soil remains.
2. In the site, a suitable size pit of propor depth is made and water should be filled fully and seem after 12 hours whether the water still remains without getting absorbed fully.

6.11 FOUR VARIETIES OF VAASTHUVULU

The place where Human being live is called as Vaashuvu. This Vsthuvu is standing on the Land selected. Hence the Land got the name of Vasthuvu. This Vaasthuvu is divided into four categories as under:

1. **Land:** This has been described in the 'Kshetra Parijnam'.
2. **Prasdam:** House which is properly built. It is called as 'soudhamu'
3. **Yanam:** The area where the Vechiles meant for Travel are kept such as Chariot, Cars, Air Planes & Ships.
4. **Satawam:** The furniture such as Cots, Chairs & Sofas for happy comfortable living.

It is necessary to know the sites which are not suitable or prohibited after examination. The locations where one should live the soil there should be tested for its color, availability of any articles or skeletons inside Vasthuvu should be known.

1. **Land:** As per Indian Sculpture Text and as per information known due to newly developed Scientific knowledge being made available with varieties of terms & methods and if one examines in an unbaised manner the following will be known.
    1. The influece of surroundings.
    2. The Physical Character of the site selected for construction.
    3. Compatability with Rules laid down for healthy living.
    4. Maintaining the Arcitecturral beauty of the construction.
    5. The construction layout is designed to suit to the necessities of life.
    6. The advantages derived in following proper Directions & levels without Digmoodhami.
    7. The effect of atmospheric changes on the construction.
    8. The effect or repercussions due to changes in the Country from time to time.

2. **Prasadam:** In this there are 2 types. The first is Hosues Owned by Humans and the second the Temples. These should be built in such a way that it is suitable to each of them. In the Houses there are:-
    1. Eka-Salas
    2. Dwi-Slatas
    3. Tri-Salas
    4. Chatus-Salas

    Those Salas which are harmful should not be built.
3. **Yanam:** The Travel Vehicles are in 3 types:
    1. Vechile Run on Earth
    2. Vechile Run on Water
    3. Vechile Run on Air

    In our country during Ramayana & Mahabharata periods, different types of Vahanas were used.

    In Samarangana Text even viechlies that could Travel on fire were said to be in use.

    There are Ships that Travel by surface of Sea and Sub-marines that travel inside sea-water.

    In Ramayna & Mahabharata periods they used Pushpaka Vimanamu & Tripuras as these belongs to Air Travel. All these Vahanas were said to be with German Country as indicated by the famaous Scientisis.
4. **Sayanam:** In this Division there are Cots, Chairs, Chakravry Chairs and many varities which were useful for domestic purposes. In certain Sculpture Texts and Samhita Grandhas, mention is made about the Sayanams that were used in different directions by humans depending upon their Status and Professional Ethics. In Mahabharata the Maya Sabha was mentioned which belongs to this category.

    Keeping the above aspects in view the human beings are always attempting to have had every article or vasthuvu is converted or shaped to his liking & convenimient so that they could spend their life happily.

6.12 SHODASA BHOO LAKSHANAM

A land site whether it is favourable for house site construction or not can be known if the shape of the Land proposed is known and whether it is good or bad for that purpose. In Vaastu Texts a mention was made about different varieties of shapes of Land on which construction of House was taken up and the Doshas or other wise attached to them were described as 'Shodasa bhoo lakshanam'.

(i) Sixteen shapes of land sites-these are as under:

1. Ayata Site

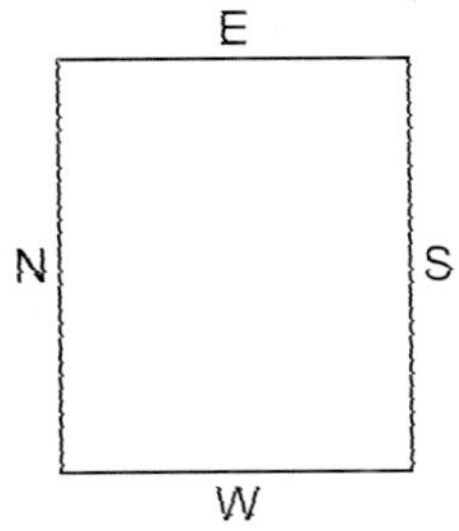

The Length is twice the Width. The Sastras said that the House built in such sites if lived will give success in all Endevours.

2. Square site

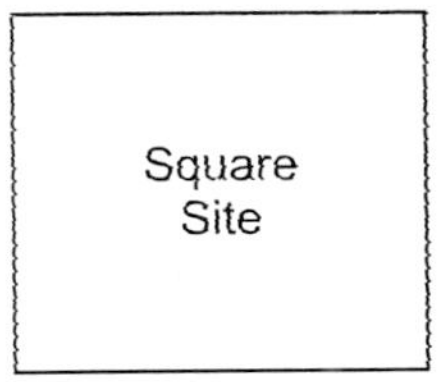

Length & Breadth are equal. This House will improve Wealth. Goddess Lakeshmi stays permanemitly.

3. Circular site

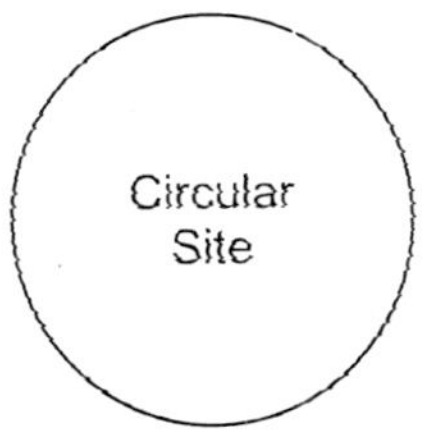

In some Texts, this type is prohibited.

4. Bhadrasanaakara site (Like sitting stool)

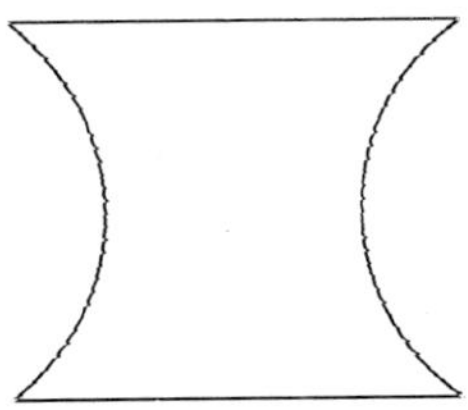

This site will give all conveniences and makes the Owner happy.

5. Chakraakara land (like a wheel)

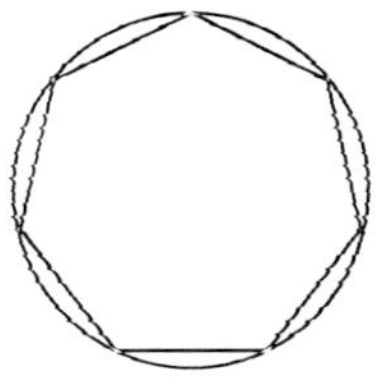

This site will lead to Poverty, loss of children and spoils the happiness.

6. Vishamabahu (Ani)

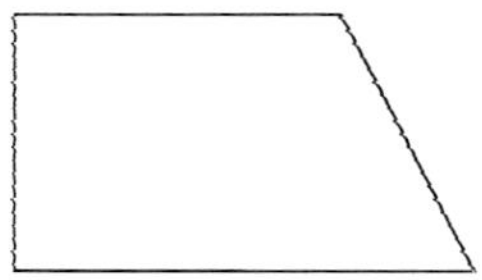

This will give Tragidies & Unhappiness.

7. Triangular shaped site

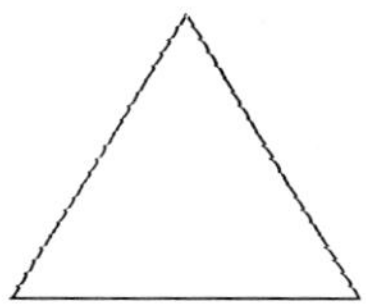

This will land up in fear from Kings and makes loss of Children.

8. Sakataakara land

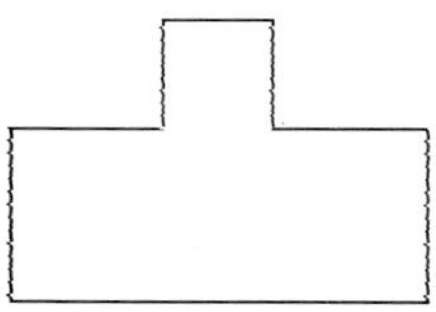

This is unfit for living.

9. Dandaakara land

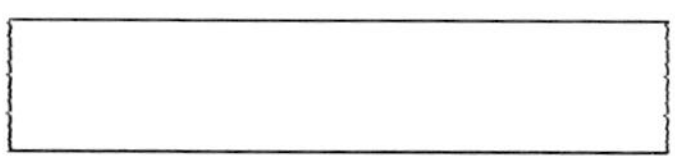

This is like a long stick. This will cause loss of cattle & loss of wealth.

10. Panavakaara land

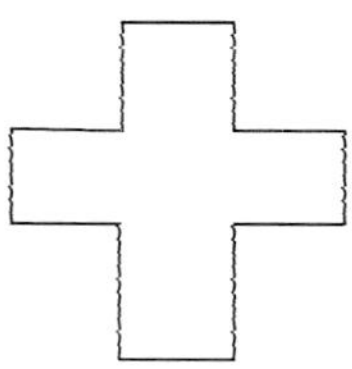

Those who live in this House will suffer from Eye diseases. Some children are born Blind.

11. Murajaakara land

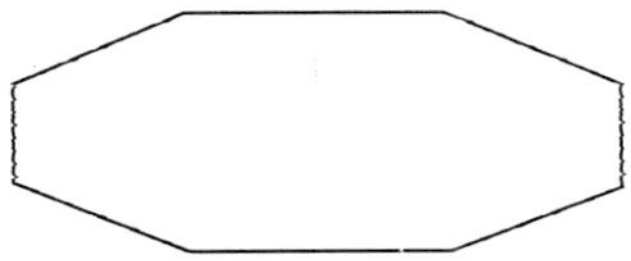

There are chances of wife expiring. Loss of happiness from Women. Either no children or children born & die or complete loss to Family.

12. Bruhanmukha site

This spoils the Wealth. Brings in Poverty Loss of Relations & causes many difficulties.

13. Vyjanaakra land

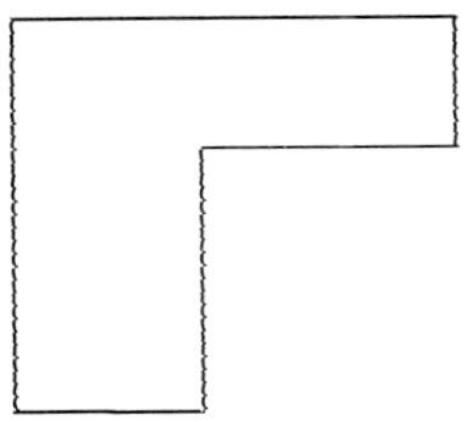

Loos of wealth, Business suffers, Loss of job.

14. Kurma prushtaakara land

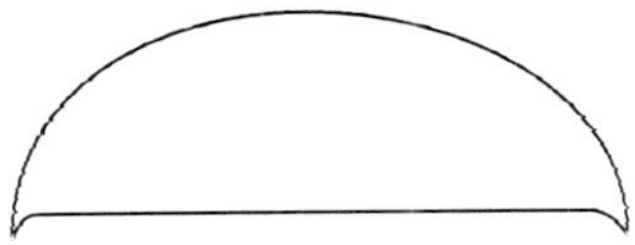

Those living will be unhappy Cruel treatement from Kings.

15. Surpaakara land

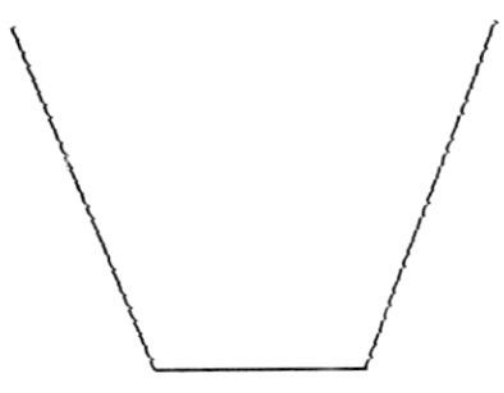

Will acquire uncurable Diseases and suffer from Poverty.

16. Kumbhakaara land

Those living will suffer from Leprosy.

6.13 VARIETIES OF ANGULAR LANDS-THEIR SUITABILITY

This Vaasthu Sastra Texts had laid down Rules for good/otherwise for construction of a House on land site from all angles and after through examination; the site chosen should be either Square or Rectangle so that it causes happiness & contribute to good results. In addition for those whose occupations are different certain shapes of Land sites were recommended to them so that they live happily.

Kshetra rupas

(a) Sqaure (b) Circle (c) Bhada peetham (d) Triangle (e) Surpam (f) Vyajanam (g) Murajam (h) Dhanus

These shapes are said to be acceptable as per Kshetra Ganita. Further there are shapes similar to Animals, Birds, Snakes, Vaasthu, Armoury & odd shapes specified in Vaasthu Texts.

The texts Rajamarthamdam, Samarangana, Silpa Ratnam lays down the shapes of Houses for persons of various occpations suitable to them. Students are advised to see these Texts.

6.14 VARIOUS SHAPES SUITABLE FOR LIVING

Shastras had laid down the following further Shapes in addition to 16 types metioned above.

1. Land with five sides.
2. Land with seven sides.
3. Land with nine sides.
4. Land with six sides.
5. Land with eight sides.

All the above types of shapes are to be modified without acute angles and should be either Square or a Rectangle in shape and used for construction, Rest of the Land should not be part of Land under construction. Compound walls are to be built & Land not required should be left out.

Samarangana Surta Dhara lays down the shape of the House to be lived in, based on individual occupation either Business or Professional.

6.15 SALYA PRAKARANAM

The Substances which are Harmful, Substances situated inside the Land have been specified in Vaasthu Sastra. The remains of living beings after death, the dust & carbon particles, iron etc which contain in the sites are harmful for living. The knowledge Sciences Text describes these matters is called Salyaparishaa.

In order to know the Salyas in the Land, this should be done with utmost care, not only with the knowledge of Sastras but one should have the experience of forces that act due to steady Meditation and in addition should have the knowledge of Prasna Sastra in Astrology.

If there are Salyas inside the Land, the forces that emanate from them causes Doshas in air & land and on those living there in. The effect of those fores clinging to Salysas also will have their influence on the Human beings living there in.

The Owner of the House should approach Sastra Pundit and question him.

1. The Owner to face either East or North and put the question. Then it is under stood that there is no Dosha of any type of the Land.
2. If the person faces the other Direction & questions, then there will be Salyas in the land positively.

6.16 THE METHOD OF DECIDING SALYAS BASED ON THE PRASNA LAGNA

If Prasma Lagna are fixed Rasis like Taurus, Leo, Scorpio & Aqurius then, it is concluded that the land selected contain Salyas.

If there are Dwiswabhava Rasis like Gemini, Virgo, Saggitarious & Pisces Salyas will be there or will not be there.

For any Lagna, 4th house, 7th house, or 10th House cantain Papa Grahas, then there will be Salyas.

Chaturdha Suddhi is very important, if Kendra & Kona have Subha Grahas, then the site selected is pure devoid of any Doshas.

6.17 JYOTHISHA-PRASNA METHOD

The Lal Kitab Text lays down that after finding out the Direction in which Salyas are found in the nominated Land based on prescribed methods and only after performing Shanthi and make the land purified before commencement of construction on the same.

Identify Salyas based on Vargaakshara method. Find out as to the Direction the Salayas existed and examined. Findout the depth at which the Salyas are found. The type of Dosha it causes and the method of readial measures proposed to be adopted, all these matters were described in grater detail in Vaasthu Texts.

If these remedial methods are taken & make the land devoid of all Doshas, before taking up construction, then that House gives calmness & happiness.

6.18 MANA PRAKARANAM

Mana means Measurement. As per Vaastu Sastra for construction Measurement is necessary. In this Sastra the decision of adoping Angula & it's importantance in the Mana differences in Kishku Pramanam, Ashtavidha Hasthalu, Dhawaar, Mushtadi Bhedalu, Purusha Pranama Aspect, Mana Advantages, Hasthopayogalu all matters of difference are made known.

In the present day period only the British Mana is only used for all practical purposes. But recently Metric Mana has come into use.

As time advances just as changes do occur in the Shastra, certain type of changes are unavoidable & do takes place even in the Mana Method of selection & adaption.

6.19 AYA PRAKARANAM

There are Methods laid down for House Construction, Sculptures and Vaastaus. Their Length and Width dimensions are most important. By having knownledge of these matters which are considered advantageous from natural surroundigns which will make the individual Prosperous and contribute happiness while living in such constructions.

To construct the Houses as per the views expressed calcutating 'Aya' is necessary 'Aya' means earnings and is in use with that understanding. For a House calculate 'Aya' and carryout constructions, such House will give advantages to the individual living there in. Some Ayas are good and some other Ayas create difficulties.

The 'Aya' is different for each direction. All materials used in house construction have to be purified in the 'Ayadisuddhi' basis. There is Lordship of 'Aya' for each Direction which are given as under:

1. For East-Dhwaja Ayam
2. For West-Vrushabha Ayam
3. For South-East Dhumra Ayam
4. For South-Simha Ayam
5. For South-West-Swarna Ayam
6. For North-West-Khara Ayam
7. For North-Gaja Ayam
8. For North-East-Kak Ayam

The Ayas of each Direction are their Own Houses. From the Owning Hosue (leaving this House) the 5th House is evemy's Houses. House is to be built accordingly. The House should not be built in sub-direction (Vidikkulu). Based on Length & Breadth, the area is calculated, this is called Kshatra Padam. This is called Padam or Pindamu. Based on these Padams, Dhwajadi Ayas' will come on calculations. The Aya is to be decided depending upon the Simhadwaram or main door and not as per Directions.

(a) If construction is done on East, South-West.	Dhwajayudham is considered as excellent.
(b) If faceing South or West construction is done.	Dhwaja & Simha Ayam, any one is excellent.
(c) If faceing West & North construction is done.	Dhawaja, Simha & Gaja Ayam, any one is excellent.
(d) If faceing West construction is done.	Dhawaj, Simha, Gaja Ayam, any one is excellent.

6.20 AYAS RESULTS

1. Dhawaja Aya: Gain of wealth
2. Dhumra Aya: Gives children
3. Simha Aya: Enjoyment of special type of pleasures
4. Swarna Aya: Highly sinful
5. Vrushaba Aya: Increase in prosperity both Money & Grains
6. Khara Aya: Enmity with women
7. Gaja Aya: Success in all auspicious functions
8. Kak Aya; Leads to death

Amsa phalam, Rasi Kutadi Phalam, Vaara Paalam, Tara phalam, Tidhi Planet Ayurdaya phalam, Directional Lordships Phalam.	For all these matters, the readers are advised to refor Vaasthu Sastra texts.
Ayas-their aspects Dwaras Shapes Vargadhi Pahlam castes, Varga details, calculation Kshetra Phala Sadhana, Mana Method of picking Ganitam of Nama Varga.	All these matters are to be examined throughout. After obtaining the required information and the site which is acceptable, only is to be under taken for construction.

6.21 DIK SADHANA

'Dik' means Disa or one which protects a place. In the land proposed for construction the Directions are fixed properly. Taking Sunrise as basis the directions are to be fixed.

In older days to determine directions, advantage was taken from Sun, Dhruvastar Krittika Star. Now a days it is done with the help of Compass.

During the period of Uttarayana & Dakshinayana, there is a difference in the timings of Sun rise & Sun set.

It is most esstential to decide the Direction based on the above aspects.

1. Methods of determining directions.
2. Improtance of determing Absolute East direction.
3. Doshas due to Dikmoodhas & their results.
4. Importance of Construction of House in the correct direction.
5. Sutra-stapana.
6. Shodasapada Vibhagamu.

If all the above matters are examined carefully to the proposed Land site and house constructed then chances of giving health, peace & prospertity increases.

6.22 SANKU LAKSHANAM

(i) Permission to go ahead with construction of House starts from 'Sankhu Stapana' (ii) Begin construction of the House. The Owner has to clean up the site make it fit for construction. (iii) A plan of the House to be constructed is to be made by consulting a Stapathi an expert in this matter, to find out:

1. Place where Vaastu Puja is to be performed.
2. As to the type of stone & materials to be used as Sankuvu.

The 'Sankuvu' is in a pointed shape which will draw its strength through that point. The forces in nature and the Prana force is drawn, through pointed end of Sankhu and kept it in the house constructed.

Just as a Child in the Mothers woomb gets food from the Ambilical chord, similarly the goddess of nature gives strength to the proposed site through Vaasthu Purusha's Ambilical chord as obtained from the pointed end of Sankhu.

The Mantra specified to be mentioned during Sun's Eclipse is recited. It is told by Ancestors that the Mantra Sakthi gets thounsand fold stronger. There are only two eclipses forming for us.

1. During Sun's Eclipse, the shadow of Sun falls on the Earth in a pointed manner similar to the shape of pointed Sankhu.
2. During Moon's Eclipse, the shadow of Earth falls on Moon in a simiarlar way.

This shadow is in the shape of Shankhu during Eclipse time. The Gravitational forces of Sun, Moon & Earth will join in one line in the form of waves. That is when forces from other planets fall on the Earth, its force increases many fold. Hence the Rituals conducted during Eclipse time on earth will give results in a similar manner. As a result of the above analysis, the shape of Sankhu has been decided.

1. Character of Sankhu.
2. Suitable or unstuiable materials for making Snakhu.
3. The place as to where Sankhu Stapama is to be done.

All these matters have to be examined as per Rules laid down in Sastras and on that basis, House is to be constructed so that it gives a happy and prospereous life.

6.23 VAASTHU PURUSHUDU

The basis of Vaasthu Sastra is Vaasthupurusha. For making Vaasthu the ingredient is Land. Those that are built on Vaasthu are called by names:

Gruham, Suddham, Harmayam, they are also called as 'Vaasthuvu':

Since it lays down Commands & Rules for making Vaasthuvu it is called as Vaasthu Sastra.

For the entire Universe, the 'Sun' is the main basis as mentioned in Bhavishyapurana. As for 'Shrauthi' Sun is proved as Vishwa Karma. Vassthu Purusha is only the 'Sun'. Due to Sun's movement Seasons are forming, timings are occurring due to changes in Atmosphere. Different conditions suitable for making Vaasthu are created and forming different Magnetic waves. The Sun's rays are examined microscopically and the fores available in those Rays were indentified and each sub-division is named after a Goddess and provided its place in Vaasthu Pada Vinyasam. It's of utmost importance to know 'Vasthupurusha'.

Story of origin of Vaasthupurusha

In a nut shell it is stated as under. There was a fight long ago, between Lord Siva and Andhakasura. In this terrible fight, a drop of swet from Lord Sivas body got turned into a big shape, which created fear alround. Since Devatas were blessed by Load Brahmna, they managed to force that Big shaped form blessed onto Earth. It had fallen on its Belley and became a Diety & occupied the whole Earth. This figure was accepted as Vasstu Purusa. Since it is homing Devathas the 'Vaasthu Purusha' is worshipped by all Human beings living on Earth.

The time of birth of Vaasthu Purusha

The origin of Vaasthu Purusha took place in Bhadrapada Bahula Vidiya Saturday, in Krittika Star, Vyatipata Yoga in Vishti sign midway of Bhadra Karana.

1. The times at which Vaashu Purusha is to be worshipped.
2. The meaning of origin of Vaasthu Purusha.
3. The Dieties contained in Vaasthu Purusha.
4. Vaasthu Pada Vinyasamu.
5. Vaasthu Padas–their advantages.
6. Positions of Vaasthu Purusha.
7. The main door positions based on Vasthupurusha.
8. Dina or kshanika Vaasthu Purusha.

All these matters are examined based on Rules laid in Vaasthu Sutras and House constructed as per norms with Main Door Location so that a happy life is led in that houses.

6.24 VAASTHU PADAS

Vaasthu Sastra is part of Jyothish Sastra and in turn Jyothsha is part of Vedas. Ancient Rishes had developed this science such as Viswakarma, Yama, Twashatra, Kasyapa Bharadwaja, Bhruguvu, Manasara, Agasthya etc. They had formulated Rules for follow up by future Generations. Those details such as Aya Padas, are essentialy to be known. There are 32 Divisions of Vaasthupadas.

Important texts in this science are Mayamata, Silpa-ratna, Mamasara contain Vaasthu Padas. The land accepted for construction irrespective of it's shape dividing into equal parts method is called 'Padam'.

The total area taken for construction is called as 'Sakalam'. If a thread is tied from North-East to South-East to South-West to North-West & to North-East, the area in between is called 'Sakalam'.

If Land is made into 4 equal parts, it is called as 'Pachakam'

If Land is made into 9 equal parts, is called as 'Peetham'.

16 equal parts: Maahapeetham

25 equal parts: Upa Peetham

36 equal parts: Ugra Peetham

49 equals parts: Sthadilam

64 equal parts: Mandookam or Chatushshati Padas.

81 equal parts: Ekaaseethi padam

100 equal parts: Aasnam or Satapada Vaasthu

Still there are 17 more (121 to 1024) for every figure from 11^2 to 32^2 there are Padas.

This sort of Division is called Vaasthu Pada Vinyasam. These have been developed for prosperity of Human beings & Animals living in such constructions.

In all Vaasthu Pada, the important are there, which are called 'Vaastuotraiya Vibhagha. These are given as under. The place where other Vaastu Pada are used are specified in Classical Texts which may be reffered to. Vaashtu Traya Vibhaga are:

1. Ekaseethi Padam-81 Divisons.
2. Chatushasti Padam-64 Divisison.
3. Satapadam-100 Divisions.

1. Ekassethi Pada Vaasthu

N.W. NORTH N.E.

Roga	Naga	Mukhta	Bhallata	Soma	Charaka	Aditi	Diti	Agni
Papaya-ksha	Rajayhksha		Prodhwi				Aadaha	Parjamya
Suosha		Rudra	Dhara			Apavatsa		Jayamta
Asura								Indra
Aruna		MITRA		BRAHMMA		ARYAMA		Ravi
Pushpa Danta								Satya
Sugreeva		Yaja	Viva			Savi		Bhrusa
Dowarika	Indra		Snan				Savita	Nabha
Pitrogana	Mruga	Bhrun Garaja	Gandha	Yama	Grohashata	Vitadha	Purosha	Anila

WEST (left) — EAST (right)

S.W. SOUTH S.E.

There are '4' Stree South Devats & '4' Puruhsa Devatas. There is no place for them. There are difference of opinion about the shape.

Ekaseethi Pada Vaasthu 81 parts & their Lordships are shown as above.

2. Chatushashti Pada Vasthu

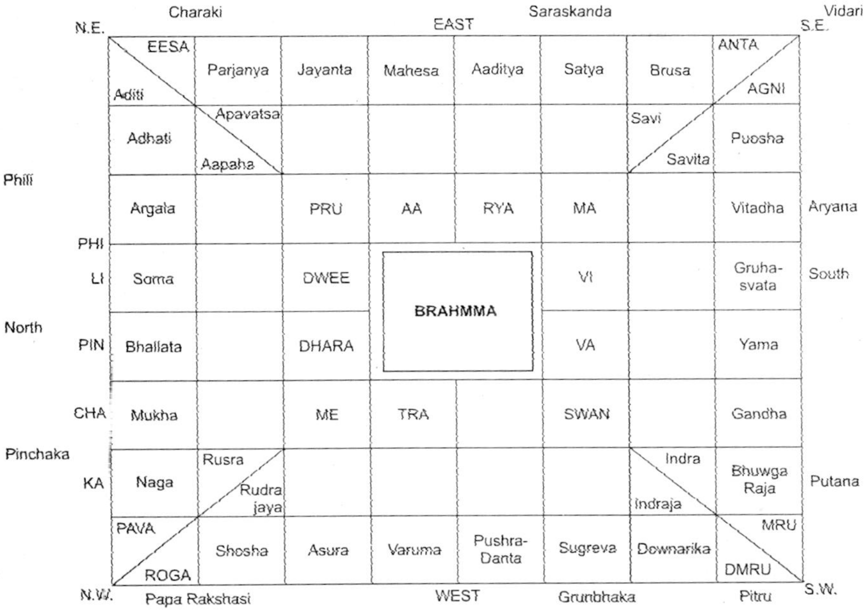

In outer Square & Angles in 28 Padas 32 Dieties are shown. Here also there are differences of opinion.

3. **Sata Pada Vasthu:** The site selected is made into 100 divisions (10 × 10). In the centre 16 divisions belong to Brahama.

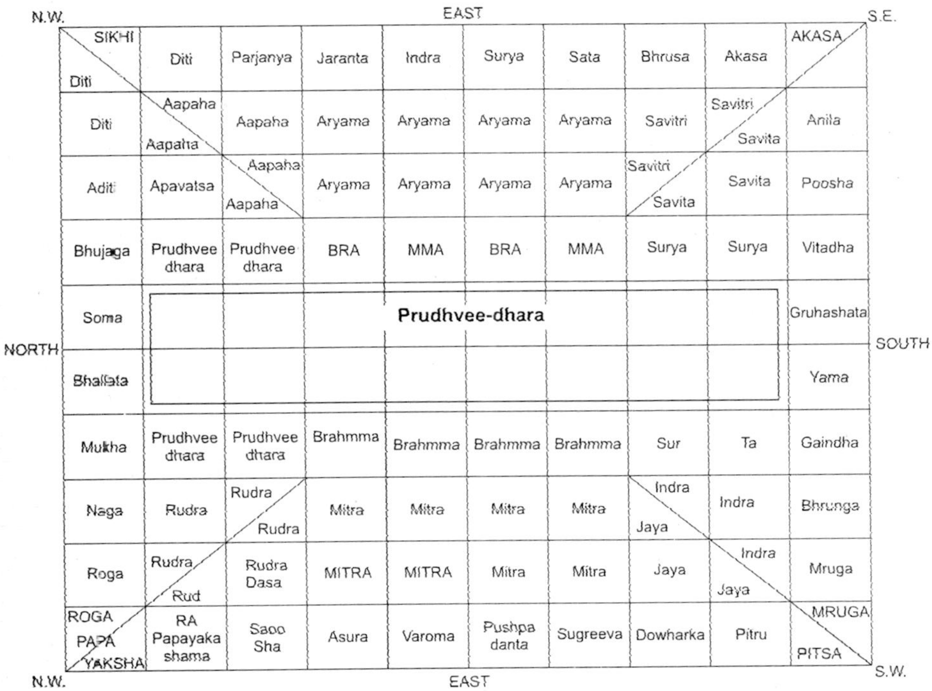

Vaasthu Padas are experience places.

1. Vaasthu Pada Marma Sandhies.
2. Vaasthu Purushanga Veeda Phalam.
3. Marmadi Veedha Phalam.

For all these matters Rules are followed as per Norms laid in Sastras. It is always better to spend the life Wealthier & Happier.

6.25 CONSTRUCTION OF SALAS

Sala means in local language as Savidi. Gruham is not meaning as Room and is not in practice. The word gruham means the total house.

Jyothisa Sastra was divided into three main divisions.

1. Siddhantam 2. Samhita 3. Hora.

1. **Siddhanta Skandhamu:** Countries, Directions, Timings and Planetary Movements etc. The information concerning these matters are fully giver.
2. **Samhita Skandhamu:** Matters concerning Muhoortha and Auspicious & Inauspicious of various functions are indicated in this division.
3. **Hora Skandhamu:** This is Predictive Astrology. It will give information regarding good & bad in an individual life in respect of all twelve Bhavas.

Matters concerning advantages in building a house as per Vassthu Norms will be known based on the area of Land. One should be aware of Rules concerning construction of Ekasala, Dwisala, Trisalas, some salas with Varandah & some without Varanda.

The shape of Sala can be as under as per requirements of Land Owner:

1. If four walls are made & covered with roof, it called Absolute Sala.
2. If three are Varandahs the Sala is called 'Sambaddam'.
3. If Salas contain three rooms it is called Samyutam.
4. If there are Varandahs between two Salas, it is called Pari Bhramam'.

Some time the word Sala gives a meaning as Gosala, Gajasala, Aswasala, Dhanyasala etc. Moveover the Bedroom (Sayana Gruham), Armoury Gruham. Kosa Gruham etc. The Gruham is used. Very wide & extensive area Salas are called Sala Prayogam. If there are small rooms all together as a unit it is called Gruha Satram. Thre are very many words equivalent to 'Gruham'.

The shapes & differences in Salas, the various areas of Salas in this are based on Directions. The Magnanimity of Sala Decision of Main Door and difference between Tri Salas Chotahsalas, the changes needed in their construction etc. Important aspects like Gurulaghu Prasthara Kramam can be found out in the Vaasthu Sastra Texts.

6.26 CONSTRUCTION OF 16 VARIETIES OF SALAS

There are 16 types.

1. Dhruvam
2. Dhanayam

9. Durmukham
10. Krooram

3. Jayam
4. Nandam
5. Kharam
6. Kaantam
7. Manoharam
8. Sumukham
11. Supaksham
12. Dhanadham
13. Kshayam
14. Aakrandam
15. Vipulam
16. Vijayam

(1)

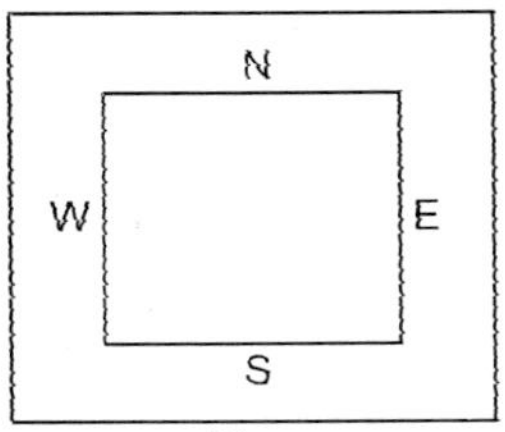

Dhruvam

(2)

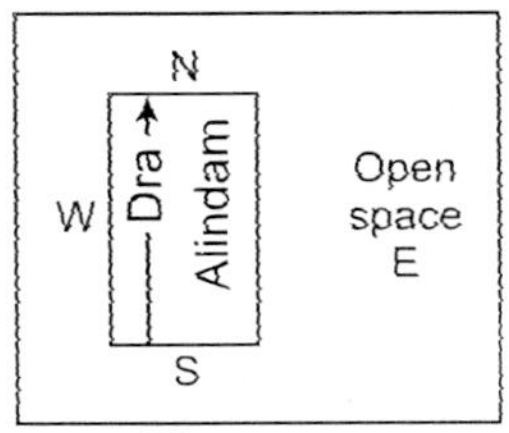

Dhaanyam

(3)

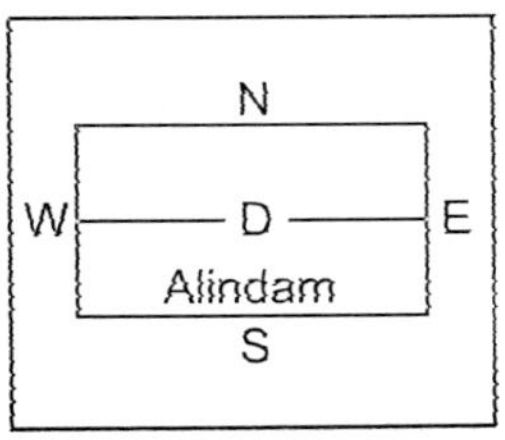

Jayam

(4)

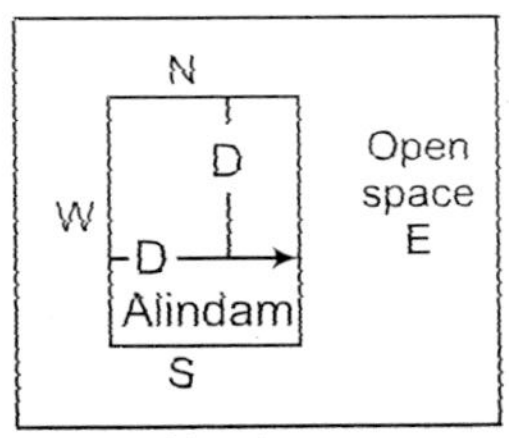

Nandam

(5)

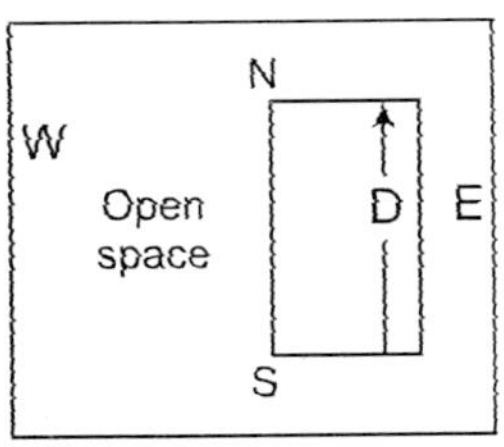

Kharam

(6)

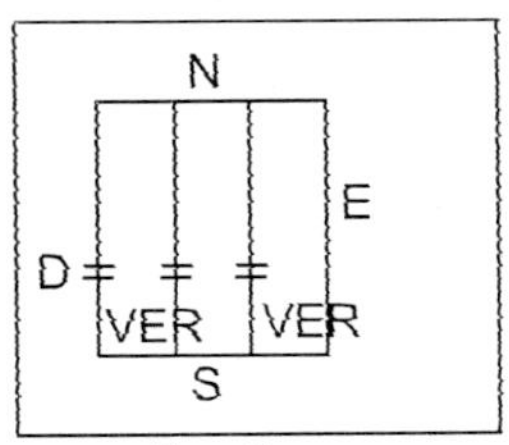

Kaantham

(7)

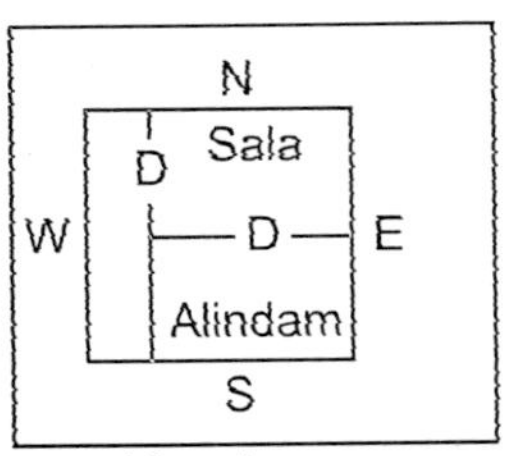

Manoharam

(8)

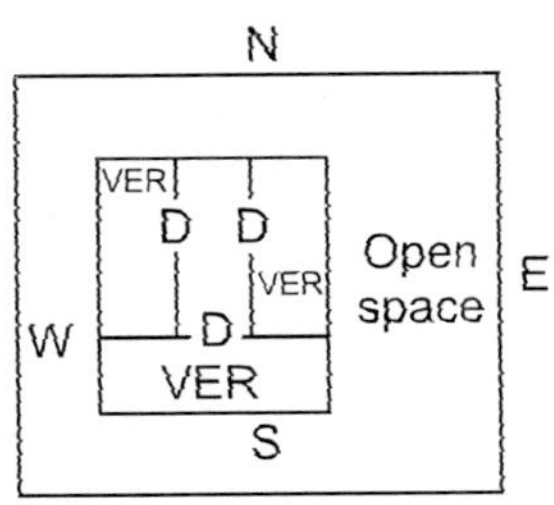

Sumukham

(9)

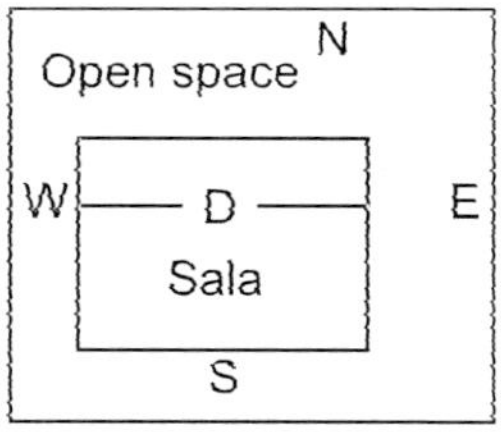

Durmukgam

(10)

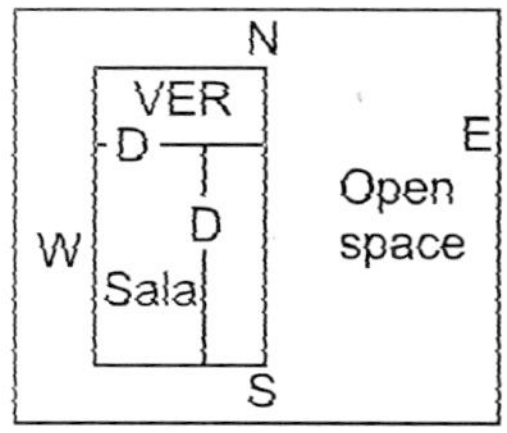

Krooram

(11)

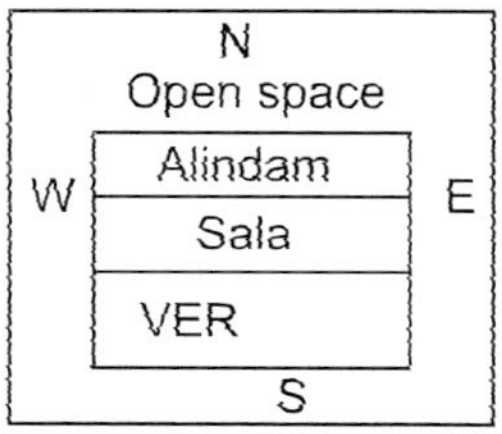

Supaksham

(12)

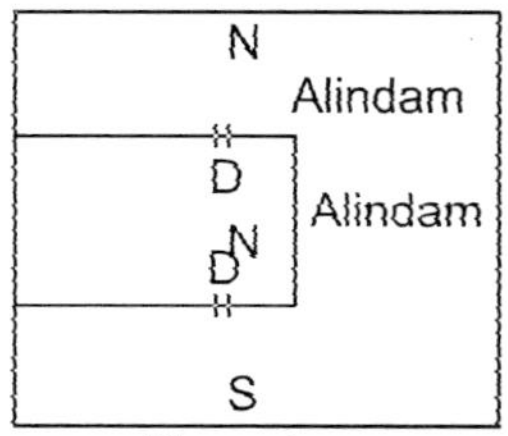

Dhanadam

(13)

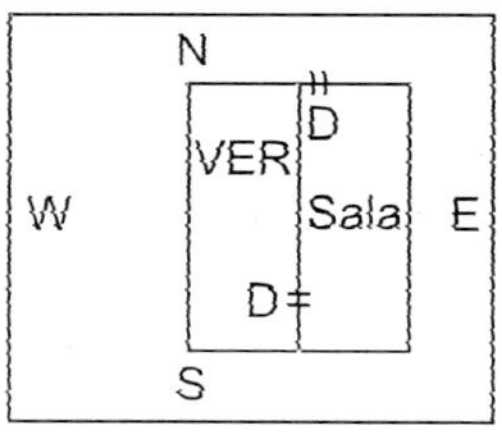

Kshayam

(14)

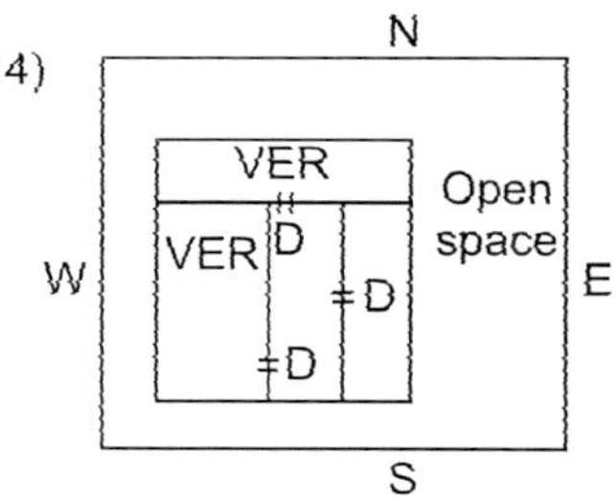

Akakramdam

(15)

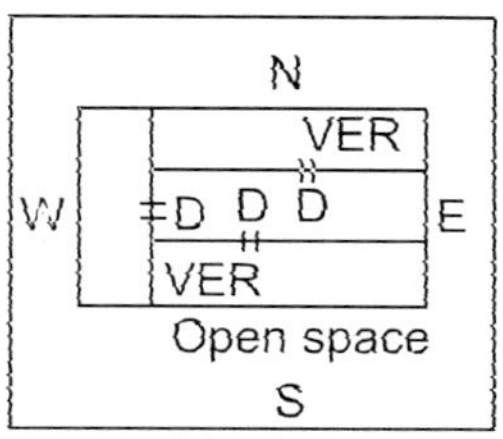

Vipulam

(16)

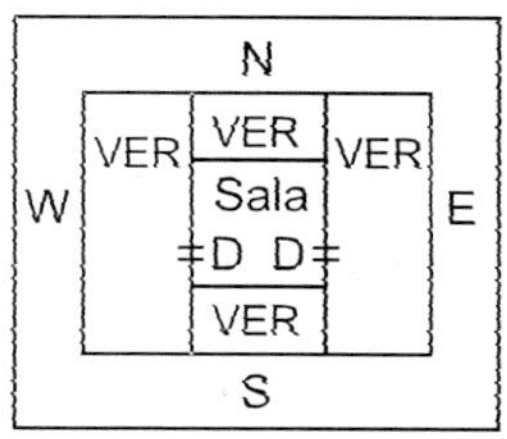

Vijayam

If sala is built as per Sastra Dharma, the advantages in construction of a house can be more.

6.27 CONSTRUCTION OF A BHAVANAM (PALACE)

The matters concerning Nature, the hidden secrets inside the Land, the changes occurring due to Rotation & Revolution of Earth, when all these are examined then the depth of Vaasthu Sastra would be understood.

For Gruha Vaathu is concerned the Ayas are defined with Vargus and the Padas are determined. Then the construction is commanced. The method of construction of House in this fashion is to be fully studied & under stood. In this there is Poorva Bhavanamu, Anthar Bhavanamu, Salaas, Storeys, Sub-Divisions in same floor etc. are to be built as per Sastra considerations. We must be aware of important matters in constructions.

1. Portion built in front of Bhavanam is called	Poorvabhavanam
2. Remaing part with all fecilities is called	Antharbhavanam
3. Those furniture that are used inside of the built house	Soopaanalu
4. Houses built above the existing house are called	Anthasthulu (Storeys)

The Rules & Regulations for of these houses should be known. The matters concerning the following.

1. Poova Bhavana construction.
2. Importance of Stambha Sthapama.
3. Method of six Pillar construction.
4. Method of eight Pillar building.
5. Construction of Palace with 10 Piller & its order.
6. Twelve pillar sthaphana order.
7. Sixten pillar stahapana method.
8. Anthar Bhavama Nirmanamu.
9. Construction of Furniture.
10. Upa-graha nishkramanamu.
11. Puja-Gruhamu
12. Character of Gosala.
13. Construction of additional Storyes.
14. Aguments inside the house.

For all these types of constructions, detailed Rules & Regulations are described fully in Vaasthu Sastra Grandhas. The Readar should also be aware of those matters.

6.28 GRUHA DOSHA PRAKARANAMU (INAUSPICIOUS MATTERS)

During middle ages due to slavery of Hindustaan at the hands of Moghuls there were lot of changes in Hindu Sasrtas in recitation. Vaasthu Sastra had come to that Stage. As part of learning it is necessary to know the Dosahs in Vasthu Sastraas. With the help of Experts house construction could be done with complete Auspiciousness.

If construction is done without following Rules laid, the persons living in the house will get exposed to all sorts of problems in health & mental happiness & attitude. Hence while constructing the house, effort should be made to fully follow the Vaasthu Sastra Rules keeping in view of the Natural surroundings. The Buildings existing around the characteristics of soil examined, the shapes of Rooms inside properly designed. The Canals and Tanks situated around to be noted and trees grown in the area got conversent. All these matters are to be looked into and construction proceded. While doing so the readers should also know the Doshas that are required to be countered and proper remedial measures taken timely. These are:

1. Doshas in Land.
2. Dikmoodha Dosha.
3. Marma Dosha.
4. Dwara Dosha.
5. Ordinary Doshas.
6. Trees & their Doshas.
7. Foundations & their Doshas.
8. Vedhas-their results.
9. House construction Ordinary & special Rules & Exceptions.
10. Characteristics of soil.
11. Land slopes.
12. High & Low places in the house land.
13. Foundation, construction of walls, Doors & Windows, place where exactly the house is to be built in the land acquired.

For all these matters, very detailed & elobarte informations are available in the texts of Vaasthu Sastra which one should make an earnest attempt to know thoroughly. The readers are advised to refer these Texts. The Doshas to be avoided & construction proceded.

6.29 MUHOORTHA FOR COMMENCEMENT OF HOUSE CONSTRUCTION

For under taking any type of work best suitable time should be selected, as per traditions of Hinduism in India. There were many occasions when it was seen that after commencement, it could not proced further due to various reasons. The reasons being, there were Doshas in the owner's Horoscope or Doshas in the Muhoortha for taking up construction. It is not advantages without fully examining these aspects. Those times & Doshas should be essentially known.

Time is Brahma Swarupa. In the beginning of Life on Earth, knowledge of Direction Country. Stars & planets were ascertained. Examination of timings for starting the job got developed into Muhoortha Bhaga and Predictive Astrology Divisions. The owners Horoscope & Gochara are to be thoroughly examined. Then only a suitable auspicious time chosen and the muhoortha selected for commcement of house construction.

In these matters such as:

1. Importance of Muhoortha.
2. Different varieties of staring construction for Foundations, Sankhu Sthaptana, Places for cement etc.
3. The Months in which the construction be taken up & their results, Tithis, Stars Weekdays, Lagnas Planetry Positions etc.
4. Matters concerning avoidable items.
5. Vaasthu Chakram (Vrushabha Chakram).
6. Gochara strength to the Land & House Owner.

7. Strength in the Horoscope.
8. The matters which are avoided for commencement of House construction.
9. Tara Balam & Yogas. Inauspicious Yogas, Ashtakavargu, Examination of Dasa & Antardasa Lords Koopakhanana, Muhoortham for digging Well, Compound wall construction if required to be done before Sanku Staapama & when to rise & fix Simhadwara.

All these matters should fully be examined & construction take up.

6.30 THE TIMING OF GRUHA PRAVESA

After completion of construction the Owner should enter the house. The time at which the Owner enters into the house should be highly Auspicious. If entered at a good timing the Native will lead a Healthy Happy & Prosperous life. If the time of entering is not Auspicious the Owner will under go inumarable diffcuilties. Hence all these aspects are to be considered and the time for entering decided.

6.31 THREE METHODS OF TIME FOR ENTERING INTO NEW HOUSE

1. New Hosue Warming is called "Apoorvapravesa"
2. Enters into House after a long periods of Travel is called "Sapoorva Pravesha"
3. Entering into a House which is Renovated after fire or damaged due natural calamities is called "Punah".

6.32 SUITABLE MONTHS FOR HOUSE WARMING BASED ON CHANDRA & SOURA MANAS

1. For a newly built House Warming Magha, Phalguna, Vaisakha & Jyestha Months are Good.
2. If done in Kaartika & Margasira months it is Mahdhyamika.
3. The periods of Guru & Sukra Moudhami are to be avoided.
4. As per Vaasthu Sastra Saura months are to be taken.
5. It is Auspicious to do between Months Magha to Jyeshtha.
6. Since Kartika & Margasira Months are close to Uttarayanam they were considered as acceptable midway.
7. The Month Sravana which is said to be Auspicious for commencement of house construction is prohibited for House Warming purposes.
8. In Uttarayana when Sun & Moon have Full Strength day is considered as auspicious with good Omen Signs that House Warming is recommended.
9. The Auspiciousness in a Month is from Panchami of Sukla Paksha to Dashami of Krishna Paksha.
10. Tithis other than Riktha, Dagdha, Amavasya & Suka Padyami are to be avoided and the remaining Tithis are Auspicious.

Ekadashi, Dwadasi, Trayodashi in Sukla Pakasha can be considered

(a) Riktha Tithis: Chaviti, Navami, Chaturdasi.

(b) Dagdha Tithis: Dwadasi on Sunday
Ekadasi on Mondy
Panchami on Tuesday
Tadiya on Wednessay
Shashti on Thrusday
Ashtami on Friday
Navami on Saturday

(i) Poorna Tithis for entering East side Main Door	Panchami, Dasami, Poornima
(ii) Nanda Tithis for entering South Main Door	Padyami, Shashti, Ekadasi
(iii) Bhadra Tithis entering West side Main Door	Vidiya, Saptami, Dwadasi
(iv) Jaya Tithis entering North side Main Door	Tadia, Ashtami, Trayodasi

The above are said to be the most Auspicious

12. Deciding Auspicious Day for the House Warming

The date on which House Warming is done & the results there on if the Day is

(i) **Sunday:** Unhappiness

(ii) **Monday when Moon in full Ksheena:** Quarrel-some

(iii) **Monday when Moon is full:** Wealthy

(iv) **Tuesday:** Burnt

(v) **Wednesday:** Advatnage of Grains coming.

(vi) **Lakshmivara (Guru) Day:** Blessed with Sons, & Cattle

(vii) **Friday:** Happiness, cause for Marriage.

(viii) **Saturday:** Likely to have Thefts.

Hence full Moon Monday, Wednesday, Thursday & Friday are auspicious.

13. (A) Deciding Auspicious Nakshatra for House Warming Function

(i) Rohni, Mrugasira, Chitta Uttara, Anuradha, Dhanishta Satabhisham, Uttarashada, Uttarabhara, Revati are excellent.

(ii) Pushyami: Medium advantage.

(iii) Punarvasu, Swati, Hastha, Aswini & Sravanam House will go to another individual.

(iv) Ardra, Krittika: House will be burnt.

(B) Decide the Time of Hosue Warming

Two types Night & Days can be done

14. Decide Lagna for House Warming

Panchamga Suddhi, Tara Balam, Chandra Balam Subha Grahas are in Lagna or Lagna is aspected by Subha Grahas and Lordship of Naturally Good Planets to Lagna.

15. Lagna to be either Stihra or Dwiswabha Rasis, the House Warming is to be done.

Chara Lagna: Not Accepted.

Mesha Langa: Gives Change.

Karkataka Lagna: Causes Destruction

Tula Lagna: Cuases diseases.

Makara lagna: Causes Destruction of Grains.

16. Results if Lagnas are based on Jama Lagna or Lagna counted from Jamama Rasi to Rasis 3,4,6,10,11 will be as under-

1. Healthy
2. Poverty
3. Become famous
4. Attain friendship
5. No children
6. Defeating evemy
7. Harm to Wife
8. Death
9. Get Disease
10. Gain strength
11. Wealthy
12. Ememity increases

Hence 2, 5, 7, 8, 9, 12 are not at all considered.

17. Position of Grahas Acceptable

(i) If Papagraha mean Sun, Ksheena Chandra, Sat, Mars, Rahu, Ketu are there in 3, 6, 11 from Lagna	Subham
(ii) If no Grahas are there in 8, 12 from Lagna	Subham
(iii) If in House 4, 5, planets are there from Lagna	It is better to perform Gruha Pravesha

18. Deciding Vama 'Ravi'

(i)	If Main Door is on East	If Sun is in 8-9-10-11-12 from Pravesh Lagna is called 'Vama Ravi'
(ii)	If Main Door is on South	If Sun is in 5, 6, 7, 8, 9 from Pravsha Lagna is called 'Vama Ravi'
(iii)	If Main Door is on West	If Sun is in 2, 3, 4, 5, 6 from Pravesh Lagna is called 'Vama Ravi'
(iv)	If Main Door is on North	If Sun is in 11, 12, 1, 2, 3 from Pravesh Lagna is called 'Vama Ravi'

When 'Vama ravi' is there Gruha Pravesha is prohibitted.

19. Suddhi of 'Kalasa' & 'Vrushabha' Chakras

(i) For house comcement: Require suddhi of Kalasa and Vrushabha Chakra.

(ii) For house warming: Require suddhi of both Charkas 'Vrushabha' & 'Kalasa'.

(a) Kalasa Chakra suddhi: Kalasa means draw a Circle, after that mark a point at centre as Sun Located Star, counted from the Star where Sun is situated (leaving Abhizin Star) as the Star in the Head.

(i) If that day's Star is same	The head will be broken.
(ii) If it is part of 4 Stars on East	Will go to foreign Countries.
(iii) If it is part of 4 Stars on South	Fearlessness.
(iv) If it is part of 4 Stars on West	Get Grains.
(v) If it is part of 3 Stars on Neck	Wealth.
(vii) If it is part of 3 Stars on bottom	Get Full Longevity.

(b) Vrushabha Chakra Suddhi: Count from the Star in which Sun is positioned to the Pravesha Star (including Abhizin Star) and if the Star is part of first-

(i) 4 Stars in the Head of Vrushabha	House gets burnt
(ii) There after 4 Stars are in foot	Vaceum
(iii) Then if the 4 Stars on the back of feet	Strength
(iv) If another 3 Stars on the Private parts	Gain of Money
(v) If another 4 Stars on the of body Right	Gains
(vi) If another 3 Stars are in the Back	Death of Swamy
(vii) If another 4 Stars are on left of the body	Poverty
(viii) If another 3 Stars are in Face	Pain-full

The Jyothsha Prakasa Text gives details of 9 Planets with reference to Lagna in all twelve Lagnas. The results are given in a Tabular format.

Readers are advised to see and pickup an Auspicious Lagna which gives good results from Subha sthithi Lagna and carry out house warming function accordingly.

20. Gruha Pravesha Vidha

(a) Before entering into the house constructed as per Vaasthu Sastra the following arrangements are to be made.

(i) Vaasthu Puja & Homam

(ii) Ishta Devata Puja

(iii) Nava Graha Puja

(iv) Give Bali to Croora Devatas

(v) Anna santhi to be done (feeding food to many persons)

(vi) In Subha Muhoortha

(vii) With Mangala Vaidyas

(viii) Married Women leading Brahmin Pundits following with all Relations, the Owner should do Gruha Pravesham.

(b) The House Owner with his Wife, Brahmins, Virgins, following with Cow & Calf with all Pump & Show of Instrument Music, House duly decorated with flowers take Clockwise Pradaskshana to the House and enter the House at the specified

Auspicious Timing. Then the Owner will Honour Silpies, Astrologer, Vaasthu Sastra Pundits, Brahmins-Pundits & well wishers to the extant, he could afford with clothes and money as Dakshina.

(c) The Gruha Pravesam to be done by Owner on its completion without delay at Subhamurtha Time.

(d) One day before Pravesha Muhoortha all works to be completed and entire house from North-East smeared with cowding and floor Decorated with coloured powder by making atractive Diagrams and walls be decked with flower Toranas.

In the South East room the Fire-place (show) is to be fxed. In the right side rooms of the House and Bed Room, furniture is to be kept & decorated with flowers.

Before Subha Muhoortha Nava Dhanyas are to be kept at the main door. Take his Wife with his Left Hand, House Owner will make Cow & Calf enter first, then Women carrying Pots with water, then Stapathi and Purohit & Brahmins duly reciting Veda Mantras with Mangala Vadyams, Owner taking Poorna Kalasa & with all relations & friends take one Pradakshina to the house from North East direction by giving Bali to all Devatas, submit to Ashta Devatas & consecrate & at appointed time approach Main Door make Devatas Cow & Calf to enter first at subha time. Then women with Poorna Kumbha with water entering with the Owner with this Wife steps into the House with Right foot first & enters the House. Then the couple will go to the Right side Bedroom and make them seated on the bed.

Then the Puja of Ganesh is performed in the middle room and Agni is lit up in S.E Room. Then Mantapa Aaradhana to Dieties performed as laid down in Sastras. All have been honoured to their satisfaction with Cloths, Money & obtain their blessings. All are given prasadam & fuly satisfied.

A day before Gruha Pravesa Puja, Vaastu Puja, Bali for Devas, etc. are to be carried out. Suitable Stars are Mrugasira, Chitta, Anuradha, Revati, Uttrashada, Rohini, Aswini, Pushyami, Abijit, Swati. Punarasu, Sravanam, Dhanshta & Satabhesham (Nakshatras-14), and good Tithis & 8th house free and naturally Bad Plaents in 3, 6, 11 from Lagna & good Planets in other phaces; Vaashu Puja, Bali Haoam etc. are to be performed. Follow Rituals as per practice in vogue, so as to lead a good life thereon.

❖❖❖

CHAPTER 7

Introduction to Prasna Sastra

7.1 THE USEFULNESS OF PRASNA SASTRA

In Prasna Jyothisha, the Astrologer makes Gochara Chakra for the moment of time the Prasna is asked and Prediction is given. Some times the Predictions are so accurate that the person putting the question will be wonderstruck. Predictions made and told which are usefull from experience points of view. Prasna Jyothisha is factual and candid. Since the problems are solved quickly or results obtained in minutes this Sastra is proved to be highly usefull. It is usefull in many occassions to correctly decide. Example:

It is usual to a Bachelor to select a correct bride among dozen offers received by him. This Sastra is usefull for Mankind at large. In another example: a person standing for Elections can get the results as to who would win by taking a figure in Two Digits or Single Digit.

7.2 HINDU TRADITIONAL METHOD

The Prasna Sastra was first written by Bhattootpaludu. He had written Commentaries on Text written by Varahamihara. The Prasna Sastra is one of the parts of Jyothish Sastra. The Text Jataka Parijata stipulate 10 states of existence for the Planets. These are.

1. Deeptha
2. Swastha
3. Mudita
4. Saantaa
5. Saktha
6. Prapeeditha
7. Deena
8. Khala
9. Vikala
10. Bheeta

How planet is posited	Called as
1. A Planet in Exaltation or in Moola Trikona	Deepthaavastha
2. A Planet is in His own House	Swasthaavastha
3. A Planet in a friends House	Muditaavastha
4. A Planet in Subha Varga	Saanthaavastha
5. A Planet not in Combustion	Sakthaavastha
6. A Planet is over powedered by other Planets	Prapeedithaavsastha
7. A Planet is in enemy's House	Deenaavastha
8. A Planet is defeated in Graha fight or have Veedha of bad planet or in papa vargus	Khalaavastha
9. A Planet in combustion by Sun	Vikalavastha
10. A Planet in debilitation or very week	Bheetaavatha

7.3 THE FOLLOWING TABLE GIVES THE RASIS & DEGREES RANGE OF EXALTATION AND MOOLA TRIKONA FOR ALL SEVEN PLANETS

(a) Deepthaavastha

S. No.	Planet	Exaltation	Moola Trikona
1	Sun	Aries (1° – 10°)	Leo (0° – 20°)
2	Moon	Taurus (1° – 3°)	Taurus (4° – 30°)
3	Mars	Capricorn (1° – 28°)	Aries (0° – 18°)
4	Mercury	Virgo (1° – 15°)	Virgo (16° – 30°)
5	Jupiter	Cancer (1° – 5°)	Sagitterius (0° – 13°)
6	Venus	Pisces (1° – 27°)	Leo (0° – 10°)
7	Saturn	Libra (1° – 20°)	Aquarius (0° – 20°)

At all times when Papa-Grahas Exhalation Dasa runs, many persons suffer & under go lot of difficulties.

(b) Swasthaavastha: The owning Houses of Planets are given as under.

S. No.	Planet	Own house
1	Sun	Leo
2	Moon	Cancer
3	Mars	Aries & Scorpio
4	Mercury	Gemini & Virgo
5	Jupiter	Sagitterius & Pisces
6	Venus	Taurus & Libra
7	Saturn	Capricron & Aqaurius

A Planet in his Own House gives happiness & cheerfullness. It some tims causes difficulties and become harmfull.

(c) Muditaavastha: These Planets when positioned in Friends Houses gives satisfaction. The count of friendly Houses, from it's Moola Trikona Rasi-situated in 1, 2, 12, 5, 9, Exaltation, 8, 4 in order are friendly Houses.

3, 6, 10, 11, 7 are Upachaya positions, these are not Mitra Sthanas. The two Rasis having Lordship of a Planet one is a friendly House and the second is Enemy House Such planets are considered as Neutral.

(d) Saanthaavastha: If Planets are in Subha Virgu, then the Native is either helpful or engage himself in doing Punya Karmas.

(e) Saktaavasha: A Planet which is not in Moudya or Combustion and is shinning all the time, it has strength, competence & dexterity and will bring honours and respects. Many Men & Women become friends. Every one likes him. The person wears good chothes and uses perfumes which are fragnant.

(f) Peedithaavastha: A Planet got defeated while fighting with another Planet. Such Planet causes separation from friends and relations, get highly disturbed, will make a person Vagabond or Tramp. He will suffer in enemy's hands causes illhealth. Even if he is King he will suffer.

(g) **Deenaavastha:** A Planet which is in Rasi & Navasmsa posited in Enemeys House, it causes unhappiness. Makes timid mentally disturbed, agony transfer from the place get over thrown from position of Status and brings dis-honour and dis-respects. Person gets defeated, gets ruined, will go to foreign Countries and can never remain neat & clean.

(h) **Khalaavastha:** If the Planet either in Rasi or Navamsa is in Conjection with Sun Kshena Moon, Mars, Mercury associated with Bad Planet Saturn, these bad planets makes the person becomes immoral, cruel and lead a difficult life.

(i) **Vikalaavastha:** When a Planet is in Moudhya or in Combustion by Sun, the person will not have stable life, become weak, separation from Wife, mental worry. Enemy's become stronger etc. will happen.

(j) **Bheetaavastha:** When a Plaent is in Debilitation a person becomes frightened face all sorts of difficulities, becomes fearfull, untrustworthyness and faces all problems.

7.4 METHOD OF MEETING THE ASTROLOGER

Planets are worshipped duly submitting pranams. Then the place where Prasna will be entertained is to be decided. The person who came to question should sit faceing East or North or Northest. He should not sit in other Directions. Varamihra stated that the Astrologer should sit under a shade of a Tree with Fruits & Flowers. Astrologer should Elect Rules concerning Sadhus. Even the plain Land where grass is grown is also good for Astrologer to sit.

The person coming to question should come with Fruits & flowers and Prayers conducted within himeself wearing Gold Chain and Diamond Ring. Then only his problems are to be mentioned to the Astrologer.

Both the Person questioning & Astrologer should fix only morning hour for consultation. Other timings are not suitable or rather prohibited.

7.5 SINCERITY OF THE QUESTIONER

The Person who has come for questioning is sincere or he came to examine the accuracy of the Astrologer will be known as per indications given below.

1. In Prasna Lagna when Moon is there and in Kendra or 7th House contain Saturn or Mercury in 7th house.
2. Mars & Mercury in Combustion, aspecting the Moon in Lagna. If the above Veedhas are noticed to the Prasna Lagna, it should be understood that the questioner is not sincere.
3. If there are Naturally Good Planet in Lagna Bhava, it should be taken that the questioner is sincere.
4. If Lagna contain Papis, it is concluded that the questioner is asking without any plan.
5. For 7th Bhava has the aspect of an a Enemy or Jup & Ven aspect, then it is to be taken that the person came is sincere.
6. If Lagna & 7th House has the Aspect of Moon/Jupiter or both, it should be understood that the person who came for questioning has no malicious intention.
7. If 7th House is aspected by an emeny and if that Planet has the aspect of Good Planets it should be under stood that the person came for questioning is sincere.

7.6 DECIDING THE LAGNA BASED ON THE QUESTION

1. For answering first question	Lagna Bhava should be taken first
2. While answering that second question	The Rasi in which Moon is there is taken as Lagna
3. For 3rd question answering	Take the Rasi in which Sun is there as Lagna.
4. Fourth question answering	Take the Rasi in which Jupiter is posited in Lagna
5. While deciding answer to fifth question	The Rasi containing Mercury & Venus are taken and who ever is stronger that Rasi is to be taken as Lagna

7.7 OMENS (SAKUNAS)

Astrologer to observe Omens & Signs and decide whether he could give favourable answers or not. On this subject the Text & Bruhat Samhita written by Varahmihara, the famous Astrologer of 6th Century may be seen on this subject.

7.8 FRUITFULLNESS OF QUESTIONS

In order to give answer to quesries indicating fruitfullness, the Astrologer should consider different Bhavas and find out aspects of Good Planets & Strength of Bhava Planets ascertained on the following basis:

1. What ever Bhava is under examination it should be examined whether:-

   (a) Anyone of the Good Planets Mercury, Jupiter, Venus.

   Or

   (b) The Bhava Lord under examination

   Remain in that Bhava or aspect that Bhava, then the Karakatwa of that Bhava will give good result.

2. If there are Subha Grahas in 2-4-7-10-12 Houses from that Bhava under consideration then that Bhava will give Good results.
3. If the Lagna is of Chatushpat Rasi or Human Sign and there is Aspect of Papa Grahas then the Karakatwas of Lagna Bhava will not give the desired good results, only unfavourable results will have to be faced.
4. In Bhavas 1-4-7-10. If Lagna Lord & his Friend are there and in addition if no Papa Grahus are not there in houses 1-4-7-8-10, then fravourable results could be predicted.
5. If in Bhava 5 or Good Planets like Mercury, Jupiter, Venus are there, there are chances of obtaining good results, one would be benefitted.
6. If there are Papa Grahas in Lagna, one would suffer from disease or gets involved in altracations and fights. If Papa Grahas are there in 4th house, there will be Enemity with relations, unhappiness and there is no harmony nor amicableness.
7. If there are Papa Grahas in 7th house, there will be obstructions or impediments for Travel, gets delayed, led into troubles. If there are Papa Grahas in 10th House then

there is Victory in the efforts. But if a Good Planet joins or aspects, then there will be indication of obstructions, but ultimately the questioner's desire gets fullfilled.

8. If Langa is in Sthira Rasis, the questioner will not be defeated and there will be no loss but the disease will continue. But will attain the anticipated honours or get the expected higher status.
9. If Chara Rasis become Lagna, one would get defeted, suffer losses Gets recovered from disease. Travel will get accomplished. But one would not get neither better position in seniority nor the anticipated Higher Post nor any improvement.
10. If Dwiswabhava Rasi become Lagna the first half considered as Sthira Rasi give prediction as Sthirarasi & if 2nd half considered as Chararasi Lagna, give predictions as for Chararasi Lagna.
11. If there are Subha Grahas either in Lagna or Varga Lagna then the questioner will achieve his desire.
12. If there are Subha Grahas in 1-4-5-7-9-10 and Papa Grahas in 3-6-11 any where, efforts get fruitfull and the person who had left can be anticipated for his return.
13. If Jupiter or Venus are either in 2nd or in 3rd house, the person who had left the house will return back. If there are Good Plaents in 4th, then also it can be told that the person will return back.
14. If either to Lagna or Chandra Rasi Mercury & Venus are there in 2/12 houses, the person who went out will return live quickly.
15. (a) If Lagna & Navasmsa Lagna are in Chararasis & if Moon is in Sthirarasi, then Enemy will come with his full force.

    (b) If Chandra is in Chararasi Lagna & if Lagna is in Sthirarasi then that enemy will not come at all based on the above analogy, given in items (a) above, the business matters can be deceided, whether from that there will be favourability from the opposition or not can be known.
16. Budha, Guru/Venus-among these two, if one is in 6, Moon in Dwiswabhava Rasi and Lagna is also in Dwiswabhava Rasi.

    The Enemy however mighty, he may/will face lot of difficulties and become sorrowful. If it is business he will be unsuccessful.
17. (a) If bad planets are in 5th & 6th the enemy will return back even if a notice is sent with disagreement, it will be accepted.

    (b) If there are Papa Grahas in 4th: Enemy even if come to the border he will return back & any case in a Court of Law he will be taken aback.
18. (a) If Jala Rasi's become Lagna and if planet is in 4th got Aspects from Subha Graha, the Enemy gets defeated.

    (b) If 4th Bhava beomes Mesha or Vrushabha and if Papa Grahas are there the Enemy will come Lock-Stock & Barrel. The court proceedings will continue.
19. (a) Bhava: 9-10-11-12-1-2 Indicate invasion.

    (b) Bhava: 3-4-5-7-8: Shows reasonableness of Defendant or Respondent.

    (c) If there are Subha Grahas between Bhavas 9-2: Indicate success.

    (d) If there are Subha Grachas between Bhavas 3-8: Indicate fear of defeat, Loosing the Court case.

20. If Subha Grahas are in first half of Virgo, Libra, Sagittarius & Aquarius and those Rasis should be 1, 12, 11: There will be Acceptance or Willingness or Treaty.
21. If Lagna is aspected by Papagraha & if Moon is 3/6/10/11 Subha Grahas in 1/4/5/7/8/9/10: The person though looks healthy & strong will suffer from illhealth.
22. If strong Moon aspect Lagna or Jupiter or Jup/Venus are positioned in 1-4-5-7-8-9-10: The person who came to question will get cured of his disease.
23. (a) Moon Aspected by Jupiter, if in 3-6-7-10-11: The questioner will get his better half in Marriage.
    (b) If same Moon is Aspected by Papa Grahas: The time has not yet ripened for getting a Marriable partner.
24. If Moon in 3-6-5-7-11 gets Aspects from Jup/Sun/Mercury: The questioner will get Married.
25. (a) If Subha Grahas are there in 1-4-5-7-9-10: Prediction to be given that the Marriage takes place.
    (b) If 7th Bhava Lord is a Good Planet: The facial outlook & character is good.
    (c) If 7th Bhava Lord is Papa Grahs: The partner will be of ordinary Beauty.
26. (a) If Sub Planets are there in 5/11: Blessed with Children.
    (b) If Lagna & Planets are in basi sankhya Rasi: Blessed with Male Child.
27. (a) Lagna, Ravi, Chandra, Guru are in sama sankya Rasis: Blessed with Female Child.
    (b) Planets some in Sthree Rasis & some in Purusha Rasis: Findout the strongest of all & give prediction accordingly.
    (c) If Saturn is in 1-3-5-7-9-11: Bllesed with Male Child.
28. (a) Guru, Sukra in Basi Rasis: Blessed with Male Child.
    (b) Guru, Chandra, Kuja in Samarasis: Blessed with Female Child.

7.9 METHODS AND RULES FOR PREDICTION IN OTHER MATTERS

The matters like, taste, dreams, rain coming, how the theif looks like, height, what is there in the closed fist, color, shape; all questions concerning human beings identifying the objects stolen-decision about which direction the lost article exist, the time of happening an event, the predictive result if a Moon's cresent is seen, results based on first Alphabet mentioned by the questioner for all these, the Methods & Rules for giving prediction are given in Prasna Jyothisha Text written by K.S. Krishna Murthy.

7.10 SIMILARLY THE PREDICTION BASED ON THE CHART PREPARED ON QUESTIONS

Predictions are written in greater detail in the following Texts, which the readers are advised to carefully examine.

1. Uttakalamrutham by Kalidas.
2. Shatpanchasika written by Prudhuyassasu S/o Varahamihra.
3. Padmaprabhuri Krutham

7.11 PRASNA JYOTHSHA WESTERN METHOD

The first point of Bhachakra of Western Method is different from the practice followed by Indians. Therefore the position of Rasis get changed.

Westerners follow Sayana method (Tropical System) and construction of Birth Chart. We prepare based on Nirayana method (The Sidereal System). Westerners do not take Rahu & Ketu. But they consider three additional planets described as udner:

(i) Uranus (Indra Chapa)

(ii) Neptune (Varuna)

(iii) Pluto (Yama)

They examine Brith Charts taking these three Planets.

In the Text Horary Astrology written by Dr. N.J. Simonite contains.

1 The method of preparing the Prasna chart.
2. The type of results given by different Planets.
3. How an individual leads the life at planets connected to the Rasis.
4. The Plaents Aspects are not uniform.
5. Longitudes & Paths of Planets are different.
6. Details regarding individuals living depending upon Rasis connected to various Planets.
7. The Aspects of Planets are varying including their Paths.
8. Details of individuals.
9. Indications of 12 Bhavas.
10. The time of occurance.

For all these subjects suitable descriptions have been given. The Reeders are advsed to go through them throughly.

Sri. K.N. Krishna murthy has indicated in his Text Prasna Jyothisa.

7.12 PRASNA JYOTHISHAM-KRIHSNA MURTHY METHOD-NEW STELLAR ASTROLOGY

There are two methods.

(a) Ask for any figure below 108 and divide the same by 12. The reminder figure is counted from Aries and which ever Rasi comes is treated as Lagna. The next Rasi is to be taken as 2nd Bhava & so on.

(b) Ask for any figure becow 108 and devide the same by 9; the full figure obtained counted from Aries gives Lagna and the figure remained as balance taken as the figure of Navamsa Lagna.

In both the methods, only when Latitude is between 14° to 18° North only when the Sayana Libra 0° will be rising. All the Bhavas will be 30° in equal Amplitude. If it is not so, the length of each Rasi wil be varying.

In this method the figure mentioned by the questioner will indicate Rasi, Star, and Dasa Bhukthy of the Planet relavent to the Star. Bhukthi starts from a fixed point. That point should be considered as Lagna. Depending upon the Latitude of the prasna Place the Cusps of the remaing Bhavas are calculated. The Ayanamsa is counted for the day in question.

Coming to Western method they only consider the time of question for predictive purposes considering the Latitude of the place of questioning the Birth Chart is prepared.

If Birth Chart is made based on figure as mentioned in Krihsa Murthy's Method the answer will conrrectly be known. The result is also accurate.

The prediction given based on Krishna Murthy method are direct to the point, accurate & satisfactory and possible to evaluate from the Rules points of view than the predictions given based on Traditional Astrological methods.

In traditional Astrology the Rasi if in Aswini Makha & Moola Stars it will be under the control of Ketu as it is in the region of Ketu. The Planet in that Rasi is said to get controlled by Ketu. Though mentioned by Astrologer then that Planet is in which Rasi also is to be told. If it is not identified then one canot say definitely as to where the Planet is situated.

Due to the above reason all the 27 Stars were given Names. Since the Lordship of Stars is among Planets for every 120° region it will have three diffent Lordships for example:

For Aswini, Makha, Moola: The Lordship goes to Ketu.

For Bharani, Pubba, Poorvashada: The Lordship goes to Venus, one Planet get Lordship of three regions.

7.13 SIGNIFIACTORS & SUBLORD METHOD

Planet may be in any Star. It is proved that the Star Lord retaiming in a Bhava will have connection to Karakatwas of that Bhava. This particular Bhava is termed as Significator to the Star Lord. Similarly if all Planets are examined, for every planet, it is found out that they have relationships with two different bhavas.

If a Planet is examined, it will indicate a Karakatwa. Whether that Planet will support for improvement or otherwise will be dependent on the Sub Lord or the Bhukthinath. If the Sub Lord or the Bhukthinath causes harm to the Karakathwaas of that Bhava then that Planet will not only be unhelpfull but also causes destruction.

7.14 REACTION OF BIRTH CHART OF HORAY ASTROLOGY

(i) Universal table of Houses.

(ii) Krishna Murthy Ephemeris for the year.

(iii) Table showing commencement of Sub Lord according the number by the consultant.

(iv) The correct time to be taken for erecting the Prasna Chart.

For giving predictions to a consultant the Astrologer should construct the Kundali for the time at which question is asked for, even if he had written any figure it will give the same results.

7.15 TABLE TO FOLLOW THE KRISHNA MURHTY METHOD

In the following table the figures given there in will indicate it's Rasi Lord, Star Lord, Sub Lord and the Longitude of the Planet from its commencement to its end D° = degrees, M = Minutes & S = Seconds

Aries:

S.No.	Rasi Lord	Nakshatra Lord	Sub Lord	From DMS	To DMS
1.	Mars	Ketu	Ketu	0-00-00	0-46-40
2.	Mars	Ketu	Venus	0-46-40	3-00-00
3.	Mars	Ketu	Sun	3-00-00	3-40-00
4.	Mars	Ketu	Moon	3-40-00	4-46-40
5.	Mars	Ketu	Mars	4-46-40	5-33-20
6.	Mars	Ketu	Raho	5-33-20	7-33-20
7.	Mars	Ketu	Jupiter	7-33-20	9-20-00
8.	Mars	Ketu	Saturn	9-20-00	11-26-40
9.	Mars	Ketu	Mercury	11-26-40	13-20-00
10.	Mars	Ketu	Venus	13-20-00	15-33-20
11.	Mars	Ketu	Sun	15-33-00	16-13-20
12.	Mars	Ketu	Moon	16-13-20	17-20-00
13.	Mars	Venus	Mars	17-20-20	18-6-40
14.	Mars	Venus	Rahu	18-6-40	20-6-40
15.	Mars	Venus	Jupiter	20-6-40	21-53-20
16.	Mars	Venus	Saturn	21-53-20	24-00-00
17.	Mars	Venus	Mercury	24-00-00	25-53-20
18.	Mars	Venus	Ketu	25-53-20	26-40-00
19.	Mars	Sun	Sun	26-40-00	27-20-00
20.	Mars	Sun	Moon	27-20-00	28-26-40
21.	Mars	Sun	Mars	28-26-40	29-13-20
22.	Mars	Sun	Rahu	29-13-20	30-00-00
23.	Venus	Sun	Rahu	0-00-00	1-13-20
24.	Venus	Sun	Jupiter	1-13-20	3-0-00
25.	Venus	Sun	Saturn	3-00-00	5-06-40
26.	Venus	Sun	Mercury	5-6-40	7-00-00
27.	Venus	Sun	Ketu	7-00-00	7-46-40
28.	Venus	Sun	Venus	7-46-40	10-00-00
29.	Venus	Moon	Moon	10-00-00	11-06-40
30.	Venus	Moon	Mars	11-06-40	11-53-20
31.	Venus	Moon	Rahu	11-53-20	13-53-20

S.No.	Rasi Lord	Nakshatra Lord	Sub Lord	From DMS	To DMS
32.	Venus	Moon	Jupiter	13-53-20	15-40-00
33.	Venus	Moon	Saturn	15-40-00	17-46-40
34.	Venus	Moon	Mercury	17-46-40	19-40-00
35.	Venus	Moon	Ketu	19-40-00	20-46-40
36.	Venus	Moon	Venus	20-46-40	22-40-00
37.	Venus	Moon	Sun	22-40-00	23-20-00
38.	Venus	Mars	Mars	23-20-00	24-06-40
39.	Venus	Mars	Rahu	26-6-40	26-6-40
40.	Venus	Mars	Jupiter	26-6-40	27-53-20
41.	Venus	Mars	Saturn	27-53-20	30-00-00
42.	Mercury	Mars	Mercury	0-00-00	1-53-20
43.	Mercury	Mars	Ketu	1-53-20	2-40-00
44.	Mercury	Mars	Venus	2-40-00	4-53-20
45.	Mercury	Mars	Sun	4-53-20	5-33-20
46.	Mercury	Mars	Moon	5-53-20	6-40-00
47.	Mercury	Rahu	Rahu	6-40-00	8-40-00
48.	Mercury	Rahu	Jupiter	8-40-00	10-26-40
49.	Mercury	Rahu	Saturn	10-26-40	12-33-20
50.	Mercury	Rahu	Mercury	12-33-20	14-26-40
51.	Mercury	Rahu	Ketu	14-26-40	15-13-20
52.	Mercury	Rahu	Venus	15-13-20	17-26-40
53.	Mercury	Rahu	Sun	17-26-40	18-6-40
54.	Mercury	Rahu	Moon	18-6-40	19-13-20
55.	Mercury	Rahu	Mars	19-13-20	20-00-00
56.	Mercury	Jupiter	Jupiter	20-00-00	21-46-40
57.	Mercury	Jupiter	Saturn	21-46-40	23-53-20
58.	Mercury	Juptier	Mercury	23-53-20	25-46-40
59.	Mercury	Jupiter	Ketu	25-46-40	26-33-20
60.	Mercury	Jupiter	Venus	26-33-20	28-46-40
61.	Mercury	Jupiter	Sun	28-46-40	29-26-40
62.	Mercury	Jupiter	Moon	29-26-40	30-00-00

S.No.	Rasi Lord	Nakshatra Lord	Sub Lord	From DMS	To DMS
63.	Mercury	Jupiter	Moon	0-00-00	0-33-20
64.	Moon	Jupiter	Mars	0-33-20	1-20-00
65.	Moon	Jupiter	Rahu	1-20-00	3-20-00
66.	Moon	Saturn	Saturn	3-20-00	5-26-40
67.	Moon	Saturn	Mercury	5-26-40	7-20-00
68.	Moon	Saturn	Ketu	7-20-00	8-6-40
69.	Moon	Saturn	Venus	8-6-40	10-20-00
70.	Moon	Saturn	Sun	10-20-00	11-00-00
71.	Moon	Saturn	Moon	11-00-00	12-6-40
72.	Moon	Saturn	Mars	12-6-40	12-53-20
73.	Moon	Saturn	Rahu	12-53-20	14-53-20
74.	Moon	Saturn	Jupiter	14-53-20	16-40-00
75.	Moon	Mercury	Mercury	16-40-00	18-33-20
76.	Moon	Mercury	Ketu	18-33-20	19-20-00
77.	Moon	Mercury	Vensu	19-20-00	21-33-20
78.	Moon	Mercury	Sun	21-33-20	22-13-20
79.	Moon	Mercury	Moon	22-13-20	23-20-00
80.	Moon	Mercury	Mars	23-20-00	24-6-40
81.	Moon	Mercury	Rahu	24-6-40	26-53-20
82.	Moon	Mercury	Jupiter	26-6-40	27-53-20
83.	Moon	Mercury	Saturn	27-53-20	30-00-00
84.	Sun	Mercury	Ketu	0-00-00	0-46-40
85.	Sun	Mercury	Venus	0-46-40	3-00-00
86.	Sun	Mercury	Sun	3-00-00	3-40-00
87.	Sun	Mercury	Moon	3-40-00	4-46-40
88.	Sun	Mercury	Mars	4-46-40	5-33-20
89.	Sun	Mercury	Rahu	5-33-20	7-33-20
90.	Sun	Mercury	Jupiter	7-33-20	9-20-00
91.	Sun	Mercury	Saturn	9-20-00	11-26-40
92.	Sun	Mercury	Mercury	11-26-40	13-20-00
93.	Sun	Mercury	Venus	13-20-00	15-33-20

S.No.	Rasi Lord	Nakshatra Lord	Sub Lord	From DMS	To DMS
94.	Sun	Mercury	Sun	15-33-20	16-13-20
95.	Sun	Mercury	Moon	16-13-20	17-20-00
96.	Sun	Mercury	Mars	17-20-00	18-6-40
97.	Sun	Mercury	Rahu	18-6-40	20-6-40
98.	Sun	Mercury	Jupiter	20-6-40	21-53-20
99.	Sun	Mercury	Saturn	21-53-20	24-00-00
100.	Sun	Mercury	Mercury	24-00-00	25-53-20
101.	Sun	Mercury	Ketu	25-53-20	26-40-00
102.	Sun	Sun	Sun	26-40-00	27-20-00
103.	Sun	Sun	Moon	27-20-00	28-26-40
104.	Sun	Sun	Mars	28-26-40	29-13-20
105.	Sun	Sun	Rahu	29-13-20	30-00-00
106.	Mercury	Sun	Rahu	0-00-00	1-13-00
107.	Mercury	Sun	Jupiter	1-13-00	3-00-00
108.	Mercury	Sun	Saturn	3-00-00	5-06-40
109.	Mercury	Sun	Mercury	5-06-40	7-00-00
110.	Mercury	Sun	Ketu	7-00-00	7-46-40
111.	Mercury	Sun	Venus	7-46-40	10-00-00
112.	Mercury	Moon	Moon	10-00-00	11-6-40
113.	Mercury	Moon	Mars	11-6-40	11-53-20
114.	Mercury	Moon	Rahu	11-53-20	13-53-20
115.	Mercury	Moon	Jupiter	13-53-20	15-40-00
116.	Mercury	Moon	Saturn	15-40-40	17-46-40
117.	Mercury	Moon	Mercury	17-46-40	19-40-00
118.	Mercury	Moon	Ketu	19-40-00	20-26-40
119.	Mercury	Moon	Venus	20-26-40	22-40-00
120.	Mercury	Moon	Sun	22-40-00	23-20-00
121.	Mercury	Mars	Mars	23-20-00	24-6-40
122.	Mercury	Mars	Rahu	24-6-40	26-6-40
123.	Mercury	Mars	Jupiter	26-6-40	27-53-20
124.	Mercury	Mars	Saturn	27-53-20	30-00-00

S.No.	Rasi Lord	Nakshatra Lord	Sub Lord	From DMS	To DMS
125.	Venus	Mars	Mercury	0-00-00	1-53-20
126.	Venus	Mars	Ketu	1-53-20	2-40-00
127.	Venus	Mars	Venus	2-40-00	4-53-20
128.	Venus	Mars	Sun	4-53-20	5-33-20
129.	Venus	Mars	Moon	5-33-20	6-40-00
130.	Venus	Rahu	Rahu	6-40-00	8-40-00
131.	Venus	Rahu	Jupiter	8-40-00	10-26-00
132.	Venus	Rahu	Saturn	10-26-00	12-33-20
133.	Venus	Rahu	Mercury	12-33-20	14-26-40
134.	Venus	Rahu	Ketu	14-26-40	15-13-20
135.	Venus	Rahu	Venus	15-13-20	17-26-40
136.	Venus	Rahu	Sun	17-26-40	18-6-40
137.	Venus	Rahu	Moon	18-6-40	19-13-20
138.	Venus	Rahu	Mars	19-13-20	20-00-00
139.	Venus	Jupiter	Jupiter	20-00-00	21-46-40
140.	Venus	Jupiter	Saturn	21-46-40	23-53-20
141.	Venus	Jupiter	Mercury	23-53-20	25-46-40
142.	Venus	Jupiter	Ketu	25-46-40	26-33-20
143.	Venus	Jupiter	Venus	26-33-20	28-46-40
144.	Venus	Jupiter	Sun	28-46-40	29-26-40
145.	Venus	Jupiter	Moon	29-26-40	30-00-00
146.	Mars	Jupiter	Moon	0-00-00	0-33-20
147.	Mars	Jupiter	Ketu	0-33-20	1-20-00
148.	Mars	Jupiter	Rahu	1-20-00	3-20-00
149.	Mars	Saturn	Saturn	3-20-00	5-26-40
150.	Mars	Saturn	Mercury	5-26-40	7-20-00
151.	Mars	Saturn	Ketu	7-20-00	8-6-40
152.	Mars	Saturn	Venus	8-6-40-	10-20-00
153.	Mars	Saturn	Sun	10-20-00	11-00-00
154.	Mars	Saturn	Moon	11-00-00	12-6-40
155.	Mars	Saturn	Mars	12-6-40-	12-53-20
156.	Mars	Saturn	Rahu	12-53-20	14-53-20

S.No.	Rasi Lord	Nakshatra Lord	Sub Lord	From DMS	To DMS
157.	Mars	Saturn	Jupiter	14-53-20	16-40-00
158.	Mars	Mercury	Mercury	16-40-00	18-33-20
159.	Mars	Mercury	Ketu	18-33-20	19-20-00
160.	Mars	Mercury	Venus	19-20-00	21-33-20
161.	Mars	Mercury	Sun	21-33-20	22-13-20
162.	Mars	Mercury	Moon	22-13-20	23-20-00
163.	Mars	Mercury	Mars	23-20-00	24-6-40
164.	Mars	Mercury	Rahu	24-6-40	26-6-40
165.	Mars	Mercury	Jupiter	26-6-40	27-53-20
166.	Mars	Mercury	Saturn	27-53-20	30-00-00
167.	Jupiter	Ketu	Ketu	0-00-00	0-46-40
168.	Jupiter	Ketu	Venus	0-46-40	3-00-00
169.	Jupiter	Ketu	Sun	3-00-00	3-40-00
170.	Jupiter	Ketu	Moon	3-40-00	3-46-40
171.	Jupiter	Ketu	Mars	4-46-40	5-33-20
172.	Jupiter	ketu	Rahu	5-33-20	7-33-20
173.	Jupiter	Ketu	Jupiter	7-33-20	9-20-00
174.	Jupiter	Ketu	Saturn	9-20-00	11-26-40
175.	Jupiter	Ketu	Mercury	11-26-40	13-20-00
176.	Jupiter	Venus	Venus	13-20-00	15-33-20
177.	Jupiter	Venus	Sun	15-33-20	16-33-20
178.	Jupiter	Venus	Moon	16-33-20	17-20-00
179.	Jupiter	Venus	Mars	17-20-00	18-6-40
180.	Jupiter	Venus	Rahu	18-6-4C	20-6-40
181.	Jupiter	Venus	Jupiter	20-6-40	21-53-20
182.	Jupiter	Venus	Saturn	21-53-20	24-00-00
183.	Jupiter	Venus	Mercury	24-00-00	25-53-20
184.	Jupiter	Venus	Ketu	25-53-20	26-40-00
185.	Jupiter	Sun	Sun	26-46-00	27-20-00
186.	Jupiter	Sun	Moon	27-20-00	28-26-40
187.	Jupiter	Sun	Mars	28-26-40	29-13-20

S.No.	Rasi Lord	Nakshatra Lord	Sub Lord	From DMS	To DMS
188.	Jupiter	Sun	Rahu	29-13-20	30-00-00
189.	Saturn	Sun	Rahu	0-00-00	1-13-20
190.	Saturn	Sun	Jupiter	1-13-20	3-00-00
191.	Saturn	Sun	Saturn	3-00-00	5-6-40
192.	Saturn	Sun	Mercury	5-6-40	7-00-00
193.	Saturn	San	Ketu	7-00-00	7-46-40
194.	Saturn	Sun	Venus	7-46-40	10-00-00
195.	Saturn	Moon	Moon	10-00-00	11-6-40
196.	Saturn	Moon	Venus	11-6-40	11-53-20
197.	Saturn	Moon	Rahu	11-53-20	13-53-20
198.	Saturn	Moon	Jupiter	13-53-20	15-40-00
199.	Saturn	Moon	Saturn	15-40-00	17-46-40
200.	Saturn	Moon	Mercury	17-46-40	19-40-00
201.	Saturn	Moon	Ketu	19-40-00	20-26-40
202.	Saturn	Moon	venus	20-26-40	22-40-00
203.	Saturn	Moon	Sun	22-40-00	23-20-00
204.	Saturn	Mars	Mars	23-20-00	24-6-40
205.	Saturn	Mars	Rahu	24-6-40	26-6-40
206.	Saturn	Mars	Jupiter	26-6-40	27-53-20
207.	Satrun	Mars	Saturn	27-53-20	30-00-00
208.	Saturn	Mars	Mercury	0-00-00	1-53-20
209.	Saturn	Mars	Ketu	1-53-20	2-40-00
210.	Saturn	Mars	Venus	2-40-00	4-53-20
211.	Saturn	Mars	Sun	4-53-20	5-33-20
212.	Saturn	Mars	Moon	5-33-20	6-40-00
213.	Saturn	Rahu	Rahu	6-40-00	8-40-00
214.	Saturn	Rahu	Jupiter	8-40-00	10-26-40
215.	Saturn	Rahu	Saturn	10-26-40	12-33-20
216.	Saturn	Rahu	Mercury	12-33-20	14-26-40
217.	Saturn	Rahu	Ketu	14-26-40	15-13-20
218.	Saturn	Rahu	Venus	15-13-20	17-26-40

S.No.	Rasi Lord	Nakshatra Lord	Sub Lord	From DMS	To DMS
219.	Saturn	Rahu	Sun	17-26-40	18-6-40
220.	Saturn	Rahu	Moon	18-6-40	19-13-20
221.	Saturn	Rahu	Mars	19-13-20	20-00-00
222.	Saturn	Jupiter	Jupiter	20-00-00	21-46-40
223.	Saturn	Jupiter	Saturn	21-46-40	23-53-20
224.	Saturn	Jupiter	Mercury	23-53-20	25-46-40
225.	Saturn	Jupiter	Ketu	25-46-40	26-33-20
226.	Saturn	Jupiter	Venus	26-33-20	28-46-40
227.	Saturn	Jupiter	Sun	228-46-40	29-26-40
228.	Saturn	Jupiter	Moon	29-26-40	30-00-00
229.	Jupiter	Jupiter	Moon	0-00-00	0-33-20
230.	Jupiter	Jupiter	Mars	0-33-20	1-20-00
231.	Jupiter	Jupiter	Rahu	1-20-00	3-20-00
232.	Jupiter	Saturn	Saturn	3-20-00	5-26-40
233.	Jupiter	Saturn	Mercury	5-26-40	7-20-00
234.	Jupiter	Saturn	Ketu	7-20-00	8-6-40
235.	Jupiter	Saturn	Venus	8-6-40	10-20-00
236.	Jupiter	Saturn	Sun	10-20-00	11-00-00
237.	Jupiter	Saturn	Moon	11-00-00	12-6-40
238.	Jupiter	Saturn	Mars	12-6-40	12-53-20
239.	Jupiter	Saturn	Rahu	12-53-20	14-53-20
240.	Jupiter	Saturn	Jupiter	14-53-20	16-40-00
241.	Jupiter	Mercury	Mercury	16-40-00	18-33-20
242.	Jupiter	Mercury	Ketu	18-33-20	19-20-00
243.	Jupiter	Mercury	Venus	19-20-00	21-33-20
244.	Jupiter	Mercury	Sun	21-33-20	22-13-20
245.	Jupiter	Mercury	Moon	22-13-20	23-20-00
246.	Jupiter	Mercury	Mars	23-20-00	24-6-40
247.	Jupiter	Mercury	Rahu	24-6-40	26-6-40
248.	Jupiter	Mercury	Jupiter	26-6-40	27-53-20
249.	Jupiter	Mercury	Saturn	27-53-20	30-00-00

7.16 TIME OF QUESTION TO BE CONVERTED TO LOCAL TIME

There is a Standard Time for one Country. The time of question should be converted to the local time. There is no necessity of looking into Sidereal Time. Since what we are taking is a figure. For every figure there is an absolute position in Nirayana Zodiac. Consider this as Lagna & Calculate the Cups for the remaning 11 Bhavas based on the Latitude of the planet.

7.17 TWELVE VIRGU CHARTS FOR ALL THE TWELVE RASI SIGNS IN BHACHAKRA

1. Signs (i) Odd/Positive/Masculine Signs (ii) Even/Negative/Female Signs.
2. Northern & Southern Signs.
3. Equinotical-Tropical Signs.
4. Fire-Earth-Air-Water-Signs.
5. Chara-Sthira-Dwiswabhava Signs.
6. Truthful & Barren Signs.
7. Mute Signs.
8. Voilent Signs.
9. Human Signs.
10. Voice Signs.
11. Four legged Animal Signs.
12. Mutable/Changeable Signs.
13. Double Bodied or Biocorporal signs.
14. Signs of short Ascension and Long Ascension.

7.18 HOW TO DO THE PREDICTION

(i) Specific Characters

(ii) Ill health

(iii) Wealth

(iv) Luckiness

(v) Love affairs

(vi) Matters which are indicative for all 12 Bhavas.

(vii) Ruling Planets etc.

Matters mentioned in para 7.17 to 7.18 above & all the above issues have been dealt in greater detail in Prasna Astrology Texts written by Sri. Krishna Murthy method and students are advised to read carefully.

7.19 THE FOLLOWING QUESTIONS WILL BE PUT FORWARD BY CONSULANT VERY FREQUENTLY

1. Whether Pass Port will be given to go to foreign Countries.
2. Will I go to foreign Countries or abroad.
3. Can I become the prime minister.
4. Auspicious time (i) To employ a Servant (ii) to Purchase an Article (iii) to Sell the Property (iv) to join Service (vi) to sign an Agreement (vi) to start business (vii) to release a Film (viii) For laying foundation Stone (ix) will I go aborad on promotion or will I go on probation (x) Which God to be Worshipped.

While examining a Horoscope from Astrological Angle the Planets which are favourable to the consulant to be observed. Then the Astrologer should pray his Guruji who had made you to get into this right & good direction elders always say.

"Guru Brahma!

Gurur Vishunu,!

Guru Devoo Maheswaraha!!"

Guru will make you adequatly powerfull for proper decision either in protecting your desire or remove the edifices involved in the Consulatns question, in the best manner.

Either the Blessings of Gurujis

Or

Jagad Guru Kanchikamakoti-Peethaadhipatulu

Or

Sri. Sankaracharya Swamijis

Alternatively select a Subha Graha & it's connected Diety relating to significators of Stars Lords situated in the Bhavas 8, 12 or 10, 11 and suitable prayers offered.

7.20 FUTURE ACTIONS

In this Krishna Murhty method many Sutras were given which will help in getting answers for different varieties of questions from the Consultants. Such of those Readers who are very much interested & enthusiastic in these matters may kindly read the texts available on this subject.

CHAPTER 8

Ayanamsa-Different Concepts

8.1

Indian Astrology is 'Nirayama' and all Western Texts on this subject are on 'Sayana' System. The difference between Nirayana and Sayana is called Ayanamsa.

In the begining the description of Nirayama System, followed by Sayana Method are discussed one by one below.

8.2 THE CONCEPT OF NIRAYANA AYANAMSA FROM ARIES

We have been seeing always in the infinite Sky, the Glittering Stars from Times Immorial. In this Clusteres of Stars, the 28 Stars identified which are usefull for purpose of counting Time. These 28 Stars are Shining in Sky moving from East to West in an Elipitcal form.

This is called Nakshatra Chakram or Nakshatra Skeleton or Bhacharka or Kanthi-Vruttamu or 'Aka-Vruttamu' or 'Rasi-Chakarm'. It has so many different Names.

These 28 Stars are counted from the Stars Aswini onwords. That is First one is Aswini Second one is Bharani and so on. These Stars are to their East always. East of Aswini is Bahrani and East of Bharani is Krittika and all are in this Fashion.

The Bha-Chakra is divided into 27 equal parts and each part is covered by 13 Degrees & 20 Minutes.

The Star 'Abhigit' is the 23rd, as its Path is only 254 Minutes, 21 Seconds. This has been merged with the 22nd Star Sravanam. The angle of Star is 26°-40′. The Starting Point of Aswini Nakshatra is called by Name ASWINYADI. This Bahchkara is divided into 12 equal prats. Each part is of 30° length on Ecliptic. For these 12 parts Names have been given from Aries. The First Point of Aries is called 'Meshadi' and the First Point in Bhachkra is called 'Aswiniyadi' and both concide together at one Point.

The three names are:

(i) Meshadi

(ii) Aswanyadi

(iii) Nirayanaaswinyadi

In English this point is called the First Point of Aries. This is a Fixed Point. There is no movement for this Point. Stars from Aswinyadi their particular positions are not in the beginning of each. They are away from their starting point. The Yoga Star of Aswini is 8° East of the starting point. Other Stars are also in the same manner positioned.

The Hindu names & Western names for 27 Star are given in the following table.

S. No.	Star-Hindu Names	Star-Equivalent in English
1.	Aswini	Arietis
2.	Bharani	Musa, Arietis-35,41
3.	Krittika	Pleiades, Aleyone
4.	Rohini	Aledberan, Hyades
5.	Mrugasira	Orionis, Deltaorions
6.	Ardra	Betelguese
7.	Punarvasu	Castor, Pollux, Geminorium
8.	Pushyami	Canneri
9.	Aslesha	Hydra
10.	Makha	Leonis, Regulus
11.	Poorva Phalguni	Leo (Delta, theta), Denebola
12.	Uttaraphalguni	Leo (Beta-93)
13.	Hastha	Virgo
14.	Chitta	Spica
15.	Swathi	Arcuturus, Bootes
16.	Visakha	Libra
17.	Anuradha	Scrpionis (Beta, Delta-P)
18.	Jyeshta	Antares
19.	Moola	Scorpionis
20.	Poorvashada	Sagittari (Delta, Epsilon)
21.	Uttaraashada	Sagittari (Beta, Omicron)
22.	Sravanam	Altair, Aqulia
23.	Dhanishta	Delphinis
24.	Satabhisham	Aquaril
25.	Poorvabhadra	Pagasis (Alpha, Beta)
26.	Uttarabhadra	Dagasus (Gaama) Andromedia (Alpha)
27.	Revati	Piscum

Revati Star is 13°-20′ away from its starting point. That is at its end only. The Revati Star has a group of 32 Stars. Revati Yoga Tara is at 10 seconds to the West of its end point. In Aswini it's bright Star is not visible nor any bright point is visible. Hence the present day observers are not able to identify even now. The Star Revati which is at end is also not succeptible for its identification. This is how the Nirayna Meashadi is described.

8.3 SAYANA MESHADI

The Sayana Meshadi shape cannot be understood unless one has a complete knowledge about a sphere. The matters concerning Astrology and to define it's Planets positions and to know clrearly in detail, the Ancestors had erected certain Spheres as the basis in the Sky, along this the first one is called Naadi Vruttam & the second one is called Kranthi Vruttam. Kranthi Vrutham is already explained in the Niraya Meshadi Paragraph. Now the, Naadi Vruttam is described.

Naadi Vrutthamu

In the Norhtern Sky there is a star called Dhruvudu. Similarly in the southern hemisphere on south direction there is another Star which is also called on the name of Dhruvudu. A circle drawn through these two points is called Mahanaadi Vrutthamu. It's angular measurement is also 360°. The circuferetance of Karanti Vrutthamu also covers 360°. When these two circles join at one point and exactly at 180° they join again when distance between them is 180°.

(In circular measurement every Ghatikas are called Naadis). Hence the circle is called as such.

Naadi Vrutthamu with Sampatha Binduvus

These two Naadi Circles are meeting once in the Eastern Spehre and a second time in Western Sphere. These points are called as Sampatha Binduvus.

The point which is in Eastern Sphere is called Sayana Meshadi. In English it is called Vernal Equinox. This point is now a days called as Vasantha Sampaatamu or Vasantha Vishuvamu.

In the Western Sphere the Sarat Vishuvamu or Sarat point is called as Sayana Tuladi or Kranthi Pathamu. This is called as Automanal Equinox. This is also called as Tuladi Sampathamu.

Kranthi Vrutthamu

Since this is moving East to West, the Sayana Meshadi point is not fixed. Every year this is moving at certain rate. When Sun comes into Sampatha Points, the Days & Night are of equal time in hours. These two Points are called as Vishuvatthus.

Current Sayana Meshadi is in Uttarabhadra Star could be told but in which part of minutes is lying could not be estbshlied, hence the Sayana Meshadi is defined as such.

8.4 THE SHAPE OF AYANAMSA

As explained earlier the difference between Sayana & Nirayana Meshadis along the Kranti Vrutthamu is called as Ayamamsa. For this there are six names.

1. Ayana Chalamsamulu
2. Ayanamsamulu
3. Chalaamsamulu
4. Bhagamulu
5. Amsamulu
6. Antharamsamulu

Even now it is to be of positive sign (Dhanat Makamulu).

While calculating Longitudes the Ayamamasas are to be added to the Planets Longitude. Sometimes these Ayamamsaas will be of negative sign. Then that Ayamamsas should be deducted from the Planets Longitude.

The movement of Vishuwat Point arrived by different methods in an year-the Ayana Gati is in seconds.

	Seconds
(a) As per Arsha Siddhanta	54
(b) As per actual observations conducted at Jaipur's Star Observatory in India	51
(c) The present day movement as per Westerners observation though powerfull Telescopes	50.26 (27)
(d) Bhaskara-II Ayanamsa	59.9
(e) Ancient Acharaya Manjunadhula's observation going purely in West direction	59.9
(f) B.V. Raman's	50.33
(g) Lahri's	50.27

For this movement when compared to earlier & later times it is much less. Hence the Manujanadhula & Others were not taken when compared to the figure based on actual observation.

Earth is Rotating along it's own North-South Druva Axis at an inclined angle to the Kranti Vruttha & also to that of the path of Moon around the Earth.

Here it is presummed that the Earth is Rotating as inclined Spindle due to Gravitational Forces of Sun & Earth it has shown its effect on the Equator and these forces have shown its effect and are acting to bring these two Planets together since Earth is Rotating in a circular fashion some difference is occurring in the movement. Hence the movement of circle of Earth is getting slower. The Gravitational Force acting with North pole as it's basis the Divya Gola Dhruvams both moving in Elliptical form for one full Rotation it is estimated by Astronomical Scientists that it would take 26,000 years based on the present rate of Ayana Gati.

How the movement of the Point of Vishuat is shown in the following diagram.

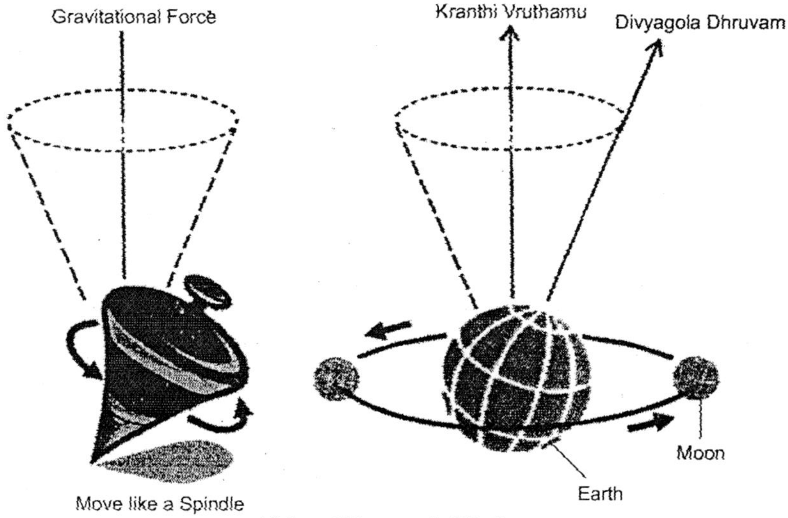

Vishuwat Movement of Earth

The cuase of Vishuwat Point moving is due to Earth's Vibrational Rotation on it's own North South Axis.

When Earth with its Axis Roating like a Spinning Top the North Pole (Uttaradhrumam) is moving in a an Ecliptieal form wedening to 47° (2 × 23° – 30′) (ie) the plane of Equatorial Line. Hence the point of Kranti Vruttam is always moving & changing. Therefore the Sarat Vishuam is always going to West. It has been found that this rate of movement is 50.26 seconds per year.

Due to change of the Vishuvat Point, there is change in the Longitude of a Planet and it gets changed to the extent of movement of Vishuvamsa, this movement as per Astronomical Seientists is said to be 26,000 years approximately for its full movement.

The following sketch shows how the plane of Earth Orbit is moving at an inclination of 23°-30′ and the movement in Ecliptical Form with North pole Roating at a total Angle of 47°.

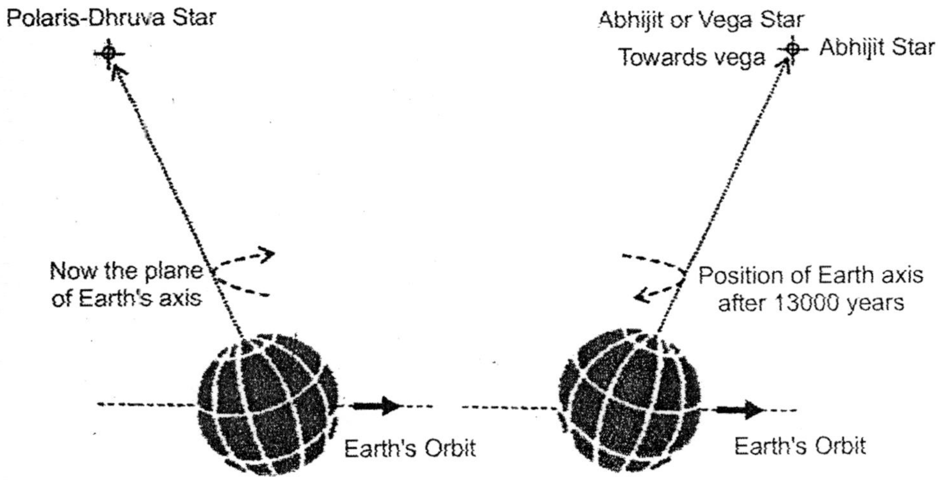

Now the North Pole is towards Polaris Dhruva Nakshatra. After 13000 years it will be towars Abhijit Star.

When old methods are not giving proper results, new methods are to introduced. When new methods are avaviable to get correct Longitudes of Planets these methods are to be used. The Almanae should be so prepared with correct Ayamasa obtained based on actual observations and should be Absolute Equitable Fixed & Accurate. There should be proper efforts in this direction.

The Calendar Reforms Committee of 1952 apponited by Govt. of India deeided that the fixed Sampatha Binduvu was at 285 AD as arrived. It was decided that the Sampata Binduvu at 285 AD was moving towards West at the rate of 50.26 seconds per year backwards. Based on this in 2019 of Sri Vilamba Nama year on Chittra Suddha Padyami (6-4-2019) the Ayanamsa is 20°-07′-5″ IST time of 05-30 AM.

CHAPTER 9

INTRODUCTION TO THE DIFFERENT METHODS ADOPTED IN PANCHAMGAMS

Sri. Kuppa Anjaneya Sastry

1. From Times Immemorial 'The Element of Time' was inter- linked with the daily activities of Human Lives and it need not be emphasized as it was the most important aspect in the Individual's life career. Examination of time/ counting of time elements remained as unavoidable at all times and in all places. World over counting of time such as hours, minutes and seconds & later days, months & years-all these units of time count remained Universal and it became the most popular method of counting from ancient times.
2. In all Cultures which ever in use World over in all the Countries, the Culture existing and practiced in India is the most appropriate and acceptable form. It has abundant knowledge. The Culture adopted by India during Vedic & Traditional Functions, remained unaffected and unaltered and it goes to prove beyond doubt that the methods adopted were worthy by their nature and can be boasted as the best. Our Mental attitude leans towards attaining stability in harnessing past and present religious and academic functions and these are the forwards for Indians and are the basis on which the Generations continued to line-up one after the other. Even the methods of counting of time for conducting their functions remained steadfast. Not only counting of time- in days ,months & years but also finding out the positions of Sun and Moon and is interlinked with Tithis, Vaaras, Nakshatras, Yogas and Karanams. All these time factors are molded to a highly specialized system which was not in existence anywhere in the World, and this is called as "PANCHAMGAM". The practice of following Panchamgam based on an Individual's position on the Earth, positions of Sun, Moon & other Planets and fixing Chara Rasis is non-existence elsewhere. The calculated details based on Siddhanta, for these factors showing daily position for a period of one year given in Panchamgam is not followed in other (Countries) cultures.
3. The Panchamgam cannot be dispensed with from the life of a Hindu Citizen. For all the functions performed at auspicious time by families, results in leading the Human life for safe conduct in all matters of business activities and other Cultural functions, Panchamgam is the most essential reference Book. Apart from the above, the Planetary position present at the time of performance of, both for the past events or for the events to be performed in future; the effect of it will be known and action taken for improving the benevolence of Planets by conducting suitable

remedial measures. At that time it is the Panchamgam that will be most usefull. The Panchamgam is a Text which contain the knowledge of both Astronomical Bodies and the Rules laid down in different Sastras.

4. Here is an important aspect. In other Countries/ cultures, Examination of Astronomical changes, finding out the Longitudes of Planets etc. is being done in respect of functions for both good and bad events which relate to either an Individual Human Being or for a function of Social nature; but examination is only limited purely for acquiring knowledge. Where is the necessity to find out the Horoscopes and give predictions, as what has to happen will necessarily be coming out and whichever is not supposed to get will never get, however much one would try and make efforts. Sometimes a Doctor examines a Patient and indicate the Nature of disease and symptoms likely to be there and the repercussions will be indicated. What is the necessity of informing this position to the Patient. The treatement is required to be indicated to the desired results. But in Astrology it is not so. The position of Planets now present and to be in future to be indicated and remedial measures suggested. Then only the efforts will be fruitful. Our Ancient Rishies have handed over this wonderful Text of Panchamgam only for this purpose.

5. But the Panchamgam gives only the Astronomical Data and the connected knowledge of Planets Longitudes. There may be any number of Astrologers, but the Planets and their position is same daily and Panchamgams in the Market should all be uniform. But they are not identical. In the present Day World there are mainly three varieties of Panchamgams are to be seen

   (a) Poorva Paddhati,

   (b) Druk Paddhati, &

   (c) Mixed Paddhati,

   In every Panchamgam there are different opinions. There are differences in Longitudes of Planets, Tithis, & Nakshatras. What is the reason for these deviations? What is the remedy? These are the questions that will be examined hence forth. This matter is related to Astronomical Data and Dharma Sastra. It is not easy to resolve the same. One has to make a deep study of the Sastra. However an effort is made to correlate on matters related to Primary Points at this stage.

6. The Siddhanta Bhaga necessary for 'Counting Time' is dependent on the Astronomical knowledge & data. The Panchamgams need the knowledge of the theoretical part of Siddhanta Bhaga and is dependent on the observed part of Astronomical Data. Such Panchamgams are called as "SIDDHANTA GRANDHAS" and have become famous. These Books are Ancient in Nature but they are up-to date in their knowledge. There are very many and it can be so so—

   Sloka: " suryaha pitamahoo vyaasaha vashishtootri paraasaraha!
   kaasyapoo naaradoo gargaha mareechirmanurangeraaha!
   lomasaha poulishchaiva chyavanoo yavanoo bhruguhu!
   Sounakaadashtaadasa heeyati jyothisaastra pravartakaaha !"

This is an important Sloka. There were 18 Astronomical Pravarthakas or Pundits who had laid down Rules for Siddhanta Bhaga. These Rishies were ancient. In the later periods in the Christian Era, there were Bhaskaracharya, Varahamihira, Bhramma Gupta and Aryabhatta etc., who were famous writers of 'Siddhanta Bhaga".

7. The meaning of Siddhanta is that the Rules framed are studied by different Personalities, examined by a group of Specialists and discussed in various Seminars and then it was put-up with it's results and then only the Rule is finalized. This is similar to an example of measurement of the distance between two selected points on surfaces. This distance can be told approximately but cannot be to it's exactness. This aspect was known to everyone. It was accepted that from the practical points of view the result arrived was almost closer to the actual but cannot be equal to its Theoretical value. Based on this analogy, it is an accepted fact that a SIDDHANTA is real in its true sense. It's actual meaning is only known to the Almighty and only the Maharshies with their Divya Drishti could find-out and start preaching but it was not within the purview of the mankind.

   We have to ultimately accept that the Astronomical and Astrological Siddhantas were fortunately given to us not by any Human beings by their examination, research and experiments but given only by the Lord Brahmma, Vasishta, Narada Rishies, which should be taken sincerely as such and We must be proud of that.

8. It is an accepted fact that there would not be any change in the Principles of Basic Siddhanta, irrespective of the fact that there may be any number of Authors or Writers on this subject; but they do not come under the purview of Siddhanta Karthas. The position is same in any Sastra.

   For instance one Writer describes the Principle in a language which is easily understood by ordinary people of average intelligence. The same Writer for people of higher intellect can add-up many more items and write a Big Book to be proud of. But there will not be any change in the Basic Siddhantas. For Example- In the present Day Siddhanta Bhaga, there are two texts available belonging to Vashiasta Rishie. These are 1). Bhruhat Vasishta Samhita 2). Laghu Vasishta Samhita. The first one was in use in Krutayuga when Vashishta taught the subject to his Grand-Son Varahamihira. The 2nd one was in Tretayuga when Mandavya Rishie taught the subject to his disciples. In both these, there was no difference in Siddhanta but there were changes in the mathematical calculations and now it is looking that there was no linkage between the two texts, unless this is examined judiciously, the fact will not be known. Taking this aspect into consideration the writer Daivagna, Sri Mandavya Somayaji had written in his Text ' Jagadeepika', a write-up as under-

   " swakruta praacheena grandhee kaalaanuguna beejam

   prasaarya sastraantharamiva praaphraa "

   meaning- that both the texts were written at different times, with a long gap of time- only after proper corrections are made, otherwise this looks like a new text, but there was no difference of opinion in Siddhanta Bhaga.

9. If there was no change in Siddhanta Bhaga, why there were differences in Panchamgas? Why so many Varieties? (How?). In order to answer these questions, they will be examined separately from their Principles. These Varieties in Panchamgas are the ones which follow the Poorva Paddhati or Old Practice. These are followed by our Ancestors based on Siddhanta then available. The Ancestors were Maharshis,

Mahatmas who followed these practices. This is the reason why we would say that everyone should follow these Panchamgas.

All of us know that the Oldest knowledge available is VEDA. To understand and recognize that Mine itself is a big job. Just like Gold is obtained atfter elaborate processing and distilling the raw material and it is not obtained in the Ornamental Fashion. To recognize this knowledge, is also a great literary job. Similar to this, from Veda Mine which is infinite and of great depth , the basic knowledge necessary for the Human beings is brought out, so that the Sutras required and necessary for writing the Panchamgas had to be formulated for the benefit of the Mankind and it cannot be explained how difficult is this job.

From that Mine of Vedas- the first Text Book of Principles and this Grandha is called as Vedanga Jyothisha. But the present day world is far away from the Hindu Sampradaya and this Grandha unfortunately became unavailable and even if available is not in it's full shape and scope. After this, the currently available Grandha is the SUYA SIDDHANTA. This is fortunately available with Commentaries as it was written by Surya Bhagavan. This is the only one which is the basis. The Panchamgas that follow the SURYA SIDDHANTA are the real ones. . But in the present days, no one is writing such Panchamgas and it is also not possible.

10. It is not possible to write Panchamgas only based on Surya Siddhanta or other Siddhanta Grandhas.

Sloka: "dharmee prateeyamaanee tu veedeena karanaatmanaa
iti kartavyataa bhaagam meemaamsaa poorayishyati"

Meaning being- that one should follow Dharma as said by Veda. to perform and adhear to that including Daily Puja Rituals or Bhrammaarpanam as are prescribed in various Texts. Similarly the information contained in Siddhanta Grandhas is taken out by Varahamihiraadi Maharshies and formulated as texts which are called as Practical Guides. Some other Rishies like Kesava/ Ganesha Daivagna Pundits had given commentaries which are convenient and easy to understand. These are like ready reckoners. With the help of these Grandhas, it had become possible for Ordinary Pundits to write Panchamgas. The present Poorva Paddhathi Panchamgas were prepared on these lines. In the present period the Grandhas such as:-

Graha Laghavam, Gana Kaananandam, Narakanteeravam,
Tithi Ratnavali, Dina Chandrika, Panchamga Manjusha, Siddhantarahasyamu.

These are available which are important Karana Grandhas.

In some places or in certain Families/ Vamsas/ Guru-Sishya paramparas, a special Karana Grandha was in use inadvertently. With the help of these Karana Grandhas, now a days the Panchamga Writers are calling them as Porva Panchamgas. The Panchamga Karthas may follow any Siddhanta Karana Grandha, but they openly say that that the Panchamgam is based on Surya Siddhata. This is also a fact from one point of view. But if the Panchamgas are based on Surya Siddhanta, why then they are differences between them is to be analyzed.

11. Planets are always are on their move. They appear/ seen, to move in a predetermined path. But actually the real position is completely different. The Planet's position and

the rate of movement varies while in motion. There are no empirical Rules laid down nor can they be specified for the purpose. Temporarily some assumptions are either made or formed out, even among them the changes are inevitable. These changes can be recognized by means of spcial examination, otherwise it is impossible.. This Natural Phenomena was known to the Ancesstors in the beginning itself and they (Surya and Others).- every one in their Siddhanta Grandhas had expressly stated with-out any doubts. The Grandhas which came after Surya Siddhanta were all made with changes that occurred from time to time. We only understand the reasons for such changes, from the Commentaries of the Author of the Text " Jagadeepika". Similarly all Karana Grandhas were also subjected to changes from time to time.

12. This sort of up-dating Karana Grandhas was in force in our Country, right from the beginning. The Surya Siddhanta was Evolved in Krita Yuga. This means that this relates to the period of about 2,60,000 years prior to us. If in case based on this, if Panchamgam was prepared, it will only relate to that period only.. But Karana Gramddhas when ever they were up-dated from time to time, and Panchamgas are written based on these, would have actually suited to them in those periods. Such changes made in Karana Grandhas are called as " Dhruk Samskaras". Based on these, the Planet's position and rate of movement there of and the calculations leading to such results are proved to be correct. Such Karana Grandhas which were modified from time to time relate to that period only and not for the current period. However these Panchamgas were considered as Poorava Paddathi Panchamgas Only.

13. Graha Ganana was in force even from the time of Evolution/ Kaliyuga starting. For every Planet the average rate of movement was calculated including making corrections based on Druk Siddhanta with the help of coefficients and as such corrections revealed, the accuracy so arrived of Planets movements Positions, were almost tallying with the practical Observations made. In these, there would be corrections relevant to the time factors elapsed. For Example based on the Grandha of' Kalyana Ganita' the time taken by Sun for one Rotation/ Revolution was equal to one Soura Year, 7 Days, 15 Ghadias, 31 Vighadias and 31 Parakalas (1-7-15-31-31). Either from the beginning of Evolution and also from the beginning of each Yuga, the Sun would have come to the first Point of Aries Sign as per Surya Siddhanta, after the lapse of this Time. In addition, right from Kaliyuga the number of Years / Days elapsed were calculated and the present Day position of Sun is arrived. For the purpose of easy additions and multiplications, certain Tabular Formats were given in the same Grandha. In the same fashion, the Tabular Formats were made and given in every type of Karana Grandhas which were varying from one another. As a result, there will be differences in these Poorava Paddhathi Panchamgas. What they had obtained was the average rate of movement. For this, corrections were made based on Druk aspects, as such coefficients are available in Karana Grandhas to obtain the Sun's actual position, but the methods being separate for each of these Grandhas. Similarly the positions of all other Planets were calculated and obtained. The positions so arrived should become equal to the position obtained as per actual observations. In the present day world, it is to be seen whether these calculations are actually tallying but the subject of which can only be examined and not meant for raising objections.

14. For every Planet the average rate of movement of each Planet varies from one to another. This aspect cannot be said as incorrect. Similarly there would differences/ variations in the methods of arriving. Example if five articles cost. twenty Rupees, the cost of eight items will be thirty two Rupees as the rate of one item was four Rupees. But by adopting the proportionate method like 8x20/5; the Rule for such method can be easily be obtained. In both these methods the basis behind it's recognition is a matter of acceptance but not for raising an objection. But in some circumstances the work is not done only on proportional methods. For Example-One Palanquin from its original position is moved and in 10 seconds it moves towards its left and in another 10 seconds it reaches its original position. There after it moves towards to its right and when it comes to its starting point the total travelling time would be 40 seconds.

    In reference to this, it cannot be told that the Palanquin speed in every second is the same. If it is not so, after travelling to some distance, it would not be possible to return to the same place by coming in the reverse direction and it would have proceeded straight only. Depending on the circumstances, the distance and time would be calculated in the Proportional methods by assumptions. Similarly in the Karana Grandhas, based on the writers intelligence/experience/, there would be approximations depending upon the requirements. keeping in mind the root elements of these Ganita Sutras one can easily understand. Otherwise it was stated that theirs, was based on their own Methods/ Sampradayas and they would not budge an inch from their argument.

15. We had earlier discussed that the Rotation/Revolution of Sun per year as per Kalyana Ganitham was 1-1-15-31-31. This could be acceptable for a period of about 500/600 years, but after 1000/2000 years, the last figures of Parakalu (Lipthas) would have to be got corrected. For this purpose the Knowledge contained in Siddhantam was absolutely necessary. The Ancient Maharshies by their, Shakthi of Tapas/ Futuristic Vision possessed by them could do these corrections easily. After a long period of time they were using instruments which were similar to the ones which are now in use in the present day world, like telescopes etc. These Implements were called as 'Nalikas' in those days. The Scientific knowledge behind these in so far as to manufacturing them and methods of putting them into the utility, is not easily available. Those Sampradayas had become extinct.

16. Now a days, we have been specifying positively that all Siddhanta Grandhas are to be made update as per actual observations for all Planets in respect of their movements. We have been mentioning that they should adopt Astronomical observations instead of depending upon the Ganita Sutras. In our Country it was established since Ancient times that this procedure was in vogue as seen from our Tantra/ Karana, Grandhas. But unfortunately since 1500/2000 years period our Country was Ruled by Foreigners as a result our knowledge, Kalas and Sampradayas had gone into the oblivion. The damage was maximum during British Rule. As a result our Bharatiya Samskruti and Sampradayas and the practice of writing Panchamgas had been completely destroyed. The practice of Astronomical Examination/ observations of Planets had been givenup. The Panchamga preparation is even now going on based on oldest Karana Grandhas. It is a redeeming factor that preparation of Panchamgas

had not been given up. This was a blessing in disguise. Having come to know the position, some Knowledgeable persons in the past Century had fortunately started their search for proper solutions.

17. There is a saying 'that Ships could become Carts and Carts become Ships'. On the same corollary, once upon a time India had been the basis to know the Knowledge about Astronomical observation of Planets more so due to the Astrological Siddhantic and Predictive Sciences. Foreigners had obtained full knowledge on these maters and now they are far advanced in these aspects and had reached a higher state than Indians. With the help of new Astronomical Large Telescopes now made by them, they have now become experts and are able to carry out their experiments correctly in establishing not only the position of Planets to the minutest value of degrees, minutes and seconds but also are able to measure their rate of movement nearest to the minutes & seconds. etc. In this field the Foreigners had full support of the Jyotish Scholars of Indians is a well known fact. There was a saying' karanamadapi bangaram'; meaning that Gold can be identified even from the mud-stuff and can be used by washing the same. So why not Indians make use of the Foreigners results of their experiments and observations?

    'why not we utilize the knowledge of Foreigners/non-Hindus, similar to the saying that when we are not getting hand pounded rice, are we not cooking the rice food with even milled rice'.

    Factually what is the advantage gained by Foreigners with the knowledge obtained in Astronomical Science, excepting that they satisfied their hunger for Scientific knowledge. Could they elevate themselves to a higher levels or put it to a superior advantage?.

    Their knowledge would be useful in determining & writing an Absolute Panchamgam by Indians. Based on that, which would be of more use to us, we could put the same into practice to achieve the four Purushaardhas in a proper way. The Inauspiciousness in day to day working could completely be mitigated or totally eliminated not only to us but to the entire world. We can achieve and lead a peaceful, safe, happy and calm life through the entire period one would live through in that manner. Hence with the help of the New knowledge, we could prepare our Panchamgas on that basis and the method is the most acceptable solution which even the learned old Scholars are agreeing. Even some are making efforts in that direction or even some Scholars had achieved in doing so.

18. Sri. Damodar Bapuji Ketkar, a Maharashtrian Pundit had made enormous efforts in this field and prepared a Grandha called ' Jyothir Ganitham'. As per this even to day this is the most closest to the Druk Ganita and one can easily arrive at the positions of Planets Longitudes very accurately. About 150 years backwards from now on the Pundits in Varanasi by name Sri. Sudhakar Dwivedi and his disciple Sri. Muralidhara Jhaji (Bihar) and Sri. Pidaparthi varu from the Andhra Pradesh – like this all experts in the Ancient Knowledge had suitably blended the ancient knowledge with that of the new knowledge of Astronomical Science and started making an effort to prepare the best Panchamgam. Such efforts were approved by Gurus like Kamakoti Peethadhipathulu as they were the protectors of the methods & practices adopted based on Sampradaya Principles. Even the Calendar Reforms

Committee appointed by the then Indian Government in 1953 for purposes of bringing out a suitable Panchamgam; had also vouchsafed that such Panchamgas are accepted even from the Principles of Sastra and based on this all Indian States had prepared and published Panchamgas in the Vernacular followed by them.

19. Therefore the Panchamgas that were prepared based on this method are called as Druk Ganita Panchamgas. Truly speaking these Druk Ganita Panchamgas should be called as True Poorva Paddhathi Panchamgams. The reason being from times immemorial all our Siddhanta/ Tantra/ Karana, Grandhas were modifying from time to time based on Druk Padhathi system. This aspect was discussed in the preceding paras. Unfortunately such practice of introduceing corrections based on Druk Siddhanta was badly affected since 5/6 Centuries. However the Panchamga which was updated based on time factor element of Druk Siddhanta can only be called as Poova Paddhathi Panchamga.

20. Druk Samskaram has to be invariably be carried out. But that element of Samskaram should be of Acceptable Standard. Some people opine that the Westerners New method of carrying out Samskaram is not acceptable to us. The intention is only to accept our ancient Indian 'NALIKAS' as per the version expressed by certain sect. So far so Good. Accordingly we will be closer to the real natural position. But we may be a bit far away from the New Methods. But in case if we completely avoid the new method, then our differences would greatly increase. Therefore in the present times the Panchamga which is called as based on Poorva Paddhthi; can only be really called as the Poorva Paddathi Panchamga in its primitive stage as per the aims set earlier. Such Panchamgas have not attained the truthfulness and has not reached the stage for which the goal is set. Its only after correcting one's own mind and reach the goal in making corrections based on the new method , then only it becomes nearer to the newly prepared Druk Siddhanta Panchamga. Even if one has adopted a different method, the ultimate goal is to reach the same point.

21. In any method, either Poorva Paddhathi or Druk Paddhathi when once the true positions of Sun and Moon are arrived, 50 % the work of Preparation of Panchamga can be said to have been completed. The difference between Moon and Sun is the Tithi and based on the position of Moon the Nakshatra is obtained. If Longitudes of Moon is added to that of Sun , the Yogam is obtained.. Half the Tithi is the Karanam. The calculation of Panchamga is proceded in that fashion. For the Day calculation, the Graha Ganita is not required.Right from the first Day the Evolution started with Sunday in the morning at 6 hours. From that time, the Days could be counted and for the present day it can be arrived. In this respect everyone in the world are on one method only which was started by the Indians long ago, which is creditable.

22. The order of week days is dependent on the seven Planets only. Temporarily the Sun and Moon are taken as Jeevatma and Parmatma respectively. Based on the rotational speed and position, the Planets order- Earth, Chandra, Budha, Sukra, Ravi, Kuja, Guru and Sani. The rate of movement for Chandra is the quickest in all the Planets and that of Sani is the slowest. In a day there are 24 Horas or Hours. For every Hora one Lord ship is given for each Planet. The world got commenced in the beginning with the Sunday as the first Hora. Second Hora was given to Venus who was just behind him. Next was given to Budha, thereafter to the Moon who are the Lords

of Horas. The fifth Hora was given to the Sani , the sixth Hora to Jupiter, seventh Hora was given to Kuja. Again for each Hora- the Lords are- in the same order- Sun, Venus,Mercury, Moon, Sani, Guru, Kuja. In this manner when three rounds are completed, when the fourth round starts, ie. 3x7=21+ 3 Horas of Sun, Venus and Mercury completed 24 Horas have elapsed. The 25 th. Hora Lord is Moon and that Day is nominated as Monday. Again – Moon. Sani, Guru, Kuja, Sun, Venus, Mercury Hora will go for 3 rounds and in the end three Horas of Moon, Sani, Guru when completed, the 3rd. Day the next will be Tuesday as that Hora belongs to Kuja (Mangal- another Name given for Kuja) Similarly all the seven Days are rotating. There is no place for Rahu and Ketu in that. The entire world is following this same order. This has no relevance to the Planets rotational aspect.

23. In so far as the Ganita used in the preparation of Panchamga, the only important part left is; the position and of the remaining five Planets starting with Kuja and also the information relating to Eclipses. In the Poorva Paddhathi Panchamgas Druk Samskaram was done for Kuja and other four Planets based on Karana Grandhas, knowing fully-well that they do not relate to the relevant period. Therefore differences were noticed in respect of Moudhyas and other matters between Druk Panchamgas and Poorva Paddhathi Panchamgas. The starting and ending of Moudhyas could only be correctly specified as they could be correctly identifiable and they belong to the category of Druk Ganitham only.

    The Eclipses will only tally based on Druk Ganitham. They can be identified with the naked Eye. In Poorva Paddhathi even if predicted as per Karana Grandhas, they will not tally, because the position and movement of Planets do not relate to the current period. Therefore for purposes of determining Eclipses, even people who were following the Poova Paddhathi have to follow, as there is no alternative but to use, the new method and are now using them.

    The remaining items are Muhurthas, Festivals and Parvadinas. These are being written by the Panchamga Kartha as they like. The Pramana Grandhas required for these items are common. Between two Authors irrespective of following any Paddhathi, if a difference has cropped up in these matters, it was due to accepted Sampradaya Bhedhas in the Main Grandhas. It can also be due to the Authors ignorance or mistakes on their part. The answer or solution (behind all) to this will be the look out of the People who are using these Panchamgas.

24. Even in Druk Panchamgas also there are differences in the mathematical portions. These are mainly relate to the Ayanamsa. The clarification on this matter is highly Technical. For the present we stop discussing on this matter. We now go in for discussing the third type of Panchamgas which are said to be of Mixed Type.

    In this Panchamgas there will not be any Samskaram made to Sun and Moon. They do it for Kuja and others. Even for this some people use Karuna Grandhas and some others use the New Tabular Formats issued for the purpose. Since there will not be any Samskaram done to Sun and Moon, there will be glaring differences in Tithi, Nakshatra, Yoga and Karana, in the Panchamgas. Consequently, there are changes in Muhoorthas, Festivals and Parvadinas.

25. Now we go into the matter as to the one which is correct? Which one is based on Technical Sastra? Which one can be accepted from the Dharma Sastra point of view?

All these questions can be answered and decided by knowledgeable persons. If one can start questioning there will always be an opposite view expressed. To justify their reasoning they can always give causative factors or they give independent commentaries on the same subject and they find ways and means and always attempt to justify their view point. The person involved in supporting an argument will not worry to know about the real truth.

Sri. Neelakhantha Pundit who gave Commentary to the Maha Bharata, during his period, had obtained Mahabharata texts from different places and examined himself each one and decided as to which one is acceptable, which is to be rejected, which one is based on Sampradayas, which one would be acceptable to the learned at that time? After thorough examination on all fronts and gave his commentary after taking a decision on that matter.

Sloka " bahoon samaahrutya vibhinna deesyaan
koosaan vinishchitya cha paatha magrayam !
praachaam gurunaa manusprutya vaacham
arabhyatee bhaarata bhaavadeepaha !!"

Our Panchamga Karthas specially those in favor of Poorva Paddhathi had no such inclination in their minds. Most of them were averse to the word " Siddhatam". Some of them were not even aware that there (was) is a Siddnanta. For some others they were not proficient in the Language to enable them to fully understand all the Poorva Granddhas. The Panchamga preparation is done as though it is a routine matter, they may be efficient in giving predictions on Jatakas and also in deciding and fixing correct Muhurthas.

26. In order to justify their method of preparing Panchamgam, they repeatedly emphasized that the Muhuthas fixed based on their Panchamga got very good results and that the predictions given on Jatakas were actually tallying with the results obtained and therefore their method of preparing Panchamgam is sacrosanct and acceptable.

In order to get a good result about the Karma, Muhurtha is not the only causative factor. There are many factors on which the results would depend up-on such as- the Place, Time, Mantra, Tantra, Dravya, Chitta, Bhakthi, Sraddha etc and many more factors to obtain results for Karma.. Besides these, there is what is called ' Prarabdham' and they should be eligible to enjoy such a fruitful results. There is one more factor- Pameswara is the Karmaphala Pradata. Whatever one would get either good or bad, is as a result of which Karma performed earlier, would not be able to decide and establish by any one.

We have a right to perform actions " karmanyevaadhikaraha". Therefore one would always vouchsafe to perform Karmas strictly based on Sastra to the extant one was aware of and to the extent possible. Whenever a Muhurta is needed, the same should be according to the prescribed norms and it should be strictly followed. It is therefore the responsibility of the Panchamga Kartha to give a Panchamga which is proper and purely made as a Sacred Grandha. It cannot be said that his Pachangam is Sacred just because the results given were good as per the Muhurtha fixed. Otherwise what would one say when the result obtained was of opposite nature. Therefore one would be very careful in these matters. The Predictive results also could fortunately tally. Similarly the treatment given to a Patient in the Medical field with ordinary knowledge are giving good results. From this point of view how far it is correct to say that it is not necessary that one should have a long experience in treating Patients or to have a deep knowledge on the Medical Science.

27. Some people say that it is their Sampradaya and their Elders/ Gurus were following from ancient times and that method is only Sacred. Sri.Madwacharya had categorically stated after careful examination of the subject based on Time elements such as Sampradaya/Shistachara stated as under:-

Slokas with meaning-

'sammarsinaha=yukthikusalaaha'.Those who have comprehensive knowledge concerning the Subject- Those who decide good and bad based on Poorva Paksha Siddhanta.

'yuktaaha=satratatparaaha' – Those who have faith in the Sastra.

'aayuktaaha= tadanushtaanatatparaaha' – Those knowledge for their benefit. who not only advise others, but also applythe same sastra conjunctions in their personal lives

'aalooshaaha= kroodhavargitaaha' – Those who do not wish that their argument should only be accepted.

' dharmatatpaaraaha= Those who have strong belief in following the path of dharma.

'itti bhraahmmanaaha'= Those who have the divine knowledge, who have the aforesaid qualities, those actions alone are acceptable and to be followed

Hence the opinion expressed by the Acharya should be taken as a Rule and followed.

Hence the argument that their Forefathers had followed or spoken cannot become a Sampradayam. The argument that the House was built by Forefathers and need not be altered and should be used as such is not correct. If it is absolutely necessary, it can be completely demolished and a new house built in its place.

In Dharam Sastra there will be many modifications, exceptions, alternatives etc. The Apasthambha Maharish had directed in his Sloka, stated that-

'yathaavaishaam dkuladharmam syaath'

Say for Example-For Female Child the Alphabets should be in odd number while naming the child. Whereas for Male Child the Alphabets should be in even number. At these moments the Kula Dharma should be observed, as the practice was in vogue & coming from Forefathers time. At this place it is not necessary in the case of Forefathers to bring the Slokas earlier discussed such as – sammarsinaha, yukataaha, aayuktaaha, need not to be analyzed. For Female Child – Saraswati, and for the Boy- Kesava names can be given.

In the past 5/6 Centuries our Country was unfortunately Ruled by Foreigners and as a result, the Educational methods, Sampradayas/ and the abundant Knowledge was completely Eclipsed. Some of our Ancestors had taken precautions to protect our Educational methods & Knowledge to the extent within their reach. They could not conduct Astronomical Observations and could not get the information from those who had conducted such observations. Having known fully these aspects, they were only using willfully the old Karana Grandhas. There is a saying –

Sloka- 'sarvanaasee samutpanee, ardham tyajayathi panditaha'

This Sloka applied to them. Such Grandhas were handed over to us. For this we should whole heartedly appreciate them. Convey our bountiful acknowledgements to them. Otherwise we would not have had these Grandhas also. During the days when Rice was not available, they had accepted the rice made out of Ragi. They lived in temporary hutments meant for workers. They had passed on the Knowledge to the maximum extent possible. Now a days we are having the benefit of new knowledge and information regarding the Astronomical Observations afresh conducted. These have to be used to the best and to our advantage. Now we are living the Independent houses and also in Multi-storied flats, and there is no necessity to live in workers sheds.

28. Now we will stop these arguments and counter-arguments and come to the understanding of Poorva Paddhathi and the main Technical differences of information as available from Druk Observations from the Powerful Telescopes and further examination of such information.

	Poorva Padhati	Druk Siddhantam
Druk Samskaram	Druk Samskaram not done for Sun and Moon. For Mars and other 4 Planets they used Karana Grandhas.	For all 9 Planets Druk Samskaram is done based on the latest Astronomical observations.
Applicability for Performance of Rituals	The tithis as obtained from Druk method are not applicable for performance of Yagnas, Yaagaas, Sraddha & Srardha karmas.	The Druk Siddhanta Tithis are only taken for performing such Functions.
Determination of Eclipses	For Eclipses they only carry out Smaskaram based on new Druk Method.	For events, it has only to be done based on the new Methods.
Traditional Grandhas vs Actual Observations	Since ancient times Karana Grandhas were used, it is called as Poorva Paddhathi.	For actual Astronomical Observations, there are observatories with Large Telescopes for greater clarity and adopting this information will be equal to the actual. Hence it is callad as Druk Siddha Paddhathi
Philosophy.	Since the timely Samskarams which were necessary were not carried out willfully in Siddhanta,Tantra, Karana Grandhas; This is not actually Poorva Paddhathi	The underlying Philosophy of corrections or samskarams is followed for all events and Planets, hence this can be called as TRUE Poorva Paddhathi and also this alone is true Druk Paddhathi.

29. Poorva Paksha/ Siddantamulu:-

(a) People who followed the Poorva Paddhathi – Sloka

1. syaaddheesoochita nirbheeja grahaiee panchaanga soodhanam !
   sabeejaiee grahanaadeenaam punyah karmani sasyathee !!
2. drukssiddha grahaa kaaleena grahaanaadeena soodhayeet !
   sastra siddha grahaagathihe adrushtaarddheeshu karmasoo !!

To obtain the best results, there are many causative remedial factors- that means- for Vrathoopavaasa, Yagna, Srahddhas , Druk Samaskara Rahita Planets/ Thiddhis are to be accepted. They opine that it's only for-Grahana(Eclipse), Graha-Samagam, Planets raising / disappearance and Moons increasing Cresent etc for these purposes Druk Samskaram has to be carried.

Siddhantam -- For causative remedial factors have no invisible force behind them. The results obtained through the self effort or by self physical performance by an individual are accepted as not the results obtained through invisible forces. By carrying out Vrathoopavasa and Yagnas, they may give results based on fortunes and that is the reason as to why they are performed. May be Eclipses are visible. Even the actions such as Snana, Dana and Srardha, performed during Eclipse Time are also the fortuitous ones. Where is the necessity that Druk Samskaram should be done for Punya Karmas during the duration of the Eclipse? Even if the Druk Ganita Siddhanta only indicate the periods of commencement and ending of Eclipse and based on the Ganita of Druk Samskara Rahita, if the Eclipse timings of starting & ending are given and in the same period it should be told to perform the Punya Karmas related to the Eclipse, why it is not said so. When the Sky is covered with Clouds during the Eclipse Timings, it is famous and recommended to do auspicious Karmas such as to perform Snana and Dana, as stipulated in the knowledge obtained through the Sastra. On the same analogy how for it is justified to advise to perform Punya Karmas during the periods of timings of Eclipse arrived based on Druk Samskara Rahita Ganitha. Therefore there is something wrong in the Causative factors mentioned above (Karikas). In opposition to this,- Sloka,

'bha chakra naabhi druksiddhee kuryarchaarddha vrataadikam !
Bha chakra naabhi drusyasya karmaamgatvee cha heetavahah !!'

There is also a saying like the one mentioned. This is mentioned in the Annexure to the Panchamga of Pidaparthis related to Siddarddha Year. What answer one would give to this aspect.

(b) For Poorva Paddhathi Persons –

The results based on Druk Siddhanta like- Jataka, Muhurtha, Yaatra & Marriages are fixed based on the positions of Planets obtained through the Druk Samskaram and for such of those Karmas the results of which depend upon an Invisible force, namely,- for Yagnaas and Srardha Cermonies, it is said that the positions of Planets is to taken which have not been carried out as per the Druk Samskara.

Siddhantam:- All actions which are like- Giving Food to Bhrahmin Pundits, Service to Gurus who had become very old, Performing Pujas to Idols and performing Homam in the Sacred Fire. These are not the Druhshta Phalas only, there may be Adrushta Phalas also. Adrushta Phalaardham is not only doing/ performing Homam in Sacred Fire with Aarani/ Dharbhasthabham. By performing Pujas or doing Worship to the Invisible Gods, are we not enjoying the good results emanating from that. Will Marriage comes under Drushta Phala only? Is it not the result of the Samskara?.

By examination of such questions, it can be concluded that the sayings of Poorva Paksha Persons are not according to the Principles laid down in the Dharma Sutra, and also are not in the famous Dharma Sruthis/ Nibhandhana Grandha, then it can be safely said that they are to be neglected.

(c) In Poorva Paddhathi –

There is a saying- ' baanaavruddhee rasa skhayayaha'.

This means that absolute increase of Thithi is 5 ghadias and absolute decrease is 6 ghadias.

Siddhantam- For all Vratataas and Sraddha Ceremonies, the Day period from Sun rise to Sun set, total period is made into 5 equal parts, the Time at the which the Vrata and Sraardha Ceremonies are to be performed, either before/ after the Noon, and unless these matters are fully examined from the six points of view (Shat Paksha Vicharana), the Time to be conducted is not decided. The procedure of Examination of Division of Day Time into 5 equal parts and Six points of view is done as laid down in 'Nibhandhana Grandhas', is one and the same in all Grandhas. The Kala Pramanamu is 6 ghadias. In Bharat Desa which is the Karma Bhumi, this Kala Pramana will always more than 5 ghadias for any Place and for any Day in India.

But in Poorva Paddhathi the absolute increase in Thithi is only 5 ghadias, and in the Shatpaksha examination, the 3rd. part which is called 'Ubhayeedyuhu' is not famous. For this purpose why all the Nibhandhana Karthas had with strong will power had all joined together & examined in thoroughness and advised that it is not in the fitness of things to follow the Natural Justice, to permit the Shatpaksha method. Hence it is stated that the Tithis Tithis of Poorva Paddhathi sect are not as per Dharma Sastra

(d) Poorva Pakshamu-

In Druk Paddhathi there is a saying:- ' vasu vruddhi dasaskhayaha'—Meaning that the absolute increase is 8 ghadias; and absolute skhya is 10 ghadias some times one Thithi will not touch the five divisions of the first day as well as the second day. This sort of position is experienced some times in the Shat Paksha examination, which is coined as 'anubhayeedyuhu'. Therefore the Sraddha ceremonies and the recurring annual Sraddha ceremonies should be carried after the Noon of the day and in such circumstances not a single day is available for performance of such ceremonies and there will be shortfall in performing Sraddha ceremony. Even if done in any other day that Sraddha is not acceptable. The Pitru Devatas will curse the individual, as he is mainly responsible.

Sloka –

'druksiddha kheeta grahaa saadhitaasu

kurvanthi Tithis Tithishupramaadaat' !

' sraaddhaadikam tatpitru saapataptee

Punyakshayaa durgate maapnuvanthi' !!

Therefore the Poorva Paddhathi Sect state that following Druk Paddhathi is not good and their Poorva Paddhathi is only the answer and the above Sloka stipulates the same.

Siddhantam-- The same position will also come as in the Poorva Paddhathi. If the Day period is much less than 30 ghadias and this position comes when ' Pramakshayam' is nearer to 6 ghadias. By careful examination of both the days, adjustments are made so that on paper at least that noon touches the Time of the Sraddha ceremony. It is a mistake. If it is not touching Noon on two adjacent days, it is not a mistake. Following Dharma only is correct. This is one factor in the six items of examination. In the circumstances, in all Grandhas of 'Kala Madhaviyadi' a mention is made specifically as to when the Sraddha Ceremony is to be performed. There should not be any shortfall in doing the Sraddha Ceremony. The saying as laid down in all the Granddhas of Poorva Paksha, whose theory was just the opposite to that of the famous Grandhas, goes to prove that the statement of Poorva Paksha People is only abominable (hateful).Therefore adopting Druk Paddhathi is highly up-held, at all times, in all places and in all circumstances, as the system is following the Principles laid down in Dharma Sutra. In fact , as we had already discussed the situation of

'Ubhayeeduhu' , that is the condition that the Thithi beginning and ending is not getting touched to the third part of the five divisions of the day, belonging to Poorva Paksha, is just opposite to the Dharma Sutras as laid down and accepted universally. Druk Paddhathi is only correct always from the points of view of Dharma

Not only in the case of Sraddha Ceremony- currently in all Nibhandhana Grandha of Dharma Sastra- the issue of 'Anubhayeedyu' condition was discussed and decisions are being taken. Hence Druk Paddhatiyee is completely' Dharmaanugunam'.

(e) Poorva Paksham–

Poorva Paddhathi Persons object the practice of Astronomical observations through Newly Established Scientific Laboratories for carrying out the Druk Siddhanta Samskaram.

Siddhanta

What is meant by Sampradayam- The Druk Paddhathi was followed from ancient times as Sampradaya, so also the Poorva Paddhathi fell short of the same Sampradaya since 5/6 Centuries as was discussed earlier.

In the present day period every one of us are habituated to use newly invented methods for everything. Even if there is an alternative we still stick on to the new methods. We are living in individual houses and also in multi-storied apartments. We are using Cement for construction purposes. We are utilizing-Rail ,Buses, Pumpsets and Electricity etc. The Offerings to all deities was stopped. Even in Dress and Language we had already become non-Indian. Why there should be strong feeling that we should use Poorva Paddhathi or should not adopt Druk Paddhathi.

Sloka- 'aavrutha saastreebhyaha pratheeyeeran (aasoodraabhyaha)'

The statement made by Aapastambha Maharshi is an advise. Meaning that the Mangalakara Vishayams or Matters resulting in the form of good, can be taken from Women including Sudra Origen.' Balashitham Subhashitam' saying is also there. Therefore it is not objectionable to accept the Good matters achieved from the newly conducted Experiments in the Established Observatories . It is most objectionable if they are not accepted. It is wise to accept such information.

Observation:

While preparing Panchamgams the important part is dependent on the correct positions of Sun & Moon. Based on this, the Thithi, Nakshtra, Yoga and Karana are arrived. Even for Sun and Moon proper corrections are required to be carried out taking the Time factor into consedaration. This method was the ancient Sampradaya for preparation of Panchamgam. It is already established that this was also the direction obtained from the Dharma Sastra.

In the Mixed Paddhathi there will be no Druk Samskaram for Sun and Moon; hence it need not be emphasized separately that the same is un-acceptable.

30. We have finally decided that timely based corrections are to be carried out as obtained from the Druk method of Observations. Even in this, there are differences of opinions. The main cause for this, is the ' Ayanamsa' which was discussed in the main para-24. What this Ayanamsa? What is the relation between ' Ayanamsa' and the 'Panchamga Ganitham'. We have to thoroughly understand this. For that purpose certain information pertaining to Astronomical Ganitham and the Important Technical Vocabulary is to be understood and is discussed below.

31. **Technical Matters concerning Ayanamsa.**

    1. Sun and other Planets move into all the 12 Rasis commencing from Mesha Sign is called as Sankramana/ Sankranthi. There are two categories- one is Sayanas and the second one is Nirayanas.
    2. In Rasi Chakra the movement of Sun will be at the steady rate, approximately 365 days for one Revolution (360 degrees) to be completed. This period is called as 'Soura Samvaschara. In Soura Mana, the Nirayana Sankramanas will always happen on the same day (Same Dates) Example- Makara Sankranthi comes always on every January 14 th.
    3. The Sayanas Sankramans are not like that. There is some basis for this. They will not come on the same date as per Nirayanas. Currently the Sayana Surya Sankramanas are occurring 24 days ahead than the Nirayana Sankramanas. This distance is increasing with the passage of Time. But after long duration of Time it can also get reduced. This change is very little. Nearly 50.26 seconds yearly. This difference in movement per year is called as 'Ayanamsa'.

At the rate of 50.26 seconds per year, for 22 years , it moves by one Degree. At this rate, for 360 Degrees, it will take 360 x60x60/50.26=360x71.62= 25,920, say 26,000 years approximately

4. Some People opine that for all times to come, this point will always move at the same rate. There after movement of the Point to 180 Degrees, the Sayanas appear to look that they are always behind Nirayanas.
5. Some others say that it will not happen in that manner. They say that the Ayanas will Increase to 27 degrees, then stop for a moment, and start decreasing. Then they go on reducing to zero degrees and go back by 27 degrees. Therefore a Total of 54 degrees Range is reached,. Then the Point moves like a Palanquin. It is Just like the Children playing with a " Bongaram and Thread', as in such movement there is a shuttling of the top surface with a pointed edge below. For this movement, at the rate of 72 years per degree, it will approximately take 4000 years for 54 degrees. This is called Dolana Siddhantam.
6. Unfortunately, no correct information is available in oldest Granddhas. Even among the latest Scientists, there are differences of Opinion. If we are required to know the Real Ayanamsa, currently if Ayanamsas are 24 degrees and for this to reach 27 degrees, another 3 degree movement is there. It will therefore take $72 \times 3 = 240$ say 250 years. Till then we have to wait for the actual observation and only then it could be done. It is not possible now to arrive at that point.
7. If the Equator is extended up-to the Star level or Celestial Meridian, it becomes the Celestial Equator. This Celestial Equator is also called as the Vishuvat Circle or Sampata Circle The Vishuvat is defined as a Point when the Day and Night periods of time are equal on that date. Each one is equal to 12 hours of Time interval. It happens when Sun comes closer to that point.
8. Earth is rotating around Sun in one year for full revolution. Even if it assumed that the Sun is moving and Earth is stable, as seen by us, this Path of the Sun rotating around Earth is called as Rasi Chakra, It has other names as Jyothis Chakra, Bhachakra and Kanthivrutta.
9. The Vishuvat Cicle and the Rasi Chakra are inclined between themselves at an angle of 23 degrees 30 minutes.. The Intersecting points are two in number. These are called as Vishuvat Points. The First one is Vasant Vishuvat and the second one is called Sarat Vishuvat.. These Points are also called as Sampata BInduvus.

   The Sun reaches Vasant Vishuvat around March 21 st. Then the Soura Vasant Rutuvu will start. Similarly the Soura Sarat Vishuvat will come when Sun comes nearer to this Point around September 22 nd. Then the Soura Sarat Rutuvu will start.
10. Factually though the Paths of Sun and Moon being separate, all calculations are made as though they are moving on the Kranthi Vruthamu. On this Circle only there are 12 Rasis each one being 30 Degrees apart.
11. Earth in a day is circling around itself at one time, ie. round it's North and South Pole and in this pattern Rotating for one year around the Sun is an universal known fact. Not only these two movements, but also there are other movements

to the Earth. In the Play of the rotation of Spindle and the Head, it is not only rotation around itself but also moving away from its Circle, making a movement like a Spring or a Coil. Therefore there are two axises on which the Spindle and the Head are moving.

One on the point touching the floor and the other is the resultant axis of its inclination as it is balancing due to rotation. The movements of Earth can be imagined similar to that. The cause being both Physical and Gravitational forces acting.

As a result the line of Equator in the sky is not constant. But is fixed on the Earth. Similarly the Celestial Meredian is also not fixed because it is moving on two Axis.

Like a flat plate inclined. If this point got inclined on one end to that extent the Vishuvat Point will also move downwards. The second point of the Vishuvat on the opposite side will consequently rise to the same extent on the Rasi Chakra.

Like this these two Vishuvat Points move on the Rasi Chakra in a year at an inclined angle, to an extent, in an angular measurement, and is called as 'Ayanamsa'. This was discussed earlier

12. If the Points of Vishuvat are constant, then for Sun to move on the Rasi Chakra will be one year. If the Vishuvat Point is inclined and getting reduced then the time taken by Sun will also getting reduced. Then Vishuvat in 72 years covers one Degree less, then Sun joins that Point one day earlier .Till now the Vasant Vishuvat had come down by 24 degrees Hence the Sun has joined that point 24 days before.
13. Now where is the starting point for measurement of Ayanamsa. For Chara Rasis, for movement of measurement there should one fixed point. All Planets with Sun and Moon are always on the move in the Sky. It is only the Stars that are constant and has no relation to the movement of the Planets. The meaning of Nakshatra is out of the words ' na sharati' & ' na chalati' . In fact all Nakshatras are, the only ones identified as brightest, among a group of Stars in the arc range of 13 Degrees 20 minutes. All the Nakshatras are assumed to be moving on the Rasi Chakra with the distance being 13 Degrees and 20 Minutes for each.
14. If Rasi Chakra in divided into 12 equal parts, one Division is one Rasi. The arc length of that Rasi is 30 Degrees. If the Range of Nakshatra is divided into 4 equal parts, each Pada will be 3 Degrees 20 Minutes. For 27 Nakshatras there are $27 \times 4 = 108$ Padas. If each all the 12 Rasis are distributed equally, there will be 9 Nakshatra Padas. Mesha Rasi starts with Aswani Nakshtra.
15. From starting point of Aswani the count begins for Ayanamsa measurement.. That means that the movement of Vishuvat starts from Aswani Nakshatra.. In fact this can be measured from any point.. In order to make it uniform and for the convenience of Astronomical observations the count starts from Aswani Nakshatra..Now present Ayanamsa is 24 degrees. Therefore the Vasant Vihsuvat came down in the Rasi Chakra by 24 degrees.
16. Therefore the Ganitham based on Vishuvats which are moving is called 'Sayana Ganitham'. Based on the Nakshatra which are fixed starts from Aswani Nakshatra is called 'Nirayana Ganitham'.

Note: The Ayana between Sayana and Nirayana is between Vishuvats and not pertaining to the Sun.

17. All the Rasis leaving Nakshatras are assumed to be moving with Vishuvats and make such arrangement of counting; then the Mesha Rasi along with the other Rais following will always be moving and that they have reached new places on the Rasi Chakra. The Planets coming to the new places is called Sayana Sankrathis.. If there is no reference to the moving Vishuvats and take only Nakshatras and Planets moving into fixed Rasis is called ' Nirayana Sankramanam'. Nirayana means the one which has no movement.

18. At sometime of the movement, the Vasant Vishvat has to come to that point ie. The Nirayana Mesha Rasi. Then along the Vasant Vishuvat , the Sayana Mesha staring also has reached that point. On this auspicious moment both Sayana and Nirayana points join together and becomes one point. Then there will not be any difference. That Moment is called as ' Ayana Sunya Kala'.

19. The Ayanamsa gets started with commencement of the Vishvat.. Nirayana and Sayanas get separated. Therefore the count of Ayanamsa starts from that Time.

20. Like that every year taking 50.26 seconds and for 72 years one degree rate, so for 24 degrees got elapsed. That means that the Vasant Vishuvat from Aswani Nakshatra had moved by 24 degrees. That means that Point has reached to the mid of Chitra Nakshatra. Therefore it is called as ' Chaitra Paksha Ayanamsamulu'. Therefore the Sayana Sankramanas are occurring 24 days earlier than Niraya Sankramanas.

21. **Important Point to be Noted:**

    1. The Ayanamsas of 50.26 seconds per year are not be taken as Sacred. How much is the value to be taken is a difficult question. There very many differences of opinions in all Astronomical Grandhas.. Some People said it is 30 seconds and some others have mentioned as 60 seconds.. Many have said as 50.26 seconds.

    2. This can be 50.26 seconds or it can be anything. However it is to be taken as an approximation only and for all times to come it cannot be stated as permanent.

32. **The Necessity of Sayana and Nirayana.**

(From Muhurtha Chintamani/ Commentary by Peeyushadhaara- pages 205-209).

Why there should be two varieties of Calculations?. But there is necessity for them. If an overall aspect is considered, for everything there are advantages and also limits.

(a) Regarding SAYANAS:

1. The Sayana movements are practically visible. One can directly observe through the powerful Telescopes installed in Astronomical Observatories.

2. The Periods of Time assessments for the Day and for the Night are decided as per Sun's Ingress (Sankramana) into the Signs. These are practically visible. The reason being:-

   (i) In the current period the Sayana Vishuvat (this is also called as Sayana Mesha Sankramana/ Meshaayanam.) falls on March 21st. Similarly the

Sayana Tula Sankramana is coming on September 22nd. On these dates everyone is fully aware, seen and established that the Day and Night periods of time are equal in the duration.

(ii) The Sayana Karkataka Sankranthi comes on June 21st. From that date the Sun will move in the Rasi Chkra to the Southern Hemisphere and this can be clearly seen. In all Places on that Day the Time period of Day time will be maximum and the Night Periods are less and there after the Time of the Night duration will be reducing and will become the Minimum on December 22nd.

(iii) The Sayana Makara Sankramana comes on December 22nd. From that Date, onwards the Sun starts moving in-to the Northern Hemisphere and every one can readily see. On that Date the duration of the Day Time is the least. The Night period is the Maximum. From that Date onwards in all Places, the duration of the day period starts increasing and it becomes Maximum on June 21st.

(iv) As a result of Sayana Makara/ Karkataka Sankramanas, The Sun's movement into Rasi Chakra gets changed from North to South This is recognized by one and all by seeing the shadow movements of Sun on the compound walls and the trees.

(v) For Astronomy Calculations/ Panchamga Ganitham, the Sayanas are more useful.

(b) Regarding NIRAYANAS.

(i) All our Religious Functions are connected with Nirayanas.

(ii) There is no difference for Thithi and Vaara, if it is either Sayana/ Nirayana

(iii) The Chaitradi Chandramana Months are linked with Nirayanas only.

(iv) The Adhika Masa/ Kshaya Months are only possible with Nirayanas. It will not happen in Sayanas.

(v) The Eclipses will happen only in Nirayanas. It is not possible in Sayanas.

(vi) The Jataka Muhurthadi Satras, Guru Pushyadi Subha Yogas, Bharani Vishkhambhadi Inauspicious Yogas, as all these have been mentioned in Nirayna Grandhas. In all day to day activities, the Nirayanas are most useful.

33. In Astronomical Observatories with help of powerful Telescopes only movements of Sayanas can be seen and not Nirayanas. If Ayanamsas are known, the value of Nirayanas can be obtained from Sayanas. Meaning that the knowledge of Ayanamsa is most essential. Based on the information available from the Astronomical Observatories about Sayanas, We can Calculate the Positions of Planets in the Nirayana System and on that basis the Nirayana Panchamgam is to be written.. Therefore every now and then we should enquire about the information on the Ayanamsas. The change in the Ayanamsa is being very minute, it should be obtained once in a year and not day to day. Now for the Hevalambi Nama Samvatsara Ayanamsas for Sravanamasam are 24 degrees 06 minutes and 49 seconds at the end of August 2018.

Sri. Madhura Krishna Murthy Sastry garu, a famous Astrologer of Rajahmundry, and also a Panchamga Kartha; and disciple Sri. Sreepada Venkata Ramana Sarma garu; had expired on 5th. April, 2016. His Ayanamsas for Durmukha Nama Samvatsaram are 20 degrees 04 minutes 00 seconds.

On the Point of Ayanamsa there are plenty of arguments and counter arguments were going on in the preceding past among the Scientists/ Pundits of Astronomical background. Though Late Sri. Madura Krishna Murthy Sastry garu is the most knowledgeable Pundit in this field, a President's Medal Awardee, no one is agreeing to his arguments. This matter being highly Technical in nature, further discussion on the disputed subject for the present is not possible.

The entire difference in Druk Panchamgam is due to the projection of different values of Ayanamsa. Currently in India specially in the Telugu speaking states there are the two Druk Paddhathi Panchamgas. We therefore acknowledge with due respects, only the Chaitra Paksha Ayanamsas as approved by the Learned Pundits in this field.

❖❖❖

CHAPTER 10

Examples

10.1 CASTING HOROSCOPE CHARTS FOR EXAMPLE

Date of Birth = 20-4-1997

Time of Birth = 8:00 PM

Place of Birth = Hyderabad

How to Calculate Lagna & 10th Bhava as per N.C. Lahari method

1. **Calculation of Lagna:** Find out Sidereal Time for time of Birth

Hyderabad – Latitude – 17°26′ Norht – Longitude – 78°27′ East.

Indian Standard Time (IST) is at the Longitude = 82°-30′

This is passing through Mirzapur, U.P.

For 1° Longitude the time difference = 4 minutes.

∵ For 4°-3′ the difference is = 1° = 4 mts

4° = 16 mts

3′ = 12 seconds

Difference in Longitude

From IST is = 82°-30′

Hyderabad Longitude = 78°-27

Difference = 4°-3′

The total time diff. is = 16 mit. 12 seconds. Hyderabad is West of IST Meridian. This time difference is to be subtracted

Time of birth is $= 8^h - 0^m - 0^s$ pm

$(-) = 0^h - 16^m - 12^s$

Hyerabad Local mean time $= 7^h - 43^m - 48^s$ pm ...(1)

From Lahari Table of Ascendants.

(a) On 20-4-1997 afternoon at 12.00 hr.

Sideral time (from page-3) $= 1^h - 51^m - 33^s$ ...(a)

(b) On date of birth the local mean time as arrived at above is

= (+)7h – 43m – 48s ...(b)

Since birth is in the evening, it should be added, if it is in the morning it should be deducted.

The Local Mean Time at Birth' Sidereal Time is

$= 9^h - 35^m - 21^s$ (a + b)

(c) For this, correction for daily variation on local time (1)

Above for 7h – 43m – 48s as per table IV in page 5 is to be added.

For 24 minutes correction = 4 seconds

For 1 hour – correction = 10 seconds

S.T. BF $9^h - 35^m - 21^s$ (a) + (b)

For 6 minutes – correction = 1 second

As per the above

For 7 hours correction is = $1^m - 9^s = 69^s$

For43–48^{s}Lminassumedas44m,thecorrectionis $69^s + 7\frac{1^s}{2} = 76\frac{1^s}{2} = 1^m - 16\frac{1^s}{2}$

Total = 77 seconds

Total Correction (+) 0h – 0m – 77 seconds = 0^h - 0^m - 77^s ...(c)

(d) For the year 1997

The correction in table no II page -4 is to be taken for Latitude.

(+) 0h – 2m – 00 second

0h – 1m – 59s ...(d)

S. T. (a) + (b) = $9^h - 35^m - 21^s$

(c) = $0^h - 0^m - 77^d$

(d) = $0^h - 2^m - 00^d$

= $9^h - 38^m - 38^s$

Adding (a + b) + (c) + (d) = 9h – 38m – 38s ...(2)

This is the total Sidereal Time of Hyderabad. Latitude 17°-26′ North. For this, Lagna has to be calculated.

As per page-26 of Table of Ascendatns for Latitude of 17°-30′, for every 3 hours, at 4 mint. difference Lagna has been given. As per this, for the total Sidereal time of 9h – 38m – 38 sec, the Lagna has to be calculated.

As per Table

For 9h – 36m value is = 6s – 27°-36′ ...(i)

For 9h – 40m value is = 6s-28°-30′

For 4m difference = 54′

For 2 mint-do = 27′ ...(ii)

For 1 min-do = 13′-30″

For 30 sec-do = 6′-45″ ...(iii)

For 3 sec-do = $36'' + 4\frac{1}{2}'' = -40\frac{1}{2}''$

For 6 sec = $40\frac{1}{2}'' \times 2 = 81'' = 1' - 21''$ ...(iv)

For 1 sec = $40\frac{1}{2}'' \div 3 = 13\frac{1}{2}''$ ...(v)

For 8 seconds = 48″ ...(vi)

∴ For sederial time

Of 9h – 38m – 38s, the Lagna from P-36 is ...(2)

As per (i) for $9^h - 36^m$ = 6s – 27° – 36′ (i)

Add value of (ii) for 2^m = (+) 27′

Add value of (iii) for 30^s = (+) 6′ – 45″

Add value of (vi) for 8^s = $(+) 1' - 34\frac{1}{2}''$

Total = 6s – 28° – 11′ – 33″ this is taken as

Lagna is = 6s – 28° – 12′ ...(A)

(33″ is more than 30″ and hence taken as 12)

Now correction for Ayamamsa as per Table at page = 6

In 1938 Ayamansa correction is = 00°-0′

In 1997 Ayamamsa correction is = (–) 00° – 49′

= 6s – 28° – 12′ – 0″ ...(B)

(A) – (B) = (–) 00° – 49′

= 6s – 27° – 23′

Lagna = Tula 27° – 23′ ...(3)

After 6 Rasis, the 7th Rasi is Tula.

2. **To calculate 10th Bhava:** For this the table of Lahri's page-8 is to be seen.

For Sidereal Time we got as per (2) = 9h – 38m – 38s

For obtaining 10th bhava

For 9h – 36m value = 3s – 28° 37′ ...(viii)

For 9h – 40m value = 3s – 29° – 39′

For 4m difference in the value is = 1° – 2

For 2m do = 0° –31′ ...(ix)

For 1m do = 0° – 15′ – 30″

For 30 sec do = 0° – 7′ – 45″ ...(x)

For 3sec do = $0° - 0' - 46\frac{1}{2}''$

For 6s difference is = 0° – 1′ – 33″ ...(xi)

For 2s do is = 0° – 0′ – 31″ ...(xii)

By adding

(viii) + (ix) + (x) + (xi) + (xii)

For $9^h - 36^m$ = $3^s - 28° - 37' - 0''$

For $0^h - 2^m$ = $0^s - 0° - 31' - 0''$

For $0^h - 0^m - 30^s$ = $0^s - 0° - 7' - 45''$

For $0^h - 0^m - 6^s$ = $0^s - 0° - 1' - 33''$

For $0^h - 0^m - 2^s$ = $0^s - 0° - 0' - 31''$

$3^s - 29° - 17' - 49''$ ...(xiii)

BF = $3^s - 29^0 - 17' - 49''$

This is rounded off t 18′.

∴ As per Table at page-6 = 3s – 29° – 18′

Deduct Ayamamsa correction for 1997

= (–) 0s – 0° – 49′

In 1997 the 10th Bhava = 3s – 28° – 29′

3. **Construct Bhava Chakra:** In Rasi Chakra every Rasi covers 30°. In Bhava Chkara some Bhavas have less than 30° & some other Bhavas have more than 30°. The cause of this is due to difference in the Longitude of Lagna & 10th Bhava. The following is the method by which the Bhava chakra is constructed.

Date of Birth = 20 – 4 – 1997

Time of birth = Night 20.00 hrs.

Place of Birth = Hyderabad

Lagna = 6s – 27° – 22′ Ist Bhava

Xth bhava = 3s – 28° – 29′ Xth Bhava

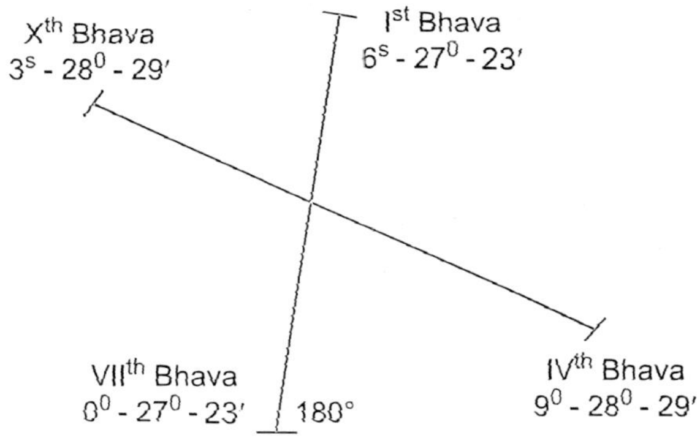

Arrive VII Bhava = 0s – 27° – 23′

Arrive IV Bhava = 9s – 28° – 29′

(a) IVth Bhava = 9s – 28° – 29′

I^{st} Bhava = 6s – 27 – 22′

Differeance for 6 Nos. of ½ Bhavas = 3s – 1° – 7′/Devide by 6.

Difference for one ½ Bhava = 0s – 15° – 11′ = 0^s-15°-11′ Half of Ist Bhava ...(i)

(b) For VIIth bhava = 0s – 27° – 22′

VIth bhava = (–) 9s – 28° – 29′

Difference of 6 Nos. of ½ bhavas = 2s – 28° – 54′

For one ½ Bhava = 2s – 28° – 54′/6

= 0s – 14° – 49′ Bhavarthamu ...(ii)

(c) The same different as of (a) will come for X[th] Bhava and VIIth Bahva	$= O_5 - 15°\text{-}11'$	...(iii)
(d) The same difference as of (b) will come for X[th] Bhava and I[st] Bhava	$= O_5 - 14°\text{-}49'$	...(iv)
Lagna is assumed as mid of I[st] Bhava	$= 6_5 - 27°\text{-}23'$	
Add one no. Bhavarthamu of item (i)	$+ O_5 - 15°\text{-}11'$	
End of I[st] Bhava & Start of IInd Bhava	$+ 7_5 - 12°\text{-}34'$	$7_5 - 12°\text{-}34'$ End of I[st] Bhava
Add two nos. of Bhavarthamulu of Item (i)		
	$+ O_5 - 15°\text{-}11'$	
	$+ O_5 - 15°\text{-}11'$	
End of IInd Bhava & Start of IIIrd Bhava	$+ 8_5 - 12°\text{-}56'$	$8_5 - 12°\text{-}56'$ End of IInd Bhava
Add two nos. of Bhavarthamulu again of item (i)		
	$+ O_5 - 15°\text{-}11'$	
	$+ O_5 - 15°\text{-}11$	
End of IIIrd Bhava & Start of IVth Bhava	$+ 9_5 - 13°\text{-}18'$	$9_5 - 13°\text{-}18'$ End of IIIrd Bhava
Add one number of Bhavartha of item (i)	$+ O_5 - 15°\text{-}11'$	
Mid of IVth Bhava	$+ 9_5 - 25°\text{-}28'$	
Add one number of Bhavartha of item (ii)	$+ O_5 - 14°\text{-}49'$	
Earth of IVth Bhava & Start of Vth Bhava	$+ 10_5 - 13°\text{-}17'$	$10_5 - 13°\text{-}17'$ End of IVth Bhava
Add two nos. of Bhavartha move of item (ii)		
	$+ O_5 - 14°\text{-}49'$	
	$+ O_5 - 14°\text{-}49'$	
End of Vth Bhava & Start of VIth Bhava	$11_5 - 12°\text{-}56'$	$11_5 - 12°\text{-}56'$ End of Vth Bhava
Add two nos. of Bhavarthas of item (ii)	$+ O_5 - 14°\text{-}49'$	
	$+ O_5 - 14°\text{-}49'$	
End of VIth Bhava & Start of VIIth Bhava	$O_5 - 12°\text{-}34'$	$O_5 - 12°\text{-}34'$ End of VIth Bhava
Add one Bhavartha of item (ii)	$+ O_5 - 14°\text{-}49'$	
Mid of VIIth Bhava	$O_5 - 27°\text{-}23'$	
Add one Bhavaatha of item (iii)	$O_5 - 15°\text{-}11'$	
End of VIIth Bhava & Start of VIIIth Bhava	$1_5 - 12°\text{-}34'$	$1_5 - 12°\text{-}34'$ End of VIIth Bhava
Add two numbers Bhavarthamulu of item (iii)	$+ O_5 - 15°\text{-}11'$	
	$+ O_5 - 15°\text{-}11'$	

End of VIIIth Bhava & Start of IXth Bhava	$2_5 - 12°\text{-}56'$	$2_5 - 12°\text{-}56'$ End of VIIIth Bhava
Add two nos of Bhavarthasmulu of item (iii)	$+ O_5 - 15°\text{-}11'$	
End of IXth Bhava & start of Xth Bhava	$+ O_5 - 15°\text{-}11'$	$3_5 - 13°\text{-}18'$ End of IXth Bhava
Add one Number of Bhavartha of item (iii)	$+ O_5 - 15°\text{-}11'$	
Mid of Xth Bhava	$3_5 - 28°\text{-}29'$	
Add one number of Bhavartha of item (iv)	$+ O_5 - 14°\text{-}49'$	
End of Xth Bhava & Start of XIth Bhava	$4_5 - 13°\text{-}18'$	$4_5 - 13°\text{-}18'$ End of Xth Bhava
Add two nos. Mars of Bhavarthamulu of item (iv)	$+ O_5 - 14°\text{-}49'$ $+ O_5 - 14°\text{-}49'$	
End of XIth Bhava & Start of XIIth Bhava	$5_5 - 12°\text{-}56'$	$5_5 - 12°\text{-}56'$ End of XIth Bhava
End of XIth Bhava & start of XIIth Bhava	55 – 12°-56′	
Add two nos. Bhavarthamulu of item (iv)	$+ O_5 - 14°\text{-}49'$	
Mid of I[st] Bhava of Lagna	$+ O_5 - 14°\text{-}49'$	
End of XIIth Bhava & Start of I[st] Bhava	$6_5 - 12°\text{-}34'$	$6_5 - 12°\text{-}34'$ End of XIIth Bhava
Add one Bhavartha of item (iv)	$+ O_5 - 14°\text{-}49'$	
Mid of Ist Bhava or Lagna	$6_5 - 27°\text{-}23'$	$6_5 - 27°\text{-}23'$ Lagna

4. Calculation of Longitudes of Plaents as per N.C. Laharis table of period 1996 to 2000 see page-16, 17, 18, 19, 20.

(i) Moon – 16th page

Nirayana Longitude at 0.5-30 hrs IST (Indian Standard Time)

On 20-4-1997 = 5s – 3° – 53′

On 21-4-1997 = 5s – 15° 57′

Difference for 24 hrs = 0s – 12° – 4′ = 724′

Birth at 8.00 pm = 20h – 0m – 0s

(–) 5h 30m 0s

The time lapsed from morning 5h 30m to birth time of 20.00 hrs. 14h – 30m – 0s = $14\frac{1}{2}$ Hours

= 14h – 30m – 0s = 14½ hrs.

As per Trirasika method

$$= \frac{14\frac{1}{2} \times 724'}{24} = 437.42$$

= 0s – 7° – 17′

Add to this value of the Longitude of Moon at 05-30 hrs

$$= (+)\ 5s - 3^\circ - 53'$$

$$5^s - 11^\circ - 10' \quad ...(1)$$

Hence Moon in Kanya Rasi = $5^s - 11^\circ - 10'$

(ii) Sun: As per page-18 in Exaltation

On 21-4-1997 = $0s - 7^\circ - 7'$

On 19-4-1997 = $0s - 05^\circ - 10'$

Difference for 48 hrs = $1^\circ - 57' = 117'$

Birth on 20-4-1997 Night at 20.00 hrs. From 19-4-1997 the number of hours lapsed from the time of birth

$$= 24 + 14\tfrac{1}{2} = 38\tfrac{1}{2} \text{ hrs}$$

As per Trirasika method

$$= \frac{117' \times 38\frac{1}{2}}{48} = 93.84375 = 1^\circ - 34'(+)$$

To this add Longitude of Sun of 19-4-1997 as on 5½ hrs.

$$(+)\ 0s - 5^\circ - 10'$$

$$0s - 6^\circ - 44'$$

∴ Sun in Airies Rasi = 6°-$44'$ in Exaltation. ...(2)

(iii) Mars: As per page-18. He is in Retrogration

On 19-4-1997 = $4s - 23^\circ - 25'$

On 21-4-1997 = $(-)\ 4s - 23^\circ - 13'$

Difference for 48 hrs = $(-)\ 12'$

$$\text{For } 38\tfrac{1}{2} \text{ hrs} = \frac{(-)12 \times 38\frac{1}{2}}{48}(-) = 9.625(-) = 10'$$

∴ Mars (Retro) on 19-4-1997 = $4s - 23^\circ - 25'$

$$(-)\qquad 10'$$

$$4s - 23^\circ - 15'$$

∴ Mars is in Leo Rasi = $23^\circ - 15'$ ...(3)

(iv) Mercury: 18th page he is in retrogression

On 20-4-1997 = $0s - 14^\circ - 39'$

On 21-4-1997 = $0s - 14^\circ - 10'$

Difference for 24 hrs. = $29'$

$$\therefore \text{ For } 14\frac{1}{2} \text{ Hours} = \frac{29' \times 14\frac{1}{2}}{24} = 17'.52 = (-)18'$$

∴ Mercury = $0s - 14^\circ - 39'$

$$(-)\quad (-)\quad 18$$

$$0s - 14^\circ - 21$$

Mercury in Retrograde in Aries = 14° – 21′ ...(4)

(v) Jupiter: In debilitation.

21-4-1997 = 9s – 24° – 24′

19-4-1997 = 9s – 24° – 07′

Difference for 48 hrs = 17′

$$\therefore \text{ For } 38\frac{1}{2} \text{ hrs} = \frac{38\frac{1}{2}\times 17}{48} = 13'.64 = 14'$$

Jupiter = 9s – 24° – 7′

∴ Jupiter in Capricorn = 24° – 21′ ...(5)

(vi) Venus:

21-4-1997 = 0s – 11° – 52′

19-4-1997 = 0s – 9° – 23′

For 48 hrs difference = 2° – 29′ = 149′

$$\text{For } 38\frac{1}{2} \text{ hrs} = \frac{38\frac{1}{2}\times 149}{48} = 119.51 = 120' = 2^\circ - 0'$$

Venus = 0s – 9° – 23′

(+) 2° – 0′

0s – 11′ – 23′

Venus is in Aries = 11° – 23′ ...(6)

(vii) Saturn: 18th page

21-4-1197 = 11s – 19° – 3′

19-4-1997 = 11s – 18° – 48′

Difference for 48 hr = 15′

$$\therefore \text{ For } 38\frac{1}{2} \text{ hrs} = \frac{38\frac{1}{2}\times 15'}{48} = 12.03 = 12'$$

Saturn = 11s – 18° – 48′

(+) 12

11s – 19° – 0′ ...(7)

Saturn is in Pisces at = 19° – 0′

(viii) Rahu 20th page

1-4-1997 = 5s – 4° – 51′

1-5-1997 = 5s – 4° – 7′

Difference for 30 days = 44′

$$\text{For } 20\frac{14.5}{24} = \frac{20.6042 \text{ days} \times 44'}{30} = 30'$$

Rahu = 5s – 4° – 51′

(–) 30

Rahu 5s – 4° – 21′

∴ Rahu in Virgo at = 4° – 21′

∴ Ketu in Pisces at = 4° – 21′ At 6 Divisions opposite ...(9)

Longitudes of lagna, 10th bhava & all planets

Lagna = 6s – 27° – 23′

10th Bhava = 3s – 28° – 29′

Sun-Exaltation = 0s – 6° – 44′

Moon = 5s – 11° – 10′

Mars (Retro) = 4s – 23° – 15′

Mercury (Retro) = 0s – 14° – 21′

Jupiter Debilitation = 9s – 24° – 21′

Venus = 0s – 11° – 23′

Saturn = 11s – 19° – 0′

Rahu = 5° – 4° – 21′

Ketu = 11s – 4° – 21′

5. Construct Rasi & Bhava Charts.

(A) Rasi Chart

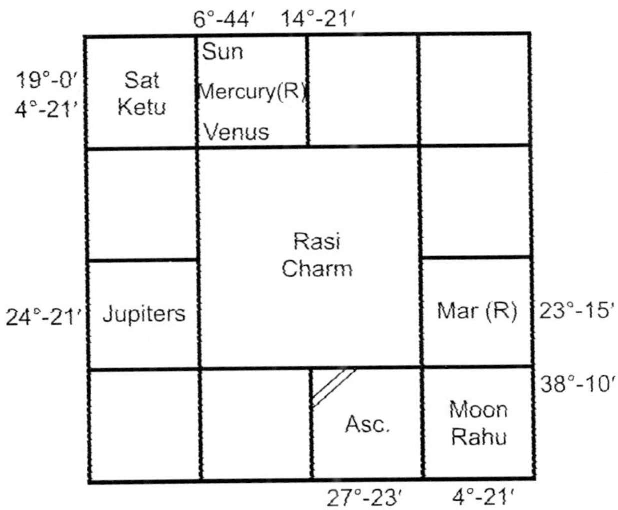

(B) Bhava Chart

Ist Bhava end = 7s – 12° – 34′

IInd Bhaa end = 8s – 12° – 56′

IIIrd Bhava end = 9s – 13° – 18′

Jupiter (9s – 24° – 21′) in IVth Bhava

IVth Bhava = 10s – 13° – 18′

Ketu = 11s – 4° – 21′ in 5th Bhava

Vth Bhava end = 11s – 12° – 56′
Saturn = 11s – 19° – 0′ in 6th Bhava
Sun = 0s – 6° – 44′ in 6th Bhava
Venus = 0° – 11° – 23′ in 6th Bhava
VI Bhava end = 0s – 12° – 34′
Mercury = 0s – 14° – 21′ in 7th Bhava
VII Bhava end = 1s – 12° – 34′
VIII Bhava end = 2s – 12° – 56′
IX Bhava end = 4s – 13° – 18′
X Bhava end = 4s – 13° – 18′
XI Bhava Mars (R) = 4s – 23° – 15′ (In 11th Bhava)
Rahu = 5s – 4° – 21′ (In 11th Bhava)
Moon = 5s – 11° – 10′ (In 11th Bhava)
XI Bhava end = 5° – 12° – 56′
XII Bhava end = 6s – 12° – 34′
Ascendnat = 6° – 27° – 22′ in Ist Bhava
Ist Bhava end = 7s – 12° – 34′

The Bhava Chart is now as under

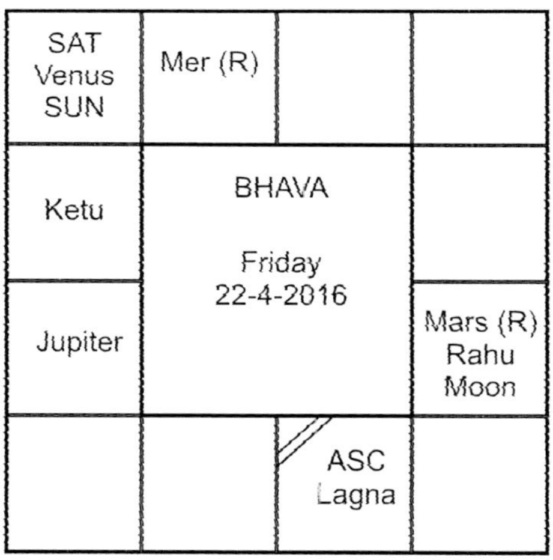

Change of planets between Rasi & Bhava chart

Placent	From	To
Rahu	12	11
Moon	12	11
Sun/Venus	7	6
Ketu	6	5

6. Method of construction of Navamsa Chart: Longitudes of Langa & Planets are given below:-

1. **Asc** = $6s - 27° - 23' = 6 \times 9 + 9 = 54 + 9 = \frac{63}{12} = 5 + (3)$ Gemini Navamsa Rasi

2. **Sun** = $0s - 6° - 44' = \frac{3}{12} = 0 + (3)$ Gemini Navamsa Rasi

3. **Moon** = $5s - 11° - 10' = 5 \times 9 + 4 = 45 + 4 = \frac{49}{12} = 4 + (1)$ Navamsa Aries Rasi

4. **Mars (Retro)** = $4s - 23° - 15' = 4 \times 9 + 7 = 36 + 7 = \frac{43}{12} = 3 + (7)$ Navamsa Libra Rasi

5. **Mercury (Retro)** = $0s - 14° - 21' = \frac{5}{12} = 0 + (5)$ Leo Navamsa Rasi

6. **Venus** = $0s - 11° - 23' = \frac{4}{12} = 0 + (4)$ Cancer Navamsa Rasi

7. **Jupiter (Neecha)** = $9s - 24° - 21' = 9 \times 9 + 8 = 81 + 8 = \frac{89}{12} = 7 + (5)$ Leo Navamsa Rasi

8. **Saturn** = $11s - 19° - 0' = 11 \times 9 + 6 = 99 + 6 = \frac{105}{12} = 8 + (9)$ Sagitterius Navamsa Rasi

9. **Rahu** = $5s - 4° - 21' = 5 \times 9 + 2 = 45 + 2 = \frac{47}{12} = 3 + (11)$ Aqurius Navamsa Rasi

10. **Ketu** = $11s - 4° - 21' = 11 \times 9 + 2 = 99 + 2 = \frac{101}{12} = 8 + (5)$ Leo Navamsa Rasi

Every longitude Sign is to be multiplied by 9. This figure to be kept separate. Find out from Planets Longitude of Degrees & Minutes, as to the Navamsa Division it falls that figure is to be added to the first multiplication product and divided by 12. The balance figure left out is the Rasi in which Planet is positioned in Navamsa Cart.

The following table will give the Navamsa Division from the Longitudes Rasi as:

Ist Navamsa is from

$0° - 0'$ to $3° - 20'$

2nd do $3° - 21'$ to $6° - 40''$

3rd do $6° - 41'$ to $10° - 00'$

4th do $10° - 01'$ to $13° - 20'$

5th do $13° - 21'$ to $16° - 40'$

6th do $16° - 41'$ to $20° - 00'$

7th do $20° - 01'$ to $23°$ – to $20'$

8th do $23° - 21'$ to $26° - 40'$

9th do $26° - 41'$ to $30° - 00'$

	Moon		Asc Sun
Rahu	Navamsa		Venus
			Mer(R) Jup Ketu
Saturn		Mars (R)	

7. Calculation of balance of Dasa at Birth (as per Vimshottari Dasa System) (1 to 6. 10 to 18 & 19 to 27)

The following Table gives the Lordships of Planets for each group of three stars and the total years assigned to that planet in Vimshuttari Dasa System.

S. No.	Planet	Stars 9th Star set-3Nos			Dasa in years
1	Sun	Krittika	Uttara	Uttarashada	6
2	Moon	Rohini	Hastha	Sravanam	10
3	Mars	Mrugasira	Chtta	Dhanishta	7
4	Rahu	Ardra	Swathi	Satabhisham	18
5	Jupiter	Dunarvasu	Visakha	Poorvabhadra	16
6	Saturn	Pushayami	Amuranam	Uttarabhadra	19
7	Mercury	Aslesha	Jyestha	Revati	17
8	Ketu	Makha	Moola	Aswani	7
9	Venus	Pubba	Poorvashada	Bharani	20
				Total	**120**

As per Longitude of Moon the Balance of Dasa is to be arrived Moon in Virgo Rasi

$= 5s - 11° - 10'$

Virgo at $= 11° - 10'$

Page 56 of 1996-2000 of condensed Ephemeris in 2nd part Virgo Rasi is shown from this:

Y – M – D

$11° - 0' =$ Moon Dasa

$= 9 - 3 - 0$

$11° - 20' =$ do $= 9 - 0 - 0$

$\therefore$ For $11° - 10'$ do Moon value gives = 9 – 1 – 15

$\therefore$ Moon Dasa balance left at Birth is on 20-4-1997 = 9 years – 1 Months and 15 days.

8. Antar Dasa calculation method

For Moon · Moon $= \frac{10 \times 10}{120} = \frac{100}{120} = 0 - 10$ Months

For Moon · Mars $= \frac{10 \times 10}{120} = \frac{70}{120} = 0 - 7$ Months

For Moon · Jupiter $= \frac{10 \times 10}{120} = \frac{160}{120} = 1 - 4$ Months

Like this all other Planets Antar dasa periods are to be calculated.

9. Vidasa calculation method

Moon · Moon · Moon $= 10 \text{ months} = 30^D \times 10^M = 300^D \times \frac{10}{120} = \frac{100}{4} = 24$ days

Moon · Moon · Mars $= 7 \text{ months} = 7^M \times 30^D = 210^D \times \frac{7}{120} = \frac{2100}{120} = 17\frac{1}{2}$ days

Moon · Mars · Rahu $= \frac{10 \times 7}{120} = 7 \text{ months} \times \frac{18}{120} = 31\frac{1}{2}$ days

Mars · Rahu · Jupiter $= \frac{7 \times 18}{120} = 12.6 \text{ months} \times \frac{16}{120} \times 30 = 504$ days

Hence the calculation is to be done taking the total years & divded by 120 Twice to get vidasa periods in days.

10.2 MARRIAGE MUHURHAM

	Boy	Girl
Date of Birth	24-7-1989	31-8-1994
Time	15:22 PM	8:00 AM
Place	Pithapuram	Kakinada
Star	Revati	Mrugasira

Place of Marrage = Kakinada as per Panchamgam of Dumukha Nama Samvatsara 2016-2017, Approved by Govt. of India. The Marriage Muhurthas are given at pages 28 to 30 are to be seen.

1. First good Stars suitable to the birth Stars of Boy & Girl are to be selected. For this table at page 39 to be seen.

   The Tara numbers given as 2, 4, 6, 8, & are only to be taken.

   For Revati/Mrugasira Stars, the Subha stars, groups are:

Aswani	Krittika	Pushami
Makha	Uttaraphalguni	Anooradiha
Moola	Uttarashada	Uttarabhadra

In Sravana Masa at page 29 on 20-8-2016:

Star Uttarabhadra is good for marriage.

Karktaka lagna = Night 3-50 hrs.min

Saturday = Bhaula Vidiya

The Chart at Muhurtha Lagna is as under on 20-8-2016

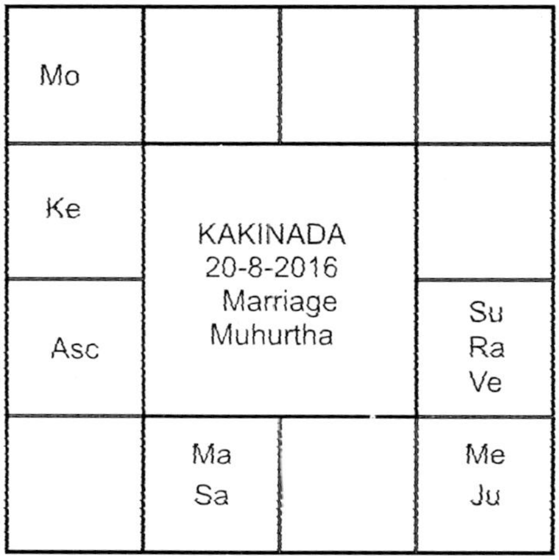

From the above chart it is seen that 7th house from Lagna is free of any planet which is good.

10.3 GRUHA PRAVESHA MUHURTHAM

Hosue Owner's Birth Star = Bharani. His Wife's Birth Star = Hastha. The Good Star groups suitable to these two Stars are as under. Place Rajahmundry.

Kristtika	Mrugasira	Puamrvasu	Aslesha
Uttaraphalguv	Chatta	Visakha	Jyeshta
Uttarashada	Dhanishta	Purvabhadra	Revati

At page 29 of Panchamgam Subha muhurthas for April Month have been given on 21-4-2016 Sukla, Chatur dasi, Guru Varam Chitta Star-Vivaha, Gruha Pravesha is given for Dhanur Lagna at 11:33 PM. This is tallying for the Couple at page 54 at 5:30 the Chart on 22-4-2016 is also compared with chart on 21-4-2016.

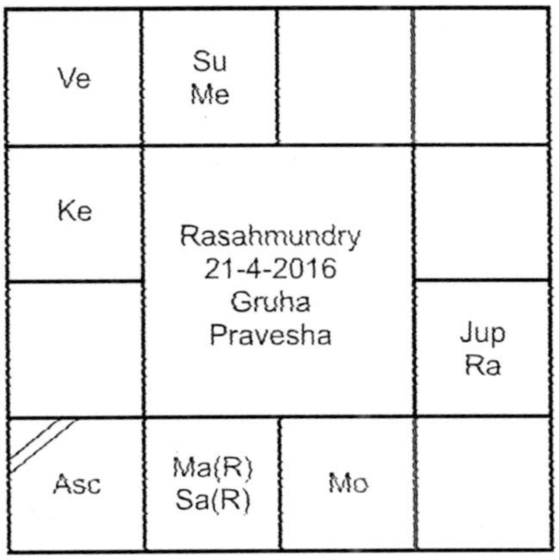

At Muhurtha time of 11:33 PM on 24-4-2016. The longitude of Moon is = 6s – 1° – 42′ in Tula Rasi. Moon in Labhasthana, Venus in 4th Hosue, Jupiter in Bhagyathana Aspecting Lagna.

7 & 8 Houses are Vaeant & Aspected by Naturally Good Planets Jupiter in Lagna. That is why this Muhurtha is Good & Auspicious.

10.4 UPANAYANA MUHURTHAM

Venue = At Rajahumdy
Vatuvu Birth star = Hastha
Father Birth star = Uttaphalguni
Mother's Birth star = Swathi

Suitable Star group for these three Stars are:

Bharani	Rohini
Poorvaphalguni	Hastha
Poorvashada	Sravamam

In Panchaamgam there was only one Muhurtha on 15-2-2017 Wednesday, Hastha star, Anna Prasana, Upanayana, Vivaha are coverd for Mesha Lagna. At 10-53. This star is an approved Star as written in the Text Muhutha Sindhuvu. The chart on that day is as under:

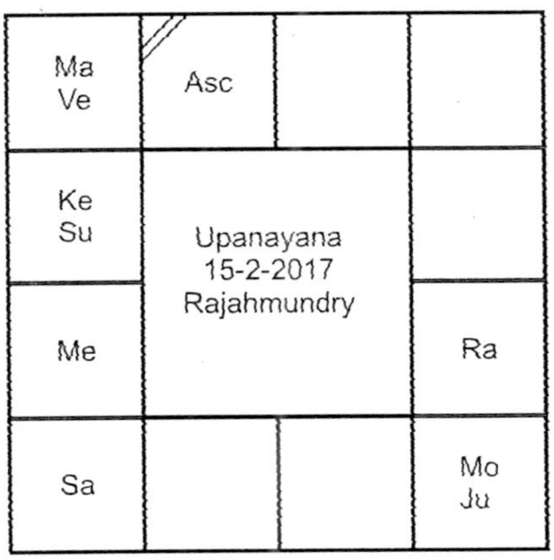

From the above Chart it is seen that Houses 7 & 8 are empty. Hence this Muhurtha is Auspicious & Very Good.

❖❖❖

CHAPTER 11

Colloquial Stanzas

11.1 English to Telugu

A

Abacus - అబేకస్

Abelean group - ఏబెల్ గూర్పులు

Aberration - విపథనము

Aberration co-efficient - విపథన గుణకము

Aberration constant - విపథన స్థిరాంకము

Aberration of light - కాంతి విపథనము

Aberration of planet - గ్రహ విపథనము

Absolute - అమూర్త, ప్రకేవల

Absolute convergence - ప్రకేవల, ఉపసరణత

Absolute curve - ప్రకేవల వక్రము

Absolute magnitude - పరమ తరము

Absolute potential - అమూర్త శక్మము

Absolute temperature - పరమ తాపక్రమము

Absolute time - ప్రకేవల కాలము

Absolute value - ప్రకేవల విలువ

Absorption - విచూషణ

Absorption bands - విచూషణ పట్టికలు

Abstract - విరుపాధిక, శుద్ధ

Abstract algebra - శుద్ధ బీజగణితము

Abstract geometry - శుద్ధ జ్యామితి

Abstract spaces - విరుపాధిక ఆకాశములు

Acceleration - త్వరణము

Acoustics - ధ్వనిశాస్త్రము

Acute angle - అల్పకోణము, లఘుకోణము

Acute angled triangle - అల్పకోణ త్రిభుజము

Addition - సంకలనము, కూడిక

Aerials - ఆకాశకములు

Aerolite - ఉల్కాపిండము

Albedo - పరావర్తన శక్తి

Aldebaran - రోహిణి

Algebra - బీజగణితము

Algebraic functions - బీజీయ ఫలములు

Alternate angle - ఏకాంతర కోణము

Alternate exterior angle - బాహ్య ఏకాంతర కోణము

Alternate interior angle - అంతర ఏకాంతర కోణము

Altitude - ఉన్నతి, ఎత్తు

Analysis - విశ్లేషణ, విశ్లేషణ గణితము

Analysis of variance - చలన విశ్లేషణము

Analytical functions - విశ్లేషణ ఫలములు

Analytical mechanics - విశ్లేషణ యాంత్రిక శాస్త్రము

Anchor ring - లంగరు వలయము

Anchormeda - దేవయాని

Angle - కోణము

Angle of depression - నిమ్నకోణము

Angle of dip - నిమజ్జన కోణము

Angle of elevation - ఉన్నత కోణము, ఊర్ధ్వకోణము
Angle of incidence - పతనకోణము
Angle of retraction - వక్రీభవన కోణము
Angle solid - ఘనకోణము
Angular - కోణీయ
Angular momentum - కోణీయ గతిభారము
Angular velocity - కోణీయ వేగము
Annual - వార్షిక
Annual equation - వార్షిక సమీకరణము
Annual parallax - వార్షిక అతివర్తనము
Annular eclipse - కంకణ గ్రహణము
Anomaly - మాంద్యత
Antares - జ్యేష్ఠ
Anticlock wise - అపసవ్య
Antiparallel - ప్రతి సమానాంతర, ప్రతిసామ్య
Aphelion - అపహేళి
Apogee - అపజ్యా
Apparent - వ్యక్త
Apparant brightness - దృశ్యదీప్తి
Apparent direction - వ్యక్తదిశ
Apparent magnitude - కేవల పరిమాణము, వ్యక్తతరము
Apparent solar time - ప్రత్యక్ష సౌరకాలము
Apparent zenith distance - వ్యక్తనత దూరము, వ్యక్తనతా
Applied mathematics - వినియుక్త గణితము
Approximate - ఆసన్న
Apsidal line - నీచోచ్చ రేఖ
Aquaril - శతభిషము
Aquarius - కుంభ
Aquila - శ్రవణము
Arc - చాపము, ధనుస్సు
Architectural acoustics - వాస్తుధ్వని విద్య
Arcturus - స్వాతి
Area - వైశాల్యము, విస్తీర్ణము
Area co-ordinates - వైశాల్య నిరూపకములు
Areal velocity - వైశాల్యవేగము
Areas under the nomal curves - సరళవక్ర విస్తీర్ణము
Aries - మేష
Arietis - అశ్విని
Arietis - 35, 41 భరణి
Arithmetic - అంకగణితము
Arithmetic mean - సంకలన మధ్యమము
Arithmetic progression - అంకశ్రేణి, సంకలనశ్రేణి
Ars conjectandi - ఊహన కళ
Artifical satellite - కృత్రిమ ఉపగ్రహము
Ascendent - లగ్నము
Associative law - సంయోజక న్యాయము
Assumptions - ఉపకల్పనలు
Asteroids - లఘుగ్రహములు
Astrolabe - నక్షత్ర యంత్రము
Astrology - జ్యోతిషము
Astronomical units - ఖగోళ శాస్త్రీయ యూనిట్
Astronomy - ఖగోళశాస్త్రము
Astro - dynamics - ఖగోళ గతిశాస్త్రము
Astro - physics - ఖగోళ భౌతికశాస్త్రము
Asymptotes - అసంపాతములు
Asymptotic line - అసంపాతీయ రేఖ
Asymptotic solution - అసంపతనీయ సాధనము
Atomic model - పరమాణు ప్రతిరూపము
Attraction - ఆకర్షణ
Auto-correlation - స్వయం సంబంధము
Autumnal equinox - తులావిషువు, తులాసంపాతము, శరద్విషువు
Axes of reference - నిరూపకాక్షములు
Axiom of choice - వరుణస్వీకృత తత్త్వము

Axioms - ఆధార తత్త్వములు

Axis - అక్షము

Azimuth - అజిమత్, దిగంశ

B

Ballistics - అస్త్రప్రయోగశాస్త్రము

Base - ఆధారము, పీఠము

Bearing - ధురాధారములు

Bicontinuity - ద్విపార్శ్వ అవిచ్ఛిన్నత

Binaries - ద్వికతారలు, యుగళతారలు

Binomial - ద్విపద

Binomial co-efficient - ద్విపద గుణకము

Binomial expression - ద్విపద సమాసము

Binomial theorem - ద్విపద సిద్ధాంతము

Biology - జీవశాస్త్రము

Biometry - జీవన మాపకము

Birational transformation - క్రమోనా మార్పులు

Bisector - ద్విభాజకము

Bi-uniformity - ద్విపార్శ్వ ఏకరూపత

Bomb ballistics - బాంబు అస్త్ర ప్రయోగ విద్య

Bootes - స్వాతి

Bounded - మర్యాదిత, సీమిత

Bounded oscillation - మర్యాదిత కంపనము

C

Calculating machine - గణిత్ర యంత్రము

Calculus - కలనశాస్త్రము

Calculus of probabilities - సంభావ్యతాకలనము

Calculus of variation - చలకలనము

Calendar - పంచాంగము

Cancer - కర్క

Caneri - ఆశ్లేష

Caneri - పుష్యమి

Canopus - అగస్త్య

Capture hypothesis - గ్రహసిద్ధాంతము

Cardioid - కార్డియాయిడ్

Cartesian co-ordinates - కార్టీసియన్ నిరూపకములు

Cartesian product - కార్టీసియన్ గుణకారసమితి

Casting out - నిష్కాసము

Castor - పునర్వసు

Catenary - కాటినెరీ

Calestial - దివ్య, ఖగోళ

Celestial equator - దివ్యనిరక్షరేఖ, విషువృత్తము

Celestial latitude - దివ్య అక్షాంశము, శరము

Celestial longitude - దివ్యరేఖాంశము, భోగము, ధ్రువకము

Celestial mechanics - ఖగోళ యాంత్రిక శాస్త్రము

Celestial objects - నభోమూర్తులు

Celestial sphere - ఖగోళము, దివ్యగోళము

Centaurus - త్రిశంకువు

Central conicoid - కేంద్రీయ ఘనశాంకము

Central projection - కేంద్ర విక్షేపము

Centre - కేంద్రము

Centre of curvature - వక్రతాకేంద్రము

Centre of gravity - గురుత్వకేంద్రము, గరిమనాభి

Centre of involution - సమవాయుతాకేంద్రము

Cepheid variables - సెఫీడ్ చలతారలు

Chance - యదృచ్ఛ

Change of axis - అక్షపరివర్తన

Change of co-ordinates - నిరూపక పరివర్తన

Chord - జ్యా

Chord line - జ్యారేఖ

Chromate aberration - వర్ణవిపథనము

Chromosphere - వర్ణమండలము

Chronometer - క్రోనోమీటరు, ఘటికాయంత్రము

Circle - వృత్తము

Circle geometry - వృత్తీయ జ్యామితి

Circle of Curvature - వక్రతా వృత్తము
Circular - వర్తుల, వృత్తీయ
Circular functions - వృత్తీయ ఫలములు
Circular lines - వర్తుల రేఖలు
Circular ornamental patterns - వృత్తీయ అలంకారములు
Circular points - వృత్తీయ బిందువులు, వర్తుల బిందువులు
Circular points at infinity - అనంతంలో ఉండు వర్తుల బిందువులు
Circum centre - పరికేంద్రము
Circum circle - పరివృత్తము
Circumference - పరిధి
Cissoid - సిస్సోయిడ్
Clockwise - సవ్యదిశ
Closed - సంవృత
Closed curve - సంవృత వక్రము
Closed interval - సంవృత అంతరము
Closed sets - సంవృత సమితులు
Cluster variables - చలనగుచ్ఛములు
Coal sack nebuls - అంగార కోశనీహారిక
Co-axial circles - ఏకాక్ష వృత్తములు
Co-efficient - గుణకము
Co-efficient of friction - ఘర్షణ గుణకము
Co-factor - కోఫాక్టర్
Collinear Points - ఏకరేఖీయ బిందువులు
Colour index - వర్ణసూచకము
Column - స్తంభము
Coma - కోమా
Combinations - సంయోజన విధానము
Comet - సంయోగములు
Commodity reveral test - ధూమకేతువు, తోకచుక్క
Commutative law - వస్తుపరివర్తన పరీక్ష
Commutative law - పరివర్తన న్యాయము, పరివర్తన నియమము
Commutative law - సంయోగ నియమము
Commutative ring - పరివర్తన మండలము
Companion star - అనుచర తార
Complementations - పూరకములు
Complementary angles - పూరక కోణములు
Comlex - కాంప్లెక్స్, సంకీర్ణ
Complex line - సంకీర్ణ రేఖ
Complex numbers - సంకీర్ణ సంఖ్యలు
Complex variable - సంకీర్ణ చలరాశి
Components - అంశములు, ఘటకములు
Composite probability - మిళిత సంభావ్యత
Computers - గణిత్రములు, గణన యంత్రములు
Concept - భావము
Conchoid - కాంగ్‌కాయిడ్
Concurrent - అనుషక్తము
Conduction of heat - ఉష్ణవాహకత
Cone - శంకు
Cone of friction - ఘర్షణ శంకు
Cone speakers - శంకుభాషులు
Confocal conics - ఏకనాభికా శాంకవములు
Conformal mapping - సదృశ చిత్రపట లేఖనము
Congruent - సర్వసమాన
Conic - శాంకవము
Conica; projection - శాంకవ విక్షేపము
Conic section - శాంకవ ఛేదము
Conical retraction - శాంకవ వక్రీభవనము
Conical surface - శకుంతలము
Conicold - ఘనశాంకవము
Conjugate - సంయుగ్మ
Conjugate points - సంయుగ్మ బిందువులు
Constant - యుతి, యోగము
Constellations - తారామండలములు, రాశులు
Contingency co-efficient - అధీనతా గుణకము

Continued fractions - శృంఖలిత భిన్నములు
Continuity - అవిచ్ఛిన్నత
Contour integral - పరివృత్తి చయనము
Contravariants - విలోమ చలరాశులు
Convergency - ఉపసరణత
Convergent series - ఉపసరణ పరంపర
Co-ordinate axes - నిరూపకాక్షములు
Co-ordinate geometry - నిరూపక జ్యామితి
Co-ordinates - నిరూపకములు
Corona - ముకుటము
Correspondence - అనురూపత
Corresponding angles - అనురూప కోణములు
Co-secant - కోటిఛేదకము
Cosine - కోటిజీవ, కో జీవ
Cosine circle - కోటిజీవ వృత్తము
Cosine series - కో జీవ పరంపర
Cosmic dust - విశ్వధూళి
Cosmic matter - విశ్వద్రవ్యము
Cosmos - విశ్వము
Co-tangent - కోటి స్పర్శజీవ
Couple - యుగ్మము
Cross fertilized - పరపరాగసిక్త
Cross multiplication - క్రాస్ గుణకారము
Cross ratio - వజ్ర నిష్పత్తి
Cryptarithmetic - గుప్తాంక గణితము
Cube - ఘనము
Cube root - ఘనమూలము
Cuneiform script - బాణాగ్రలిపి
Curvature - వక్రత
Curved space - వక్ర ఆకాశము
Curves - వక్రములు
Curvilinear co-ordinates - వక్రరేఖీయ నిరూపకములు
Cusp - సూచీముఖము
Cyclic - చక్రీయ
Cyclical component - చక్రభాగము
Cyclic quadrilateral - చక్రీయ చతుర్భుజము, వృత్తీయ చతుర్భుజము
Cycloid - సైక్లాయిడ్
Cygnue 61 - హంస
Cylinder - స్థూపము
Cylindrical co-ordinates - స్థూపీయ నిరూపకములు
Cylindrical projection - స్థూప విక్షేపము
Cylindrical surface - స్థూప తలము

D

Dark line spectrum - కృష్ణరేఖా వర్ణమాల
Dark nebulae - కృష్ణ నీహారికలు
Data - దత్తాంశములు
Data line - తారీఖురేఖ
Decimal fraction - దశాంశ భిన్నము
Decimal notation - దశాంశ సంకేతనము
Decimal point - దశాంశ బిందువు
Decimals - దశాంశములు
Declination - క్రాంతి
Declination circle - ద్యుజ్యావృత్తము
Deductive system - తార్కిక కల్పన
Definition - నిర్వచనము
Degree - తరగతి, డిగ్రీ
Degree of freedom - స్వేచ్ఛతాతరము
Delphini - ధనిష్ఠ
Delta orions - మృగశిర
Demand - అర్థన
Demand analysis - అర్థన విశ్లేషణ
Denebola - ఉత్తరఫల్గుణి
Denominator - హారము

Density - సాంద్రత

Dependent variable - పరతంత్ర చలరాశి

Derivative - వ్యుత్పన్నము

Design of experiment - ప్రయోగరచన

Determinants - నిర్ధారకములు

Deviation - విచలనము

Diagonal - వికర్ణము

Diameter - వ్యాసము

Different equation - అంతర సమీకరణము

Differential calculus - అంతరీకరణ కలనము

Differential co-efficient - అంతరీకరణ గుణకము

Differential equation - అంతరీకరణ సమీకరణము

Differential geometry - అంతరీకరణ జ్యామితి

Differential ratio - అంతరీకరణ నిష్పత్తి

Differentiation - అంతరీకరణము

Digits - అంకెలు

Dimension - వ్యాప్తి, పరిమాణము, విమా

Dimensional analysis - విమా విశ్లేషణ

Diophantine equations - డయోఫాంటస్ సమీకరణములు

Dip - నతి, నిమజ్జత

Direction cosines - నిర్దిష్ట కోటిజీవలు

Direct proportion - అనులోమ అనుపాతము

Displacement - స్థానాంతరత

Displacement of the first point of Aries - అయనాంశ

Distance of a planet from the centre of earth - శీఘ్రకర్ణము

Diurnal - దైనిక

Diurnal rotation - దైనిక పరిభ్రమణము

Diurnal rotation of earth - భూదైనిక పరిభ్రమణము

Divergence - అపసరణత

Divergent series - అపసరణ పరంపర

Divident - భాజ్యము, విభాజ్యము

Division - భాగాహారము

Divisor - భాజకము

Dot multiplication - బిందు గుణకారము

Duality - ద్వైత స్వభావము

Dwarfs - వామనములు

Dynamics - గతిశాస్త్రము

Dynamics of a particle - కణగతిశాస్త్రము

E

Earth - భూమి

Eccentric circle - ఉత్కేంద్ర వృత్తము

Eccentricity - ఉత్కేంద్రత

Eccentric orbit - ఉత్కేంద్ర కక్ష్య

Eclipse - గ్రహణము

Eclipsing stars - గ్రహణ తారలు

Eclipsing variables - ఆచ్ఛాదిత చలతారలు

Ecliptic - క్రాంతి వృత్తము

Econometrics - అర్థమితి శాస్త్రము

Economics - అర్థశాస్త్రము

Eigen functions - యుక్తఫలములు

Eigen function expansion - యుక్తఫలముల వ్యాకోచనము

Electric charge - విద్యుదావేశము

Electric potential - విద్యుచ్ఛక్మము

Electro-dynamics - విద్యుద్గతిశాస్త్రము

Electro-magnetic theory - విద్యుదయస్కాంత సిద్ధాంతము

Electronic computers - ఎలక్ట్రానిక్ గణిత్రములు

Ellipse - దీర్ఘవృత్తము, విలోపము

Ellipsoid - ఎలిప్సాయిడ్

Elliptic functions - విలోప ఫలములు, దీర్ఘవృత్త ఫలములు

Elliptic geometry - విలోప జ్యామితి, దీర్ఘవృత్త జ్యామితి

Elliptic orbit - విలోప కక్ష్య, దీర్ఘవృత్త కక్ష్య

Empirical - అనుభవగర్భిత

Energy - శక్తి

Envelope - వేష్టనము

Epicycle - ప్రాక్ప్రక్రమము
Ephemeris meridian - పంచాంగరేఖ
Ephemeris time - పంచాంగ కాలము
Equation - సమీకరణము
Equation of centre - మందఫలము
Equation of time - కాల సమీకరణము
Equator - నిరక్షరేఖ
Equiangular spiral - సమానకోణ సర్పిలము
Equinoctial - విషుదర్శని
Equinoctial point - విషుబిందువు
Equinox - విషువు, అయనము
Era - శకము
Error - ప్రమాదము
Estimate - అంచనా
Euclidean space - యూక్లిడ్ ఆకాశము
Euclid's Elements - యూక్లిడ్ ఎలిమెంట్స్
Evening star - సందెచుక్క
Even number - సరిసంఖ్య
Event - సంఘటన
Evolute - అంతర్జూరి
Evolution - పరిణామము
Exact equations - సమగ్ర అంతరీకరణ సమీకరణములు
Exactly similar representating- వాస్తవిక ప్రతిరూపము
Ex-centre - బాహ్యకేంద్రము
Expanding universe - వ్యాకోచద్విశ్వము
Expansion of determinants - నిర్ధారక వ్యాకోచము
Expectation of life - జీవిత ప్రత్యాశ
Experiment - ప్రయోగము
Exponent - ఘాతాంకము
Exponential functions - ఘాత ఫలములు
Exponential series - ఘాతాంకీయ పరంపర, ఘాత పరంపర
Expression - సమాసము
Exterial angle - బాహ్యకోణము

F

Factor - కారణాంకము, విభాజకము
Factor analysis - కారణాంక విశ్లేషణ
Factorization - విభాజకీకరణము
Factor reversal test - కారణాంశ పరివర్తన పరీక్ష
False coin - కూటనాణెము
Fermat numbers - ఫర్మాసంఖ్యలు
Field of force - బలక్షేత్రము
Field potentia - క్షేత్రశక్మము
Finite geometry - పరిమిత జ్యామితి
Fire balls - అగ్నిగోళములు
First point of Aries - మేషాది బిందువు
First point of Libra - తులాది బిందువు
First quadratic differential from - ప్రథమవర్గ అంతరీకరణ రూపము
Flat - చిపిట
Flat spaces - చిపిట ఆకాశములు
Fluid - ద్రవము
Fluid mechanics - ద్రవయాంత్రిక శాస్త్రము
Flux - density - ప్రవాహ సాంద్రత
Focal length - నాభ్యంతరము
Focal of conic - శాంకవనాభులు
Focus - నాభి
Force - బలము
Force of mortality - మృతిబలము
Forecast - పూర్వనిర్దేశము
Form co-efficient - ఆకృతిగుణము
Form function - ఆకృతి ఫలము
Formula - సూత్రము
Four dimensional - చతుఃపరిమాణిక
Fourier series - ఫోరియర్ పరంపర
Fraction - భిన్నము

Fragmentation ballistics - శకలాస్త్ర ప్రయోగము
Frequency - పౌనఃపున్యము
Frequency division - పౌనఃపున్య విభజనము
Friction - ఘర్షణ
Frustum of a pyramid - కత్తిరించిన గోపురము
Fuel - ఇంధనము
Function - ఫలము
Functional determinent - ఫల నిర్ధారకము
Function theory - ఫలవాదము
Fundamental trihedron - మూల త్రితలము

G

Galactic collision - క్షీరపథ సంఘర్షణ
Galaxy - గెలాక్సీ, మందాకిని, క్షీరపథము, పాలపుంత
Gamma functions - గామా ఫలములు
Gauss curvature - గౌస్ వక్రత
Gaussian law of errors - గౌస్ ప్రమానియమము
Gemini - మిథునము
Geminorium - పునర్వసు
Geminorum - నక్షత్రద్వికము
General - వ్యాపక
General solution - వ్యాపక సాధనము
Generalized co-ordinates - విశాలీకృత నిరూపకములు
Generating line - జనకరేఖ
Genus - జాతి
Geodesic - హ్రస్వతమరేఖ
Geodesic curve - హ్రస్వతమ వక్రము
Geometrical mean - గుణోత్తర మధ్యమము
Geometrical progression - గుణోత్తర శ్రేణి
Geometry - క్షేత్రగణితము, జ్యామితి
Geometry of three dimensions - త్రిమాత్రయ జ్యామితి
Giants - బృహతుల్లు
Gibbous - న్యుబ్జ
Gnomon - శంకు
Gravitation - గురుత్వాకర్షణము
Gravitational co-efficient - గురుత్వాకర్షణ గుణకము
Gravitational constant - గురుత్వ స్థిరాంకము
Gravitational field - గురుత్వాకర్షణ క్షేత్రము
Great circle - గురువృత్తము, మహావృత్తము
Greatest Common Measure -
అపవర్తనాంకము, గరిష్ఠ సామాన్య భాజకము (గ.సా.భా.)
Groups - కూర్పులు, పుంజములు
Gyro-compass - వృద్ధి ప్రతికృతులు
Gyroscope - గైరోస్కోప్, భ్రమణదర్శకము

H

Harmonic - స్వరాత్మక, హరాత్మక
Harmonic conjugate - హరాత్మక యుగళము
Harmonically - హరాత్మకముగ
Harmonic functions - స్వరాత్మక ఫలములు
Harmonic mean -
స్వరాత్మక మధ్యమము, హరాత్మక మధ్యమము
Harmonic motion - హరాత్మక గతి
Harmonic pencil - హరాత్మక శలాక, స్వరాత్మక శలాక
Harmonic progression - హరాత్మక శ్రేణి
Harmonic range - స్వరాత్మక రేంజి
Harmonic section - స్వరాత్మక ఛేదము
Harmonic triangle - హరాత్మక త్రిభుజము
Heat index - తాపసూచకము
Heliometer - హేళిమాపకము
Helix - హెలిక్స్
Highly composite numbers - అతివిభాజ్య సంఖ్యలు
Hilbert space - హిల్బర్ట్ ఆకాశము
Holder inequalities - హోల్డర్ హెచ్చుతగ్గులు
Homogeneous - సమఘాత
Homogeneous equations - సమఘాత సమీకరణములు

Horizontal - క్షితిజ
Horizontal plane - అంబుతలము
Horocycle - హోరోవృత్తము
Horoscope - హోరాచక్రము, రాశిచక్రము
Horse head nebula - అశ్వశిర నీహారిక
Hour angle - నతకాలము
Hour circle - హోరావృత్తము
Hydra - ఆశ్లేష
Hydrodynamics - ద్రవగతిశాస్త్రము
Hydrostatics - ద్రవస్థితిశాస్త్రము
Hyperbola - అతిపరాస
Hyperbolic function - అతిపరాస ఫలములు
Hyperbolic orbit - అతిపరాసీయ కక్ష్య
Hyperboloid - ఘనఅతిపరాస
Hypotenuse - కర్ణము
Hypothesis - కల్పన

I

Identities - సర్వసమతత్త్వములు
Identity - సర్వసమత
Igniter - ప్రజ్వాలకము
Implicit differentiation - అవ్యక్తఫల అంతరీకరణము
Implicit functions - అవ్యక్త ఫలములు
Improper fraction - అపక్రమ భిన్నము, అయుక్త భిన్నము
In-centre - అంతర కేంద్రము, అంతఃకేంద్రము
Incidence - అపాతము
Incircle - అంతర్వృత్తము
Inclination - నిమ్నత
Indefinite integration - అనిశ్చిత చయనీకరణము
Independent variable - స్వరాత్మక
Indeterminate equations of first degree - అనిశ్చిత ప్రథమ తరగతి సమీకరణములు
Indeterminate equations of first degree in many unknowns - బహుపద అనిశ్చిత ప్రథమ తరగతి సమీకరణములు
Indeterminate equations of second degree - రెండవ తరగతి అనిశ్చిత సమీకరణములు
Index - సూచిక
Index number - సూచక సంఖ్య, సూచ్యంకము
Index number theory - సూచీసంఖ్యా సిద్ధాంతము
Inequalities - హెచ్చుతగ్గులు
Inertia - జడత్వము
Inertia of large numbers - పెద్ద సంఖ్యల జడత్వము
Inferior conjunction - అధమయోగము
Infinite geometric progression - అనంత గుణోత్తర శ్రేణి
Infinite limit - అనంత అవధి
Infinite product - గుణకార పరంపర
Infinite regression - అనంత పరంపరదోషము
Infinite series - అనంతపరంపర
Infinitesimal - సూక్ష్మరాశి
Infra red - పరశ్శోణ
Inner angle - అంతరకోణము
Inner planets - అంతర్గ్రహములు
Inscribed circle - అంతర్లిఖిత వృత్తము
Insurance - భీమా
Integers - పూర్ణాంకములు
Integral calculus - చయన కలనము
Integral equations - చయన సమీకరణములు
Integral test - చయనీయ పరీక్ష
Integration - చయనీకరణము
Intelligent quotient - బౌద్ధిక గుణ్యము
Inter continental ballistic missiles - అంతరఖండ విక్షేపాస్త్రములు
Internal ballistics - అంతర అస్త్ర ప్రయోగము
Interpolation - పద నిశ్చయము

Inter stellar dust - అంతర్నక్షత్ర ధూళి

Inter stellar gas - అంతర్నక్షత్ర వాయువు

Invariance - అచలత, నిర్వికృతి

Invariant - అచలరాశి

Inverse - విలోమ

Inverse functions - విలోమ ఫలములు

Inverse proportion - విలోమ అనుపాతము

Involute - బహిర్వల్లి

Involution - సమన్వయత, సమవాయత

Involution pencil - సమన్వయ శలాక, సమవాయతా శలాక

Ionization - అయనీకరణము

Ionosphere - అయనావరణము

Irrational - కరణీయ

Irrational numbers - కరణీయ సంఖ్యలు

Isogonal conjugates lines - సమానకోణ సంయుగ్మ రేఖలు

Isogonal conjugates - తుల్యకోణ సంయుగ్మములు

Isomorphic - ఏకరూప

Isosceles triangle - సమద్విభుజ త్రిభుజము

J

Jiba - జీబ

Jupiter - గురుడు, గురుగ్రహము, బృహస్పతి

K

Kinematics - శుద్ధగతిశాస్త్రము

Kinematics of particle - కణశుద్ధగతిశాస్త్రము

Kinetic energy - చలనశక్తి

Kinetic theory - అణుచలన సిద్ధాంతము

L

Lamina - ఫలకము

Laplace's equation - లాప్లాస్ సమీకరణము

Latin square - లాటిన్ చతురస్రము

Latitude - అక్షాంశము, శరము

Lattice points - జల బిందువులు

Latus recium - ఉల్థానము

Law of inverse squares - విలోమవర్గ న్యాయము

Leo - సింహ రాశి

Leonis - మఘ

Leonis - పుబ్బ

Leonis - ఉత్తర

Lens - కటకము

Lever - ఉచ్చాలకము

Libra - తుల

Libration - తోలనము

Life Insurance - జీవితభీమా

Light - కాంతి, జ్యోతి

Light year - కాంతి వత్సరము, జ్యోతిర్వత్సరము

Limacon - లిమేసాన్

Limit - అవధి

Limiting point - అవధి బిందువు

Limit of a sum - సంకలన అవధి

Line - రేఖ

Line co-ordinates - రేఖా నిరూపకములు

Linear - రేఖీయ

Linear differential equation - మొదటి తరగతి అంతరీకరణ సమీకరణములు

Linear equation - ఏకవర్ణ సమీకరణము

Linear sets of points - రేఖీయ బిందు సమితి

Line at infinity - అనంతదూరరేఖ

Line geometry - ఋజురేఖా జ్యామితి

Lines of curvature - వక్రతా రేఖలు

Linkage - శృంఖలా సంధానము

Liquid fuels - ద్రవేంధనములు

Loaded dice - కూట పాచికలు

Local time - స్వదేశకాలము

Locus - బిందుపథము
Logarithmic functions - లాగరిదమ్ ఫలములు
Logarithmic series - లాగరిదమ్ పరంపర
Logarithm - లాగరిదమ్
Longitude - రేఖాంశరేఖ
Loop - పాళి
Loud speakers - ఉచ్చభాషులు
Lunar eclipse - చంద్రగ్రహణము
Lunar phases - చంద్రకళలు
Lower transit - అథమ ప్రతరణము
Lower limit - అథమ అవధి
Lowest common multiple - కనిష్ఠ సామాన్య గుణిజము (క.సా.గు.)

M

Magellanic cloud - నీహారికా మేఘము
Magic square - కూట చతురస్రములు
Magnetic field - అయస్కాంత క్షేత్రము
Magnetic perturbation - అయస్కాంత క్షోభములు
Magnetic poles - అయస్కాంత ధ్రువములు
Magnifying power - అధికీకరణ సామర్థ్యము
Magnitude - పరిమాణము, తరము
Major arc - గురుచాపము
Mars - అంగారకుడు, కుజుడు
Mathematical anecdotes - గణిత కథలు
Mathematical economics - గణిత అర్థశాస్త్రము
Mathematical fallacies - విపరీత గణితము
Mathematical induction - గణిత అనుగమనము
Mathematical logic - గణిత తర్కము
Mathematical physics - గణిత భౌతికశాస్త్రము
Mathematical prodigies - అద్భుత గణకులు
Mathematical puzzles and recreation - గణిత చిక్కుప్రశ్నలు, వినోదములు
Mathematical tables - గణిత పథకములు
Mathematics - గణితము
Matrix - మాత్రిక
Matrix theory - పంజరవాదము
Matter - ద్రవ్యరాశి
Maximum - గరిష్ఠ
Maximum power - గరిష్ఠ ఘాతము
Mean solar time - మధ్యమాన సౌరకాలము
Mean value - మధ్యమాన విలువ
Mean value theorem - మధ్యమ మూల్యసిద్ధాంతము
Mechanic - యాంత్రిక శాస్త్రము
Median - మధ్యగత
Mercury - బుధుడు
Meridian - మధ్యాహ్నరేఖ, యామ్యోత్తర రేఖ
Meridian circle - యామ్యోత్తర వృత్తము
Meteor - ఉల్క
Meteor crater - ఉల్కాబిలము
Meteorite - ఉల్కాపిండము
Meteor shower - ఉల్కాపాతము
Meteor swaram - ఉల్కాకూటము
Method of least square - కనిష్ఠవర్గ విధానము
Metric space - పరిమేయాకాశము
Micrometer - సూక్ష్మమాపకము
Microscope - సూక్ష్మదర్శిని
Milky way - ఆకాశగంగ, క్షీరపథము, పాలపుంత, మందాకిని
Minimum - కనిష్ఠ
Minor arc - లఘుచాపము
Models - ప్రతికృతులు
Modern geometry - నవీనజ్యామితి
Modulus - మాపాంకము (మా)
Moment of force - బల బిభ్రమిష
Moment of interia - జడ బిభ్రమిష

Moment of momentum - గతిభార విభ్రమిష
Momentum - గతిభారము
Moon - చంద్రుడు
Morning star - వేగుచుక్క
Mortality table - ఆయుర్దాయ పట్టికలు
Multinomial theorem - బహుపద సిద్ధాంతము
Motion - గమనము, గతి, చలనము
Multiples - గుణిజములు
Multiple stars - బహుళతారలు
Multiplication - గుణకారము
Multiplication table - గుణకార పట్టికలు
Multivariables - బురాశి
Musa - భరణి

N

Nadir - పాతాళబిందువు
Nebulae - నీహారికలు, నెబ్యులాలు
Nebular hypothesis - నీహారికావాదము
Negative - ఋణ
Negative roots - ఋణమూలములు
Neptune - వరుణుడు
Nine point circle - నవబిందువృత్తము
Nodal point - యుగళబిందువు
Node - పాతము
Nomogram - నోమోగ్రామ్
Non-algebriac - అబీజీయ
Non-algebriac numbers - అబీజీయ సంఖ్యలు
Non-differentiable - వ్యుత్పన్నరహిత
Non-enumerably infinite - అగణ్య అనంత
Non-Euclidean geometry - యూక్లిడేతర జ్యామితి
Normal - అభిలంబరేఖ
Normal curve - సరళవక్రము
Normal plane - లంబతలము
Normal population - సరళలోకము
Normal section - అభిలంబ ఛేదనము
North polar distance - ఉత్తర ధ్రువాంతరము
North frigid zone - ఉత్తర శీతమండలము
North pole - ఉత్తర ధ్రువము
North temporate zone - ఉత్తర సమశీతోష్ణ మండలము
Novae - నవీనములు, నవతారలు, నోవాలు
Number - సంఖ్య
Numerator - లవము
Nutation - అక్షవిచలనము, అక్షస్పందనము

O

Object glass - వస్తుకటకము
Oblique - తిర్యక్
Oblique axes - తిర్యక్ అక్షములు
Oblique cylinder - తిర్యక్ స్థూపము
Oblique prism - తిర్యక్ ప్రిజమ్
Obliquity of the ecliptic - పరమాపక్రాంతి
Observation - అవలోకన, అవేక్షణ
Observational - అవలోకనాత్మక
Observatory - వేధశాల
Obtuse angle - గురుకోణము
Octaheron - అష్టతలకము
Odd - బేసి
Odd number - బేసి సంఖ్యలు
Official statistics - అధికారిక సాంఖ్యకీయ ప్రచురణ
One-to-one corresponding - ఒకటికొకటి అనురూపత
Open interval - వివృత అంతరము
Operation - పరికర్మము
Opposition - షడ్భాంతరము
Optical double - దృశ్యయుగళములు
Optic - చాక్షుషశాస్త్రము
Orbit - కక్ష్య, కక్ష

Ordinate - కోటి

Origin of the solar system - సౌరకుటుంబ ఉత్పత్తి

Orionis - ఆర్ద్ర

Orionis - మృగశిర

Ortho-center - లంబకేంద్రము

Orthogonal - సమకోణీయ, లంబకోణీయ

Orthogonal involution - సమకోణీయ సమన్వయత

Orthogonal pencil - సమకోటియశలాక

Orthogonal projection - సమకోణీయ విక్షేపము

Osculating plane - పరిస్పర్శతలము

Osculating sphere - పరిస్పర్శగోళము

Outer planet - బాహ్యగ్రహములు

P

Parabola - పరాస

Paraboloid - పెరాబొలాయిడ్, ఘనపరాస

Parallax - అతివర్తనము, లంబనము

Parallax method - లంబన విధానము

Parallel - సమానాంతర, సామ్య

Parallel postulate - సమానాంతర స్వీకృతతత్త్వము

Parallel projection - సమానాంతర విక్షేపము

Parallelogram - సమానాంతర చతుర్భుజము

Parallelogram law of forces - సమానాంతర చతుర్భుజ నియమము, సమానాంతర చతుర్భుజ సంయోజన సూత్రము

Parallelepiped - సమానాంతర ఘనము

Parameter - పెరామీటరు, ప్రాచలము

Parameter group - ప్రాచలకూర్పు (పుంజము)

Parsec - పరశకము

Partial - అంశిక, ఖండ

Partial derivative - అంశిక వుత్పన్నము

Partial differential equation - ఆంశిక అంతరీకరణ సమికరణము

Partial eclipse - ఖండగ్రహణము

Partial integration - ఆంశిక చయనీకరణము, ఖండ చయనీకరణము

Particle - కణము

Pascal triangle - పాస్కల్ త్రిభుజము

Pedal curve - పాదవక్రము

Pedal line - పాదరేఖ

Pegasi - పూర్వాభాద్ర

Pegasi - ఉత్తరాభాద్ర

Pellian equation - పెల్లియన్ సమీకరణములు

Pencil - శలాక

Pencil of rays - రశ్మి శలాకము

Pendulum - లోలకము

Penultimate convergent - ఉపాంత ఉపసరణ

Perihelion - పరిహేళి

Perigee - పరిజ్యా

Period - ఆవృత్తి

Period-luminosity curve - ఆవర్తన దీప్తివక్రము

Periodic co-efficient - ఆవర్తన గుణకము

Periodic comet - ఆవర్తన ధూమకేతువు

Periodic function - ఆవర్తన ఫలములు

Periodic time - ఆవర్తన కాలము

Permutations - ప్రస్తారములు

Permutation groups - క్రమచయ కూర్పులు, ప్రస్తారపు కూర్పులు

Prepetual day - నిరంతర దినము

Prepetual night - నిరంతర రాత్రి

Prespective drawing - యథాదర్శన జ్యామితి

Preturbation - పరిక్షోభము

Phases - కళలు

Phenomena - దృశ్య సంఘటన

Philosophy of organism - అవయవి దర్శనము

Photographic magnitude - ఛాయాచిత్ర మహత్వములు
Photo sphere - కాంతిమండలము
Physical double - భౌతిక యుగళములు
Physics - భౌతికశాస్త్రము
Pisces - మీన
Piscium - రేవతి
Place value - స్థానమూల్యము
Plane - తలము
Plane geometry - సమతల జ్యామితి
Plane ornamental groups - తలములోని అలంకార కూర్పులు
Plane trigonometry - సమతల త్రికోణమితి
Planet - గ్రహము
Planetary - గ్రహకక్ష్య
Planing - యోజన
Pleides - కృత్తిక
Pluto - ప్లూటో, యముడు
Point - బిందువు
Point co-ordinates - బిందు నిరూపకములు
Point line configurations - బిందురేఖా విన్యాసములు
Point of contact - స్పర్శబిందువు
Point of incidence - ఆపాతబిందువు
Point of intersection - సంపాతబిందువు, ఛేదకబిందువు, ఖండన బిందువు
Polar axis - ధ్రువాక్షము
Polar caps - ధ్రువము కూటములు
Polar co-ordinates - ధ్రువీయ నిరూపకములు
Polar reciprocal - ధ్రువీయ వ్యుత్క్రమము
Polar surface - ధ్రువతలము
Pole - ధ్రువము
Pole of ecliptic - కదంబము, ధ్రువకదంబము
Pole star - ధ్రువ నక్షత్రము
Pollux - పునర్వసు
Polygon - బహుభుజి
Polyhedron - బహుతలకము
Polynomials - బహుపదములు
Population - లోకము
Position vector - స్థల సదిశరాశి
Positive - ధన
Positive electric charges - ధన విద్యుదావేశములు
Positive integers - ధన పూర్ణాంకములు, ధనపూర్ణ సంఖ్యలు
Positive fractions - ధనభిన్నములు, ధన భిన్నాంకములు
Positive roots - ధనమూలములు
Postulates - స్వీకృత తత్త్వములు
Potential - శక్మ (ము)
Potential energy - శక్మశక్తి, స్థానశక్తి
Potential flow - శక్మప్రవాహము
Potential theory - శక్మవాదము
Power - ఘాతము
Precession - విషుచలనము
Pressure - ప్రేషము
Prime number - ప్రధాన సంఖ్య
Principle of least action - ప్రధాన అభిలంబరేఖ
Prism - ప్రిజమ్
Probability - సంభవనీయత, సంభావ్యత
Probability density - సంభావ్యతా సాంద్రత
Probability distribution - సంభావ్యతా విభజనము
Probability theory - సంభవనీయతావాదము, సంభావ్యతావాదము
Probit analysis - ప్రోబిట్ విశ్లేషణ
Product - గుణకార లబ్దము
Progressions - శ్రేఢులు
Projection - విక్షేపము
Projective configurations - విక్షేప విన్యాసములు
Projective co-ordinates - విక్షేప నిరూపకములు

Projective geometry - విక్షేపక జ్యామితి
Projective transformations - విక్షేపక మార్పులు
Prominences - జ్వాలలు
Proof - ఉపపత్తి
Propeller - నోదకము
Proper fraction - క్రమభిన్నము, యుక్తభిన్నము
Proportion - అనుపాతము
Proposition - ప్రమేయము
Pure matematics - శుద్ధ గణితము
Pyramid - పిరమిడ్
Pyramidal numbers - గోపురపు సంఖ్యలు

Q

Quadrangle - చతుష్కోణము
Quadrant - పాదము, చతుర్థము
Quadratic equations -
రెండవ తరగతి సమీకరణములు, వర్గ సమీకరణములు
Quadrilateral - చతుర్భుజము
Qualitative - గుణాత్మక
Quantitative - పరిమాణాత్మక
Quantum thoery - క్వాంటం సిద్ధాంతము
Quaternions - చతుష్కములు, చతుష్క సంఖ్యలు
Quotations from mathematicians -
గణితవేత్తల దివ్య వచనములు
Quotient - భాగఫలము

R

Radian - రేడియన్
Radiant - వికిరణ బిందువు
Radiation - వికిరణము
Radical axis - మూలాక్షము
Radioactive elements - రశ్మ్యుద్గారక మూల ద్రవ్యములు
Radio astronomy - రేడియో ఖగోళ శాస్త్రము
Radio star - రేడియోతార
Radius - వ్యాసార్థము
Radius of curvature - వక్రతా వ్యాసార్థము
Radius of torsion - విమోచన వ్యాసార్థము
Radius of vector - రేడియస్ వెక్టార్, శ్రుతి
Radio-metric - వికిరణమాపక
Radix - రేడిక్స్, మూలాంకము, మూలసంఖ్య
Random - యాదృచ్ఛిక
Randomization - యాదృచ్ఛికీకరణము
Randomized blocks - యాదృచ్ఛికీకృత ఖండములు
Random numbers - యాదృచ్ఛిక సంఖ్యలు
Random residue - యాదృచ్ఛికావశేషము
Random samples - యాదృచ్ఛిక ప్రతిరూపములు
Random sampling numbers-
యాదృచ్ఛిక ప్రతిరూప సంఖ్యలు
Random variable - యాదృచ్ఛిక చలరాశి
Ratio - నిష్పత్తి
Rational - అకరణీయ
Rational numbers - అకరణీయ సంఖ్యలు
Reaction - ప్రతిక్రియ
Real numbers - వాస్తవ సంఖ్యలు
Reciprocal - వ్యుత్క్రమము
Reciprocal numbers - వ్యుత్క్రమ సంఖ్యలు
Reciprocation - పరస్పరత
Rectangle - దీర్ఘచతురస్రము
Rectangular - లంబాక్ష, ఆయతాక్ష
Rectangular co-ordinance - లంబాక్ష నిరూపకములు
Rectangular hyperbols - ఆయత, అతిపరావ, లంబ
అతిపరావ
Reductio ad absurdum - అనిష్టాపత్తి
Reflecting telescope - పరావర్తన దూరదర్శిని
Reflection - పరావర్తనము, ప్రతిబింబము

Reflex angle - పరావృత కోణము
Refracting telescope - వక్రీభవన దూరదర్శిని
Refraction - వక్రీభవనము, భుగ్నత
Regular hexagon - క్రమషడ్భుజి
Regular polygon - క్రమబహుభుజి
Regular polyhedron - క్రమ బహుతలకము
Regulus - రెగ్యులస్
Regulus - మఘ
Relative - సాపేక్ష
Relative acceleration - సాపేక్ష త్వరణము
Relative frequency - సాపేక్ష పౌనఃపున్యము
Relative velocity - సాపేక్ష వేగము
Relative theory - సాపేక్షతావాదము
Raplication - పునరావృత్తి
Repulsion - అపకర్షణ
Residue - అవశేషము
Retrograde motion - వక్రగతి
Reversing layer - ప్రత్యావర్తనస్తరము
Revolution - భ్రమణము, భగణము
Rhombus - రాంబస్
Right angle - లంబకోణము, సమకోణము.
Right ascension - విషువాంశ
Right circular cylinder - లంబవృత్త స్థూపము
Right Prism - లంబ ప్రిజమ్
Rigid body - దృఢవస్తువు
Rigid dynamics - దృఢవస్తు గతిశాస్త్రము
Rigour - నిష్ఠురత
Ring - కంకణము, మండలము
Risks - హానిభయములు
Roots - మూలములు
Rotation - పరిభ్రమణము
Row - వరుస
Rule - సూత్రము, నియమము
Rule of three - త్రైరాశికము

S

Sagittari - పూర్వాషాఢ
Sagittari - ఉత్తరాషాఢ
Sagittarius - ధనుస్సు
Samples - ప్రతిరూపములు
Saros - గ్రహణయుగము
Satellite - ఉపగ్రహము
Saturn - శని
Saturn's rings - శనికంకణములు
Scalar - స్కేలార్, అదిశరాశి
Scalar field - అదిశరాశి క్షేత్రము
Scales of notation - సంకేతిక మానములు, సంఖ్యా మాపములు
Science of perspective drawing - యథాదర్శన శాస్త్రము
Scorpio - వృశ్చిక
Scorpionis - అనురాధ
Scorpionis - జ్యేష్ఠ
Scorpionis - మూల 34, 35
Screw motion - మరచలనము
Seasons - ఋతువులు
Seasonal component - ఋతుభాగము
Secant - ఛేదకము
Secular variation - కాలాంతర చలనము
Segment - ఖండము
Self consistant - ఆత్మావిరుద్ధము
Self conjugate - స్వసంయుగ్మ
Self fertilised - స్వపరాగసిక్త
Semi circle - అర్ధవృత్తము
Semilatus rectum - ఉత్థానార్ధము

Sequence - వరుస
Squential sampling - క్రమాత్మక ప్రతిరూపకరణము
Series - పరంపర
Set - సమితి
Set theory - సమితివాదము
Sextant - షష్ఠకము
Shells - గోళకములు
Shock waves - అఘాత తరంగములు
Shooting stars - శర నక్షత్రములు
Short axis - హ్రస్వాక్షము
Siderial clock - నక్షత్ర గడియారము
Siderial day - నక్షత్ర దినము
Siderial parallax - నక్షత్ర అతివర్తనము
Siderial period - నక్షత్ర భ్రమణకాలము
Siderial spectrum - నక్షత్ర వర్ణమాల
Siderial time - నక్షత్ర కాలము
Similar triangles - సరూప త్రిభుజములు
Similarity - సారూప్యము
Simple continued fractions - సరళ శృంఖలిత భిన్నము
Simple fraction - సరళ భిన్నము, సరళ భిన్నాంకము
Simple connected - సరళ సంబద్ధ
Simultaneous - సమకాలీన
Simultaneous equations - సమకాలీన సమీకరణములు
Sine - జీవ జ్యా
Sine tables - జీవకోష్టకములు, జీవపట్టికలు
Single valued functions - ఏకమూల్య ఫలములు
Singular point - అసాధారణ బిందువు
Singular solution - అసాధారణ సాధనము
Sirius - సిరియస్, మృగవ్యాధుడు
Slope - నిమ్నము
Small circle - అల్పవృత్తము, లఘువృత్తము
Small samples - అల్ప ప్రతిరూపములు

Solar - సౌర
Solar day - సౌరదినము
Solar eclipse - సూర్యగ్రహణము
Solar parallax - సౌరాతివర్తనము
Solar prominences - సౌరజ్వాలలు
Solar radiation - సూర్య వికిరణము
Solar spectrum - సూర్యవర్ణమాల
Solar system - సూర్యకుటుంబము
Solar telescope - సౌర దూరదర్శిని
Solar time - సౌరకాలము
Solid - ఘనరూపము
Solid sphere - ఘనగోళము
Solstice - అయనము
Solstitical point - అయన బిందువు
Solution - సాధనము
Sound - ధ్వని
Southern cross - విశ్వామిత్రుడు
South polar distance - దక్షిణ ధ్రువాంతరము
South pole - దక్షిణ ధ్రువము
Slope - నిమ్నము
Space - ఆకాశము
Space curve - ఘనవక్రము
Space satellites - కృత్రిమ ఉపగ్రహములు
Special theory of relativity - ప్రత్యేక సాపేక్షతావాదము
Spectral analysis - వర్ణమాలా విశ్లేషణ
Spectrograph - వర్ణమాలా చిత్రము
Spectro - heliograph - వర్ణమాలా హేళిలేఖిని
Spectroscope - వర్ణమాలా దర్శిని
Spectroscopic parallax - వర్ణమాలాలంబనము
Spectrum - వర్ణమాల
Speed - ద్రుతి
Sphere - గోళము

Sphere - geometry - గోళీయ జ్యామితి
Spherical - గోళము
Spherical co-ordinates - గోళీయ నిరూపకములు
Spherical curve - గోళీయ వక్రము
Spherical harmonic functions - గోళీయ హరాత్మక ఫలములు
Spherical surface - గోళతలము
Spherical triangle - గోళీయ త్రిభుజము
Spherical trignometry - గోళీయ త్రికోణమితి
Spheroid - గోళాభము
Spica - చిత్ర
Spinning top - బొంగరము
Spiral - సర్పిలము
Spiral line - సర్పిల రేఖ
Spiral nubula - సర్పిల నీహారిక
Spots - కళంకలములు, మచ్చలు
Square - చతురస్రము, వర్గము
Square root - వర్గమూలము
Squaring of a circle - వృత్తచతురస్రీకరణము
Stable equilibrium - స్థిర సమతాస్థితి, స్థిర తోలనస్థితి
Standard deviation - క్రమవిచలనము
Standard meridian - ప్రమాణ మధ్యాహ్న రేఖ
Standard time - ప్రమాణ కాలము
Star - నక్షత్రము, తార
Star clusters - తారాగుచ్ఛములు
Star polyhedra - నక్షత్ర బహుతలకములు
Statics - స్థితిశాస్త్రము
Stationary - స్థావర
Statistical mechanics - సాంఖ్యక యాంత్రిక శాస్త్రము
Statistical quality control - సాంఖ్యక గుణనియంత్రణ
Statistics - సాంఖ్యకశాస్త్రము
Stellar - నాక్షత్ర
Stellar astronomy - నక్షత్ర ఖగోళశాస్త్రము
Stellar displacement - నక్షత్ర స్థానాంతరత
Stereographic projection - ఘనచిత్రీయ నిక్షేపము
Stochastic process - యాదృచ్ఛిక ప్రక్రియ
Stochastic variable - స్టాకేస్టిక్ చలరాశి
Straight angle - ఋజుకోణము
Straight line - ఋజురేఖ
Stream function - ప్రవాహ ఫలము
Sub group - ఉపకూర్పు, ఉపపుంజరము
Sub lunar point - చంద్రోపబిందువు
Sub normal - ఉప అభిలంబము
Subset - ఉపసమితి
Sub tangent - ఉపస్పర్శరేఖ
Substraction - వ్యవకలనము
Sum - సంకలనరాశి
Summability - సంకలనీయత
Summer solstice - కటకాయనము
Sun - సూర్యుడు
Sundial - సూర్యఘటి
Sun spots - సూర్యకళంకములు, రవికంకళంకములు
Super giants - అతి బృహత్తులు
Superior conjunction - ఉత్తమ యోగము
Supemova - సూపర్నోవా, అతినవతార
Supplementary angles - సంపూరక కోణములు
Symbol - సంకేతము
Symmedian point - సంమధ్యబిందువు
Symmetry - సౌష్ఠవము
Synodic period - గ్రహయుతి, శుక్రయుగము
Synodic time - పారిషద కాలము
Synthetic - సంయోజిత
Synthetic propellents - సంయోజితనోదకద్రవ్యములు

T

Table - కోష్టకము, పట్టిక
Tabulation - కోష్టరచన
Tangent - స్పర్శజీవ, స్పర్శజ్యా, స్పర్శరేఖ
Tangent plane - స్పర్శతలము
Tangential - స్పర్శీయ
Tangential co-ordinates - స్పర్శీయ నిరూపకములు
Tangential equation - స్పర్శీయ సమీకరణములు
Taylor series - టేలర్ పరంపర
Telescope - దూరదర్శిని
Temperature - తాపక్రమము
Tensor - టెన్సార్
Tensor calculus - టెన్సార్ కలనము
Tensor multiplication - టెన్సార్ గుణకారము
Terminal ballistics - అంతిమ అస్త్ర ప్రయోగము
Terrestrial - పావన
Terrestrial day - పావన దినము
Terrestrial phenomena - భౌమ్యసంభవములు
Terrestrial time - పావన కాలము
Terrestrial year - పావన సంవత్సరము
Tetrahedron - చతుస్తలకము
Theodolite - తియోడలైట్
Theory of attributes - లక్షణవాదము
Theory of equations - సమీకరణవాదము
Theory of functions of complex variable - సంకీర్ణ చలనరాశి ఫలవాదము
Theory of groups - కూర్పు (పుంజ) వాదము
Theory of lattice points - జాలబిందువాదము
Theory of numbers - సంఖ్యావాదము
Theory of summability - సంకలనీయతా సిద్ధాంతము
Theory of wave propagation - తరంగ ప్రాపణ సిద్ధాంతము
Theta functions - తీటా ఫలము
Three dimensional - త్రిపరిమాణిక, త్రివిమా
Three dimensional curve - త్రిపరిమాణిక వక్రము
Three dimensional geometry - విమాత్రాయ జ్యామితి
Three dimensional space - త్రిపరిమాణిక ఆకాశము
Third order contact - మూడవ తరగతి సంస్పర్శ
Tidal fiction - స్రోతో ఘర్షణ
Tidal waves - స్రోత్రో తరంగము
Tides - స్రోతస్సుల
Time - కాలము
Time reversal test - కాలపరివర్తన పరీక్ష
Time series - కాలశ్రేణి
Topological transformations - టోపాలజీ మార్పులు
Topology - టోపాలజీ, స్థలశాస్త్రము
Topology of point sets - బిందు సమూహముల టోపాలజీ
Torsion - విమోటనము
Torus - లంగరు వలయము
Total eclipse - పూర్ణ గ్రహణము
Tractrix - ట్రాక్ట్రిక్స్
Trajectory - విక్షేప పథము
Transfinite arithmetic - క్రాంతపరిమిత అంకగణితము
Transfinite numbers - క్రాంత పరిమిత సంఖ్యలు
Transit instrument - క్రాంతి యంత్రము
Transit of venus - శుక్రప్రతరణము
Translation - స్థానాంతరత
Transparency - పారదర్శకత
Transverse - తిర్యక్
Transverse axis - తిర్యక్ అక్షము
Trapezium - ట్రెపీజియమ్
Trend - ఉన్ముకత
Triangle - త్రిభుజము
Triangular inequalities - త్రిభుజ హెచ్చుతగ్గులు

Triangular numbers - త్రిభుజ సంఖ్యలు

Triangular prism - త్రిభుజ ప్రిజమ్

Trigonometry - త్రికోణమితి

Trigonometric functions - త్రికోణమితి ఫలములు

Trigonometric ratios - త్రికోణమితీయ నిష్పత్తులు

Trilinear - త్రిరేఖీయ

Trilinear co-ordinates - త్రిరేఖీయ నిరూపకములు

Triple stars - త్రికతారలు

Tropical - సాయన

Tropical day - సాయన దినము

Tropical year - సాయన సంవత్సరము

True zenith distance - నిజ నతకోణము

Twilight - సంధ్య

U

Unified field theory - ఏకీకృత క్షేత్రవాదము

Uniform - ఏకరూప

Uniform angular velocity - ఏకరూప కోణీయ వేగము

Uniform convergence - ఏకరూప వికరణ

Uniform functions - ఏకరూప ఫలములు

Uniform velocity - ఏకరూప వేగము

Unit - ఏకాంకము, యూనిట్, రూపము

Unit acceleration - యూనిట్ త్వరణము

Unit cell - యూనిట్ సెల్

Unit force - యూనిట్ బలము

Universal law of gravitation - విశ్వ గురుత్వ సిద్ధాంతము

Universe - విశ్వము

Unstable equilibrium - అస్థిర సమతాస్థితి

Upper transit - ఉత్తమ ప్రతరణము

Uranus - ఇంద్రుడు

Ursa major - సప్తర్షి

Ursa minior - అల్ప సప్తర్షి

V

Variable - చలనరాశి

Variable - చలతారలు

Variable stars - విచలనము

Variance - విచలనము

Vector - వెక్టర్, సదిశరాశి

Vector space - సదిశరాశి ఆకాశము

Vega - అభిజిత్తు

Velocity - వేగము

Velocity potential - వేగశక్మము

Venus - శుక్రుడు

Vernal equinox - వసంత విషువు, వసంత సంపాతము

Vertical - ఉదగ్ర

Vertical angle - శీర్షకోణము

Vertical plane - ఉదగ్రతలము

Vertex - శిఖరము, శీర్షము

Vertex of angle - కోణ శీర్షము

Vertex of cone - శంఖు శీర్షము

Vibration - కంపనము

Vibration figure - కంపన చిత్రము

Visual magnitude - దృశ్య పరిమాణము

Vital statistics - జీవసాంఖ్యకము

Volume - ఘనపరిమాణము

W

War head - ఆయుధ శీర్షము

Wav϶ length - తరంగదైర్ఘ్యము

Wave theory of light - కాంతి తరంగ వాదము

Weighed multiples - ధారాంకిత గుణకములు

Weighed ratio - భారవర్ధిత నిష్పత్తి

Weight - బరువు

Window readers - గవాక్ష వాచకములు

Winter solstice - మకరాయనము

With respect to x - అపేక్షయా

Work - పని

Z

Zenith - మస్తకము

Zenith - నతాంశ, మస్తకాంశ

Zero - శూన్యము, శూన్యాంకము

Zets functions - జీటా ఫలములు

Zodiac - రాశిచక్రము

Zodiacal belt - శింశుమార చక్రము

Zone - మండలము

11.2 Telugu to English

అక్షవిచలనము - Nutation

అక్షస్పందనము - Nutation

అక్షాంశము, అక్షాంశ లేఖ - Lattitude

అగణ్య అనంత - Non-enumerably infinite

అగస్త్యుడు - Canopus

అగ్నిగోళము - Fire ball

అగ్రము - Amplitude

అచలరాశి - Invariant

అజిమత్ - Azimuth

అణుచలన సిద్ధాంతము - Kinetic theory

అతినవతార - Super nova

అతినీలలోహిత వికిరణము - Ultra-violet radiation

అతిపరాస - Hyperbola

అతిపరాస ఫలములు - Hyperbolic functions

అతిపరాసీయ కక్ష్య - Hyperbolic orbit

అతిబృహత్తులు - Super giants

అతివర్తనము - Parallax

అతి విభాజ్య సంఖ్యలు - Highly composite numbers

అధికరాశి - Scalar

అధికరాశి క్షేత్రము - Scalar field

అధమ అవధి - Lower limit

అధమ ప్రతరణము - Lower transit

అధమ యోగము - Interior conjunction

అధర దిక్కు - Vertically lower

అధికీకరణ సామర్థ్యము - Magnifying power

అద్భుత గణకులు - Mathematical prodigies

అనంత అవధి - Infinite limit

అనంత ఋజురేఖ - Infinite straight line

అనంత గుణోత్తర శ్రేణి - Infinite geometric progression

అనంత దూరరేఖ - Line at infinity

అనంతపద పరంపర సంకలనము - Summation of infinite number of terms

అనంత పరంపర - Infinite series

అనంత పరంపర దోషము - Infinite regression

అనంత పరంపరల ఉపసరణత - Convergence of infinite series

అనంత పారిమాణిక క్షేత్రము - Infinite dimensional space

అనంత బిందువులు - Infinite points

అనంతమునందున్న ఋజురేఖ - Straight line at infinity

అనంతములో ఉండు వర్తుల బిందువులు - Circular points at infinity

అనంతరేఖ - Infinite line

అనంత వర్తుల బిందువులు - Infinite circular points

అనంత సంఖ్యలు - Infinite numbers

అనిశ్చిత చయనీకరణము - Indefinite integration

అనిశ్చిత ప్రథమ తరగతి సమీకరణము - Indeterminate equation of the first degree

అనిష్టాపత్తి - Reduction and absurdum

అనుచర తార - Companion star

అనుపాతము - Proportion

అనుపాత సంబంధము - Proportionality

అనుభవ గర్భిత - Empirical

అనురూప కోణములు - Corresponding angles

అనురూపత - Correspondence

అనులోమ అనుపాతము - Direct proportion

అనుషక్తములు - Concurrents

అనురాధ - Scorpionis
అపకర్షణ -, Repulsion
అపక్రమ భిన్నము - Improper fraction
అపజ్యా - Apogee
అపవర్తనాంశము - Greater common measure
అపసరణత - Divergence
అపసరణ గుణకార పరంపర - Divergent multiple series
అపసరణ పరంపర - Divergent series
అపసవ్య - Anti-clockwise
అపహేళి - Aphelion
అపేక్షయా - With respect to
అబీజీయ - Non-algebraic
అబీజీయ సంఖ్యలు - Non-algebraic numbers
అబేకస్ - Abacus
అభిజిత్తు - Vega
అభిలంబ ఛేదనము - Normal section
అభిలంబ రేఖ - Normal
అభ్యుప గమనము - Approach
అమూర్త - Absolute
అమూర్తశక్మము - Absolute potential
అయన బిందువు - Solstitial point
అయనావరణము - Ionosphere
అయనీకరణము - Ionization
అయస్కాంత క్షేత్రము - Magnetic field
అయస్కాంత క్షోభములు - Magnetic perturbations
అయస్కాంత ధ్రువములు - Magnetic poles
అయస్కాంత స్థితి - Magnetic conditions
అయుక్త భిన్నము - Improper traction
అర్థనము - Demand
అర్థన విశ్లేషణ - Demand analysis
అర్థమితిశాస్త్రము - Econometrics
అర్థశాస్త్రము - Economics
అర్థ ఆవర్తన - Quasi periodic
అర్థ వృత్తము - Semi circle
అల్పకోణ త్రిభుజము - Acute angled triangle
అల్పకోణము - Acute angle
అల్ప ప్రతిరూపములు - Small samples
అల్పవృత్తము - Small circle
అల్ప సప్తర్షులు - Ursa-minor
అవధి - Limit
అవధి బిందువు - Limiting point
అవధి భావము - Conception of limit
అవధి మూల్యము, అవధి విలువ - Limit value
అవయవ దర్శనము - Philosophy of organism
అవలోకనాత్మక - Observation
అవలోకనాత్మక ఖగోళశాస్త్రము - Observational astronomy
అవశేషము - Residue
అవిచ్ఛిన్నత - Continuity
అవిచ్ఛిన్న ఫలములు - Continuous functions
అవిచ్ఛిన్న భిన్నములు - Continued fractions
అవిచ్ఛిన్న మార్పుల జ్యామితి - Geometry of continuous transformations
అవిదిత ఫలము - Unknown function
అవినాభావ వాదము - Theory of Null hypothesis
అవేక్షణ - Observation
అవ్యక్త గణితము - Algebra
అవ్యక్తఫల అంతరీకరణము - Implicit differentiation
అవ్యక్త ఫలములు - Implicit functions
అశ్వశిర నీహారిక - Horse head nebula
అశ్విని - Arietis
అసంపతనీయ సాధనము - Asymptotic solution
అసంపాతములు - Asymptotes
అసంపాతీయ రేఖ - Asymptotic line
అసాధారణ బిందువులు - Singular solution

అసాధారణ సాధనము - Ballistics

అస్థిర సమతాస్థితి - Unstable equilibrium

అష్టతలకము - Octahedron

ఆ

ఆంశిక - Partial

ఆంశిక అంతరీకరణ సమీకరణము - Partial differential equation

ఆంశిక అయునీకరణము - Partial integration

ఆంశిక వ్యుత్పన్నము - Partial derivative

ఆకర్షణ - Attraction

ఆకాశకములు - Aerials

ఆకాశగంగ - Milkyway

ఆకాశము - Space

ఆకృతి గుణకము - From co-efficient

ఆకృతి ఫలము - Form function

ఆఘాత తరంగములు - Shock waves

ఆచ్ఛాదిత చలతారలు - Eclipsing variables

ఆత్మావిరుద్ధము - Self consistent

ఆధారతత్వములు - Axioms

ఆధారము - Base

ఆధికారిక సాంఖ్యికీయ ప్రమరణ -Official statistics

ఆధీనతా గుణకము - Contingency co-efficient

ఆధునిక గణితము - Modern Mathematics

ఆపాత బిందువు - Point of incidence

ఆపాతము - Incidence

ఆయన అతిపరావ - Rectangular hyperbola

ఆయతాక్షము - Rectangular axis

ఆయుధ శీర్షము - War head

ఆయుర్దాయ పట్టికలు - Mortality tables

ఆర్ద్ర - Orionis

ఆవర్తన కాలము - Periodic time

ఆవర్తన గుణకము - Periodic co-efficient

ఆవర్తన దీప్తి - Period luminosity

ఆవర్తన దీప్తి వక్రము - Period luminosity curve

ఆవర్తన ధూమకేతువు - Periodical comet

ఆవర్తన ఫలములు - Periodic functions

ఆవృత్తి - Period

ఆశ్లేష - Hydra, caneri 1, 2 - 49, 50

ఆసన్న - Approximate

ఆసన్న ఫలితము - Approximate result

ఆసన్న మూల్యము, ఆసన్న విలువ - Approximate value

ఇ

ఇంద్రుడు - Uranus

ఇంధనము - Fuel

ఈ

ఈజిప్టు దేశపు గణితము - Egyptian mathematics

ఉ

ఉచిత ప్రతిరూపములు - Proper samples

ఉచ్ఛభాషులు - Loud speakers

ఉచ్ఛాలకము - Lever

ఉత్కేంద్ర కక్ష్య - Eccentric orbit

ఉత్కేంద్రత - Eccentricity

ఉత్కేంద్ర వృత్తము - Eccentric circle

ఉత్తమ ప్రతరణము - Up␣er transit

ఉత్తమ యోగము - Superior conjunction

ఉత్తర - Leonis

ఉత్తర ధ్రువము - North pole

ఉత్తర ధ్రువాంతరము - North polar distance

ఉత్తర ఫల్గుణి - Denebola

ఉత్తర శీతమండలము - North frizid zone

ఉత్తర సమశీతోష్ణ మండలము - North temperate zone

ఉత్తరాభాద్ర - Pegasi

ఉత్తరాషాఢ - Sagittari
ఉత్థానము - Latus rectum
ఉత్థానార్ధము - Semi latus rectum
ఉత్పాదకములు - Generations
ఉదగ్ర - Vertical
ఉదగ్రతలము - Vertical plane
ఉన్నతకోణము - Angle of elevation
ఉన్నతి - Altitude
ఉన్ముఖత - Trend
ఉప లంబము - Sub-normal
ఉపకల్పనలు - Assumptions
ఉపకూర్పు - Sub-group
ఉపగ్రహము - Satellite
ఉపపత్తి - Proof
ఉపపుంజము - Sub-group
ఉపరితలీయ సిద్ధాంతములు - Surface theories
ఉపసమితి - Sub-set
ఉపసరణ గుణకార పరంపర - Convergent multiple series
ఉపసరణత - Convergence
ఉపసరణ పరంపర - Convergent series
ఉపసరణ వరుస - Bio convergent sequence
ఉప స్పర్శరేఖ - Sub-tangent
ఉపాంత ఉపసరణ - Penultimate convergent
ఉభయ అభిలంబము - Common normal
ఉర్సామేజోరిస్ - Ursa majores
ఉల్క - Meteror
ఉల్కల కూటమి - Meteor swarm
ఉల్కాపాతము - Meteor shower
ఉల్కాపాత స్ఫోటనము - Meteor shower explosion
ఉల్కాపిండము - Aerolite, meteorite
ఉల్కాబిలములు - Meteor craters
ఉష్ణవాహకము - Conduction of heat

ఊ

ఊర్ధ్వకోణము - Angle of elevation
ఊహనకళ - Ars conjectandi

ఋ

ఋజుకోణము - Straight angle
ఋజుగతి - Straight motion
ఋజురేఖ - Straight line
ఋజురేఖా జ్యామితి - Line geometry
ఋజురేఖా ప్రావణ సిద్ధాంతము - Theory of linear propagation
ఋణ అకరణీయ సంఖ్యలు - Negative rational numbers
ఋణ పూర్ణాంకములు - Negative integers
ఋణ భిన్నాంకములు - Negative fractions
ఋణ మూలములు - Negative roots
ఋణసంఖ్య - Negative number
ఋతుభాగము - Seasonal component
ఋతువులు - Seasons

ఎ

ఎత్తు - Altitude
ఎలక్ట్రానిక్ గణితములు - Electronic calculators, Electronic computers
ఎలిప్సాయిడ్ - Ellipsoid

ఏ

ఏకనక్షత్రములు - Single stars
ఏకనాభికా శాంకవములు - Confocal conics
ఏకమూల్య ఫలములు - Single valued functions
ఏకరూప - Uniform, Isomorphic
ఏకరూప ఉపసరణత - Uniform convergence
ఏకరూప ఉపసరణ పరంపర - Uniform convergent
ఏకరూప కోణీయవేగము - Uniform angular velocity

ఏకరూప పరంపర - Uniform series

ఏకరూప ఫలము - Uniform function

ఏకరూప వేగము - Uniform velocity

ఏకరూప సమితులు - Uniform sets

ఏకరేఖీయ బిందువులు - Collinear points

ఏకలవ భిన్నాంకము - Unit numerator fraction

ఏకాంకము - Unit

ఏకాంతరకోణము - Alternate angle

ఏకాక్ష వృత్తములు - Co-axal circles

ఏకీకృత క్షేత్రవాదము - Unified field theory

ఏబెల్ కూర్పులు - Abeleian groups

ఒ

ఒకటికొకటి అనురూపత - One to one correspondence

క

కంకణ గ్రహణము - Annular eclipse

కంకణములు - Rings

కంపన చిత్రము - Vibration figure

కంపనము - Vibration

కక్ష (కక్ష్య) - Orbit

కటకము - Lence

కటకాయనము - Summer solstice

కణగతిశాస్త్రము - Dynamics of a particle

కణము - Particle

కణ శుద్ధ గతిశాస్త్రము - Kynamatics of a particle

కత్తిరించిన గోపురము - Frustum of a pyramid

కదంబము - Pole of ecliptic

కనిష్ఠ - Minimum

కనిష్ఠ క్రియాసూత్రము - Principle of least action

కనిష్ఠ వర్గ విధానము - Method of least squares

కనిష్ఠ సామాన్య గుణిజము (క.సా.గు.) - Lowest common multiple (LCM)

కరణీయ - Irrational

కరణీయ సంఖ్య - Irrational number

కరణీయ సంఖ్యలు అవధులుగా పొందుట - Irrational numbers as limits

కర్కా - Cancer

కర్ణవర్గ సిద్ధాంతము - Theorem of phythagores

కలనశాస్త్రము - Calculus

కళంకములు - Spots

కళలు - Phases

కాంగ్‌కాయిడ్ - Conchoid

కాంతి - Light

కాంతికిరణ వక్రీభవనము - Refraction of light rays

కాంతి తరంగవాదము - Wave theory of light

కాంతి మండలము - Photosphere

కాంతివత్సరము - Light year

కాంతి విద్యుత్ ఘటములు - Photo-electric cells

కాంతి విపథనము - Aberration of light

కాంప్లెక్స్ - Complex

కాటినెరీ - Catenary

కారణాంకము - Factor

కారణాంక విశ్లేషణ - Factor analysis

కారణాంక పరివర్తన పరీక్ష - Factor reversal test

కార్టీసియన్ గుణకార సమితి - Cartesian product

కార్టీసియన్ నిరూపకములు - Cartesian co-ordinates

కార్డియాయిడ్ - Cardioid

కార్యకర లక్షణము - Operating characteristic

కాలనిరూపకములు - Time co-ordinates

కాలపరివర్తన పరీక్ష - Time reversal test

కాలము - Time

కాలశ్రేణి - Time series

కాల సమీకరణము - Equation of time

కాలాంతర చలనము - Secular variation

కుంభ - Aquarius

కుజుడు - Mars

కూట చతురస్రములు - Magic squares

కూట నాణెము - Flase coin

కూటపాచికలు - Loaded dice

కూర్పులు - Groups

కూర్పు వాదము - Theory of groups

కృత్తిక - Aleyone, Pleides

కృత్రిమ ఉపగ్రహము -
Artificial satellite, Spare satellite

కృష్ణ నీహారికలు - Dark nebulae

కృష్ణరేఖా వర్ణమాల - Darkline spectrum

కేంద్రము - Centre

కేంద్ర విక్షేపము - Central projection

కేవల పరిమాణము - Absolute magnitude

కో జీవ - Cosine

కో జీవ పరంపరలు - Cosine series

కోటి - Ordinate

కోటి భేదకము - Co-secant

కోటిజీవ - Cosine

కోటిజీవ వృత్తము - Cosine circle

కోటి స్పర్శజీవ - Corangent

కోణము - Angle

కోణశీర్షము - Vertex of an angle

కోణీయ - Angular

కోణీయగతిభారము - Angular momentum

కోణీయ వేగము - Angular velocity

కోణీయవేగ సదిశరాశి - Vector of angular velocity

కో ఫాక్టర్ - Co-factor

కోమా - Coma

కోష్టకము - Table

కోష్టరచన - Tabulation

క్రమచయ కూర్పులు - Permutation groups

క్రమబాహుతలకము - Regular polyhedral

క్రమబహుభుజి - Regular polygon

క్రమభిన్నము - Proper fraction

క్రమవిచలనము - Standard deviation

క్రమషడ్భుజి - Regular hexagon

క్రమాత్మక ప్రతిరూపకరణము - Sequential sampling

క్రాంతపరిమిత అంకగణితము - Transfinite arithmetic

క్రాంత పరిమిత సంఖ్యలు - Transfinite numbers

క్రాంతి - Declination

క్రాంతి యంత్రము - Transit instrument

క్రాంతి వృత్తము - Ecliptic

క్రాస్ గుణకారము - Cross multiplication

క్రమోనామార్పులు - Birational transformations

క్రోనోమీటరు - Chronometer

క్వాంటం సిద్ధాంతము - Quantum theory

క్షితిజము - Horizon

క్షీరపథము - Milkyway

క్షీరపథ వికిరణము - Milkway radiation

క్షేత్రగణితము - Geometry

క్షేత్రశక్మ - Field potential

క్షోభము - Perturbation

ఖ

ఖండములు - Segments

ఖండగ్రహణము - Partial eclipse

ఖండ చయనీకరణము - Partial integration

ఖగోళ గతిశాస్త్రము - Astro - dynamics

ఖగోళ భౌతికశాస్త్రము - Astro - physics

ఖగోళము - Celestial sphere

ఖగోళ యాంత్రిక శాస్త్రము - Celestial mechanics

ఖగోళశాస్త్రము - Astronomy

ఖగోళ శాస్త్రీయ యూనిట్ - Astronomical unit

గ

గణిత అనుగమనము - Mathematical induction

గణిత అర్థశాస్త్రము - Mathematical Economics

గణిత కథలు - Mathematical anecdotes

గణిత చిక్కు ప్రశ్నలు - వినోదములు - Mathematical puzzles and recreations

గణితతర్కము - Mathematical logic

గణిత పఠకములు - Mathematical tables

గణిత భౌతికశాస్త్రము - Mathematical physics

గణితము - Mathematics

గణిత విశ్లేషణ - Mathematical analysis

గణితవేత్తల దివ్యవచనములు - Quotations from Mathematicians

గణిత్రములు - Calculators, computers

గణిత్ర యంత్రములు - Calculating machines

గతిభార బిభ్రమిష - Moment of a momentum

గతిభారము - Momentum

గతిశాస్త్రము - Dynamics

గతి - Motion

గమనము - Motion

గరిమనాభి - Centre of gravity

గరిష్ఠ - Maximum

గరిష్ఠ, కనిష్ఠ మూల్యములు - Maximum and minimum values

గరిష్ఠ ఘాతము - Maximum power

గరిష్ఠ సామాన్య భాజకము (గ.సా.భా.) - Greater common multiple (GCM)

గవాక్ష వాచకములు - Window readers

గామా ఫలములు - Gamma functions

గెలాక్సీ - Galaxy

గుణకము - co-efficient

గుణకాల పట్టికలు - Multiplication tables

గుణకారము - Multiplication

గుణకార లబ్ధము - Product

గుణకార లబ్ధము యొక్క వ్యుత్పన్నము - Derivative of a product

గుణాత్మక - Qualitative

గుణిజములు - Multiples

గుణోత్తర మధ్యమము - Geometrical mean

గుణోత్తర శ్రేణి - Geometrical progression

గుప్తాంక గణితము - Crypt arithmetic

గురుకోణ త్రిభుజము - Obtuse angled triangle

గురుకోణము - Obtuse angle

గురుచాపము - Major arc

గురువృత్తము - Great circle

గురుత్వకేంద్రము - Centre of gravity

గురుత్వ క్షేత్రము - Gravitational field

గురుత్వ తులాయంత్రము - Gravitational balance

గురుత్వ స్థిరరాశి - Gravitation invariant

గురుత్వ స్థిరాంకము - Gravitational constant

గురుత్వాకర్షణము - Gravitation

గురుత్వాకర్షణ క్షేత్రము - Gravitational field

గురుత్వాకర్షణ గుణకము - Gravitational co-efficient

గురుత్వాకర్షణ స్థిరాంకము - Gravitional constant

గురుడు - Jupiter

గైరోకంపాస్ - Gyrocompass

గైరోస్కోప్ - Gyroscope

గోపురపు సంఖ్యలు - Pyramidal numbers

గోళకములు - Shells

గోళఖండము - Segment of a sphere

గోళతలము - Spherical surface

గోళము - Sphere

గోళ సమీకరణము - Equation of a sphere

గోళీయ - Epherical

గోళీయ జ్యామితి - Ephrical geometry

గోళీయ త్రికోణమితి - Spherical trignometry

గోళీయ త్రిభుజములు - Spherical triangles
గోళీయ నక్షత్ర బృందము - Globular star cluster
గోళీయ నిరూపకములు - Spherical co-ordinates
గోళీయ వక్రము - Spherical curve
గోళీయ హరాత్మకము - Spherical harmonics
గోళీయ హరాత్మక ఫలములు - Spherical harmonic functions
గాస్ ప్రమాద నియమము - Gaussian law of errors
గ్రహకక్ష (కక్ష్య) - Gauss curvature
గ్రహకక్ష్యా వేగము - Planetary orbit
గ్రహణతారలు - Velocity in the orbit
గ్రహణ తారలు - Eclipsing stars
గ్రహణము - Eclipse
గ్రహణయుగము - Soras
గ్రహము - Planet
గ్రహముల ఋజుగతి - Direct motion of planets
గ్రహముల వక్రగతి - Retrograde motion of planets
గ్రహయుతి - Synodic period
గ్రహవిపథనము - Aberration of planet
గ్రహ సిద్ధాంతము - Capture hypothesis

ఘ

ఘటికాయంత్రము - Chronometer
ఘన అతిపరావ - Hyperboloid
ఘనకోణము - Solid-angle
ఘనచిత్రీయ విక్షేపము - Stereographic projection
ఘనపరావ - Paraboloid
ఘనము - Volume
ఘనము - Cube
ఘనమూలము - Cube root
ఘనరూపము - Solid
ఘనశాంకవము - Conicoid
ఘర్షణ - Friction
ఘర్షణ గుణకము - Co-efficient of friction
ఘర్షణ శంకు - Cone of friction
ఘాతపరంపర - Exponential series
ఘాత ఫలములు - Exponential functions
ఘాతము - Power
ఘాతాంకము - Exponent
ఘాతాంకీయ పరంపర - Exponential series

చ

చంద్రకళలు - Lunar phases
చంద్రగ్రహణము - Lunar eclipse
చంద్రుడు - Moon
చంద్రోప బిందువు - Sub-lunar point
చక్రభాగము - Cyclic component
చక్రీయ - Cyclic
చక్రీయ చతుర్భుజము - Cyclic quadrilateral
చతుఃపరిమాణిక - Four dimensional
చతురస్రము - Square
చతుర్భుజము - Quadrilateral
చతుస్తలకము - Tetrahedron
చతుష్కము - Quaternion
చతుష్క సంఖ్యలు - Quaternions
చతుష్కోణము - Quadrangle
చయన కలనము - Integral calculus
చయన సమీకరణములు - Integral equations
చయనీకరణము - Integration
చయనీకరణ గుణకము - Integral co-efficient
చయనీకరణ స్థిరాంకము - Integral constant
చయనీయ పరీక్ష - Integral test
చలకలనము - Calculus of variation
చలతారలు - Variable stars
చలన గుచ్ఛములు - Cluster variables
చలనము - Motion

చలన విశ్లేషణము - Analysis of variance
చలనశక్తి - Kintetic energy
చలరాశి - Variable
చాక్షుష శాస్త్రము - Optics
చాపము - Arc
చిత్ర - Spica
చిపిట - Flat
చిపిట ఆకాశములు - Flat spaces
ఛాయాచిత్ర మహత్వము - Photographic magnitude
ఛేదకము - Secant
ఛేద్యక జ్ఞానము - Knowledge of projection

జ

జడ విభ్రమిష - Moment of inertia
జనక చతురస్రము - Generating square
జనక రేఖ - Generating line
జాతి - Genus
జాలబిందువులు - Lattice points
జాలబిందువాదము - Theory of lattice points
జీటాఫలములు - Zeta functions
జీవ - Sine
జీవకోష్టకము - Sine table
జీవనమాపనము - Biometry
జీవపట్టికలు - Sine tables
జీవశాస్త్రము - Biology
జీవసాంఖ్యికము - Vital statistics
జీవితప్రత్యాశ (అక్షాంశ) - Expectation of life
జీవితభీమా - Life insurance
జీబ - Jiba
జ్యా - Chord, sine
జ్యామితి - Geometry
జ్యామితీయు - Geometrical
జ్యారేఖ - Chord line
జ్యేష్ఠ - Antares, Scropionis
జ్యోతి - Light
జ్యోతిర్వత్సరము - Light year
జ్యోతిర్వేగము - Velocity of light
జ్యోతిషము - Astroloy
జ్వాలలు - Prominences

ట

టెన్సార్ - Tensor
టెన్సార్ కలనము - Tensor calculus
టెన్సార్ గుణకము - Tensor co-efficient
టేలర్ పరంపర - Tayler series
టోపాలజీ - Topology
టోపాలజీ మార్పులు - Topological transformations
ట్రాక్టిక్స్ - Tractrix
ట్రెపీజియమ్ - Trapezium

డ

డయోఫాంటస్ సమీకరణములు - Diophantine equations
డెజార్గ్ విన్యాసము - Desargues arrangement

త

తరంగదైర్ఘ్యము - Wavelength
తరంగ ప్రాపణ సిద్ధాంతము - Theory of wave propagation
తరగతి - Degree
తలము - Plane
తాపక్రమము - Temperature
తాపసూచకము - Heat index
తారామండలములు - Constellations
తారీఖు రేఖ - Date line
తార్కిక కల్పన - Deductive system
తియోడలైట్ - Theodolite
తిర్యక్ - Oblique, Transverse

తిర్యక్ అడుములు - Oblique axes, Transverse axes
తిర్యక్ అఘాతములు - Transverse impulses
తిర్యక్ నిరూపకములు - Oblique co-ordinates
తిర్యక్ ప్రిజమ్ - Oblique prism
తిర్యక్ రేఖ - Oblique line
తిర్యక్ స్థూపము - Oblique cylinder
తీటాఫలములు - Theta functions
తుల - Libra
తులాదిబిందువు - First point of Libra
తులావిషువు - Autumnal equinox
తులాసంపాతము - Autumnal equinox
తుల్యకోణ సంయుగ్మములు - Isogonal conjugates
తృతీయ వ్యుత్పన్నము - Third derivative
తోలనము - Libration
త్రికతారలు - Triple stars
త్రికోణమితి - Trigonometry
త్రికోణమితి ఫలములు - Trigonometric fuctions
త్రికోణమితీయ నిష్పత్తి - Trigonometric ratio
త్రిపరిమాణిక - Three dimensional
త్రిపరిమాణిక ఆకాశము - Three dimensional space
త్రిపరిమాణిక జ్యామితి - Three dimensional geometry
త్రిపరిమాణిక చక్రము - Three dimensional curve
త్రిభుజ అంతర కేంద్రము - In-centre of triangle
త్రిభుజ గురుత్వ కేంద్రము - Centre of gravity of a triangle
త్రిభుజ పరికేంద్రము - Circumcentre of a triangle
త్రిభుజ ప్రిజమ్ - Triangular prism
త్రిభుజము - Triangle
త్రిభుజ లంబకేంద్రము - Ortho-centre of a triangle
త్రిభుజసంఖ్యలు - Triangular numbers
త్రిభుజ హెచ్చుతగ్గులు - Triangular inequalities
త్రిరేఖీయ - Trillinear
త్రిరేఖీయ నియామకములు - Trillinear co-ordinates
త్రిశంకువు - Centaurus
త్రైరాశికము - Rule of three
త్వరణము - Acceleration

ద

దక్షిణ ధ్రువము - South pole
దక్షిణ ధ్రువాంతరము - South polar distance
దత్తాంశములు - Data
దశాంశ బిందువు - Decimal point
దశాంశ భిన్నము - Decimel fraction
దశాంశములు - Decimals
దశాంశ సంకేతనము - Decimal notation
దిగంశ - Azimuth
దివ్య - Celestial
దివ్య అక్షాంశము - Celestial latitude
దివ్య నిరక్షరేఖ - Celestial equator
దీర్ఘచతురస్రము - Rectangle
దీర్ఘవృత్త ఫలములు - Elliptic functions
దీర్ఘవృత్తము - Ellipse
దీర్ఘావర్తన ధూమకేతువు - Long period comet
దూరదర్శిని - Telescope
దృఢవస్తువు - Rigid body
దృఢవస్తు గతిశాస్త్రము - Rigid dynamics
దృశ్యదీప్తి - Apparent brightness
దృశ్యపరిమాణము - Visual magnitude
దృశ్య యుగళములు - Optical doubles
దృశ్య సంఘటనలు - Phenomena
దేవయాని - Andromeda
దైనిక పరిభ్రమణము - Diurnal rotation
ద్యుజ్యావృత్తము - Declination circle
ద్రవగతిశాస్త్రము - Hydrodynamics
ద్రవము - Fluid
ద్రవయాంత్రిక శాస్త్రము - Fluid mechanics

ద్రవస్థితి శాస్త్రము - Hydrostatics
ద్రవేంధనములు - Liquid fuels
ద్రవ్యరాశి - Matter
ద్రుతి - Speed
ద్వికతారలు - Binaries
ద్వితీయ అంతర విధానము - Method of second difference
ద్విపద - Binominal
ద్విపద గుణకము - Binominal co-efficient
ద్విపద సమానము - Binominal expression
ద్విపద సిద్ధాంతము - Binominal theorem
ద్విపార్శ్వ అవిచ్ఛిన్నత - Bicontinuity
ద్విపార్శ్వ ఏకరూపత - Bi-uniformity
ద్విభాజకము - Bisector
ద్వైతస్వభావము - Duality
ధన - Positive
ధన అకరణీయ సంఖ్య - Positive rational number
ధన పూర్ణసంఖ్య, ధనపూర్ణాంకము - Positive integer
ధనభిన్నము, ధనభిన్నాంకము - Positive fraction
ధనమూలము - Positive root
ధనవిద్యుదావేశము - Positive electric charge
ధనసంఖ్య - Positive number
ధనిష్ఠ - Delphini
ధనుస్సు - Sagittarius
ధనుస్సు (చాపము) - Arc
ధురాధారములు - Bearings
ధూమకేతువు - Comet
ధ్రువ కదంబము - Pole of the ecliptic
ధ్రువకము - Celestial longitude
ధ్రువతలము - Polar surface
ధ్రువనక్షత్రము - Pole star
ధ్రువము - Pole
ధ్రువము కూటములు - Polar caps
ధ్రువాక్షము - Polar axis
ధ్రువీయ నిరూపకములు - Polar co-ordinates
ధ్రువీయ వ్యుత్క్రమము - Polar reciprocal
ధ్వని - Sound
ధ్వనిశాస్త్రము - Acoustics

న

నక్షత్ర అతివర్తనము - Siderial parallax
నక్షత్ర గడియారము - Siderial clock
నక్షత్ర ద్వికము - Geminorum
నక్షత్రము - Star
నక్షత్ర వర్ణమాల - Siderial spectrum
నక్షత్ర స్థానాంతరత - Stellar displacement
నక్షత్రాంతర ద్రవ్య సంచయము - Inter stellar matter
నతకాలము - Hour angle
నతాంశ - Zenith distance
నతి - Dep
నభోమూర్తులు - Celestial bodies, Celestial objects
నరదలు కోసిన తుపాకి - Rifled gun
నవతార - Nova
నవబిందువృత్తము - Nine point circle
నవీన జ్యామితి - Modern geometry
నవీనము - Nova
నాక్షత్రకాలము - Siderial time
నాక్షత్ర ఖగోళశాస్త్రము - Stellar astronomy
నాక్షత్రదినము - Siderial day
నాక్షత్ర భ్రమణకాలము - Siderial period
నాక్షత్ర యంత్రము - Astrolable
నాభి - Focus
నాభ్యంతరము - Focal length
నిజ నతకోణము - True zenith direction
నిమజ్జన - Dip
నిమజ్జనకోణము - Angle of dip

నిమ్నత - Inclination
నిమ్నము - Slope
నిరంతర దినము - Perpetual day
నిరంతర రాత్రి - Perpetual night
నిరక్షరేఖ - Equator
నిరుపాధిక - Abstract
నిరుపాధిక ఆకాశములు - Abstract spaces
నిరూపక జ్యామితి - Co-ordinate geometry
నిరూపక పరివర్తన - Change of co-ordinates
నిరూపకములు - Co-ordinates
నిరూపకాక్షములు - Co-ordinates axes; Axes of reference
నిర్దిష్ట కోటిజీవలు - Direction cosines
నిర్ధారకములు - Determinants
నిర్ధారక వ్యాకోచము - Expansion of determinants
నిర్వచనము - Definition
నిర్వికృతి - Invariance
నిశ్చిత చయనీకరణము - Definite integration
నిష్కాపము - Casting out
నిష్ఠురత - Rigour
నిష్పత్తి - Ratio
నీచోచ్చరేఖ - Apsidal line
నీహారికలు - Nebulae
నీహారికా మేఘము - Magellanic cloud
నీహారికావాదము - Nubular hypothesis
నెబ్యులాలు - Nebulae
నోదకము - Propeller
నోమోగ్రాములు - Nomograms
నోవా - Nova
న్యుబ్జ - Gibbous

ప

పంచాంగ కాలము - Ephemeris time
పంచాంగము - Calender
పంచాంగ రేఖ - Ephemeris meridian
పంజరవాదము - Matrix theory
పట్టకము - Prism
పతనకోణము - Angle of incidence
పదనిశ్చయము - Interpolation
పని - Work
పరంపర - Series
పరతంత్ర చలరాశి - Dependent variable
పరపరాగసిక్త - Cross fertilized
పరమతము - Absolute magnitude
పరమతాపక్రమము - Absolute temperature
పరమాణు ప్రతిరూపము - Atomic model
పరమాపక్రాంతి - Obliquity of the ecliptic
పరశకము - Parsec
పరశ్శోణ - Infra red
పరస్పర అనురూపత - Mutual correspondence
పరస్పరత - Reciprocation
పరస్పర బహిష్కాసంభవములు - Mutually exclusive events
పరస్పర లంబములు - Mutually perpendiculars
పరాలోక త్రిభుజములు - Triangles in perspective
పరావర్తనము - Reflection
పరావర్తన దూరదర్శిని - Reflecting telescope
పరావర్తన శక్తి - Albedo
పరావృతకోణము - Reflex angle
పరాస - Parabola
పరాసరూపము - Paraboloid
పరికర్మములు - Operators
పరికేంద్రము - Circum centre
పరిక్షోభము - Perturbation
పరిజ్యా - Perigee
పరిధి - Circumference

పరిమాణము - Evolution
పరిభ్రమణము - Rotation
పరిమాణము - Magnitude
పరిమాణాత్మక - Quantitative
పరిమితి జ్యామితి - Finite geometry
పరిమేయాకాశము - Metric space
పరివర్తన నియమము - Commutative law
పరివర్తన న్యాయము - Commutative law
పరివర్తన మండలము - Commutative ring
పరివృత్త చయనము - Contour integral
పరివృత్తము - Circum circle
పరిస్పర్శగోళము - Osculating sphere
పరిస్పర్శ తలము - Osculating plane
పరిహేళి - Perihelion
పరిహేళిగతి - Perihelion motion
పాతము - Node
పాతాలబిందువు - Nadir
పాదత్రిభుజము - Pedal triangle
పాదబిందువులు - Pedal points
పాదము - Quadrant
పాదరేఖ - Pedalline
పాదవక్రము - Pedal curve
పారదర్శకత - Transparency
పారిషద ఆవృత్తి - Synodic period
పారిషద కాలము - Synodic time
పార్థివ ప్రమాణము - Terrestrial standard
పాలపుంత - Milkyway
పాళీ - Loop
పాస్కల్ త్రిభుజము - Pascal triangle
పిడివాదము - Dogmatism
పిరమిడ్ - Pyramid
పుంజములు - Groups
పునరావృత్తి - Repilation
పునర్వసు - Geminorium, Castor, Pollux
పుబ్బ - Leonis 70, 71
పుష్యమి - Caneri
పూరక కోణములు - Complementary angles
పూరకములు - Compliments
పూర్ణగ్రహణము - Total eclipse
పూర్ణాంకములు - Integers
పూర్వనిర్దేశము - Forecast
పూర్వాభాద్ర - Pegasi
పూర్వాషాఢ - Sagittari
పెద్ద సంఖ్యల జడత్వము - Inertia of large numbers
పెరాబొలాయిడ్ - Paraboloid
పెల్లియన్ సమీకరణములు - Pellian equations
పౌనఃపున్యము - Frequency
పౌనఃపున్య విభజనము - Frequency division
ప్రకృతి నియమములు - Law of nature
ప్రకేవల - Absolute
ప్రకేవల ఉపసరణత - Absolute convergence
ప్రకేవల కాలము - Absolute time
ప్రకేవల వక్రములు - Absolute curves
ప్రకేవల విలువ - Absolute value
ప్రజ్వలక పదార్థము - Igniter
ప్రతికృతులు - Models
ప్రతిక్రియ - Reaction
ప్రతిబింబము - Reflection
ప్రతిరూపములు - Samples
ప్రతిరూప సంఖ్యలు - Random sampling numbers
ప్రతిసమానాంతర - Antiparallel
ప్రతిసామ్య - Antiparallel

ప్రత్యావర్తన స్తరము - Reversing layer
ప్రత్యేక సాపేక్షతావాదము - Special theory of relativity
ప్రథమవర్గ అంతరీకరణ రూపము - First quadratic differentia form
ప్రధాన అభిలంబరేఖ - Principal normal
ప్రధాన సంఖ్యలు - Prime numbers
ప్రమాణ కాలము - Standrad time
ప్రమాదము - Error
ప్రమేయము - Proposition
ప్రయోగము - Experiment
ప్రయోగరచన - Design of experiment
ప్రవాహఫలము - Stream function
ప్రవాహసాంద్రత - Flux density
ప్రస్తారములు - Permutations
ప్రాక్చక్రము - Epicycle
ప్రాచలకూర్పు - Parameter group
ప్రాచలము - Parameter
ప్రేషము - Pressure
ప్రోబిట్ ఎనాలిసిస్ - Probit analysis
ప్లూటో - Pluto
ఫర్మా సంఖ్యలు - Format numbers
ఫలకము - Lamina
ఫలకములు - Layers
ఫలముల అవిచ్ఛిన్నత - Continuity of functions
ఫలములు - Functions
ఫలవాదము - Function theory
ఫలిత త్వరణము - Resultant acceleration

బ

బరువు - Weight
బలక్షేత్రము - Field of force
బలబిభ్రమిష - Moment of force
బలము - Force
బలయూనిట్ - Unit force
బలశ్రుతి - Vector of force
బహిర్లతి - Involute
బహిర్వృత్తము - Outer circle
బహు ఆవర్తన ఫలములు - Multiperiod functions
బహుతలకము - Polyhedron
బహుపద అనిశ్చిత ప్రథమ తరగతి సమీకరణములు - Indeterminate equations of the first degree in many unknowns
బహుపదములు - Polynominals
బహుపద సమాసములు - Multinominal expressions
బహుపద సిద్ధాంతము - Multinominal theorem
బహుభుజి - Polygon
బహురాశి - Multivariable
బహుళతారలు - Multiple stars
బాంబు అస్త్ర ప్రయోగ విద్య - Bomb ballistics
బాణాగ్రలిపి - Cuneiform script
బాహ్య ఏకాంతర కోణము - Alternate exterior angle
బాహ్యకేంద్రము - Ex-centre
బాహ్యకోణము - Exterior angle
బాహ్య గ్రహములు - Outer planets
బిందుపథము - Locus
బిందువు - Point
బిందు సమూహముల టోపాలజీ - Topoloy of point sets
బీజగణితము - Algebra
బీజీయ ఫలములు - Algebraic functions
బుధుడు - Mercury
బృహత్తులు - Giants
బేసి సంఖ్యలు - Odd numbers
బౌద్ధిక గుణ్యము - Intelligent quotient
బొంగరము - Spinning top
భగణము - Revolution
భరణి - Musa, Arietis 35, 41

భాగఫలము - Quotient
భాగహారము - Division
భాజకము - Divisor
భాజ్యము - Dividend
భారవర్ధిత నిష్పత్తి - Weighted ratio
భారాంకిత గుణములు - Weighed multiples
భిన్న పరికర్మములు - Manipulations of fractions
భిన్నములు - Fractions
భీమా - Insurance
భుగ్నత - Refraction
భూమి - Earth
భూదైనిక పరిభ్రమణము - Diurnal rotation of the earth
భోగము - Celestial longitude
భౌతిక యుగళములు - Physical doubles
భౌతికశాస్త్రము - Physics
భౌమ్య సంభవములు - Terrestrial phenomena
భ్రమణము - Revolution
భ్రమణ దర్శకము - Gyroscope

మ

మండలము - Zone, Ring
మందఫలము - Equation of the centre of a planet
మందాకిని - Milkyway, Galaxy
మకరాయనము - Winter solstice
మఘ - Leonis, Regulus
మధ్యకాల గ్రహయుగము - Synodical period
మధ్యగత - Median
మధ్యమ మూల్యసిద్ధాంతము - Mean value theory
మధ్యమానము - Mean value
మధ్యమాన సౌరకాలము - Mean solar time
మధ్యాహ్నరేఖ - Meridian
మరచలనము - Screw motion
మర్యాదిత - Bounded
మర్యాదిత కంపనము - Bounded oscillation
మహావృత్తము - Great circle
మస్తకము - Zenith
మాంద్యత - Anomaly
మాత్రిక - Matrix
మాపాంకము - Modulus
మిథునము - Gemini
మిళిత సంభావ్యత - Composite probability
మీన - Pisces
ముకుటకము - Corona
మూల - Scorpionis 84, 85
మూలత్రితలము - Fundamental trihedron
మూలములు - Roots
మూలసంఖ్య - Radix
మూలాంకము - Radix
మూలాక్షము - Radical axis
మూడవ తరగతి సంస్పర్శ - Third order contact
మృగవ్యాధుడు - Sirus
మృగశిర - Orinois, Delta orions
మృతిబలము - Force of mortality
మెత్త - Pallet
మేష - Aries
మేషాది బిందువు - First point of Aries
మొదటి తరగతి అంతరీకరణ సమీకరణములు - Linear differential equations

య

యథాదర్శన జ్యామితి - Perspective drawing
యథాదర్శన శాస్త్రము - Science of perspective drawing
యదృచ్ఛ - Chance
యముడు - Pluto
యాంత్రికశాస్త్రము - Mechanics

యాదృచ్ఛిక - Random
యాదృచ్ఛిక చలరాశి - Random variable
యాదృచ్ఛిక ప్రక్రియ - Stochastic process
యాదృచ్ఛిక ప్రతిరూపములు - Random samples
యాదృచ్ఛిక సంఖ్యలు - Random numbers
యాదృచ్ఛికావశేషము - Random residue
యాదృచ్ఛికీకరణము - Randomization
యాదృచ్ఛికీకృత ఖండములు - Randomized blocks
యానకము - Medium
యామ్యోత్తర రేఖ - Meridian
యామోత్తర వృత్తము - Meridian circle
యుక్తభిన్నము - Proper fraction
యుగళతారలు - Binaries
యుగళబిందువు - Nodal point
యుగ్మము - Couple
యుతి - Conjunction
యూక్లిడ్ ఆకాశము - Euclid cpace
యూక్లిడ్ ఎలిమెంట్స్ - Euclid elements
యూక్లిడేతర జ్యామితులు - Non-euclidena geometries
యూనిట్ - Unit
యూనిట్ త్వరణము - Unit acceleration
యూనిట్ బలము - Unit force
యూనిట్ సెల్ - Unit cell
యోగము - Conjunction
యోజన - Planning

ర

రవి కళంకములు - Sun spots
రవిబింబ శుక్రతరణము - Transit of venus over sun
రశ్మిశలాకము - Pencil of rays
రశ్మ్యుద్గారి మూల ద్రవ్యములు - Radio-active elements
రాంబస్ - Rhombus
రాశిచక్రము - Zodiac
రాశులు - Constellations
రూపము - Unit
రెండవ అభిలంబరేఖ - Binormal
రెండవ తరగతి అనిశ్చితి సమీకరణములు - Indeterminate equations of second degree
రెండవ తరగతి వ్యాపక సమీకరణములు - General equations of second degree
రెండవ తరగతి సమీకరణములు - Quadratic equations
రేఖ - Line
రేఖాంశము - Meridian
రేఖాంశ రేఖ - Meridian
రేఖా నిరూపకములు - Linear co-ordinates
రేఖీయ - Linear
రేఖీయ బిందుసమితి - Linear sets of points
రేడియో ఖగోళశాస్త్రము - Radio astronomy
రేడియన్ - Radian
రేడియస్ వెక్టర్ - Radius vector
రేడియోతార - Radio star
రేవతి - Piscium
రోహిణి - Aldebaran

ల

లంగరు వలయము - Anchor ring, Torus ring
లంబకేంద్రము - Ortho-centre
లంబకోణము - Right anlge
లంబతలము - Normal plane
లంబనము - Parallax
లంబన విధానము - Parallax method
లంబప్రిజమ్ - Right prism
లంబవిక్షేపము - Orthogonal projection
లంబవృత్త స్థూపము - Right circular cylinder
లంబాక్ష - Rectangular
లంబాక్ష నిరూపకములు - Rectangular co-ordinates

లక్షణవాదము - Theory of attributes
లఘుకోణము - Acute angle
లఘుగ్రహములు - Asteroids
లఘుచాపము - Minor arc
లఘువృత్తము - Small circle
లవము - Numerator
లాగరిదమ్ పరంపర - Logarithmic series
లాగరిదమ్ ఫలములు - Logarithmic functions
లాటిన్ చతురస్రము - Latin square
లాప్లాస్ సమీకరణము - Laplace's equation
లిమేసాన్ - Limacon
లోకము - Population
లోలకము - Pendulum

వ

వక్ర ఆకాశము - Curved space
వక్రగతి - Retrograde motion
వక్రత - Curvature
వక్రతాకేంద్రము - Centre of curvature
వక్రతారేఖ - Line of curvature
వక్రతావృత్తము - Circle of curvature
వక్రతా వ్యాసార్థము - Radius of curvature
వక్రములు - Curves
వక్రరేఖీయ నిరూపకములు - Curvilinear co-ordinates
వక్రీభవన కోణము - Angle of refraction
వక్రీభవన దూరదర్శిని - Refracting telescope
వక్రీభవనము - Refraction
వక్రీభవన స్థిరరాశి - Refraction constant
వజ్రనిష్పత్తి - Cross ratio
వరణ స్వీకృత తత్త్వము - Axiom of choice
వరుణుడు - Neptune
వర్గము - Square
వర్గమూలము - Square root
వర్గ సమీకరణము - Quadratic equation
వర్ణమండలము - Chromosphere
వర్ణమాల - Spectrum
వర్ణమాలాచిత్రము - Spectrograph
వర్ణమాలా దర్శిని - Spectroscope
వర్ణమాలాలంబనము - Spectroscopic parallax
వర్ణమాలా విశ్లేషణము - Spectral analysis
వర్ణమాలా హేళిలేఖిని - Spectro-heliograph
వర్ణవిపథనము - Chromatic aberration
వర్ణసూచకము - Colour index
వర్తుల - Circular
వర్తుల బిందువులు - Circular points
వర్తుల రేఖలు - Circular lines
వసంతవిషువు, వసంత సంపాతము - Vernal equinox
వస్తు కటకము - Object glass
వస్తుపరివర్తన పరీక్ష - Commodity reversal test
వామనములు - Dwarfs
వార్షిక - Annual
వార్షిక అతివర్తనము - Annual parallax
వార్షిక సమీకరణము - Annual equation
వాస్తవసంఖ్యలు - Real numbers
వాస్తవిక ప్రతిరూపము - Exactly similar
వాస్తుధ్వని విద్య - Architectural acoustics
వికర్ణము - Diagonal
వికిరణ బిందువు - Radiant
వికిరణమాపక - Radiometric
వికిరణము - Radiation
విక్షేపక జ్యామితి - Projective geometry
విక్షేపక నిరూపకములు - Projective co-ordinates
విక్షేపక మార్పులు - Projective transformations
విక్షేప పథము - Trajectory
విక్షేపము - Projection

విచలనము - Deviation, variance
విచూషణము - Absorption
విచూషణ పట్టికలు - Absorption bands
విద్యుదావేశములు - Electric charges
విద్యుదయుస్కాంత సిద్ధాంతము - Electro-magnetic theory
విద్యుద్గతిశాస్త్రము - Electro-dynamics
విద్యుచ్ఛక్రము - Electric potential
వినియుక్త గణితము - Applied mathematics
విపథనము - Aberration
విపథన గుణకము - Co-efficient of aberration
విపథన స్థిరాంకము - Aberration constant
విభాజకము - Factor
విభాజకీకరణము - Factorization
విభాజ్యము - Dividend
విమా - Dimension
విమాత్రయ జ్యామితి - Geometry of three dimensions
విమా విశ్లేషణము - Dimensional analysis
విమోటనము - Torsion
విమోటన వ్యాసార్థము - Radius of torsion
విలోపకక్ష (కక్ష్య) - Elliptic orbit
విలోప జ్యామితి - Elliptic functions
విలోప ఫలములు - Ellipse
విలోపము - Inverse
విలోమ - Inverse proportion
విలోమ అనుపాతము - Contravariant
విలోమ చలరాశి - Inverse functions
విలోమ ఫలములు - Law of inverse squares
విలోమ వర్గన్యాయము - Open interval
వివృత అంతరము - Generalized co-ordinates
విశ్లేషణ - Analysis
విశ్లేషణ గణితము - Analysis
విశ్లేషణ ఫలములు - Analytical functions
విశ్వగురుత్వ సిద్ధాంతము - Universal law of gravitation
విశ్వద్రవ్యము - Cosmic matter
విశ్వధూళి - Cosmic dust
విశ్వము - Universe
విశ్వామిత్రుడు - Southern cross
విషుచలనము - Precession of the equinoxe
విషుదర్శని - Equinoctical
విషుబిందువు - Equinoctial point
విషువాంశ - Right ascension
విషువులు - Equinoxes
విషువృత్తము - Celestial equator
వృత్తచతురస్రీకరణము - Squaring of a circle
వృత్తము - Circle
వృత్తీయ - Circular
వృత్తీయ జ్యామితి - Geometry of a circle
వృత్తీయ ఫలములు - Circular functions
వృత్తీయ బిందువులు - Circular points
వృద్ధి ప్రతికృతులు - Growth models
వృశ్చిక - Scorpio
వెక్టర్ - Vector
వెక్టర్ గణితము - Vector mathematics
వెక్టర్ బీజగణితము - Vector algebra
వేగము - Velocity
వేగుచుక్క - Morning star
వేధ - Observation
వేధశాల - Observatory
వేష్టనము - Envelope
వైశాల్య నిరూపకములు - Areal co-ordinates
వైశాల్యము - Area
వైశాల్య వేగము - Areal velocity
వ్యక్త - Apparent
వ్యక్తతరము - Apparent magnitude

వ్యక్తదిశ - Apparent direction

వ్యక్తనతదూరము, వ్యక్తనతాంశ - Apparent zenith distance

వ్యవకలనము - Subtraction

వ్యాకోచద్విశ్వము - Expanding universe

వ్యాపక - General

వ్యాపక సాధనము - General solution

వ్యాసము - Diameter

వ్యాసార్థము - Radius

వ్యుత్క్రమము - Reciprocal

వ్యుత్క్రమ సంఖ్య - Reciprocal number

వ్యుత్పన్నములు - Derivatives

వ్రాలిన గోపురము - Leaning tower

శ

శంకు - Cone

శంకుతలము - Conical surface

శంకుభాషలు - Cone speakers

శంకువు - Gnomon

శంకు శీర్షము - Vertex of a cone

శకము - Era

శకలాస్త్ర ప్రయోగము - Fragmentation ballistics

శక్తి - Energy

శక్మ - Potential

శక్మ ప్రవాహము - Potential flow

శక్మవాదము - Potential theory

శక్మశక్తి - Potential energy

శతభిషము - Aquaril

శని - Saturn

శని కంకణములు - Saturn's rings

శర నక్షత్రములు - Shooting stars

శరము - Lattitude, Celestial lattitude

శరద్విషువు - Autumnal equinox

శలాక - Pencil

శాంకవ ఛేదము - Conic section

శాంకవ నాథులు - Conic fool

శాంకవము - Conic

శాంకవ వక్రీభవనము - Conic refraction

శాంకవ విక్షేపము - Conical projection

శాంకవ శీర్షము - Vertex of a cone

శింశుమార చక్రము - Zodiacal belt

శిఖరము - Vertex

శీఘ్రకర్ణము - Distance of a planet from the centre of the earth

శీర్షకోణము - Vertical angle

శీర్షము - Vertex

శుక్రతరణము - Transit of Venus

శుక్రయుగము - Synodic period

శుక్రుడు - Venus

శుద్ధగణితము - Pure mathematics

శుద్ధ గతిశాస్త్రము - Kinematics

శుద్ధజ్యామితి - Abstract geometry

శుద్ధ బీజగణితము - Abstract algebra

శూన్యము, శూన్యాంకము - Zero

శృంఖలా సంధానము - Linkage

శృంఖలిత భిన్నము - Continued fraction

శ్రవణము - Aquila

శ్రుతి - Radius vector

శ్రేఢులు - Progressions

ష

షడ్వస్తు సమస్య - Six body problem

షడ్భాంతరము - Opposition

షష్టకము - Sextant

స

సంకలన అవధి - Limit of a sum

సంకలన మధ్యమము - Arithmetic mean
సంకలనము - Addition
సంకలన రాశి - Sum
సంకలన శ్రేణి - Arithmetic progression
సంకలనీయత - Summability
సంకలనీయతా సిద్ధాంతము - Theory of summability
సంకీర్ణ - Complex
సంకీర్ణ ఋజురేఖ - Complex line
సంకీర్ణ చలరాశి - Complex variable
సంకీర్ణ చలరాశి ఫలవాదము - Theory of functions of a complex variable
సంకీర్ణ సంఖ్య - Complex number
సంకేతము - Symbol
సంకేతిత మానములు - Scales of notation
సంఖ్యలు - Numbers
సంఖ్యామానములు - Scales of notation
సంఘటన - Event
సందెచుక్క - Evening star
సంధ్య - Twilight
సంపాత బిందువు - Point of intersection
సంపూరక కోణము - Supplementary angle
సంభవనీయత - Probability
సంభవనీయతావాదము - Probability theory
సంభావ్యత - Probability
సంభావ్యతాకలనము - Calculus of probabilities
సంభావ్యతా వాదము - Mathematical theory of probability
సంభావ్యతా విభజనము - Probability distribution
సంభావ్యతా సాంద్రత - Probability density
సంమధ్య బిందువు - Symmedian point
సంయుగ్మ - Conjugate
సంయుగ్మ బిందువులు - Conjugate points
సంయోగ నియమము - Law of combination
సంయోగములు - Combinations
సంయోజక న్యాయము - Law of association
సంయోజన విధానము - Combinational method
సంయోజిత - Synthetic
సంయోజిత నోదక ద్రవ్యములు - Synthetic propellants
సంవృత అంతరము - Closed interval
సంవృత వక్రము - Closed curve
సంవృత శాంకవము - Closed conic
సంవృత సమితి - Closed set
సదిశరాశి - Vector
సదిశరాశి ఆకాశము - Vector space
సదిశరేఖ - Vector line
సదృశచిత్రపట లేఖనము - Conformal mapping
సమకాలిక సమీకరణములు - Simultaneous equations
సమకాలీన - Simultaneous
సమకోణము - Right angle
సమకోణీయ - Orthogonal
సమకోణీయ విక్షేపము - Orthogonal projection
సమకోణీయ శలాక - Orthogonal pencil
సమకోణీయ సమన్వయము - Orthogonal involution
సమకోణీయ సమవాయత - Orthogonal involution
సమగ్ర సమీకరణము - Perfect equation
సమఘాత - Homogeneous
సమఘాత నిరూపకములు - Homogeneous co-ordinates
సమఘాత సమీకరణము - Homogeneous equation
సమతల జ్యామితి - Place geometry
సమతల త్రికోణమితి - Plane trigonometry
సమద్విబాహు (బాహు) త్రిభుజము- Isosceles triangle
సమన్వయత - Involution
సమన్వయ శలాక - Pencil of involution
సమవాయత - Involution
సమవాయతా కేంద్రము - Centre of involution

సమవాయతా శలాక - Pencil of involution

సమానకోణ సర్పిలము - Equi angular spiral

సమానాంతర - Parallel

సమానాంతర చతుర్భుజ నియమ (న్యాయ)ము - Parallelogram law of forces

సమానాంతర చతుర్భుజము - Parallelogram

సమానాంతర చతుర్భుజ సంయోజన సూత్రము - Parallelogram law of forces

సమానాంతర ఘనము - Parallelopiped

సమానాంతర రేఖలు - Parallel lines

సమానాంతర స్వీకృతతత్వము - Parallel postutate

సమానాంతర విక్షేపము - Parallel projection

సమాసము - Expression

సమితి - Set

సమితివాదము - Set theory

సమీకరణము - Equation

సమీకరణ వాదము - Theory of equations

సమ్మధ్యగతలు - Symmedians

సమ్మధ్య బిందువు - Symmedian point

సరళభిన్నము, సరళ భిన్నాంకము - Simple fraction

సరళలోకము - Normal population

సరళవక్రము - Normal curve

సరళవక్ర విస్తీర్ణము - Area of normal curve

సరళశృంఖలిత భిన్నము - Simple continued fraction

సరళ సంబద్ధ - Simply connected

సరిసంఖ్య - Even number

సరూప త్రిభుజములు - Similar triangle

సర్పిల నీహారిక - Spiral nebula

సర్పిలము - Spiral

సర్పిలరేఖ - Spiral line

సర్వసమత - Congruence, Identity

సర్వసమతత్త్వములు - Identities

సవ్యదిక్కు - Clockwise

సహజజ్ఞానము - Intuition

సాంఖ్యిక గుణ నియంత్రణ - Statistical quality contro

సాంఖ్యిక యాంత్రిక శాస్త్రము - Statistical machanics

సాంఖ్యిక శాస్త్రము - Statistics

సాంద్రత - Density

సాధనము - Instrument, solution

సాపేక్ష - Relative

సాపేక్ష త్వరణము - Relative acceleration

సాపేక్ష పౌనఃపున్యము - Relative frequency

సాపేక్ష యాంత్రికశాస్త్రము - Relative mechanics

సాపేక్ష వేగము - Relative velocity

సాపేక్షత - Relativity

సాపేక్షతా వాదము - Relativity theory

సామ్య - Parallel

సాయన - Tropical

సాయన దినము - Tropical day

సాయన సంవత్సరము - Tropical year

సావన - Terrestrial

సావన కాలము - Terrestrial time

సావన దినము - Terrestrial day

సావన సంవత్సరము - Terrestrial year

సింహ - Leo

సిస్సాయిడ్ - Cissoid

సీమిత - Bounded

సూక్ష్మదర్శిని - Microscope

సూక్ష్మమాపకము - Micrometer

సూక్ష్మరాశి - Infinitesimal

సూచకసంఖ్య - Index number

సూచి - Index

సూచీముఖము - Cusp

సూచీ సంఖ్యా సిద్ధాంతము - Index number theory

సూచ్యంకము - Index

సూపర్‌నోవా - Super nova
సూపర్‌నోవా స్ఫోటకము - Supernova explosion
సూర్యకళంకము - Sunspot
సూర్యగ్రహణము - Solar eclipse
సూర్యఘటి - Sun dial
సూర్యమందఫలము - Equation of centre
సూర్యవర్ణమాల - Solar spectrum
సూర్య వికిరణము - Solar radiation
సూర్యుడు - Sun
సెఫీడ్ చలతారలు - Cepheid variables
సైక్లాయిడ్ - Cycloid
సౌరకాలము - Solar time
సౌరకుటుంబ ఉత్పత్తి - Origin of solar system
సౌరకుటుంబము - Solar system
సౌరజ్వాలలు - Solar prominences
సౌరదినము - Solar day
సౌరదూరదర్శిని - Solar telescope
సౌరమాన - Solar
సౌరాతివర్తనము - Solar parallax
సౌష్ఠవము - Symmetry
స్కేలార్ - Scalar
స్టాటిస్టిక్ - Statistic
స్టొకేస్టిక్ చలరాశి - Stokastic variable
స్తంభము - Column
స్తూపతలము - Cylindrical surface
స్తూపము - Cylinder
స్తూపవిక్షేపము - Cylindrical projection
స్తూపీయ - Cylindrical
స్తూపీయ నిరూపకములు - Cylindrical co-ordinates
స్థలమూల్య భావము - Place value
స్థలశాస్త్రము - Topology
స్థలసదిశరాశి - Position vector
స్థానమూల్యము - Place value
స్థానశక్తి - Potential energy
స్థానాంతరము - Translation
స్థావర - Stationary
స్థితిశాస్త్రము - Statics
స్థిరతోలనస్థితి - Stable equilibrium
స్థిరరాశి - Constant
స్థిరాంకము - Constant
స్థిర సమతాస్థితి - Stable equilibrium
స్పర్శజీవ - Tangent
స్పర్శ జ్యా - Tangent, Chord of contact
స్పర్శతలము - Tangent plane
స్పర్శద్వయము - Double contact
స్పర్శబిందువు - Point of contact
స్పర్శరేఖ - Tangent
స్పర్శీయ - Tangential
స్పర్శీయ నిరూపకములు - Tangential co-ordinates
స్పర్శీయ సమీకరణము - Tangential equation
స్రోతస్సులు - Tides
స్రోతోఘర్షణ - Tidal friction
స్రోతో తరంగములు - Tidal waves
స్వతంత్ర చలరాశి - Independent variable
స్వదేశ కాలము, ప్రమాణ కాలము - Local time, standard time
స్వపరాగసిక్త - Self fertilized
స్వయం సంబంధము - Auto-correlation
స్వరాత్మక - Harmonic
స్వరాత్మకచ్ఛేదము - Harmonic section
స్వరాత్మక ఫలములు - Harmonic functions
స్వరాత్మక మధ్యమము - Harmonic mean
స్వరాత్మక రేంజి - Harmonic range
స్వరాత్మక వరుస - Harmonic sequence

స్వరాత్మక శలాక:- Harmonic pencil
స్వసంయుగ్మ - Self conjugates
స్వాతి - Arcturus, bootes
స్వీకృత తత్త్వములు - Postulates
స్వేచ్ఛాతరము - Degree of freedom

హ

హంస - Cygnus 61
హరాత్మకగతి - Harmonic motion
హరాత్మక త్రిభుజము - Harmonic triangle
హరాత్మక మధ్యమము - Harmonic mean
హరాత్మకముగ - Harmonically
హరాత్మక యుగళము - Harmonic conjugate
హరాత్మక శలాక - Harmonic pencil
హరాత్మక శ్రేణి - Harmonic progression
హానిభయము - Risk
హారము - Denominator
హిల్బర్ట్ ఆకాశము - Hilbert space
హెచ్చుతగ్గులు - Inequalities
హెలిక్స్ - Helix
హీలిమాపకము - Heliometer
హోల్డర్ హెచ్చుతగ్గులు - Holder indqualities
హ్రస్వతమరేఖ - Geodesic
హ్రస్వతమ వక్రము - Geodesic curve
హ్రస్వాక్షము - Short axis

11.3 English to Hindi

A

Abacus गिनती सिखने का यंत्र, गणनायंत्र

Abelean group विनिमय प्रणाली को संबंधित

Aberration पथान्तरण

Aberration w-efficient पथान्तरण गुहाक

Aberration constant पथान्तरण गुणक

Aberration of light प्रकाश का पथान्तरण

Aberration of planet ग्रह का पथान्तरण

Absolute पूर्ण

Absolute convergence पूर्ण केन्द्रामिमुखता

Absolute curve पूर्ण घुमाव

Absolute magnitude पूर्ण महत्व

Absolute potential पूर्ण संभावित

Absolute temperature पूर्ण तापक्रम

Absolute time पूर्ण काल

Absolute value पूर्ण मान

Absorption आमेलन/अवशोषण

Absorption bands आमेलन समुदाय/अवशोषित वर्णक्रम

Abstract संक्षेप

Abstract algebra आदर्श बीजगणित

Abstract geometry आदर्श रेखागणित

Abstract spaces आदर्श अन्तर (स्थान)

Acceleration गति-वृद्धि/त्वरण

Acoustics ध्वनिशास्त्र

Acute angle न्यून कोण

Acute angled triangle न्यून कोणीय त्रिभुज

Addition योग, जोड़, कुल

Aerials काल्पनिक, हवाई, उन्नत

Aerolite टूटता तारा

Albedo प्रकाशानुपात धवलता

Aldeberan रोहिणी तारा

Algebra बीजगणित

Algebraic functions बीजगणितीय पद

Alternate angle विकल्प (पक्षान्तर) कोण

Alternate exterior angle विकल्प बाह्य कोण

Alternate interior angle विकल्प अन्त:स्थ कोण

Altitude ऊँचाई, महत्व

Analysis विघटन, विभाजन, वाक्य विश्लेषण

Analysis of variance भिन्नता का विश्लेषण

Analytical functions भेद का विश्लेषण/विभाजन

Analytical mechanics विश्लेषणात्मक यांत्रिकी

Anchor ring छल्ला, लंगर की अंगुठी

Anchormeda/Anchord लंगर

Angle कोण

Angle of depression न्यूनता का कोण

Angle of dip निम्मजुन कोण

Angle of elevation उन्नत कोण

Angle of incidence आपतन कोण

Angle of retraction खिचाव कोण

Angle solid पुष्ट कोण

Angular कोणीय

Angular momentum कोणीय गति

Angular velocity कोणीय वेग

Annual वार्षिक

Annual equation वार्षिक साभ्य/समीकरण

Annual parallax वार्षिक लम्बन

Annual eclipse वार्षिकी ग्रहण

Anomaly अनियमितता/अव्यवस्था

Antares वृश्चिक में सबसे अधिक महत्व का एक लाल तारा

Anti clockwise घड़ी की विपरीत दिशा में

Anti parallel समानान्तर के विपरीत

Aphelion किसी ग्रह का सूर्य से सबसे दूर का स्थान

Apogee किसी ग्रह के ग्रह पथ में पृथ्वी से सबसे दूरा का स्थान

Apparent प्रकट, स्पष्ट, प्रत्यक्ष, दिखौवा

Apparent brightness स्पष्ट चमकीलापन

Apparent direction स्पष्ट दिशा

Apparent magnitude स्पष्ट मात्रा

Apparaent solar time स्पष्ट/प्रत्यक्ष सौर काल

Apparent zenith distance स्पष्ट शिरोबिंदू दूरी

Applied mathematics अनुप्रायोगिक गणितशास्त्र

Approximate अति समीप, प्राय: शुद्ध, अअत समान

Apsidal line अर्द्धवृताकार या बहुभुजीय रेखा

Aquaril कुंभ

Aquarius कुंभ राशि

Aquila नक्षत्र मण्डल/तारा मंडल

Arc वृतखण्ड, चाप, कमान

Architectural acoustics शिल्पविद्या सम्बन्धी ध्वनिशास्त्र

Arcturus ध्रुव तोर के पास उतरी तारामण्डल में एक पीला तारा

Area क्षेत्रफल

Area coordinates क्षेत्र निर्देशांक

Areal velocity क्षेत्र वेग

Areas under the normal curve सामान्य घुमाव के तहत क्षेत्रफल

Aries मेष राशि

Arietis अश्विनी

Arithmetic अंकगणित

Arithmetic mean अंकगणितीय परिमाण

Arithmetic progression अंकगणितीय प्रभाव

Artificial satellite कृत्रिम उपग्रह

Ars conjectandi कल्पना की कला

Ascendent प्रधान प्रबल

Associative law संयुक्त/संगत विधि

Assumptions मान्यताएं कल्पनाएं

Asteroids तारें

Astrolabe ऊँचाई नापने हेतु एक पुशतन औजार

Astrology फलित ज्योतिष, नक्षत्र विधा

Astronomical units खगोल विधा सम्बन्धी इकाई

Astro-dynamics खगोलीय गतिविधा

Astro-physics खगोलीय भौतिक विज्ञान

Asymptotes ऐसी रेखाएं निरन्तर रूप से घुमाव पहुचती है लेकिन उससे कभी मिलती नहीं

Asymptatic line साथ-साथ या समानन्तर रेखा

Asymptatic solution समानान्तर हल

Atomic model परमाणु सम्बन्धी नमूना

Attraction आकर्षण प्रलोभन

Auto correlation अपना परस्पर सम्बन्ध

Autumnal equinox शरत्काल का सम्पात (21 मार्च व 23 सितम्बर का दिन) जब रात व दिन बराबर होते है।

Axes of reference निर्देश कुहार

Axiom of choice पसंद का स्वयं सिद्ध प्रमाण

Axioms स्वत: सिद्ध प्रमाण, सिद्धान्त

Axis केन्द्र अक्षरेखा

Azimuth किसी आकाशीय पिण्ड से निकलता हुआ शिक्षित का चाप जो देशान्तर का लम्वत वृत के मध्य हो

B

Ballistics शस्त्र फैकन की विधा

Base आधार मूल (आश्रय)

Bearing प्रतिष्ठाद्ध छवि, ढंग, व्यवहार (स्थिति) अभिप्राय

Bicontinuity दोहरी निरन्तरता

Binaries दोहरे (द्विगुणी) जोड़े

Binomial द्विपद (बीजगणितीय)

Binomial co-efficient द्विपद गुणक

Binomial axpression द्विपदीय अभिव्यक्ति

Binomioaal theoren द्विपदीय प्रमेय

Biology जीव विज्ञान

Biometry जीव (प्राणी) विज्ञान का सांख्यकी एवं मात्रात्मक अध्ययन

Bisational transformation दोहरा तर्कसंगत रूपान्तरण

Bisector समद्विभाजक

Bi-uniformity दोहरी समानता

Bomb ballistics बम फैंकन की विधा

Bootes ध्रुव तारे के पास उत्तरी तारा मण्डल

Bounded सीमित, मर्यादित, बन्धा हुआ

Bounded oscillation सीमित कम्पन

C

Calculating machine गण्ना यन्त्र

Calculus मूत्रकृच्छ, शरीर में पथरी पड़ना, कलन (गुणना करने की विशेष विधि)

Calculus of probabilities अधिसंभावनाओं की गणना

Calculus of variation भेद/रूपान्तर/परिवर्तन की गणना

Calendar कर्क राशि विस्फोट (नासूर)

Caneri

Caneri

Canopus दक्षिणी तारा मण्डल में एक चमकीला तारा

Capture hypothesis गिरफ्तारी की कल्पना

Cardioid वृत की परिधि पर बिंदू से बना हृदयाकार का घुमाव

Cartesian co-ordinace कार्तीय निर्देशांक

Cartesian product रेन डेस्कार्टिज का उत्पाद

Casting out धातु को गलाकर ढलाई किया हुआ

Caster उद्‌बिलाव से प्राप्त एक पदार्थ, मसाले की बोतल, टेबल कुर्सी के पाये में लगा पहिया

Catenary समान रूप के लोचदार तन्तुओं से बना घुमाव

Celestial दिव्य, सुन्दर, स्वर्गीय, आकाशीय

Celestial latitude दिव्य अक्षांश रेखा

Celestial mechanics दिव्य यन्त्र विधा

Celestial objects ग्रह मण्डल

Centaurus एक पौराणिक प्राणी जिसके कमर से नीच का भाग घोड़े का व उपर का भाग मनुष्य का होता है।

Central consicoid

Central projection केन्द्रीय प्रलम्बता

Centre केन्द्र

Centre of curvature वक्रता केन्द्र

Centre of gravity गुरुत्वाकर्षण केन्द्र

Centre of involution पेचीदगी/फसावट केन्द्र

Cepheid variables

Chance दैव, योग, अवसर, घटनाक्रम, संभावना

Change of axis अक्ष रेखा का परिवर्तन

Chord चापकर्ण

Chord line चाप कर्ण रेखा

Chromate aberration चटक रंग पथान्तरण

Chromosphere रंगीला चित्र मण्डल

Charomometer ठीक-ठीक समय बताने वाली एक छोटी घड़ी

Circle वृत

Circle geometry वृत ज्यामिति/रेखा गणित

Circle of curvature वक्रता का वृत

Circular वर्तुलाकार चक्राकार परिपत्र

Circular function वर्तुलाकार कार्य सम्पादन/पद

Circular or namental pattern वर्तुलाकार विभुषक आकार/नमूना

Circular points वर्तुलाकार बिन्दु

Circular ponts at infinity श्रनन्तता पर वर्तुलाकार बिन्दु

Circum centre चारों ओर केन्द्र

Circum circle चारो ओर वृत

Circumference परिधि

Cissoid दो असीमित शाखाओं वाला समतल घुमाव

Clockwise बांयी से दांयी ओर वर्तुलाकार घड़ी की दिशा में घुमना

Closed अन्त, समीप, सीमित, संकुचित

Closed curve संकुचित घुमाव

Closed interval संकुचित/सीमित अन्तर

Closed sets सीमित समूह

Cluster variables अनित्य समुदाय

Coal sack nebuls काली निहारिकाएं

Co-axial circle सह-धुरीय वृत

Co-efficient of friction घर्षण का गुणक

Co-factor सह-कारक

Collinear points एक रेखिक बिन्दू

Colour index वर्ण चिन्ह, वर्ण प्रदर्शक सिद्धान्त

Column खंभा, आश्रय, परिमाण पृष्ठ का स्तम्भ

Coma अल्प विराम, अप्राकृतिक निद्रा, धमुकेतु के चतुर्दिक धुंधला घेरा

Combinations संधि, संयोग, संसर्ग, जुड़ाव

Comet पुच्छल तारा

Commodity reversal test द्रव्य मान जांच

Commutative law विनिमय सम्बन्धी विधि

Commutative ring विनियम पदार्थ

Companion star सहचर सितारे/नक्षख

Comlementations परिपूरकता, सम्पूर्णता

Complementary angles पूरक कोण

Complex संयुक्त, मिश्रित

Compelx line संयुक्त रेखा

Complex number संयुक्त संख्या

Complex variable संयुक्त

Comparents साधक अंगभूत

Composite probability मिश्रित अधिसंभावना

Computers गणना यन्त्र, गणक

Concept सामान्य विचार

Concoid एक समलत घुमाव

Concurent एकीभूत, सहमत, समवर्ती

Conduction of heat उष्मा का संचालन

Cone शंकु

Cone of friction घर्षण की नोकदार आकृति

Cone of speakers स्पीकर्स की नोकदार आकृति

Confocal conics

Conformal mappnig अनुकूलनीय आलेख

Congruent योग्य, अनुरूप

Conic सूच्याकार, गावदुम

Conica projection शंक्वाकार प्रलम्बता, उंचाई निकास

Conic section शंक्वाकार भाग

Conical retraction शंक्वाकार खिंचाव

Concial surface शंक्वार सतह, धारातल

Conicold

Conjugate क्रिया पद के रूप में चलना

Conjugate points क्रिया पदीय बिन्दु

Constant स्थिर, निरन्तर दृढ

Constiliations नक्षत्र मण्डल

Contingency co-efficient आकस्मिक गुणक

Continued fractions सतत् अंक

Continuity सतता, निरन्तरता

Contour integral सम्पूर्ण परिधी रेखा

Contravariants परस्पर विरोधी

Convergency केन्द्राभिमुखता

Convergent series परिचित, निपूर्ण क्रम/शृखला

Co-ordinate axes समान पदीय कुहार

Co-ordinate geometry समान पदीय रेखा गणित

Co-ordinates नियामक

Corena सूर्य, चन्द्रमा या नक्षत्र के चारों ओर का प्रभामण्डल

Correspondence अनुरूपता, सादृश्य, पत्रव्यवहार

Corresponding angle तुल्य, युक्त या अनरूप कोण

Co-secant सह कोण्ज्या या छेदन रेखा

Cosine सह द्विज्या

Co-sine circle सह द्विज्या वृत

Cosine series सह द्विज्या क्रम या शृंखला

Cosmic dust एहिक, लौकिक या जगत सम्बन्धी धूली

Cosmic matter एहिक या लौकिक पदार्थ

Cosmes क्रमबद्ध, नियम बद्ध

Co-tengent सह स्पर्श रेखा

Couple जोड़ा, युगल

Cross fertilized प्रति उपजाउं, संकर उत्पति

Cross multiplication वज्रगुणन

Cross ratio प्रतिसम्बन्ध या प्रमाण

Cryptaithmetic गुप्त अंकगणित

Cube धन

Cube root धननुल

Cuneiform scrept फन्नी के आकार का

Currature वक्रता, घुमाव

Curved space चाप

Curves वक्राकार

Curvilinear co-ordinates वक्राकार नियामक

Cusp शिखा, चोटी

Cyclic चक्रवत

Cyclical component क्रमिक साधक

Cyclic quadrilateral चतुरभुजीय चक्र

Cycloid अण्डाकार वृत

Cygnue

Clyinder वर्तुलाकार, बेलनाकार

Cylindrical co-ordinates बेलनाकार या वर्तुलाकार नियामक

Cylindrical projection बेलनाकार प्रलम्बता या उंचाई

Cylindrical surfcac बेलनाकार सतह या धरातल

D

Dark line spectrum गहरी सतरंगी

Dark nebulae घनी निहारिका

Data स्वीकृत तत्व, निर्दिष्ट सिद्धान्त

Data line निर्दिष्ट रेखा

Decimal fraction दशमलव अंक

Decimal notation दशमलव गणना

Decimal point दशमलव बिन्दू

Decimals दशमलव

Declination नीचे की ओर झुकाव

Declination circle नीचे की ओर झुकाव वाला वृत

Deductive system वियोजक प्रणाली

Definition परिभाषा, लक्षण, व्याख्या

Degree अंश, अक्षांश तापमान का अंश

Degree of freedom स्वतन्त्रता की स्थिति

Deipline

Delta orions डेल्टा (Δ ग्रकि वर्णमाला का चतुर्थ अक्षर), नदी का उपजाउ मुहाना

Demand मांग

Demand analysis मांग का विश्लेषण

Denkbola सिह नक्षत्रमण्डल की पूंछ पर एक चमकीला तारा

Denominator हर, भिन्न में भाजक संख्या अर्थात रेखा के नीचे का अंक

Density घनत्व

Dependent variable आश्रित अनित्य

Derivative गौण, यौगिक

Design of experiment प्रयोग का प्रयोजन

Determinats स्थिर, सिद्ध, निश्चित

Deviation अतिक्रम मूल

Diagonal कर्ण

Diameter व्यास

Different equation असमान समीकरण

Differential calculus भेदकर या विशेषक कलन

Different efficient विशेषक गुणक

Different equation विशेषक गुणक

Differential geometry विशेषक ज्यामिति/रेखागणित

Diofferential ratio विशेष प्रमाण

Differentiation भेदकरण

Digits अंगुल भर, ईकाई का अंक

Dimension परिमाण, मात्रा, अंश

Dimensional enalysis परिमाण सम्बन्धी विशलेषण

Diophantine equations बीजगणितीय समीकरण

Dip निमज्जन, डुनाव

Direction cosines अनुपूरक कोण की द्विज्या

Direct proportion प्रत्यक्ष प्रमाण या अनुपात

Displacement विस्थापन

Displacement of the first point of Aries मेष राशि के प्रथम बिन्दु का विस्थापन

Distance of a planet from the centre of earth पृथ्वी के केन्द्र से किसी उपग्रह की दूरी

Diurnal दैनिक

Diurnal rotation दैनिक परिभ्रमण

Divergence विस्तार, विचलन

Divergent series विभिन्न क्रम/शृंखला

Divident भाग, पृथकरणीय

Division विभाजन

Divisor भाजक

Dot multiplication सूक्ष्म गुणन

Duality द्वैध अवस्था

Dwarfs वामन, बौना

Dynamics गतिविधा

Dynamices of particle कण की गति विधा

E

Earth पृथ्वी

Ecentric circle विषम वृत

Ecentricity विषमता

Ecentric orbit ग्रहण अन्धकार

Eclipsing stars ग्रहण करने वाले पिण्ड

Eclipitc ग्रहण सम्बन्धी

Econometrics अर्थमापक विधि

Economics अर्थशास्त्र

Eigen function इंजीयन पद

Eigen function expansion ईंजिनयन पद विस्तार

Electric charge विद्युत भार

Electric potential विद्युत संभावना

Electro dyanmics विद्युत चालक गतिविधा

Electro magnetic theory विद्युत चुम्बकीय सिद्धान्त

Electronic computers विद्युत चालित कम्प्युटर्स

Ellipse दीर्घवृत

Ellipsoid दीर्घवृतज

Elliptic functions अण्डाकार पद

Elliplic geometry अण्डाकार ज्यामिति/ रेखागणित

Elliplic orbit अण्डाकार ग्रहपथ

Empirical प्रयोग सिद्ध

Energy उर्जा, शांक्ति तेज

Envelope पत्रावरण, लिफाफा

Epicycle छोटा वृत जिसका केन्द्र बड़े वृत की परिधि पर हो

Ephemeris mesidian एंचाग या जन्त्री मध्याह्म

Ephemeris time जन्त्रीकाल, पंचाग काल

Equation साम्य, समीकरण

Equation of centre केन्द्र का साम्य या समीकरण

Equator काल का समय या समीकरण

Equiangular spiral भू-मध्य/विषुवत रेखा

Equinoctial समोणीय कमानी

Equniotical point सम्पातीय, दिन व रात बराबर होने वाली का सम्पातीय बिन्दु

Equinox सम्पात (21 मार्च व 23 सितम्बर का दिन जब रात व दिन बराबर होते है)

Era युग, काल, विशिष्ट काल

Error भ्रम, दोष

Estimate मूल्य निरूपण, आंकलन

Eucidean space यूक्लीडियन दूरी/अन्तर/स्थान

Euclids elements यूक्लीड के तत्व (एक यूनानी गणितज्ञ के ना से प्रसिद्ध रेखागणित)

Evening star शुक्रतारा

even number सम संख्या

Event वृतान्त, घटना

Evalute विस्तार करना, क्रमिक आविर्भाव करना

Evolution विवरण, विस्तार, क्रमिक आविर्भाव

Exact equations विशुद्ध साम्य, यथार्थ समीकरण, उचित समीकरण

Exactly similar representatings यथावत समान प्रतिरूप

Ex-centre बाह्म केन्द्र

Expanding universe विस्तृत खगोल

Expansion of determinants निर्धारकों का विस्तार

Expectation of life जीवन की प्रत्याशा

Experiment प्रयोग

Expenent अर्थप्रदर्शक बीजगणित का अंक

Expanential functions बीज गणितीय पद

Expression आकृति

Exterial angle बाह्म कोण

F

Factor भाज्य

Factor analysis भाज्य विघटन/विभाजन

Factorization भाजन

Factor reversal test भाज्य परिवर्तन जांच

False coin जाली सिक्का

Fermant number विराम अंक

Field of force बल का क्षेत्र

Field potentia संभावित क्षेत्र

Finites geometry परिमित रेखा गणित

Fire balls दाहक गोले

Firest points of aeries मेष राशि का मुख्य प्रथम बिन्दु

First point of libra तुला राशि का मुख्य प्रथम बिन्दु

First quadratic differential from मुख्य वर्ग विशेषक रूप

Flat समतल, नीरस, बन्दबुद्धि

Flat spaces समतल स्थान

Fluid द्रव/तरल पदार्थ

Fluids mechanices तरल/द्रव पदार्थ गति विज्ञान

Flux density प्रवाह घनत्व

Focal lenght केन्द्रीय लम्बाई

Focal conic केन्द्रीय सूच्याकार

Focus केन्द्र

Force बल

Force of mortabity प्राणघातक बल

Forecast अनुमान, भविष्यवाणी

Form co-efficient सादृश्य गुणक

Form function समान पद

Four dimensional चतुष अंशीय

Formula सुत्र, नियम, विधि

Fourier series फुर्ये श्रेणी [आवृत्ति फलन को ज्या और त्रिज्या में प्रस्तुत करती है]

Fagmentation ballistics कण गतिविज्ञान

Frequency आवृति

Frequency division आवृति खण्ड

Friction घर्षण

Frustum of a pyramid किसी पिरामिड का समानान्तर आधार

Fuel ईधन

Function पद, कार्य सम्पादन, कार्य

Functional determinent कार्यकारी निर्धारक

Function theory कार्य सिद्धान्त

Fundamental trihedran मौलिक/आधारभूत समान भुजाओं वाला त्रिभुज

G

Galactic collision आकाश गंगा की टक्कर

Galaxy आकाश गंगा

Gamma functions गामा पद

Gauss curvature चुम्बकीय क्षेत्र की घनत्व ईकाई की वक्रता

Gaussian law of error मूल/भ्रम की गॉसियन विधि

Gemini मिथुन राशि, जुड़वा

Geminorium मिथुन राशि का क्षेत्र

General विस्तृत व्यापक, सामान्य

General solution आम संयोग, साधारण घोल

Generalised co-ordinates सामान्य नियामक

Generating line उत्पादन रेखा

Genus नर्ग, प्रकार जाति, गण

Geodesic भू-मण्डल नाप सम्बन्धी

Geometrical mean रेखा गणित सम्बन्धी परिमाण/मध्यमान

Geometrical progression गुणोत्तर श्रेणी (यथा 2, 4, 8, 16, 32, 64)

Geometry रेखागणित

Geometry of three dimensions तीन परिमाणों लम्बाई, चौड़ाई की रेखागणित

Giants असाधारण, अलौकिक, महाकाय

Giffous उन्नोदन, उभरा हुआ

Gnomon रेखागणित की एक आकृति, सूर्यघड़ी की एक कील

Gravitation गुरुत्वाकर्षण, केन्द्र की ओर आकर्षण

Gravitational co-effient गुरुत्वाकर्षणीय गुणक

Gravitational constant गुरुत्वाकर्षणीय दृढ़

Gravitational field गुरुत्वाकर्षणीय क्षेत्र

Great circle विशाल वृत (पृथ्वी का)

Greatest common measure महतम समापवर्तक

Groups समूह, समुदाय

Gyre compass वर्तुलाकार गति में विस्तार

Eyroscope गति के सिद्धान्त के प्रदर्शित करने का एक विशेषयन्त्र, चर्खी

H

Harmonic अनुरूप

Harmonic conjugate अनुरूप क्रियापद

Harmonically अनुरूप ढंग से

Harmonic functions अनुरूप पद

Harmonic mean अनुरूप गति

Harmonic progression अनुरूप प्रभाव/विकास

Harmonic range अनुरूप क्रम/श्रेणी

Harmonic section अनुरूप वर्ग

Harmonic triangle अनुरूप त्रिभुज/त्रिकोण

Harmonic motion आवृत्त गति

Harmonic pencil आवृत्त कुंचिका

Heat index उष्मा सूचकांक

Heliometer सौरमीटर

Helix घुमौवा पदार्थ (घड़ी की कमानी के सदृश)

Highly composite number महत्व समष्टी संख्या

Hilbert space हिलबर्ट स्थान

Hoder inequalities विषमता धारक

Homogenous समान जातीय

Homegenous equations समान जातीय समीकरण

Horizontal क्षितिज के समानान्तर, समतल

Horizontal plane क्षितिज के समानांतर तल

Horocycle कालचक्र

Horoscope जन्मपत्रिका

Horse head nebula घोड़े के सिर के आकार की आकाश गंगा

Hour angle काल मापक कोण

Hour circle खगोलीय ध्रुवों से गुजरने वाला विस्तृत वृत

Hydra अनेक फन वाला जलीय सर्प

Hydrodynamics जलीय गति विज्ञान

Hydrostatistics स्थिर तरल पदार्थों के दबावव समतल/संतुलन का विज्ञान

Hyperbola एक विशिष्ट प्रकार का रेखागणितोय चाप

Hyperbolic functions अतिश्योक्ति पूर्ण पद/ अतिपरवलीय पद

Hyperbolic orbit अतिश्याकिक्त पूर्ण अतिपरवरतीय घूर्णन या ग्रहपथ

Hyperbolcid अतिपरवलीय चाप वाला

Hypotenuse कण

Hypothesis अनुमान कल्पना प्रतिज्ञा

I

Identities एकरूपताएं, समानताएं

Idnetity एकरूपता, समानता

Igniter गरम करने वाला सुलगाने वाला

Implicit differentiation अनुमित अलगाव

Implicit functions अनुमति पद

Improper functions अनुचित पद भिन्न अंक जिसमें हर से अंश बड़ा होता है।

In-centre अंकित वृत का केन्द्र

Incidence प्रकाश किरण का तल पर आपतन, घटना, क्रम, विस्तार

Incircle वृत के अन्दर

Inclination झुकाव

Indefinite integration अंनन्त/असीमित युग्मन

Independent variables अनाश्रित अनित्य

Indeterminate equations of first degree प्रथम अंश के अतिरहारित असीमित समीकरण

Indeterminate equation of fireat degree in many unknowns अनेक अज्ञातों में प्रथम डिग्री के असीमि/अनिर्धारित समीकरण

Indeterminate equations of second degree द्वितीय अंश के असीमित/अनिर्धारित समीकरण

Index सूचकांक

Index number सूचकांक संख्या, घातांक

Index number theory घातंक सिद्धान्त

Inertia जड़ता, निष्क्रियता

Inequalities विषमताएं, भिन्नताएं, असादृश्य

Inertia of large number बड़ी संख्या में जड़त्व

Infinite product अनंत उत्पाद

Inferior conjution न्यून/अनुतम अन्यय, योग, संसर्ग, समुच्चय

Infinite limit अनंतसीमा

Infinite unit अनन्त/असीमित उत्पाद

Infinite regression अनन्त/असीमित प्रतीय गमन

Infinite series अनन्तर शृंखला

Infinitesimal असीमित रूप से लघु

Infra red दृश्य सोक्ट्रम के आखिरी लाल सीमा से परे

Inner angle अन्तरस्थ कोण

Inner planets अन्तरस्थ/गुप्त ग्रह

Insecibed circle अंकित वृत

Insurnace बीमा, रक्षा

Integres पूर्णांक

Integral calculus पूर्णकलन

Integral equations पूर्ण समीकरण

Integral test पूर्ण जांक

Integration जोड़ने का कार्य, युग्मन

Intelligent quotient निपूर्ण भजनफल

Intesnal ballistics आन्तरिक/अभ्यन्तर स्थित बैलिस्टिक्स

Interpolation क्षेपक भरने का कार्य

Inter stellar dust अन्तर तारा धूली

Inter stellar gas परस्पर तारों की गैस

Invariance

Invariants

Inverse उलटा, उलटी स्थिति

Inverse functions उलटे पद

Inverse propation उलटा परिमाण (भाग, अंश)/अनुपात

Involute अन्तरामिभुख

Involution फंसावट, पेचीदगी

Invlution pencil अन्तराभिमुखी किरणों की रेखा जो एक बिन्दु पर मिलती है।

Ionization विद्युत शक्ति उत्पन्न करना गति मान प्रमाणुओं से

Ionosphere आयन माण्डल

Irrational विवेकरहित, न्याय विरुद्ध, अर्तकसंगत

Irrational numbers ऐसी संख्या जो प्राकृत संख्या के अनुरूप न हो

Isogonal conjugates lines तुल्य कोण क्रिया पद रेखाएं

Isognoal conjugates तुल्य कोण क्रिया पद

Isomerphic अफीम तुल्य

Isosceles triangle समद्विबहुत त्रिभुज

J

Jiba जहाज का तिकोना पाल

Jupiter बृहस्पति ग्रह, इन्द्रदेवाता

K

Kinematics बल के प्रसंग के बिना गति विज्ञान

Kinematics of particles कणों की गति विज्ञान

Kinetic energy गतिज ऊर्जा

Kinetic theory अणुगतिंक सिद्धांत

L

Lamina धातु की परत

Laplace's equation लेप्लेस समीकरण

Latin square लेटिन वर्ग

Latitude अक्षांश

Lattice points जालक बिंदू

Latus recium

Law of inverse squares प्रतिलोम वर्ग का नियम

Leo सिंह

Lens लेंस

Lever उत्तोलक

Libra तुला

Libration एक मशीन जो चंद्रमा के किसी हिस्से का निरीक्षण करें

Life Insurance जीवन बीमा

Light प्रकाश

Light year प्रकाश वर्ष (एक वर्ष में प्रकाश द्वारा तय की जाने वाली दूरी, जो लगभग 9.4607 × 10 km में होती है)

Limacon

Limit सीमा

Limiting point सीमित बिंदू

Limit of a sum किसी राशि की सीमा

Line रेखा

Line co-ordinates निर्देशांक

Linear रेखीय

Linear differential equation रेखिय अवकल समीकरण

Linear equation रेखिक समीकरण

Linear sets of points रेखिक बिदूओं का जोड़ा

Line at infinity अनंत रेखा

Line geometry रेखिक ज्यामिति

Lines of curvature वक्रता रेखा/वक्रता की रेखाएं

Linkage श्रृंख्ला, कड़ी

Liquid fuels तरल ईंधन

Loaded dice जोखिम भरा

Local time स्थानीय समय

Locus बिंदूपथ/ठिकाना

Logarithmic functions लघुगुणक फलन

Logarithmic series लघुगुणक श्रृंखला/लघुगुणक क्रम

Logarithm लघुगुणक

Longitude रेखांश/देशांतर

Loop कुंडली

Loud speakers जोर से बजने वाली मशीन/ध्वनि विस्तारक मशीन

Lunar eclipse चंद्र ग्रहण

Lunar phases चन्द्रमा की कलाएं

Lower transit निम्न पारगमन/निम्न गमन

Lower limit निम्न सीमा

Lowest common multiple सबसे छोटी संख्या जो दो तथा अधिक संख्या से गुणा/गुणित हो

M

Magellanic cloud मेजलेनिक बादल (अंतरिक्ष की दो आकाश गंगाए)

Magic square एक वर्ग के सभी वर्गाकार खानों का योग बराबर है।

Magnetic field चुंबकीय क्षेत्र

Magnetic perturbation चुंबकीय पर्टबेशन

Magnetic poles चुंबकीय ध्रुव

Magnifying power आवर्धन क्षमता

Magnitude परिमाण, मात्रा

Major arc दीर्घ चाप/प्रमुख चाप

Mars मंगल ग्रह

Mathematical anecdotes गणितीय उपख्यान/गणितीय कहानियां

Mathematical economics गणितीय अर्थशास्त्र

Mathematical fallacies गणितीय पतन

Mathematical induction गणितीय प्रेरण/प्रेरण गणित

Mathematical logic तार्किक गणित/तर्क गणित/गणितीय तर्क

Mathematical physics गणितीय भौतिकी

Mathematical prodigies गणितीय कांतुक

Mathematical puzzles and recreation गणितीय पहेलियां एवं मनोरंजन

Mathematical tables गणितीय पहाड़ें/पहाड़े

Mathematics गणित/अंकगणित/अंकशास्त्र

Matrix संख्याएं स्तंभ, रेखा में व्यवस्थित/मैट्रिक्स

Matrix theory मैट्रिक्स सिद्धांत/पद्धति

Matter पदार्थ, भौतिक द्रव्य

Maximum अधिकतम

Maximum power अधिकतम क्षमता

Mean solar time सूर्य की गति के समय की गणना/मध्यक सौरकाल

Mean value मध्यकाल/औसत मूल्य

Mean value theorem माध्यमान प्रमेय

Mechanic मेकेनिक/यांत्रिक/मशीन ठीक करने वाला

Median माध्यिका/अंत:स्थ

Mercury मर्करी/पारा

Meridian मध्याह्न/देशांतर रेखा

Meridian circle मध्याह्न रेखा

Meteor उल्का/टुटता तारा

Meteor crater ज़मीन पर टुटते तारें से हुआ गड्ढ़ा/उल्का गड्ढ़ा

Meteorite उल्का पिंड

Meteor shower उल्का बौछार/उल्का पिंडों की बौछार

Meteor swargrn उल्का दल/उल्का झुंड

Method of least square न्यूनतम वर्ग की विधि

Metric space समष्टिक दूरी/दो बिंदुओं के मध्य दूरी

Micrometer सुक्ष्मदर्शी

Microscope छोटी से छोटी वस्तु (जैसे कोशिका) मापन हेतु उपयोग में लेने हेतु यंत्र

Milky way आकश गंगा

Minimum न्यूनतम

Minor arc लघुचाप

Models प्रतिकृति, प्रतिचित्र, आकार

Modern geometry आधुनिक ज्यामिति

Modulus मापांक

Moment of force बल आघूर्ण

Moment of interia जड़त्व आघूर्ण

Moment of momentum संवेग आघूर्ण

Momentum गति, वेग, चाल

Moon चंद्रमा

Morning star शुक्र तारा, सुबह का तारा

Mortality table मृत्यु सारिणी

Multinomial theorem बहुपद प्रमेय

Motion गति

Multiples गुणज

Multiple stars अनेक तारें/तारों का समूह

Multiplication गुणन, गुणा

Multiplication table पहाड़ा

Multivariables बहुचर

Musa

N

Nadir पतन

Nebulae निहारिकाएं (ऐसे बादल जिसमें धूल, हाइड्रोजन, हीलियम और अन्य आयनीकृत प्लास्मा गैसे उप. हो)

Nebular hypothesis नेबुलर परिकल्पना/निहारिका परिकल्पना

Negative नकारात्मक

Negative roots खराब जड़े

Neptune वरूण, जल देवता

Nine point circle नौ बिंदू वृत्त

Nodal point केन्द्रिय बिंदू

Node ग्रंथि, गांठ

Nomogram सरेखन

Non-algebriac गैर बीजिय

Non-algebriac numbers गैर बीजिय संख्या

Non-differentiable अपरिवर्तनीय, अलग न होने योग्य

Non-enumerably infinite अनंत तक न गिनने वाली संख्या

Non-Euclidean geometry अयुक्लिड ज्यामिति (किसी समानांतर अभिगृहित को किसी वैकल्पिक बिंदू से परिभाषित किया जाए)

Normal सामान्य

Normal curve सामान्य वक्र

Normal plane समान्य सतह/सामान्य विमान

Normal population सामान्य जनसंख्या

Normal section सामान्य खंड/सामान्य अनुभाग

North polar distance उत्तर ध्रुवीय दूरी

North frigid zone उत्तरी मैदान का क्षेत्र/उत्तरी शीतकटिबंध क्षेत्र

North pole उत्तरी ध्रुव

North temperate zone उत्तरी समशीतोष्ण क्षेत्र

Novae नया तारा/नयी चीज़

Number संख्या

Numerator मीटर, अंश, अंशगणक

Nutation सिर का इशारा, शिखावर्तन, पृथ्वी की धुरी का दोलन

O

Object glass शीशा/कैमरें का शीशा

Oblique परोक्ष/तिरछी रेखा

Oblique axes तिर्यक् अक्ष/(ऐसा बिंदू जिसमें समन्वय प्रणाली का अक्ष समान न हो)

Oblique cylinder एक ऐसा बेलन (सिलेंडर) जो किसी पक्ष का आधार बनें।

Oblique prism एक ऐसा धन जो किसी पक्ष के 90° का कोण न बनाएं। तिर्यक प्रिज़्म

Obliquity of the ecliptic तिर्यक सूर्यपथ/सूर्य का एक पथ जो पृथ्वी को रोशनी देता है।

Observation अवलोकन/देखभाल

Observatory आकाश लोचन, बेधशाला

Obtuse angle अधिककोण

Octaheron अष्टफलकीय

Odd अजीब/विषम

Odd number विषम संख्या

Official statistics अधिकारिक आंकड़े

One-to-one corresponding अलग-अलग पत्राचार

Open interval खुला अंतराल (दो सदस्य संख्याओं के बीच कोई समुच्चय)

Operation चीर-फाड़, जंगी कार्रवाई

Opposition विरोधी/विपक्ष

Optical double दूरबीन/ऐसे दो तारें का जोड़ा जिन्हें दूरबीन से देखने पर एक-दूसरे के समीप दिखते है।

Optic प्रकाशिकी

Orbit परिक्रमा/ग्रहपथ

Ordinate कोटि

Origin of the solar system सौर मंडल उत्पत्ति

Orionis मृग/मृग नक्षत्र

Ortho-center लंब केंद्र

Orthogonal आयतीय

Orthogonal involution लंबकोणीय अंतर्वलन

Orthogonal pencil लंबकोण बनाना/खींचना

Orthogonal projection लंबकोणीय प्रक्षेपण

Osculating plane किसी समतल पर बने वक्र की बिंदूओं की स्पर्श रेखा पर मिलान

Osculating sphere

Outer planet बाहरी ग्रह

P

Parabola परवलीय, अनुवृत्त

Paraboloid ठोस अनुवृत्त

Parallax लंबन, विस्थापना भास

Parallax method लंबन विधि

Parallel समानांतर

Parallel postulate समानांतर आसन

Parallel projection समानांतर प्रक्षेण

Parallelogram समानांतर चतुर्भुज

Parallelogram law of forces समांतर चतुर्भुज के बल नियम

Parallelepiped समांतर षट्फलक

Parameter मानदंड, मापदंड

Parameter group पैरामीटर समूह

Parsec दिग्विकला/खगोल विज्ञान की एक दूरी जो लगभग 3.26 प्रकाश वर्ष (3.086×10.13 km) के बराबर है।

Partial आंशिक

Partial derivative आंशिक व्युत्पन्न

Partial differential equation आंशिक अवकल समीकरण

Partial eclipse आंशिक ग्रहण, खंड ग्रहण

Partial integration आंशिक समाकलन

Particle कण

Pascal triangle पास्कल त्रिभुज

Pedal curve पेडल वक्र/पदिक वक्र

Pedal line पेडल रेखा

Pegasi पेगासी/कवि की उमंग

Pellian equation

Pencil पेंसिल

Pencil of rays

Pendulum लोलक

Penultimate convergent पारमार्थिक अभिसरण

Perihelion सूर्य समीपक/जब ग्रह सूर्य के निकट हो

Perigee पृथ्वी समीपक/जब ग्रह पृथ्वी के निकट हो

Period अवधि, काल, युग

Period-luminosity curve अवधि ज्योति वक्र

Periodic co-efficient आवधिक सहप्रभावकारिता

Periodic comet आवधिक धूमकेतु

Periodic function आवृत्ति फलन

Periodic time आवधिक समय

Permutations क्रम संचय/क्रम परिवर्तन

Permutation groups क्रमचय समूह

Prepetual day बिना अवधि के दिन

Prepetual night

Prespective drawing

Preturbation

Phases अवस्था, चरण

Phenomena घटना, दृष्टिगत वस्तु

Philosophy of organism जीवदर्शन

Photographic magnitude

Photo sphere सूर्य का बाह्य प्रभामंडल

Physical double द्वि भौतिकी/दोहरा भौतिकी

Physics भौतिकी

Pisces मीन राशि

Piscium (Latin word) मछली

Place value स्थानिक मान/स्थानीय मूल्य

Plane विमान, समतल स्थान

Plane geometry समतल ज्यामिती

Plane ornamental groups विमान सजावट समूह

Plane trigonometry समतल त्रिकोणमिति

Planet ग्रह

Planetary ग्रह संबंधी/भ्रमणकारी

Planing समतल बनाना

Pleides कृत्रिका

Pluto प्लूटों/सूर्य का नौवां ग्रह

Point बिंदु

Point co-ordinates निर्देशांक

Point line configurations बिंदू रेखा विन्यास/दो इलेक्ट्रॉनिक माध्यमों को जोड़ना

Point of contact संपर्क बिंदु

Point of incidence घटना का बिंदु

Point of intersection प्रतिच्छेद बिंदु

Polar axis ध्रुवीय अक्ष

Polar caps ध्रुवीय टेपीयां/किसी ग्रह के ध्रुव के चारों ओर बर्फ या अन्य जमे पदार्थ का क्षेत्र

Polar co-ordinates ध्रुवीय निर्देशांक

Polar reciprocal ध्रुवीय व्युत्क्रम

Polar surface ध्रुवीय सतह

Pole ध्रुव

Pole of ecliptic किसी ग्रह पर ध्रुव

Pole star ध्रुव तारा

Pollux मिथुन (तारामंडल का सबसे रोशन तारा)

Polygon बहुभुज

Polyhedron बहुतल/बहुफलक

Polynomials बहुपद

Population आबादी/जनसंख्या

Position vector स्थिति सदिश

Positive सकारात्मक

Positive electric charges सकारात्मक विद्युत आवेश

Positive integers सकारात्मक आंकड़े

Positive fractions सकारात्मक भिन्न/सकारात्मक अंश

Positive roots सकारात्मक मूल

Postulates तत्व

Potential स्थितिक

Potential energy स्थितिज ऊर्जा

Potential flow विभव प्रवाह

Potential theory विभव सिद्धांत

Power ऊर्जा/शक्ति

Precession अग्रगमन, अयन (खगोल विज्ञान में ग्रह घूर्णन में अक्ष का घूर्णन)

Pressure दाब/दबाव

Prime number अभाज्य संख्या

Principle of least action न्युनतक क्रिया नियम

Prism प्रिज़्म (पारदर्शी प्रकाश अवयव)

Probability संभावना/अनुमान/प्रायिकता

Probability density संभावित घनत्व

Probability distribution संभावित वितरण

Probability theory प्रायिकता सिद्धांत

Probit analysis प्राबिट विश्लेषण

Product उत्पाद/वस्तु

Progressions प्रगति/बढ़ाव

Projection प्रक्षेपण

Projective configurations प्रक्षेप्य विन्यास

Projective co-ordinates प्राक्षेपीय निर्देशांक

Projective geometry प्राक्षेपीय ज्यमिती

Projective transformations प्रक्षेप्य परिवर्तन

Prominences प्रसिद्धि/बहिर्गत भाग

Proof प्रमाण, जांच

Propeller प्रेरण शक्ति

Proper fraction उचित भिन्न/भिन्न का वह रूप जो इकाई से कम हो)

Proportion अनुपात

Proposition प्रस्ताव

Pure mathematics सैद्धांतिक गणित

Pyramid पिरामिड, शंभुकार स्तंभ

Pyramidal numbers पिरामिड संख्याएं

Q

Quadrangle चतुष्कोण

Quadrant वृत्त का चतुर्थ भाग, कोण मापने का यंत्र

Quadratic equations चतुष्कोणीय समीकरण

Quadrilateral चतुर्भुज

Qualitative गुणात्मक

Quantitative संख्यात्मक/मात्रात्मक

Quantum thoery क्वांटम सिद्धांत

Quaternions चतुष्क

Quotations from mathematicians गणितज्ञों से उद्धरण

Quotient भागफल

R

Radian रेडियन

Radiant चमकीला, प्रकाशमान

Radiation विकारिण, विकिर्ण

Radical axis मूलाक्ष

Radioactive elements रेडियोधर्मी तत्व

Radio astronomy रेडियो खगोलिकी/रेडियो खगोल विज्ञान

Radio star रेडियो स्टार

Radius त्रिज्या, अर्द्धव्यास

Radius of curvature वक्रता त्रिज्या

Radius of torsion विमोटन/मरोड़/व्यावर्तन की त्रिज्या

Radius of vector सदिश की त्रिज्या

Radio-metric रेडियो मेट्रिक

Radix सूत्र, मूलांक

Random यादृच्छिक

Randomization यादृच्छिकीकरण

Randomized blocks यादृच्छिक ब्लॉक/यादृच्छिक खंडक

Random numbers यादृच्छिक संख्याएं

Random residue यादृच्छिक अवशेष

Random samples यादृच्छिक प्रतिदर्श

Random sampling numbers यादृच्छिक प्रतिचयन संख्याएं

Random variable यादृच्छिक चर

Ratio अनुपात

Rational तर्क संगत, तर्क संबंधी

Rational numbers तर्क संगत-संख्याएं

Reaction प्रतिक्रिया

Real numbers वास्तविक संख्याएं

Reciprocal पारस्परिक

Reciprocal numbers पारस्परिक संख्याएं

Reciprocation विनिमय करना

Rectangle आयत, समकोण

Rectangular आयताकार, समकोण

Rectangular co-ordinance आयताकार निर्देशांक

Rectangular hyperbols समकोणीय अतिपरवल

Reductio ad absurdum असंगति प्रदर्शन

Reflecting telescope परावर्ती दूरदर्शक

Reflection प्रतिबिंब, परावर्तन

Reflex angle परावर्तन कोण

Refracting telescope अपवर्तिक दूरदर्शक

Refraction अपवर्तन

Regular hexagon समषट्भुज

Regular polygon समबहुभुज

Regular polyhedron समबहुफलक

Regulus धातुक

Regulus मघा (नक्षत्र)

Relative संबंधी

Relative acceleration त्वरण-संबंधी/सापेक्ष त्वरण

Relative frequency आवृत्ति संबंधी/सापेक्ष आवृति

Relative velocity वेग संबंधी/सापेक्ष वेग

Relative theory सिद्धांत संबंधी/सापेक्ष सिद्धांत

Raplication प्रतिकृति

Repulsion प्रतिकर्षण/विकर्षण

Residue अवशेष

Retrograde motion प्रतिगामी गति

Reversing layer उत्क्रमण परत

Revolution परिक्रमण/परिक्रमा

Rhombus विषमकोण

Right angle समकोण

Right ascension दायां आरोहण (खगोलीय माप)

Right circular cylinder लंब वृत्तीय बेलन

Right Prism लंब प्रिज़्म

Rigid body दृढ़ पिण्ड

Rigid dynamics पिण्ड गतिकी

Rigour कठोरता, दृढ़ता

Ring अंगुठी वृत्त

Risks जोखिम/खतरा

Roots मूल/आधार

Rotation चक्कर/नियमित आवर्तन

Row पंक्ति

Rule नियम, शासन

Rule of three त्रैराशिक

S

Sagittari धनु राशि

Sagittarius धनु राशि

Samples नमूना

Saros

Satellite उपग्रह

Saturn शनि ग्रह

Saturn's rings शनि ग्रह का बाहरी चक्र

Scalar अदिश

Scalar field अदिश क्षेत्र

Scales of notation

Science of perspective drawing परिप्रेक्ष्य चित्रकारी विज्ञान

Scorpio वृश्चिक

Scorpionis Scorpionis वृश्चिक राशि/बिच्छु

Screw motion पेंच गति

Seasons मौसम, युग

Seasonal component मौसमी घटक

Secant काटने वाला/छेदिका

Secular variation धर्म निरपेक्ष बदलाव/ दीर्घकालिक विचरण

Segment खंड/भाग

Self consistant स्व-संगत/आत्म संगत

Self conjugate स्व-संयुग्मी

Self fertilised स्व-निषेचित/स्व-निषेचन

Semi circle अर्धवृत्त

Sernitatus rectum अर्धनाभि लंब

Sequence क्रम/अनुक्रम

Squential sampling अनुक्रमिक नमूने

Series श्रेणी/श्रृंख्ला

Set वस्तुओं का समूह/समुच्चय

Set theory समुच्चय सिद्धांत

Sextant षष्ठक

Shells शंख, सींप, गोले

Shock waves आघात तरंगे

Shooting stars उल्का

Short axis लघु अक्ष

Siderial clock/sidereal नाक्षत्र घड़ी

Siderial day नाक्षत्र दिन

Siderial parallax नाक्षत्रिक लंबन

Siderial period नाक्षत्रकाल

Siderial spectrum नाक्षत्रिक वर्णोक्रम

Siderial time नाक्षत्रिक काल

Similar triangles समरूप त्रिभुज

Similarity समानता, समरूपता

Simple continued fractions सरल वितत भिन्न

Simple fraction सरल भिन्न

Simple connected सरल संपर्क/सरल जुड़ाव

Simultaneous समकालिक/समक्षणिक

Simuitaneous equations युगपत समीकरण

Sine जीवा/रेखा विशेष

Sine tables ज्या सारिणी

Single valued functions एक मूल्यक फलन

Singular point एक बिंदू/विचित्र बिंदू

Singular solution विचित्र हल

Sinus लुब्धक तारा

Slope ढाल/असम भूमि

Small circle लघु वृत्त

Small samples लघु नमूने

Solar सौर

Solar day सौर दिवस

Solar eclipse सूर्य ग्रहण

Solar parallax सौर लंबन

Solar prominences सौर प्रमुखता

Solar radiation सौर विकिरण

Solar spectrum सौर वर्णक्रम

Solar system सौर परिवार, सौर मंडल

Solar telescope सौर दूरबीन

Solar time सौर समय

Solid ठोस

Solid sphere ठोस क्षेत्र

Solstice अयनकाल/उच्चतम शिखर

Solstitical point एकांत बिंदु/अयनांत बिंदू

Solution हल/परिणाम/घोल

Sound ध्वनि

Southern cross दक्षिणी पार/त्रिशंकु

South polar distance दक्षिण ध्रुवीय दूरी

South pole दक्षिणी ध्रुव

Slope ढ़ाल, झुकाव

Space रिक्त स्थान, अंतरिक्ष

Space curve आकाशवत्वक्र

Space satellites आकाशीय उपग्रह

Special theory of relativity विशेष सापेक्षतावाद का सिद्धांत

Spectral analysis वर्णक्रमीय विश्लेषण

Spectrograph स्पेक्ट्रमलेखी

Spectra-heliograph स्पेक्ट्रमी तापमापी

Spectroscope स्पेक्ट्रोस्कोविक लंबन

Spectroscopic parallax स्पेक्ट्रोस्कोपिक लंबन

Spectrum वर्णक्रम/रंगावली

Speed गति

Sphere क्षेत्र

Sphere-geometry ज्यामिति-क्षेत्र

Spherical गोलाकार

Spherical co-ordinates गोलीय निर्देशांक

Spherical curve गोलाकार वक्रता

Spherical harmonic functions गोलाकार प्रांसदिक फलन

Spherical surface गोलीय सतह

Spherical triangle गोलीय त्रिभुज

Spherical trignometry गोलिय त्रिकोणमिति

Spheroid उपगोल, अंडाकार आकृति

Spica कंटक

Spinning top लट्टु (खेलने योग्य चक्करी)

Spiral कुंडली, सर्पिल रेखा

Spiral line सर्पिल रेखा/कुंडलित रेखा

Spiral nubula कुंडलित निहारिका

Spots दाग, धब्बे, निशान

Square वर्ग, समचतुर्भुज

Square root वर्गमूल

Squaring of a circle चक्र का वर्ग
Stable equilibrium स्थिर संतुलन
Standard deviation मानक विचलन
Standard meridian मानक भूमध्य रेखा
Standard time मानक समय
Star तारा
Star clusters तारा समूह/तारा गुच्छा
Star polyhedra षट् नक्षत्र
Statics स्थैतिकी
Stationary स्थिर, स्थायी
Statistics सांख्यिकी, आंकड़े
Stellar नक्षत्रीय, तारकीय
Stellar astronomy नक्षत्रीय खगोल विज्ञान
Stellar displacement नक्षत्र विस्थापन
Stereographic projection त्रिविम प्रक्षेपण
Stochastic process प्रसंभाव्य प्रक्रम
Stochastic variable प्रसंभाव्य चर
Straight angle ऋजु कोण
Straight line सीधी रेखा
Stream function धारा फलन
Sub group उप समूह
Sub lunar point उपचंद्र बिंदू
Sub norma उप मानदंड
Subset उपसमुच्चय
Sub tangent अध: स्पर्शी
Substraction व्यवकलन, शेष
Sum राशि, जोड़
Summability संकलनीयता
Summer solstice उत्तरायण
Sun सुरज, रवि
Sundial धूप घड़ी
Sun spots झाई, सुर्य कलंक
Super giants उच्च राक्षस
Superior conjunction बेहतर संयोजन
Supernova अधिनव तारा
Supplementary angles संपूरक कोण
Symbol प्रतीक, चिन्ह
Symmedian point समाध्यिका बिंदू
Symmetry सममिति/समरूपता
Synodic period संयुक्ति काल
Synodic time संयुक्ति समय
Synthetic कृत्रिम संश्लेषित
Synthetic propellents कृत्रिम पदार्थ

T

Table तालिका, मेज
Tabulation तालिका बनाना, सारिणीकरण
Tangent स्पर्श रेखा, स्पर्शी
Tangent plane स्पर्श तल
Tangential स्पर्श–रेखीय
Tangential co-ordinates स्पर्शरेखीय निर्देशांक
Tangential equation स्पर्शरेखीय समीकरण
Taylor series टेलर श्रेणी (किसी फलन को अनंत पदों व योग सेनिरूपित करती हो)
Telescope दूरबीन, दूरदर्शी
Temperature तापक्रम/तापमान
Tensor प्रदिश (सदिश, अदिश, प्रदिश के मध्य रेखिक संबंध बताती है)
Tensor calculus प्रदिश कलन
Tensor multiplication प्रदिश गुणनफल
Terminal ballistics टर्मिनल प्राक्षेप्य
Terrestrial पार्थिव लांकिक
Terrestrial day स्थलीय दिन
Terrestrial phenomena स्थलीय घटना
Terrestrial time स्थलीय समय

Terrestrial year स्थनलीय वर्ष

Tetrahedron चतुष्फलक

Theodolite सर्वेक्षण उपकरण

Theory of attributes विशेषता का सिद्धांत

Theory of equations समीकरण सिद्धांत

Theory of functions of complex variable संयुक्त फलन का सिद्धांत

Theory of groups समूहों का सिद्धांत

Theory of lattice points जालक बिंदू का सिद्धांत

Theory of numbers संख्याओ का सिद्धांत

Theory of summability संकलनीयता/सामायता का सिद्धांत

Theory of wave propagation तरंग संचरण का सिद्धांत

Theta functions थींटा फलन

Three dimensional त्रिविमीय/त्रि आयामी

Three dimensional curve त्रिविमीय वक्र

Three dimensional geometry त्रिविमीय ज्यामिति

Three dimensional space त्रिविम समष्टि

Third order contact त्रिकोटि संपर्क

Tidal fiction ज्वारीय कल्पना

Tidal waves ज्वारीय तरंग

Tides ज्वार, ज्वार-भाटा

Time समय, काल

Time reversal test कालोत्क्रमण परीक्षण

Time series समय-सारिणी

Topological transformations ऊष्णकटिबंधीय रूपांतरण

Topology संस्थिति/किसी स्थान की प्राकृतिक दशा का वर्णन

Topology of point sets किसी बिंदू की सांस्थिति

Torsion ऐंठन, मरोड़

Torus वलय, पुष्पासन

Total eclipse पूर्ण ग्रहण

Tractrix तुल्य स्पर्शवक्र

Trajectory प्रक्षेप वक्र

Transfinite arithmetic अनित्य अंकगणित/अपरिमित अंकगणित

Transfinite numbers अपरिमित संख्याएं

Transit instrument योग्योत्तर यंत्र

Transit of venus शुक्र पारगमन

Translation अनुवादन

Transparency पारदर्शीता

Transverse अनुप्रस्थ

Transverse axis अनुप्रस्थ अक्ष

Trapezium असमांतरभुज, समलम्ब

Trend दौर, प्रचलन

Triangle त्रिभुज

Triangular inequalities त्रिकोणीय विषमताएं

Triangular numbers त्रिकोणीय संख्याएं

Triangular prism त्रिकोणीय प्रिज़्म

Trigonometry त्रिकोणमिति

Trigonometric functions त्रिकोणमिति फलन

Trigonometric ratios त्रिकोणमिति अनुपात

Trilinear त्रिरेखीय

Trilinear co-ordinates त्रिरेखीय निर्देशांक

Triple stars तीन तारें

Tropical उष्णकटिबंधीय

Tropical day सौर दिन/उष्णकटिबंधीय दिवस

Tropical year सौर वर्ष

True zenith distance शिरो बिंदू दूरिता

Twilight सूर्यास्त का समय/धुंधला प्रकाश

U

Unified field theory एकीकृत क्षेत्र सिद्धांत

Uniform वर्दी, एकसमान

Uniform angular velocity एकसमान कोणीय वेग

Uniform convergence एकसमान केन्द्रमिमुखता

Uniform functions एकसमान फलन
Uniform velocity एकसमान वेग
Unit इकाई
Unit acceleration गति वर्धन इकाई
Unit cell इकाई कणिका
Unit force इकाई बल
Universal law of gravitation सार्वत्रिक गुरूत्वाकर्षण का नियम
Universe सार्वत्रिक, सार्वभौमिक
Unstable equilibrium अस्थिर संतुलन
Upper transit ऊपरी पारगमन
Uranus वरूण ग्रह
Ursa major सप्तीर्यमंडल
Ursa minior ध्रुव मत्स्य तारामंडल

V

Variable परिवर्तन शील
Variable अस्थित
Variable stars परिवर्ती तारक
Variance मतभेद, परिवर्तन
Vector सदिश
Vector space सदिश बीजगणित
Vega वीगा
Velocity वेग, गति
Velocity potential वेग विभव
Venus शुक्र ग्रह
Vernal equinox वसंत विषुव
Vertical लंबवत्, अधीलंब, ऊर्ध्वाधर
Vertical angle लंबकोण, ऊर्ध्वाधर कोण
Vertical plane ऊर्ध्वाधर तल
Vertex शीर्ष
Vertex of angle शीर्ष कोण
Vertex of cone शीर्ष का शंकु
Vibration कंपन
Vibration figure कंपन आंकड़े
Visual magnitude दृश्य परिमाण
Vital statistics जीवनांक, जीवन, संबंधी आंकड़े
Volume आयतन

W

War head मुखास्त्र, स्फोटक शीर्ष
Wave length तरंग दैर्ध्य
Wave theory of light प्रकाश का तरंग सिद्धांत
Weighed multiples भारित गुणक
Weighed ratio भारित अनुपात
Weight भार
Window readers विंडो रींडर
Winter solstice शीत अयनांत
With respect to x x के संबंध में
Work कार्य, काम

Z

Zenith शीर्षबिंदू
Zenith पराकाष्ठा, ऊर्ध्वाबिंदू
Zero शुन्य, जीरो
Zets functions जींटा फ़लन
Zodiac राशि मंडल
Zodiacal belt राशि चक्र बेल्ट
Zone जीन, क्षेत्र

CHAPTER 12

Library of Literature

1. Pedda Balasiksha-Panchamga Parvamu in Telugu.
2. Jyothisha Sastra, Pradhamika Amsalu Ist Year M.A. Paper-II, P.S.T. University Correspondence Course, Hyderabad, in English.
3. Jataka Mani Manjusha, English by Dr. Challa Somasundaram.
4. Muhurtha Sindhuvu; Late Vadrevu Surya Narayana Murthy in Telugu.
5. Vasthu Sastramu Ist Year Paper M.A. Jyothisham, Correspondance course P.S.T. University, Hyderabad in English.
6. Prasna Jyathisham; Krishna Murthy Padhdhati; Sri K.N. Krishna Murthy in Telugu.
7. Ayanamsa Churcha, Anuvadam, Late Madhira Krishna Murthy Sastry in Telugu.
8. Computation of Planetary Position and Almanac 20-22 March, 2009, I-Serve, Hyderabad in English.
9. Panchamga Siddhanta, 30 GSM, d–1-2-2007, I-Serve, Hyderabad in English.
10. Table of Ascendants by Late N.C. Lahiri.
11. Condensed Ephimeris by Late N.C. Lahiri.
12. Durmukha Nama Samvastsara Panchamgam (2016-17), Bharata Prabhutwa Sammata Sastryeeta Sanatana, written by Sri. Pidaparthi Subrahmanya Sastry Garu, and sons Podagatlapalli, in Telugu.
13. Dwadasa Lagnamulaku Yogavayoga Nirnayam, Dr. Challa Sama Sundaram in Telugu in 2017.
14. Effects in Astrology Jeeva Sarrera-Dr. N.V.R.A. Raja in English.
15. Effects in Astrology Kalaamsa-Guna, Dr. N.V.R.A. Raja in English.
16. Vishnu Dharmottaramaha Puranamu, Dwiteeya Khandamu, Anuvadamulu by Sri. Kattari Venkata Ramana Deeshutulu, Publishers, Sri. Venkateswara Arshabharati Trust, Ashoknagar, Hyderabad 500020 in Telugu.